"A panoramic overview of film and filmmakers which covers the achievements—technical, economic and aesthetic—of three quarters of a century of cinema. Robinson is especially thorough on the early days: from 1895 when the Lumière brothers first experimented with the Cinematographe in the basement of the Brand Café in Paris, to the titanic achievements of D. W. Griffith, the efflorescence of German Expressionism in such Weimar masterpieces as *Metropolis* and *The Cabinet of Dr. Caligari,* to the dazzling success of Eisenstein in post-revolutionary Russia. While his concerns are chiefly artistic, commercial factors are not overlooked—the rise and fall of the Hollywood studio system and the impact of the two World Wars and the Depression on audience tastes and film budgets are carefully considered."

—*The Kirkus Reviews*

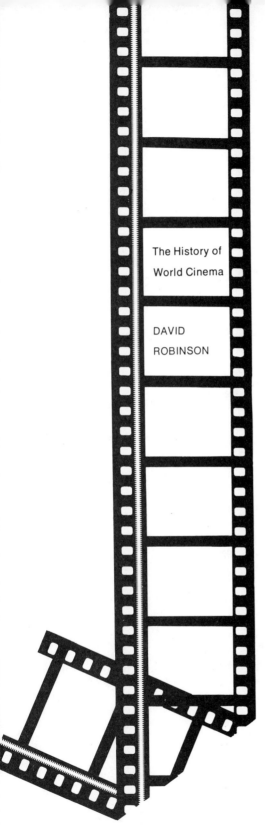

The History of

World Cinema

DAVID
ROBINSON

𝔰𝔡

STEIN AND DAY
Publishers
New York

FIRST STEIN AND DAY PAPERBACK EDITION 1974

First published in the United States of America in 1973
Library of Congress Catalog No. 76-187546
Printed in the United States of America
Stein and Day/Publishers/Scarborough House,
Briarcliff Manor, New York 10510
ISBN 0-8128-1753-2
SECOND PRINTING, 1978

CONTENTS

ILLUSTRATIONS

viii · Illustrations

PREFACE

It is a fairly reckless undertaking to try to compress the history of the cinema's first three quarters of a century into a book of this size, which possibly explains why there has been no new general history of the cinema in English since before the Second World War. Twenty-five years ago it might have seemed more feasible; but today the sheer bulk of cinema is so immense. It is practically impossible even to estimate the number of films of all kinds made since 1895, but the figure may well be in the region of a quarter of a million. If we suppose that a bare five per cent of these are worth passing attention (and in fact the cinema's proportional record of artistic successes is probably no lower than that), the task of covering all movie history, from Lumière to Andy Warhol, from German Expressionism to the Cinema Nôvo of Brazil, from the Austro-Hungarian Empire to Ghana and Vietnam, is overwhelming. And the bulk increases faster and faster, as more and more film-makers find the possibility of expression, in almost one hundred territories of the world.

Apart from the problem of quantity, of course, cinema history is generally more complex than that of any other art. In the first chapter of this book I write, 'the cinema involves an aesthetic, a technology, an economy and an audience; and all four of these elements will condition what moving images appear upon the screen at any particular place and in any period'. It is fairly pointless to write about cinema history only in terms of aesthetic judgment, simply to apportion praise and blame for artistic achievement or failure. It is true that in the end what will count is the dominating artistic personality of the author of any film (and though mostly we take the director to be the author, at times the writer, the actor, the producer, the designer or the cameraman may also claim that role). The history of the cinema would have been different, certainly, if artists like Méliès, Linder, Griffith, Eisenstein, Vertov, John Ford or André Bazin had not been the men they were and had not found themselves in a particular historical situation. Equally though the cinema would have been different but for businessmen like Pathé or Mayer; or technicians like the Lumières, Lauste, Chrétien. Technology profoundly affects the art; and economics condition technology. Sound revolutionised the cinema; yet sound pictures were introduced as a result of particular economic circumstances. The wide screen, again, revolutionised aesthetics; but the wide screen only originated in answer to the economic threat of television. It was the social climate in America after the First World War that determined the nature and content of the films made in those years in Hollywood; and it was the economic temper of America in those same years that led to Hollywood's overwhelming dominance in the world's cinemas; and the combination of circumstances had profound effects upon the development of films and life styles and international relations in the succeeding years.

To this historical complexity is added a characteristic of cinema creation that is, again, unique in the arts. Almost universally, in capitalist and socialist societies alike, film-making is conducted within a division, often an antagonism, of interests. Films cost, and can occasionally earn, a great deal of money; and so film production is invariably under the control of experts in money and the mysteries of finance. Yet in the end films have to be made by artists. The financiers necessarily seek the predictable and safe, while the artist must be dedicated to the search for adventures, imponderables. The financier tends to be committed to conservative and reactionary values, while the artist more often than not is on the side of the new and radical. This contradiction can have many different results, not frequently happy, upon what finally emerges from the complicated process of making a film.

I have tried in tracing the story of seventy-five years of films to balance these multiple considerations, which can at any point impel (or retard) the progress of the art of cinema. Sometimes one influence will be more apparent; sometimes another. I can only hope that most of the time I have found some sort of logic to the story. Not that there is invariably logic in history. It is every historian's ambition to capture the sweep of history. Unfortunately history is inclined to leap, hobble, double back, repeat itself, stop still and indeed do anything in the world but sweep.

What I hope to have achieved is, indeed, an outline of film history – a skeleton chart, with a few landmarks dotted in, on which the reader can plot his own experiences of cinema. I hope there are not, as a result, too many lists of films and names. But if there are (and generally I have consciously compressed those areas where there is plenty of literature already available in English) then I hope it will drive the exasperated reader to the further reading indicated in the Bibliography. Though, of course, I would prefer to think that he were sent there by enthusiasm rather than exasperation.

July 1972

Early poster for Lumière Cinématographe, 1896.

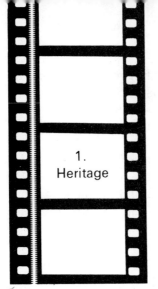

1.
Heritage

It is convenient to date the history of the cinema from 28 December 1895 – a chilly Saturday night when the Lumière Brothers of Lyon gave the first show of their 'Cinématographe' before a paying public, at number 14, Boulevard des Capucines, in Paris. They had rented for the purpose the basement below the Grand Café, a resplendent establishment in white and gold plaster-work, which was itself beneath the first-floor premises of the Jockey Club. The basement had been transformed into a *divan*, the Salon Indien, but it had not proved a great attraction, so the Lumières were able to rent it, equip it with a hundred café chairs, and charge one franc per head for the twenty-minute show.

It is useful to have such a date to commemorate; but it is misleading; for the cinema was a complex evolution rather than an invention. The cinema involves an aesthetic, a technology, an economy and an audience; and all four of these elements will condition what moving images appear upon the screen at any particular place and in any particular period. The aesthetic, technology, economy and audience which resulted, in 1895, in motion pictures as we now know them and which shaped the early years of the medium, have their origins long before the Lumières and the Salon Indien.

Since the last quarter of the eighteenth century the European public (and, in turn, the American public) had been increasingly awakened to visual experience. The whole iconography of the common man was enriched by

the advent of cheap printing. With the appearance in
England in 1842 of the first all-illustrated weekly newspaper, *The Illustrated London News*, people came more and
more to derive their experience of the world around them
from images.

Optical entertainments of ever-increasing elaboration
flourished in the century preceding the appearance of the
motion picture. The shadow show, which had made various
more or less abortive invasions from the East in the past,
leapt to fashion in the 1770s, when one Ambroise or Ambro-
gio brought his show to London, and the 1780s, when Goethe
organised a shadow theatre at Trefurt and Dominique
Séraphin, in 1784, opened what was to become the most
celebrated of all French shadow shows. Séraphin, whose
theatre continued to flourish – long after his own death in
1800 – until 1870 had countless rivals and imitators, and
throughout the century, through most of Europe, showmen toured with little fit-up 'galanty shows'. In 1887, at
Rudolph Salis's Chat Noir, Henri Rivière began the series
of shadow dramas and *épopées* which lasted until the year
after the Lumière show. Other artistic revivals in the
twentieth century culminated in the union of *ombres
chinoises* and cinema in the silhouette films of Lotte
Reiniger.

The rational temper of the last quarter of the eighteenth
century produced a passion for shows and exhibitions of
every kind, among which paintings of dramatic proportion
or content were inordinately popular: the paintings of such
an artist as Benjamin West, for instance, were almost
invariably presented as a public *show*. The 1780s saw two
significant attempts to add extra spectacular qualities to
the painter's two-dimensional and static medium. An
Edinburgh portrait painter, Robert Barker, conceived the
idea of surrounding the spectator with a gigantic cylin-
drical painting, ingeniously illuminated to enhance the
illusion of reality. The craze for 'Panoramas' – as Barker's
invention, patented in 1787, was called – rapidly spread
throughout all the capitals of Europe. Panoramas continued
to flourish into the 1860s and 1870s; and as late as 1960 a
50-year-old panorama of the battle of Borodino was successfully re-launched in Moscow.

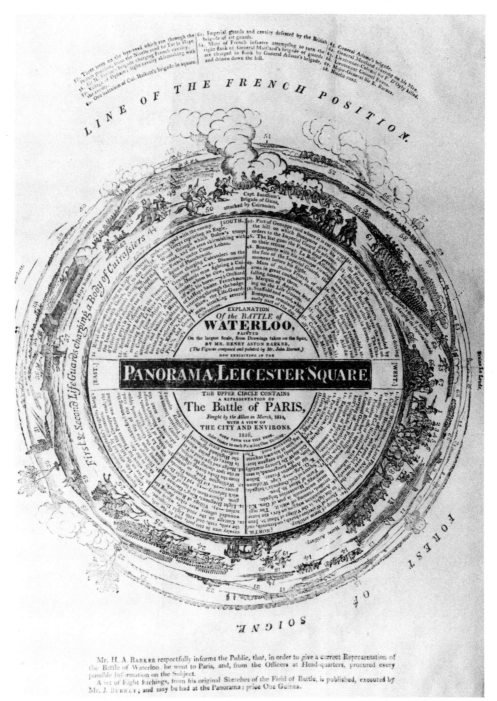

Plan of Robert Barker's Panorama of the Battle of Waterloo, 1815.

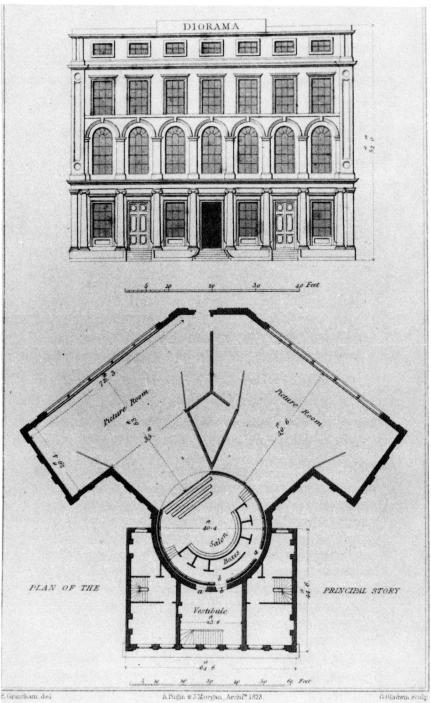

DIORAMA

5   10   20   30   40 Feet

PLAN OF THE   PRINCIPAL STORY

Picture Room

Picture Room

Salon

Boxes

Vestibule

5   10   20   30   40   50   60 Feet

R.Grantham del   A.Pugin & J.Morgan, Archt.ᵗˢ 1823.   G.Gladwin sculp.

Elevation and plan of Daguerre's Diorama in Park Square East, London, showing the arrangement for moving the entire auditorium and audience from one picture to the other.

Some years before Barker, in 1781, the Alsatian painter and scene designer Philippe Jacques de Loutherbourg opened in London the *Eidophusikon*, an entertainment in which a form of painting created, like stage settings, out of three-dimensional elements, was enhanced by ingenious and romantic effects of lighting. De Loutherbourg's ideas were further elaborated by Louis Jacques Mandé Daguerre (1789–1851) who with Claude-Marie Bouton opened his first Diorama in Paris in July 1822 and his second in Regent's Park, London, in September 1823. In the Diorama, a picture of which certain parts were more or less translucent was illuminated from before and behind by a highly sophisticated arrangement of lamps and shutters to produce effects of changing light (dear to the age of Turner and Constable) and transformations.

Polyorama Panoptique, c. 1850: an optical toy which presented the Diorama in miniature form.

The popularity of the Diorama was reflected in the production of miniature adaptations in the form of peepshows for parlour use. The nineteenth century displayed a great taste for peepshows of all kinds; and as we shall see, the earliest motion picture films were shown in a peepshow apparatus.

6 · Heritage

Of all the optical entertainments of this period, the magic lantern was the most popular; and it is with the magic lantern that the technology of the cinema proper begins. The magic lantern worked upon the principle that a brightly illuminated object placed before an objective or magnifying lens will project its inverted image onto a screen in a darkened chamber, the image being enlarged according to the relative distances of the screen and the object from the lens. The principle is still employed in the cinema projector: in its basic form the most elaborate projector is still a magic lantern, while the film and film moving apparatus is a sophisticated equivalent of the simple lantern slide.

The magic lantern had been known at least since the seventeenth century, and throughout most of Europe was toured from village to village by itinerant showmen. These early exhibitions must have been limited, with slides of rough glass painted in opaque colours and feebly illuminated by candles; but with access to better illuminants and more suitable methods of making the slides, the magic lantern came into its own in the nineteenth century. Especially popular in Germany and France, it saw its apogee in England. The noble lanterns of gleaming brass

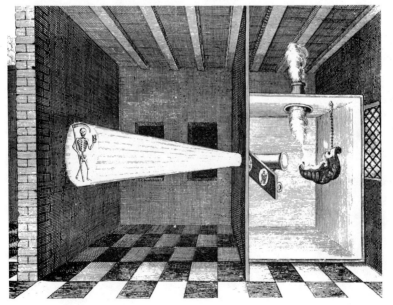

The Magic Lantern, 1761. Illustration from Athanasius Kircher's *Ars Magna Lucis et Umbrae.*

The magic lantern in the home, c. 1840.
A Dioramic print, the image on the screen appearing only
when the picture is illuminated from behind.

English triunial magic lantern, c. 1890.

and polished mahogany created by the English opticians were equalled nowhere else. Equipped with lime-lights, they could effortlessly project a clear image across the Albert Hall. They had often as many as three or four lamps and lenses, so as to produce elaborate effects of dissolving or superimposition. In this way the lanternist could produce effects of transformation more effectively and much more effortlessly than Daguerre with all his Diorama equipment. The zenith was reached between 1870 and 1900, when countless manuals on the lanternist's art were published.

From the start the lantern showman was dissatisfied with the still image; and over the decades there were constant attempts to give movement to the phantoms on the screen. Some of the most elaborate were those of the Belgian showman Etienne Robertson in Paris in the 1790s and his follower Philipstahl in London in the early years of the nineteenth century. Their favourite device was the Phantasmagoria, a system for moving the lantern nearer or further away from the screen while automatically maintaining the focus. The effect was a dramatic enlargement or diminution of the images on the screen, suited to the Gothick flavour of their entertainments. A disciple of Philipstahl, Henry Langdon Childe, developed the effects that could be obtained by projecting two dissolving or superimposed images. Both the Phantasmagoria and Childe's Dissolving Views were later to indicate directions of cinema technique.

As the century went on, a great deal of ingenuity was applied to obtaining effects of movement by means of mechanical lantern slides, which, with levers, ratchets and a variety of sliding glass panels gave an impression of movement. From the 1860s, however, lanternists made various attempts to achieve these effects by a more sophisticated technique. The phenomenon known as 'the persistence of vision', which is the primary physical principle on which the cinema is based, had been observed in ancient times. The retina of the eye retains an impression for a fraction of a second after the image producing the impression has been removed. Hence, for instance (as all children know) a lamp rapidly whirled round and round in the darkness will appear to be a continuous circle of light. The phenomenon was the subject of learned papers by the British physicists Peter Mark Roget and Michael Faraday, the Belgian Joseph Plateau and the Austrian Simon Stampfer. A number of optical toys were devised to demonstrate the principle. Plateau and Stampfer independently conceived the idea of a disc with a series of drawings around the edge representing successive phases of a single, restricted, repetitive action – animated cartoons of a sort.

Label from a box containing phenak-isticopes, c. 1833, depicting the mode of operation.

The disc was spun on an axle, and the images were viewed in a mirror through slots cut in the disc's perimeter, which permitted momentary and apparently static vision of the separate images. The effect was to fuse the individual drawings into the impression of a continuous movement.

A more convenient form of this ingenious device was suggested by W. Horner in 1834. In his Zoetrope, the images were arranged on a band inside a drum and were viewed as it was rapidly spun through slits cut in the upper half of the drum opposite the individual images. The Zoetrope became a popular toy after 1860; but its principle was vastly improved by Emile Reynaud (1844–1918) in his brilliant Praxinoscope of 1876. For the slots, which admitted only a very small proportion of the images' light to the eye,

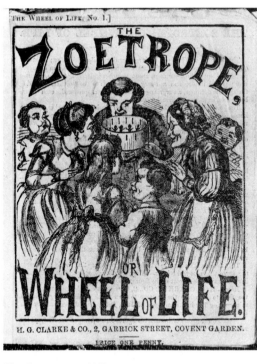

The Zoetrope, c. 1860.

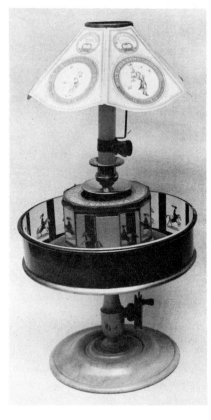

Emile Reynaud's Praxinoscope, 1876.

Reynaud substituted a polygonal drum of mirrors which, as it spun at the centre of the outer drum of images, momentarily reflected their rapid succession, giving a bright and clear impression of movement.

Reynaud continued to make refinements and improvements to his Praxinoscope, culminating in the 'Praxinoscope à Projections'. Here the images were transparent, a bright light was passed through them, and the images reflected off the spinning mirrors were passed through a projecting lens onto a screen. In 1892 Reynaud presented in Paris an elaborate entertainment which he called 'Pantomimes Lumineuses'; by using a continuous band of images for projection it came a significant stage nearer to the cinema. Little sketches were played on the screen by figures whose movements were no longer restricted to the cyclic limits of the phases of a single action. With the 'Pantomimes Lumineuses' the cinema had almost arrived.

Machinery for operating Reynaud's *Pantomimes Lumineuses*, 1892.

One element alone was missing. Reynaud, like the modern animated film-maker, was obliged to *draw* his images, frame by frame. The film proper was to depend upon photography.

The origins of the photographic camera are clearly linked to those of the magic lantern. In the lantern an object is illuminated inside a box and projected by refraction onto a screen in a darkened room *outside* the box. In the *camera obscura*, first described at about the same time as the magic lantern, a brightly illuminated scene is projected by refraction onto a screen *inside* a darkened box or chamber. Throughout the eighteenth and early nineteenth century artists made much use of the *camera obscura*, tracing with a pencil the outlines of a scene thus projected and diminished onto a screen of convenient dimensions. Inevitably they longed for, and ultimately sought, means of mechanically or chemically fixing the projected image, in order to dispense with the labour of manually tracing it. A number of chemists, among them the Englishman Thomas Wedgwood, applied themselves to the problem, but Joseph Nicéphore Niepce (1765–1833) seems to have been the first to succeed, in 1826, in fixing an image on a sensitised plate. Niepce went into association with Louis Jacques Mandé Daguerre (of the Diorama), and experiments continued throughout the 1830s and after the death of Niépce in 1833. But as with the cinema itself, the perfection of photography was more a race to the solution of known problems, than an invention. In 1839 Daguerre's perfected process was bought by the French Government a few weeks after Henry Fox Talbot had announced his 'Calotype' process. As the century progressed, the several advantages of these processes were combined and developed to increase the convenience, the speed and the sensitivity of photography.

Muybridge's arrangement for photographing a horse in motion, 1877–8.

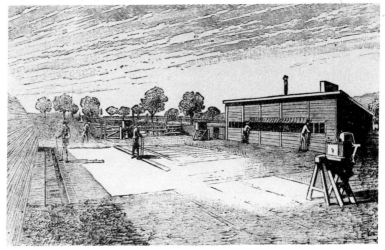

As early as 1849 Plateau suggested the use of Daguerreotypes with a Phenakistiscope; but none of a number of patents and proposals of the 1860s and 1870s reached a solution to the problem of how to take a series of photographs in the rapid succession necessary to reconstitute the appearance of a moving image of an action. Such a device as Heyl's Phasmatrope, demonstrated in Philadelphia in 1870, depended upon photographs obtained by the agonising process of posing models for each individual successive phase of an action. The problem was to be solved eventually by a number of scientists and photographers who had no primary interest at all in synthesising images to produce an impression of motion, but simply sought means to analyse movement.

Eadweard Muybridge (1830–1904) was an Englishman who had gone to the United States in the 1850s, changed his name from the more mundane Edward James Muggeridge, and eventually set up as a photographer. In 1873 he was asked by Governor Leland Stanford of California to produce some instantaneous photographs of one of his favourite race horses. Despite an interruption of his work whilst he was charged with murdering his wife's lover, Muybridge continued with a long series of experiments. By 1877 he had arrived at the solution of setting up a battery of cameras alongside a track, their shutters being released in turn as the horse set off a trigger by touching a cord as it passed each camera. Initially Muybridge's aim was to produce instantaneous single photographs; the production of rapid series was incidental. Over the next few years however Muybridge produced and published innumerable series of photographs of every kind of human or animal motion. In the early 1880s he took the step of re-synthesising his analyses of motion, projecting the short cycles of movement he had recorded by means of a projecting phenakistiscope, which he called a zoöpraxiscope.*

In the course of his travels in Europe, where he was fêted as a celebrity, Muybridge met Etienne Marey (1830–1904) with whom he had been in correspondence for some years. A physiologist, Marey had long been concerned with the graphic recording of various forms of animal mechanism. Certain problems had eluded his solution. For instance, in order to graph the movements of a bird in flight, he had devised an elaborate harness, which certainly recorded the bird's movements, but at the same time hampered and conditioned its flight. He had presented the problem to Muybridge, but the photographs of birds in

*The projected images were still not, properly speaking, photographic: Muybridge was obliged to re-draw them onto the glass discs he used in his projector, copying them by hand from his photographic originals.

flight which Muybridge brought with him to Paris in 1881 were far from satisfactory for Marey's purposes. Marey thereupon profited from an experiment by the astronomer Janssen, who in 1874 had devised a 'photographic revolver'. Intended to record the passage of the planet Venus, this ingenious camera made a successive series of exposures on a single plate, which revolved to expose only one small area of its sensitised surface each time the shutter was opened. In 1881–2 Marey contrived a *fusil photographique* on similar principles, which was capable of taking a series of twelve instantaneous photographs in rapid succession in the course of one second. For some years after this, Marey followed a different line of research, recording moving figures by means of multiple superimposed exposures on a single fixed plate; but in 1888 the appearance of roll film marketed by the Eastman Kodak company made it possible for him to devise a *chronophotographe*, a camera capable of taking a long sequence of photographs on a continuous strip of film. In 1893 he suggested the construction of a projector, to re-synthesise the movements he had thus analysed. But by this time a great many other inventors, rich and poor, scientists and dabblers, visionaries and realists, had foreseen the possibilities of a camera which would analyse and a projector which would reconstitute movement on a screen. Among them were Marey's own assistant Georges Demenÿ, and in England William Friese-Greene and the French-born Louis-Aimé-Augustin Leprince, who seemed teasingly near to solutions of the essential problems when he mysteriously disappeared in 1890.

In 1888 Thomas Alva Edison (1847–1931) met Muybridge, whose zoöpraxiscope evidently gave him the idea for a machine that could record and reproduce images as his phonograph recorded and reproduced sound. He promptly charged his English-born laboratory head, W. K. L. Dickson, with the task of developing something on these lines, and issued the first of a series of *caveats* designed to protect the tentative researches carried on at his establishment at West Orange, New Jersey.

In Paris for the Universal Exhibition of 1889, Edison met Marey, and from him seems to have derived the idea of using roll film. A fourth *caveat* of November 1889 first mooted the idea of perforating the film to secure accurate registration of the image as frame succeeded frame. (This was a problem that had continued to baffle Marey and Demenÿ.) By the autumn of 1890 Dickson had succeeded in taking rapid (up to 40-frames-per-second) sequences of photographs, with a device christened and patented as the Kinetograph. In July 1891 Edison patented the Kinetoscope, a peepshow device in which the images of the Kinetoscope were viewed in motion.

Edison's Kinetoscope, 1892.

From this point dates the production (though not projection) of motion picture films. By February 1893 a curious studio had been built in the grounds of the Edison laboratory. Known as the Black Maria, this was a tar paper hut, with a roof that opened to let in the sun and a pivot so that it could be turned to take best advantage of the light at any time of the day. Inside, at one end stood the heavy Kinetograph camera; at the other, circus and music hall artists were invited to perform brief extracts from their repertoires. Annie Oakley, along with other artists of Buffalo Bill's circus including Colonel Cody himself, the prize-fighters James Corbett and Peter Courtney and the strong man Eugene Sandow were among the first stars of the world's first film studio.

In August 1894 the Kinetoscope Company was founded by Messrs Raff and Gammon to exploit the new marvel on behalf of the Edison laboratories; but before this, in April 1894, the first of many 'Kinetoscope Parlours' had been opened, on Broadway. The film's first public were the patrons of penny arcades – at first in the cities of the U.S.A. but very soon in the old world too – who dropped small coins into peepshow apparatuses to peer through eye-pieces at films that lasted no more than forty or fifty seconds.

Money ultimately has always been the most effective motive for the development of the cinema. It was as much as anything the enthusiasm of the public and the consequent and persuasive tinkle of coins in the cash-boxes of the Kinetoscopes which gave impetus to the final stage of the race to produce an apparatus which could project moving pictures. The takings of the Kinetoscopes were limited by the fact that only one spectator could be accommodated at any one time by a single machine. One solution was suggested by the Photozootrope devised by Henri Joly and advertised by Charles Pathé, in which a single machine had four peepholes and showed two films; but the real solution, quite clearly, was projection.

Technically, as we have seen, the Lumière brothers won the race to combine the principle of the Kinetoscope with the old magic lantern. As well as luck, perhaps, they had advantages over many of their rivals in being rich manufacturers, with the economic resources to develop, protect and exploit their discoveries. Louis (1864–1948) and Auguste (1862–1954) Lumière had gone into their father's photographic factory in Lyon in 1882, when they were respectively eighteen and twenty, and had built up the firm's tottering fortunes through the success of their 'étiquette bleue' photographic plates.

Seeking a direction for further expansion, their father, Antoine Lumiere, is said to have suggested the manufacture of films for the Edison Kinetoscope. The brothers set about the problems of devising a camera, and by February 1895 were able to patent a device which would both photograph *and project* films. An additional patent in March perfected the *Cinématographe*, a machine of neat mahogany and brass which is still a miracle of elegance and compactness.

Throughout the rest of 1895 they were occupied in giving carefully publicised demonstrations to photographic societies. At the June Congress of the Société française de la Photographie, they filmed the delegates. In October they decided the time was ripe to exploit their scientific discovery as a popular spectacle. Negotiations with the Musée Grévin and the Folies-Bergères came to nothing, and a proposal to rent a room over the Théâtre Robert-Houdin – soon to play an important role in the development of the cinema – was abandoned. The Lumières settled on the Salon Indien; and on 28 December 1895 the cinema's official world premiere took place. The event went practically unnoticed. The journalists who had been invited all had better things to do with their Saturday night, and no notices appeared in the Paris papers. Indeed, when in 1924 the City of Paris wanted to commemorate the event with a plaque on the site of the Grand Café, which had disappeared the previous year, no-one could remember its exact date. The public of 1895, however, were not too slow in taking up the novelty; and by January, there were queues for the twenty-minute shows at the Salon Indien.

Within weeks of the Lumières, the English inventors Birt Acres (1854–1918) and Robert William Paul (1870–1943) were able to give projections. Paul was a scientific instrument maker of Hatton Garden. In 1894 he was approached by two Greeks who asked him to copy the Edison Kinematograph for them. Paul went on to produce a large number of these counterfeit machines on his own account; and when Edison retaliated by refusing to supply films to people not in possession of Edison machines, Paul set about

Lumière's
Cinématographe
in operation,
1895.

making a camera in collaboration with Acres. By May 1895 they had patented a camera and were shooting films. By the end of the year they were projecting them; and commenced regular showings in the programme of the Alhambra music hall a fortnight after Lumière's representative, the former illusionist and ombromane, Félicien Trewey, presented the Cinématographe at the Empire.

In Germany, Max Skladanowsky (1863–1939), a member of a family of showpeople who had long specialised in optical entertainments of various kinds, had been experimenting on independent lines; and in fact the first public show of his Bioskop at the Berlin Wintergarten predated the Salon Indien première. His machine was however an elaborate affair using two parallel film strips and two lenses, and so hardly qualifies as a film projector in the sense we have come to understand it.

In America Thomas Armat and C. Francis Jenkins had developed a projection device, the Phantoscope, efficient enough to demonstrate by the end of 1895. Edison and his representatives gained control of the Armat and Jenkins patents, and introduced a projector which they called the Edison Vitascope. The first public showings of the Vitascope took place at Koster and Bial's music hall, 34th Street, New York, over two months before the Lumière Cinématographe made its first appearance in America, at B. F. Keith's music hall.

By the end of 1896 the cinema had spread throughout all Europe and the United States, through the agency of music hall proprietors and enterprising fairground showmen.

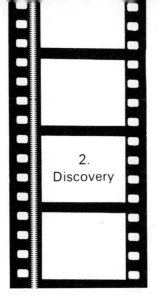

2.
Discovery

The *cinématographe* was still a long way from the cinema. The inventors of 1895–6 had provided a machine, not a medium. The ability to record and subsequently project a moving photographic image was a technological achievement for which there was as yet no evident use, and certainly no aesthetic principles. From time to time someone would throw out grandiose notions of the use that could be made of the cinema; and in 1896 Edison declared, rather boldly in view of the fact that films still ran no more than a minute and were mute:

> I believe that in coming years by my work and that of Dickson, Muybridge, Marie (sic) and others who will doubtlessly enter the field, that grand opera can be given at the Metropolitan Opera House at New York without any material change from the original, and with artists and musicians long since dead.

This statement must be taken as implying no more than a recognition of the value of the cinema as a recording instrument, not as a realisation of its nature as a *theatrical* medium.

Georges Méliès (1861–1938), a magician and proprietor of the Théâtre Robert-Houdin, who was to become the cinema's first true artist, recalled that when he tried to buy a *cinématographe* from Antoine Lumière, the old man refused him: 'Young man, you should thank me. This invention is not for sale, but if it were it would ruin you. It can be exploited for a while as a scientific curiosity; beyond that

Programme of Proctor's Pleasure
Palace, March 1897, including the
Lumière Cinématographe. Items 8 and
10 in the Lumière programme employed
trick effects of reversing the film.
Marie Dressler, starring in the same
bill, was to become a notable star of
films almost forty years later.

Programme Continued.

7   JAMES BALLARD, THE BARD

Of Red Oak, Montgomery County, Iowa, U. S. A.

The Poetical Lecturer, and Only Living Rival of the Charming Cherry Sisters, who holds the World's Record for having written 44,678 lines of poetry (?), and has thus far escaped with his life. The Cherry Sisters are very envious since Mr. Ballard has broken loose in New York.

1. An Eloquent Ode to New York.
2. Gestures, with Rhymes and Tones.
3. The Mind.
4. A Word to the Critics.
5. " Look Out !" (Tune—" Oh, Do !").
6. " Spirit of Progress."
7. " The Bachelor's Consolation."
8. " The Cuckoo " (and it is).
9. " Squeak Ta-a-a It."—Marvelous Bird Imitation.
10. " Chirwain Tit-tit-tit " (another bird of a song).

(This is Mr. Ballard's first engagement in the Effete East.)

8   THE ROGERS BROTHERS

The Famous German Comedians
(Their first engagement at the Pleasure Palace).

9   MISS MARIE DRESSLER

And her Supporting Company, in the Musical and Farcical Spasm, in One Act, by A. R. Phillips, entitled

TESS OF THE VAUDEVILLES

(With apologies to " Tess of the D'Urbervilles ").
Music by Frederick Clifton.   Words by Frederick Backus.

THE CHARACTERS.

SALLY, alias Tess of the Vaudevilles.............................Miss MARIE DRESSLER
MR. SMITH, alias Angel Food...................................FREDERICK BACKUS
MR. BROWN, alias Alec Stoughtenbottle........................FREDERICK CLIFTON

SCENE—A swell apartment on Cherry Hill.

Sixth week of the Scientific Marvel,

10   THE LUMIÈRE CINEMATOGRAPH

The Most Perfect Device yet Invented for the Photographic Portrayal of Life in Motion.

1. The Baby's First Lesson in Walking.
2. The Electrical Carriage Race from Paris to Bordeaux.
3. A Gondola Scene in Venice.
4. The Charge of the Austrian Lancers.
5. Fifty-Ninth Street, opposite Central Park.
6. A Scene near South Kensington, London.
7. The Fish Market at Marseilles, France.
8. German Dragoons Leaping the Hurdles
(Also a reverse view of this picture).
9. A Snow Battle at Lyons, France.
10. Negro Minstrels Dancing in the London Streets.
11. A Sack Race Between Employees of Lumiere & Son's Factory, Lyons.
12. The Baths of Minerva, at Milan, Italy
(Also a droll effect obtained by reversing the film).

it has no commercial future'. The story is almost certainly apocryphal, but it does accurately illustrate how far were most of the first exhibitors from realising that they had a medium for artistic expression in their hands, and not just a new optical toy. Méliès, after all, only wanted it to add to his repertory of conjuring tricks; and it is significant that Albert Hopkins' massive handbook of *Magic*, published in 1897, includes moving pictures alongside stage illusions.

For the earliest exhibitors what mattered was the phenomenon: the pictures moved. Their audiences, as we know from contemporary reviews of film shows, were so enchanted to notice that even the backgrounds moved, the leaves on the trees and the waves on the beach, that they were fairly unconcerned with what they saw. Any familiar scene or action was exciting in itself: *High Seas at Brighton*, *Arrival of a Train*, *Workers Leaving a Factory*, *Men Playing Cards* or, for the big thrills, *Demolition of a Wall* or *The Turn-out of the Leeds Fire Brigade*. The subjects were suggested by lantern slides, picture post-cards and stereoscope slides rather than by the theatre, literature or other entertainment or narrative media.

But if the theatrical nature of the medium was not at first obvious, the cinema was still quickly associated with the theatre. The first exhibitors of motion pictures were music hall proprietors, always eager to discover novelties for their audiences, who looked to them for variety and strangeness in the very mixed bills of twenty or thirty acts which they provided. In Paris the Lumière Cinématographe was booked in the Eldorado Music Hall; and the Olympia and the *caf'concert* Ba-ta-clan were also soon showing films. In London the Lumières opened at the Empire and Paul at the Alhambra; and both ran for many months. In the U.S.A. Edison's Vitascope had a triumphant première at Koster and Bial's.

In England, where the film 'turns' on the music-hall bills came characteristically to be devoted to topical reportage, the variety theatres continued to include them right through the First World War, when 'The Latest War Pictures' provided a distinct attraction. In America it was apparently otherwise: films had gone so much out of fashion in vaudeville by the early years of the century that

The Edison Vitascope in a music hall, 1896.

Fairground cinema, c. 1902.

Travelling cinema showmen, c. 1902. The Mottershaw family.

they were placed at the end of the programme in continuous performances, to act as 'chasers' to repel spectators from seeing the bill round twice.

The reputation of the cinema suffered a severe blow in May 1897. It was still novelty enough to provide a sideshow at the smart 'Bazar de la Charité', a grand annual social event when all the aristocracy of Paris gathered to raise money for good causes. A projectionist's carelessness began a conflagration which blazed through the flimsy and inflammable stalls and side-shows of the Bazar. The 140 fatal victims included the Duchesse d'Alençon. Although it would be a mistake to over-estimate the set-back this melancholy occurrence produced in the exploitation of the cinema, it certainly discouraged some more timid sections of the audience, and opened the door to police and local authority control of cinema shows, not only in France, but also in England and America, where the event was spectacularly reported.

By this time however animated pictures had ceased to be a scientific discovery and had become – thanks more to the response of the audience than the will of the first exhibitors – a show. Throughout Europe, from Ireland to Russia, the cinema passed into the hands of travelling fairground showmen. The transition was natural enough: for many generations the rustic audience had discovered what was happening in the cities and the great world through the annual fairs. For the showmen it was no great leap to transform their puppet shows, fit-up theatres, waxwork exhibitions into Electric Theatres and Bioscopes. For several years the fairground cinemas prospered without competition. Fit-ups became larger and grander and more resplendent with electric lights and steam organs. Both in England and France the best showmen were highly conscientious about the quality of their shows. It was common for the travelling showmen to film street scenes in the towns where they stopped, as a sure attraction to local audiences; and some of them, like the Englishman Walter Haggar, whose horror-drama *The Life of Charles Peace* (1905) remains a classic of the British primitive cinema, became significant producers. In England the fairground theatres lingered on till the eve of the First World War, much longer than in France where the advent of static, permanent cinemas around 1905–6 put the fairground showmen out of business, or forced them to the 'respectability' of regular cinemas.

America, with its larger territories and looser rural communities, had a different tradition of fairs from Europe, and tended to pass directly from the music-hall stage of exhibition to the store cinema. The move towards exclusively cinema shows was helped forward by a vaudeville strike in 1900, when some proprietors stayed open by putting on programmes consisting only of films. In the United States, the motion pictures had first seen (figuratively speaking) the light of day in peepshow arcades; Kinetoscope Parlours became a habit. It was a fairly logical step to enclose the arcade, or to screen off one end of it to make a small cinema. The first such auditorium, the Electric Theatre in Los Angeles, was opened by Thomas L. Tally in 1902, and led to a large-scale conversion of arcades and small stores to five-cent film theatres. From 1905 permanent cinemas began to mushroom throughout the world. In America, where the film had firmly established itself as the entertainment of the working classes, the first 'Nickelodeon' was opened in 1905, in Pittsburgh. (The name, cunningly evoking both the socio-economic

Le Gaumont Palace

Le Plus Grand Cinéma
du Monde

The Gaumont
Palace, Paris
c. 1912. From a
contemporary
advertisement.

level and the aspirations of the theatre, caught on to become a generic name for the first movie houses.) Within three years there were 10,000 such in the States.

In France, where the world's first permanent film theatre had been opened by the Lumières in 1897, energetic building of new theatres began in 1905–6. In England, a regular 'Daily Bioscope' was operating in Bishopsgate, London, from 1904; many old halls and theatres such as the Balham Empire were converted; and in 1908 the first theatre in Britain specifically for cinema shows, the tiny Central Hall, Colne, Lancashire, was built. In Russia it even proved necessary after 1905 to introduce legislation to limit the proliferation of cinemas in large towns, by laying down a statutory minimum distance between neighbouring film theatres.

The Gaumont
Studios, c. 1912.

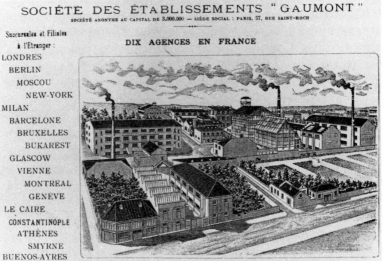

SOCIÉTE DES ÉTABLISSEMENTS "GAUMONT"

SOCIÉTÉ ANONYME AU CAPITAL DE 3.000.000 — SIÈGE SOCIAL : PARIS, 57, RUE SAINT-ROCH

Succursales et Filiales
à l'Etranger :

LONDRES
BERLIN
MOSCOU
NEW-YORK
MILAN
BARCELONE
BRUXELLES
BUKAREST
GLASCOW
VIENNE
MONTRÉAL
GENÈVE
LE CAIRE
CONSTANTINOPLE
ATHÈNES
SMYRNE
BUENOS-AYRES

DIX AGENCES EN FRANCE

Usines des Établissements Gaumont en Exploitation — Paris, 12, rue des Alouettes, 19ᵉ

The development of new forms of exhibition, longer performances, and a vastly growing audience, affected the structure of the industry. In the early days showmen had simply bought films outright, at a fixed price per foot, from producers. Inevitably there was also a brisk market in second-hand films, the prices graded according to the age and condition of prints. As cinemas became permanent and static, and audiences proved willing to patronise one or two or even seven changes of programme in a week, outright purchase was no longer economic, and the first steps were taken towards the present system of film renting. Wherever films were shown, film exchanges began to grow up, hiring out films on a sliding scale of charges according to the age of the copy and the exclusivity of the hire.

Within a very few years of the Lumières' first public show, motion pictures had become very big business indeed. The earliest producers in England and France had mostly been happy potterers, enthusiastic photographers and ingenious instrument makers who had created little films at the cost of a pound or so in their own backyards, and been astonished at the profits that could accrue from a success. Rapidly they were supplanted by new men who saw the advantage of gaining monopolistic control in this new form of entertainment.

The most remarkable of these was perhaps Charles Pathé (1863–1957), who in the space of little more than a decade built up a vast empire which assured France an almost total domination of world cinema in the years before the war; and which even today leaves its traces in most countries of the world. The son of a butcher, Pathé began his career in show business by exhibiting the Edison Phonograph in fairgrounds. Subsequently he began to market counterfeit phonographs and kinetoscopes. As ruthless in his dealings with collaborators as with his rivals, and fortunate in securing large capital investment, he was soon manufacturing equipment and raw stock, and producing films at his studios in Vincennes, the largest and best equipped of the era. This was the first example in the cinema of a complete vertical monopoly organisation. Pathé had control of production, distribution, and, by the acquisition and creation of cinemas, exhibition. Expansion was horizontal also however. The firm had agents in every country where films were known. The years 1903–1909 saw Pathé as the dominant figure in the world's film industry.

In America the Nickelodeon boom boosted production. The old companies, Edison, Vitagraph and Biograph, all dating from the very beginning of the cinema, were joined by new firms who set up their 'factories' in New York, Chicago and Philadelphia. The use of the term 'factory' indicates the nature of and approach to films in America in the early years of the century. They were industrial commodities, uniformly one-reel in length (from five to ten minutes in running time) produced at a regular production-line rate of one or two a week according to the size of the factory, sold and advertised by trade-marks. Films were produced in great secrecy because each company cheerfully plagiarised the ideas of others. Outlays were modest, profits huge.

1909 saw the start of a ferocious struggle for control of the booming film industry. Since the early days of the cinema, Edison had attempted to impose his patents on motion picture equipment. On 1 January 1909 the Motion Picture Patents Company was established. Nine producers – Edison, Biograph, Vitagraph, Essanay, Selig, Lubin, Kalem and the French firms of Méliès and Pathé – together with the distributor George Kleine, pooled their patents claims and in return each received a licence. Edison was paid a royalty on all films sold. George Eastman, the major manufacturer of film stock, contracted to supply only members of the Patents Company. Levies were imposed on exhibitors in consideration of the right to use projectors and films; and there were sanctions to prevent them from showing the product of non-Trust producers. A year later the Patents Company established the General Film Company, through which they endeavoured to gain a total monopoly of film exchanges.

These attempts at domination of the U.S. film industry produced, predictably, a vigorous reaction from independent producers. The agents of the Patents Company were prepared to resort to violence and intimidation in the pursuit of non-Trust producers; and the independents retaliated with no less determination. In 1913 William H. Fox – a distributor who had been forced into production when the Trust refused to supply his film exchange – brought action against the Motion Picture Patents Company under anti-Trust legislation.

By 1914 the Trust had ceased to be in any way effective; but there had been some significant side-effects from its activities. Fleeing from the Trust's strong-arm men, film producers had sought new locations for production. The West Coast near Los Angeles offered not only proximity to the Mexican Border in case of sudden flight, but also a good climate, cheap labour and real estate, and reliable sunshine for photography. Hollywood became the centre of American film production.

Vigorous competition and the need to grab the markets shook the American cinema out of its production-line approach; and the years after 1909 saw an appreciable improvement in the range and standard of films. Another exploitable asset was discovered at the same time. Although French film-makers had quite often filmed celebrated artists of the theatre and music hall, in general players – whether in French, British, American, German, Italian or Scandinavian films – had remained anonymous. This suited the producers, who rightly reckoned that players would demand more money if their names were used as an audience draw. It also suited the actors, who were by and large ashamed of their participation in the 'galloping tin-types' as films were derisively named in the States.

Audiences however liked to identify individual players. Since their heroes had no names they invented them – 'The Biograph Girl', 'The Vitagraph Girl', 'Little Mary'. The producers held out against identifying their artists – even though fans wrote countless letters to the studios asking for information about their favourites – until 1910, when one of the independent producers, Carl Laemmle of the I.M.P. Company, wanted to advertise his capture of 'The Biograph Girl', Florence Lawrence. He therefore staged a stunt, 'denying' non-existent rumours of the lady's death; and in consequence Miss Lawrence, the first film star, was mobbed by excited fans who tore off fragments of her clothing for souvenirs. Thus was created a new factor in cinema economics that was to grow in importance over the next half-century. Interest in the stars was fostered by fan magazines that began to appear at this time. 'When you can name all the leading players immediately they appear on the screen', advised an early issue of the English magazine *The Pictures* (22 June 1912), 'motion-pictures will bring you more enjoyment than ever. The best way to learn the identity of your favourite photoplayers is to get photographic post-cards of them.' The appearance of the film star was not solely an American phenomenon. Other film-producing countries – but notably Italy and Russia – produced their stars, some of whom like the Russian Ivan Mosjoukine, the Italian Lyda Borelli and the Danish Asta Neilsen were to achieve international celebrity and economic importance.

While the cinema was thus evolving its characteristic organisational and economic form, film-makers were discovering techniques and aesthetic principles. Presented with a new medium, no-one could define, *a priori* and complete, its nature and its rules. They had to be discovered, bit by bit, generally by reference to existing media and to that pre-history which has been described in Chapter 1. The structural peculiarities, the dramatic potential, the whole artistic nature of the film medium, were only to be developed gradually over many years; but within a surprisingly short time after the first Lumière show the full range of *optical* techniques had been realised or indicated.

The compositional possibilities of the image were explored. For several years, long after the discovery of the story film, film-makers retained a preference for using the screen like a stage proscenium. The entire scene was viewed from a fixed, head-on position; all figures were shown in full-length, from head to feet; characters entered and left the screen as they entered and left the stage. Yet too much can be made of this, and of the innumerable legends about cameramen reproached because the framing cut off the feet or the legs of a figure.

For in fact audiences and film-makers alike were well accustomed to the very sophisticated approaches of late nineteenth-century photography, which regularly used close-ups, mid-shots and any variation of framing. Georges Sadoul, the French historian, has pointed out that in one of the first Lumière films, *Arrivée d'un train*, the composition – the train moving diagonally across the screen – is characteristic of a good still photograph; while the fact that the movement of the action is from the rear-ground to the foreground of the picture, means that the composition changes from long shot to medium shot to medium close shot within the same strip of film. Likewise, at least two of the first Lumière films, *La Conversation de Lagrange et Janssen* and *Le Déjeuner de bébé*, employ mid shot, viewing the figures within them only from the waist upwards. By 1900 the English film maker George Albert Smith had made deliberate use of extreme close-up for comic effect (*Grandma's Reading Glass*).

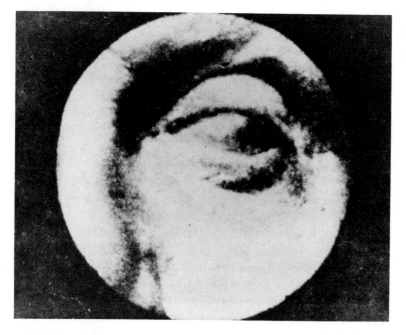

G. A. Smith: *Grandma's Reading Glass.* Britain, 1900.

Victorian photography offered the film-maker a whole repertory of photographic tricks which were to be exploited extensively in the early years of this century. For instance, in 1897 G. A. Smith *patented* the application of double exposure to cinematograph films; and energetically used the effect in films like *The Corsican Brothers, Photo-*

graphing a Ghost, Faust and Mephistopheles and other one-minute spectacles.

Other tricks in the cameraman's repertoire had direct links with the nineteenth-century spectacle theatre. In 1896 a Lumière cameraman operated his *cinématographe* whilst sailing in a gondola down the Grand Canal. The resulting shot, prototype of the travelling shot, when projected onto the screen gave the impression that the scenery of Venice itself moved before the audience's gaze, an effect that had been produced in the theatre by the roller panorama, or by panoramic lantern slides. (The effect was later used to great effect and profit in the well-loved and famous Hale's Tours, which flourished between 1904 and 1912. Devised by a former Kansas City Fire Chief, the auditorium was constructed in the form of a railway car in which the audience sat and looked through an observation window at a screen on which the moving panorama was projected.) At a very early date, at least as early as 1901 according to trade advertisements, tripods were fitted with a swivel head; the image obtained by turning the camera in this way is to this day known as the panoramic, or 'pan', shot.

The backward or forward (tracking) movement of a camera nearer to or further away from the object photographed was already predicted by the phantasmagoria lantern of the end of the eighteenth century; and when in 1901 a tracking camera was used by Georges Méliès it was for exactly the same purpose as the old phantasmagoria, to produce magical effects of the enlargement and diminution of the image (*L'Homme à la tête de caoutchouc*). (In this connection it is interesting to note that primitive audiences, who have never before seen films, are often unable to perceive tracking-in as being an approximation of the viewpoint and the object, but see only an effect of enlargement in a single plane.) Before this, in the 90s, dramatic tracking effects had been achieved by strapping the film camera onto the front of moving locomotives.

Other discoveries of film technique, however, were exclusive and peculiar to the motion picture film. In 1896 a Lumière cameraman filming at the Baths of Minerva in Milan discovered that if he filmed with his camera upside

Georges Méliès: *L'Homme à la tête de caoutchouc.* France, 1901.

In this brilliant little trick film, Méliès, in the role of an enthusiastic but eccentric scientist, is seen placing his own head upon a table, and attaching to it an indiarubber tube and bellows, with which he inflates the head, as if it were a balloon, to vast size. He repeats this and finally the head explodes. The accompanying illustrations show how Méliès borrowed from other sources and other techniques.

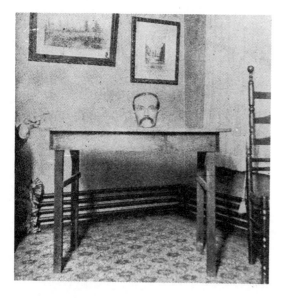

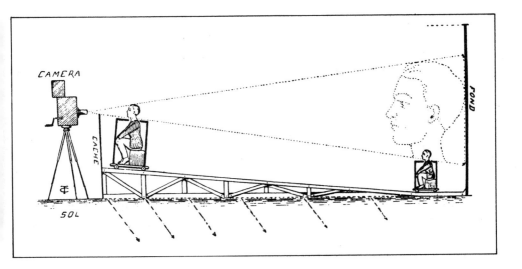

An illustration of the technique of superimposition, from the chapter on 'Trick Photography' in Albert Hopkins' *Magic* (1896), a book with which Méliès is known to have been familiar. A mid-19th century illustration of a phantasmagoria lantern is compared with Méliès's own arrangement for filming the head against a black background, preparatory to superimposing it on the scene already filmed. The old lantern showman produced effects of a growing image by moving their projectors *away from* the screen; Méliès achieved the effect in filming by moving the object *towards* his camera.

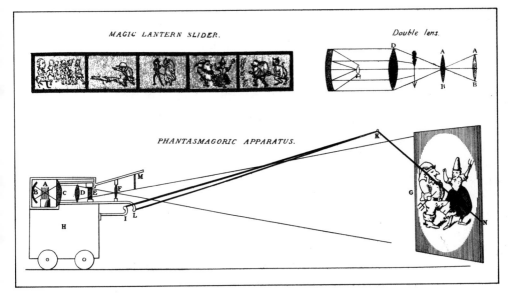

down, the action could subsequently be projected in reverse. The trick of substitution – stopping the camera and in some respect changing the scene being photographed before re-starting it – which is basic to most cinema trick-work, was discovered as early as 1895, when an Edison cameraman used it to produce a convincing effect of the beheading in *The Execution of Mary Stuart*. By 1900, then, the film's visual vocabulary had been recognised. Only gradually was the idea of a syntax appreciated, the notion that the essence of cinema is the juxtaposition of shots into an expressive continuum.

The first films, as we have seen, were literally animated photographs, each one a single shot of a single scene or action. Their repertory was analagous to that of the photographs marketed for use in the stereoscope, which enjoyed particular vogues in the 1860s and again in the 1890s. They might be scenic actualities; they might present a single visual joke (an English film of 1898, R. W. Paul's *Come Along, Do!* is directly taken from a favourite stereoscope slide, in turn taken from a comic song inspired by a narra-tive painting which was itself inspired by the painted Venus in the 1862 International Exhibition). They might present costume tableaux. More extraordinarily they would restage topical events – the Assassination of President McKinley, the Dreyfus Court-martial, or more ambitiously, with the use of models, the Eruption of Mount Pelée or the Wreck of the 'Maine'. There was no conscious attempt to deceive with these reconstructions: they were simply equivalent to the artists' impressions of news events which illustrated *The Illustrated London News* or *L'Illustration* or the more rakish daily press before half-tone photographic reproduc-tion came into general use.

It did not require a large inventive effort – given the example of the theatre, or of series-illustrations in maga-zines, or of the stereoscope repertory itself, which often included 'sets' of a particular subject – to assemble whole series of these *tableaux vivants*. Thus at Easter 1898 two rival American exhibitors both presented *Passion of Our Lord* (allegedly shot, respectively, at Oberammergau and Horitz; in fact one was shot on the roof of a New York theatre, though the other could conceivably have been shot at

Horitz by a Lumière cameraman). The dozen or so tableaux followed the precise method of the stereoscope series *La Passion de Notre Seigneur*, which had been available since the 1860s, neatly packed in boxes of twelve and daintily hand-coloured, as indeed were the films themselves. A year later the French director Georges Méliès was using similar techniques for secular stories – his reconstruction of *L'Affaire Dreyfus*, a *Cendrillon*, a *Jeanne d'Arc* in ten scenes. The method rapidly became general for story films. Each shot still represented a single, self-contained scene, with its own setting, its own entrances and exits, beginning and end. The only link between them was the same sort of logical and chronological logic as between the scenes of a play.

The first significant step towards a conception of montage as we know it – towards the discovery of a specific syntax for motion pictures – was, it appears, Edwin S. Porter's (1870–1941) *The Life of An American Fireman*, made at the end of 1902 or the beginning of 1903. Fire and the activities of the fire service were a popular subject for the early film-makers as they had been with magic lantern showmen. Only a month or so before Porter's film the English director James Williamson (1855–1933) had made *Fire!* which brought the old tableaux-scene method much nearer to an idea of montage. Porter's film however *is* montage. Taking random scenes of fires and firemen, and shooting some additional material of his own, he assembled a dramatic film:

> Porter's decision to construct a story film from previously shot material was unprecedented. It implied that the meaning of a shot was not necessarily self-contained but could be modified by joining the shot to others . . .
>
> The events which form the climax of *The Life of an American Fireman* are rendered in three stages. A dramatic problem is set in the first shot which is not resolved till the end of the third. The action is carried over from shot to shot and an illusion of continuous development is created. Instead of splitting the action into three self-contained sections joined by titles – which is how Méliès might have tackled the situation

– Porter simply joined the shots together. As a result the spectator felt that he was witnessing a single continuous event.

By constructing his film in this way, Porter was able to present a long, physically complicated incident without resorting to the jerky, one-point-at-a-time continuity of a Méliès film. But the gain derived from the new method is more than a gain in fluency. For one thing it gives the director an almost limitless freedom of movement since he can split up the action into small, manageable units. In the climax of *The Life of an American Fireman*, Porter combined the two hitherto separate styles of film-making: he joined an actuality shot to a staged studio shot without apparently breaking the thread of the action.

Another equally fundamental advantage of Porter's method of assembly is that the director is able to convey a sense of time to the spectator . . . An operation taking a considerable length of time is compressed into the space of a one-reeler without, apparently, any discontinuity in the narrative: only the significant parts of the story are selected and joined to form an acceptable, logically developing continuity.*

At one point in the drama, for emphasis, Porter cut in a close-up of a fire alarm being sounded.

The film, quite suddenly, had discovered a new story-telling method. In *The Great Train Robbery*, registered for copyright at the end of 1903, Porter used his editing technique with even greater freedom and sophistication, introducing the idea of parallel and overlapping action. One scene shows us the bandits making off towards the crime; the next shows the rescue of the telegraph operator, whom they have left bound and gagged, by his little daughter; the next is a dance hall, into which the exhausted but now freed operator suddenly bursts with news of the impending robbery. The film is naive enough by our standards; but the enthusiasm with which audiences throughout the world greeted its appearance indicates how momentous were Porter's discoveries. Audiences knew only that the

*Karel Reisz, *The Technique of Film Editing* (London, 1953).

Edwin S. Porter:
The Great Train Robbery.
U.S.A., 1903.
Series of stills illustrating
editing principle adopted
by Porter. [*footage*].

1   [14] *Title:* The Great Train Robbery Copyright
    Dec. 1904.
2   [70] *Long shot:* Telegraph room. As a train
    passes window bandits hold up telegraph
    operator. They hide under a table as the
    train halts, then knock out and tie up
    operator. Bandits leave.
3   [37] *Medium long shot:* Train draws up to a
    water feed. Bandits approach train and
    assault driver when he attempts to escape.
4   [63] *Medium long shot:* Inside train. Guard
    surprised by bandits, who shoot him. They
    blow up the strong box.
5   [49] *Medium long shot:* Rear view of moving
    engine. Bandit overpowers driver. Fireman
    attempts to hit second bandit with shovel,
    but is overpowered and thrown over side of
    train.
6   [22] *Medium long shot:* Oblique view of side of
    train. Driver is made to get down at gun-
    point. The engine is slipped.
7   [22] *Medium long shot:* Other side of train,
    a less oblique view. Passengers dismount and
    are held up. One who tries to escape is shot.
    The bandits rob the passengers and make off.
8   [18] *Medium long shot:* Side view of engine.
    The bandits, carrying their loot, climb
    rapidly onto the engine and drive it off into
    the distance.

9   [17] *Medium long shot:* Side view of engine. Bandits leap from train, with loot, and run off into wooded siding. *Camera pans to follow them into woods.*

10   [52] *Long shot:* The woods. Bandits move forward between trees, mount horses and ride away. *Camera pans to follow them.*

11   [53] *Medium long shot:* The telegraph office. Operator lying unconscious on floor. His little daughter comes in with his lunch, sees him on floor, tries to revive him, unties him, throws water in his face. He revives.

12   [74] *Medium long shot:* Barn dance in progress. After some time it is interrupted by the entry of the now-recovered operator, who leads the whole party out.

13   [37] *Medium long shot:* The woods, a road. Pursuit towards camera with gunfire. One man is shot, falls off horse. Another dismounts to aid him.

14   [61] *Long shot:* The woods. Bandits sharing loot are surprised by pursuers. All bandits are shot and the loot recovered.

15   [7] *Close up:* Moustachio'd man. He raises hand holding pistol into view, points it at the audience; and fires.

film stirred and excited them more than anything they had seen on the screen before: few of them perhaps recognised that the drama and emotional power were generated by Porter's juxtaposition of shots and images, rather than the individual content of those shots.

Film-makers, clearly, did analyse Porter's discovery; for though the tableau film survived for many more years, Porter's style of editing became common practise. By 1905 the English director Cecil Hepworth (1874–1956) was editing with extreme sophistication and fluidity in his *Rescued by Rover*, a dramatic chase film about a brave dog's rescue of a baby kidnapped by a wicked gypsy woman.

The cinema had finally to discover that it was an art. The new medium was uniquely fortunate in bringing forth within a few weeks of the Lumière show its first great artist. Georges Méliès' films are the earliest which still retain their artistic validity today. Films which he made almost seventy years earlier were still being run in commercial cinemas in Paris in the 1970s. Such durability is all the more remarkable when it is considered that in contrast to his contemporaries he was (and became much more so in the course of his career) something of a reactionary.

Méliès happily was not convinced by the rebuff of Lumière *père*, when he attempted to buy a *cinématographe* in 1895–6. He bought a projector from R. W. Paul in London, devised a camera in collaboration with an associate, and was in business (so easy was it in those days) as a film producer. Within a matter of weeks he had made his discovery – revolutionary then, however obvious it may now seem – that scenes could be *staged* for the camera in a theatrical way: the film-maker need not restrict himself to moving snapshots taken from life.

Méliès's role as inventor of the *spectacle cinématographique* and of *vues composées* is a matter of historical record. What captivates us today is the content of these *spectacles* and *vues*, the way in which Méliès' lively and unique vision, working over a whole field of popular, late nineteenth-century theatre, turned it into a new, singular and enduring art.

When he made his first film in April or May 1896, he was thirty-four years old. Born in 1861, the son of a rich footwear manufacturer, he enjoyed a sound literary education. He had done his military service, and later a stint as a caricaturist on the satirical journal *La Griffe*. The year that decided his career however was 1884–5 when his parents sent him to London to perfect his English. He took the opportunity to absorb new theatrical impressions. To avoid the strain the regular drama placed upon his small command of the language, he frequented those entertainments – of which London in the eighties offered plenty – where there was not much talk and plenty to see. Most of his time however was spent at Maskelyne and Cooke's Marvellous and Mysterious Entertainment at the Egyptian Hall. Here he developed a passion for magic, which eventually led him, in 1888, when his own considerable fortune had been augmented by a wealthy marriage, to lease the Théâtre Robert-Houdin. As a magician and prestidigitator he proved a worthy successor to the founder of the theatre.

Installed in his own theatre he was not only proprietor and manager, but producer, actor, designer, author and conjuror. The entertainments he presented reveal the variety of his theatrical interests, and prefigure the character of his films. Conjuring in the French tradition of Robert-Houdin met the newer, more sceptic English style of Maskelyne and Cooke. The pantomime-spectacles of the Eden and Châtelet theatres (from which Méliès was often to recruit his *corps de ballet*) fused with the more Anglo-Saxon manner of the Alhambra ballet and the London pantomimes.

By the time of the Lumière projections at the Grand Café, Méliès had been in command of his own theatre for seven years. At first he regarded the new invention as a novel addition to his repertory of spectacle and magic. Soon it was to supplant the magic theatre as his primary interest. As a film-maker Méliès delighted in his own versatility. Again he was producer, director, scenarist, designer, sometimes cameraman and generally actor. He designed and built the world's first true film studio, an outsize glass-house at Montreuil-sous-Bois. There, between 1896 and 1914, he made well over one thousand films, ranging from action-packed three-minute *trucs* to twenty-minute stories and spectacles.

It was as a magician that he arrived at his most important and influential discoveries. Making films with an eye to incorporating them in the programmes of the Théâtre Robert-Houdin, and approaching them with all the ingenuity of a professional stage magician, he quickly found out the whole range of camera trickery. But his quality lies much deeper than ingenuity. His trick films have marvellous pace and rhythm and variety. Insects turn into voluptuous Edwardian beauties; devils come and go in puffs of smoke; the magician produces from small but very mysterious coffers the furnishings of a whole palace, or an entire Châtelet chorus-line. The trick films have their own surrealism, as *Off to Bloomingdale Asylum* (1901):

> An omnibus arrives drawn by an extraordinary mechanical horse. On the top are four negroes. The horse kicks and upsets the negroes, who are changed into white clowns. They slap each other's faces and by the blows become black again. They kick each other and become white once more. Finally they are all merged into one large negro, and when he refuses to pay his car fare the conductor sets fire to the omnibus and the negro bursts into a thousand pieces.*

In the *féeries* and fantasy films the same trick techniques were wedded to *mises-en-scène* conceived in a florid Victorian baroque of peculiar appeal. Their subjects indicate how much the *féeries* were inspired by the Alhambra or the Châtelet ballets – two versions of *Cendrillon* (1899, 1912), *Le Royaume des fées* (1903), *Barbe Bleue* (1901), *Le Palais des mille et une nuits* (1905), *La Fée Carabosse* (1906). The fantasies *Le Voyage à travers l'impossible* (1904), *200,000 lieues sous les mers* (1907) *A la conquête du Pôle* (1912) and – the earliest and most famous – *Le Voyage dans la lune* (1902), endearingly combined Jules Verne with the Châtelet fairies.

The film that established Méliès on the international, and particularly the American, market, was *Le Voyage dans la lune*. The wit, brilliance and charm of its little tableaux

*Méliès Catalogue, 1901.

Georges Méliès: c. 1928.

Georges Méliès: *200,000 lieues
sous les mers*. France, 1906.

were a revelation to movie-goers still accustomed to pictures of street-scenes and crude realisations of comic-strip gags. Méliès indicated possibilities of organisation and art not yet conceived. His films were enthusiastically bought, and still more enthusiastically pirated in America. Méliès was encouraged – and also forced for his own protection – to open a New York branch of his Star Film Company. The reputation which he commanded in the first decade of the century is indicated by the fact that he was elected President of the Congrès International des Editeurs de Films in February 1909, at which every leading film-maker in the world was present.

But the Congress was ominous. Already there were signs of the future: the battles for control of a major industry in which men like Méliès were ill-armed. Moreover Méliès was already falling behind in his methods. He was unable to change his highly personal ways. By the time of the First World War, the international audience which had adored *Le Voyage dans la lune* had tired of him. They already preferred the thrillers of Feuillade, the new American comedies, films which took in a wider world than Méliès' tiny stage could reproduce. Production had become no cheaper and the work of pirates and imitators and under-cutters had affected profits. The cinema was the reserve of big business and a dangerous place for the solitary artist. Méliès became a thrall in the Pathé Empire, and after 1913 was forced to give up production altogether. He turned his studio into a theatre where he struggled on for a few years. In 1923 in an access of despair he sold all his negatives to a manufacturer for the sake of the celluloid, which is why barely fifty films survive out of the thousands which he produced.

In the late twenties he was discovered, poor and aged, keeping a draughty gift kiosk on the Gare Montparnasse. Ultimately he and his wife (and former leading lady) were found a place in the home for cinema veterans where Méliès spent the last years in some kind of comfort, and honoured by a new generation. He died in 1938, three years before Edwin S. Porter, who had spent his later years as an obscure factory mechanic. The cinema has never been a grateful child.

There was something a little ironic about the motto of Méliès Star Film Company: 'Le monde à la portée de la main'. The world of pasteboard and plaster which he created on the stage of his little glass-house studio was impossibly claustrophobic – this was part of its never-never charm. Other film-makers were meanwhile fascinated by the possibilities for realism which the cinema offered.

Edwin S. Porter's *The Great Train Robbery* (1903) was itself significant of the direction the American story film was taking. The cinema found its audiences largely in the poorer urban communities; this form of mute drama was especially attractive to the vast immigrant population with neither money nor a strong command of the English language. It is a curious phenomenon that socially depressed audiences do not as a rule seek, as might be expected, escapist entertainment (which historically has proved the ideal of bourgeois societies). The English music hall for instance had strongly realist roots. So did the American cinema in the first stages of evolution of story films. The favourite plot motives observed by the historian Lewis Jacobs* were crime, the penalties and romantically ennobling effects of poverty, the horrors of drink, the role of women, and other themes derived from the realities of urban life. But film-makers, particularly after being driven West by the harassments of the Motion Pictures Patents Company, discovered another America, the open spaces of the West which had so much momentous recent history to provide stories about the settlers' battles with the Indians and the environment. With the 'Western' came a new appreciation of the pictorial scope of the screen, the recognition of an epic potential in the silent drama.

The humble British producers of the early days had made an odder compromise with realism. Fascinated by the trick techniques exploited by Méliès, but lacking his extravagant notions and possibilities for *mise-en-scène* they had tended to stage tricks in natural locations: their own front gardens, the countryside near Brighton, side streets in provincial suburbia. English film-makers had also developed one of the cinema's most potent dramatic motifs: the chase.

*Lewis Jacobs, *The Rise of the American Film* (New York, 1939).

The master of the genre was Alfred Collins who worked for the British branch of the Gaumont Company (*The Runaway Match, or, Marriage by Motor; Welshed, A Derby Day Incident*, both made in 1903) though other companies such as the Sheffield Photo Company (*Daring Daylight Burglary*) and James Williamson (*Fire!*, 1903; *Stop Thief!* 1901) also made a speciality of them.

Both these tendencies in British film-making at the turn of the century were annexed by Ferdinand Zecca in France. Zecca (1864–1947), a former monologuist in *caf'* concerts, took over direction of Pathé's production around 1900. With great flair he plagiarised everybody and tried everything. At first he recognised a taste for realism which he obliged with *Histoire d'un crime* (1901) and *Les Victimes de l'alcoolisme* (1902), a dramatic five-minute résumé of Zola's *L'Assommoir*. In 1903 he made a *Passion* which showed a marked advance on the 1898 productions. With his collaborators, who included Gaston Velle, a former prestidigitator and specialist in trick films, Lucien Nonguet, Louis Gasnier and Georges Hatot, he cheerfully turned his hand alike to *sujets piquants*, to *féeries* and science fiction in the Méliès manner, to realist themes and romantic tales, to reconstructions of topical events.

At the Vincennes Studios, Zecca and his collaborators, employing the chase for comic purposes (more often than not the English directors used it for its dramatic and suspense effects) brought it to an art. Using professional acrobats, and all the trickery learned from Méliès, the pursuits of *Dix femmes pour un mari*, *La Course à la perruque*, *La course aux tonneaux* (all 1905) achieved a hysterical and surreal fantasy, with crocodiles of policemen running up walls, across roofs and tumbling like packs of cards into rivers. These *courses* developed extraordinary rhythm and fluidity, and brought new refinements to the art of editing.

One of the acrobats recruited for the *courses* shot in Pathé's Vincennes Studios was André Deed (1884–193?). Before being engaged by Pathé, Deed had worked in Méliès's studio at Montreuil, where he had learned much about the craft of films and comic magic; and he was the first comedian to make full use of all the technical possibilities of accelerated motion, substitution and other camera

trickery. Beyond this, though, Deed brought to the cinema a tradition of clowning that derived from the Italian pierrot and the Augustes of the circus ring. He was the first cinema comedian to employ the structured gag. In 1908 Deed went to Italy to work for the Itala Film Company; but by that time the Pathé Studios had a whole stable of comedians whom they starred in series that were immensely popular throughout the world: Charles Prince, Louis-Jacques Boucot, Dranem, Roméo Bosetti, who ran Pathé's new Comica Studio in Nice devoted exclusively to comedy production, Little Moritz, Sarah Duhamel, Cazalis, Léon Durac, who created a series about Nick Winter, a comic detective based irreverently on the popular Nick Carter.

The Pathé Studios' greatest discovery was Max Linder (1882–1925), who shaped the whole future of film comedy. A serious but not very successful dramatic actor, in about 1905 he changed his name from Gabriel Levielle to mitigate the shame of picking up a living as an extra in films. After

André Deed: *Cretinetti al cinema.* Italy, 1911.

Deed's defection, Linder was given his own series, in which he gradually developed his screen character: the elegant young boulevardier with sleek hair, neatly rakish moustache, elegant cutaway, beautiful cravat, splendid silk hat and trim walking cane. The screen Max was resourceful, intelligent and usually able to get out of the scrapes into which his roving eye invariably led him. He broke entirely from the tradition of the Pathé clowns – naturals thrown into a world of frenetic and exaggerated activity. Max's comedy lay in the contrast between his own normality and elegance and the lunacy of the adventures that befell him. His performance was measured and controlled, and imposed upon all his films a distinctive, oddly syncopated rhythm.

Despite his stage origins, Linder perfectly understood the visual needs and possibilities of the silent screen. His invention was prodigious. He could conceive endless variations upon a single simple activity like taking a bath or wearing a pair of new shoes. Rarely repeating himself in

Max Linder, c. 1910.

the course of more than four hundred films, he built up a vast repertory of gags which has hardly been enlarged by the film comedians who have followed him.

The Gaumont Studios competed vigorously with the Vincennes comedies. The guiding artistic force was Louis Feuillade (1873–1925), later to achieve his greatest distinction in quite another genre of film production. The Gaumont comedies tended to more extravagant use of trick techniques. The principal Gaumont clowns were Onésime (a character created by Ernest Bourbon but taken over by Marcel Levesque), Calmo, Léonce Perret (later to be a distinguished director), and two child comedians, Bébé Abeilard and Bout-de-Zan.

The influence of the French comedies rapidly spread to other countries, notably Russia and Italy, which apart from Deed (Tontolini) boasted a whole range of comedians of its own, among them Ferdinando Guillaume, Marcel Fabre and Emilio Vardannes. In Germany a popular series was built around the character of the Jewish 'Meyer', played by another clown subsequently to achieve distinction as a director, Ernst Lubitsch (1892–1947).

French film producers also sought more apparent ways to art than these essentially popular forms. In 1906, Pathé, in a further bid to assume monopoly of all areas of film activity, formed the Société Cinématographique des Auteurs et Gens de Lettres (S.C.A.G.L.) with a view to filming the classics of the modern theatrical and literary repertory. Two years later the Société Film d'Art was formed by the Frères Lafitte, with partial control, inevitably, by Pathé. The Film d'Art commissioned original scenarios from all the greatest living writers, and signed contracts with stars of the Comédie Française, including Bernhardt and Mounet-Sully. In 1908 the company presented its first programme, in which the main item was *L'Assassinat du Duc de Guise*, directed by Le Bargy and Calmettes, written by Henri Lavedan, and with a musical accompaniment by Camille Saint-Saëns. In its day the film was startling for the restraint and psychological perception of the acting, as well as for its lavish décors and costumes. The Société Film d'Art went pretty rapidly into liquidation (helped there, it is said, by Pathé politics); but every French producer aimed to emulate its literary and decorative distinction. The most interesting of the films which resulted from the vogue were several with Bernhardt (*La Reine Elisabeth*, *La Dame aux camélias*), *Madame sans gêne*, (1911) with Réjane, and a number of films directed for Pathé by the gifted Albert Capellani (1870–1931): *L'Arlésienne*, *Le Roi s'amuse*, *Les Mystères de Paris*, *Les Misérables*. Gaumont's series of 'Films Esthétiques' included *Aux lions les chrétiens* (1910).

The *film d'art* had a profound influence in other film-producing countries. In Italy, where Pathé founded Film d'Arte Italiana, the cinema hired actors like Amleto Novelli and Lydia de Roberti, and filmed Shakespeare, Dante, Bulwer Lytton and Sienkiewicz. In Britain actors as distinguished as the younger Irving (*The Bells*), Cyril Maude (*Beauty and the Barge*, from his stage success), Ellaline Terriss and Seymour Hicks (*David Garrick*) and Charles Wyndham (a rival *David Garrick*) deigned to appear in films. Cecil Hepworth, only recently the director of *Rescued by Rover* (1905), made a speciality of dignified, pedestrian adaptations from Dickens and other well-loved Victorian novelists. With varying success, Sir Johnstone Forbes-Robertson played Hamlet for Hepworth; Sir Herbert Tree played Henry VIII for Will Barker; Frank Benson Richard III; and Godfrey Tearle Romeo, for Gaumont.

In Denmark *Trilby* and *Madame sans gêne* were filmed; and in Germany the Autorenfilm was inaugurated with an adaptation for the screen of Lindau's *Die Anderen*. In Russia the great vogue for costume films (*Death of Ivan the Terrible*, *Demon*, *Eugene Onegin*, *1812*) outlasted the fashion in other countries, since they proved to be reasonably proof against the severe Tsarist censorship. The fact that Hungarian film production on any scale began in the *film d'art* period gave a lasting character to its national cinema – a predilection for literary subjects that was acquired in the years before the First World War and still survives. The leading players of the Budapest National Theatre found it quite natural to play for the cinema.

The advent of the *film d'art* was a mixed blessing. On the

Louis Mercanton: *La Reine Elisabeth*. France, 1912. Sarah Bernhardt.

one hand it undoubtedly brought to the cinema literary and theatrical styles which could be severely inhibiting to the development of the cinema's visual and intellectual development. At its very worst it had a kind of over-upholstered pretension which all too often survives today in commercial 'prestige' productions. But at the same time it served to give the cinema a social and intellectual respectability that attracted the interest of a new audience and brought to the films artists of a different calibre from the first barnstorming generations.

Italy, under the influence of the *film d'art*, developed a style of costume spectacle which gave the Italian cinema a brief international pre-eminence in the years preceding the First World War. Italy had had her own inventor of 1895, Filoteo Alberini (1865–1937). In the first decade of the new century, Alberini's Cines company had a characteristic output of comedies, under the French influence and often with comedians recruited in France, and of dramas which tended to the fashionable 'decadent' style, with *femmes fatales* played by, or in the manner of, the majestic Lyda Borelli.

A taste for historic themes had been evinced as early as 1905, with Alberini's *Il Sacco di Roma*. In 1907 Arturo Ambrosio (1869–1960) made *Marcus Lycinus* and Mario Caserini (1874–1920) *Otello*. After 1909 and the foundation of Film D'Arte Italiana, however, production of costume spectacles began in earnest: Cines' *Beatrice Cenci*, *Lucrezia Borgia* and *Joan of Arc*, Italia's *Count Ugolino*, *Isabella of Aragon*, *Catherine, Countess of Guise*, Ambrosio's *La Schiave di Cartagine, Nerone, Tasso*, Aquila's *Tra le Spire della Rivoluzione Francese*. Many of these subjects were to be made again and again in subsequent years. In 1912 Enrico Guazzoni's *Quo Vadis?* reached new heights of spectacular extravagance, with its thousands of extras, conflagration of Rome and a positive menagerie of lions to devour the Christians. Outside Italy the fame of this early super-production overshadowed that of a much more meritorious work which emerged in 1914, on the eve of the First World War. The authorship of *Cabiria* was credited to Gabriele d'Annunzio, then at the height of his fame; but it seems likely that the poet did little more than sign the work of

Giovanni Pastrone: *Cabiria*. Italy, 1914.

Giovanni Pastrone (1883–1959). An extremely elaborate narrative was expertly controlled and constructed. Vast décors were successfully combined with actual locations. No previous film had made such sustained use of sophisticated camera movement or lighting effects. It was a film which in so many ways anticipates the Griffith of *Intolerance* that to this day it remains an intriguing mystery whether or not the American master came under the direct influence of the Italian film. The early Italian cinema never surpassed *Cabiria*. After the beginning of the war the costume spectacle became an empty formula, though so deeply rooted as a tradition in the Italian studios that it has survived to this day.

Until 1912 producers and exhibitors in America and Great Britain stuck loyally to the one-reel film, with a running time of between five and fifteen minutes. The two-, three- and four-reel subjects which began to arrive from the Continent after the *film d'art* vogue were at first only reluctantly accepted in the United States as some sort of foreign extravagance. Producers at home who attempted to make subjects in multiple reels could only anticipate discouragement. In 1911 for instance D. W. Griffith decided that the story of *Enoch Arden* was important enough to justify two reels; but it was only the insistence of audiences which shifted the distributors from their decision to release it as two separate parts.

In 1912 Adolph Zukor (born 1873), then an exhibitor, had a startling success with the four-reel *La Reine Elisabeth*, starring Sarah Bernhardt. Failing to interest the Motion Picture Patents Company in the possibility of producing ambitious 'feature films', as the multi-reelers were known, Zukor launched his Famous Players in Famous Plays film company, with the name of Charles Frohman, the eminent Broadway impresario, to give it lustre. One producer after another followed Zukor's lead into feature production; but the issue was finally settled in 1913 by the overwhelming success in America of *Quo Vadis?* Far from being unable to concentrate for more than the length of one reel, as the conservative producers and exhibitors had argued, the public thrilled to the Italian film's nine reels and more than two hours' running time. It was given an unprecedented launching, in a legitimate theatre, the Astor, and with the astronomical admission price of $1.50. Within a short time there were twenty-three road shows of *Quo Vadis?* in North America, playing in legitimate theatres.

Thus the success of a group of European films contributed to the revolution which was to assist the American film industry to gain that world-wide domination which to this day has not wholly been relinquished.

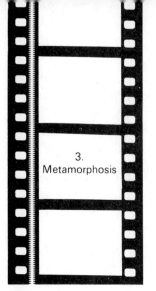

3.
Metamorphosis

The outbreak of the First World War in August 1914 effectively removed European competition and confirmed America's absolute domination of the world's cinema; but the war was not the only cause. Even before 1914, France through the persistence of out-dated production formulas, had begun to slip from the industrial pre-eminence which reached its peak around 1910. The British cinema had never really succeeded in progressing from the artisan to the industrial stage of development; her film-makers had lost the pioneering lead of 1900, and fallen into a habit of stagey literary adaptation which was to persist for many years. In Italy *Cabiria* was the magnificent swan song of a style of production that was declining into stereotype. America meanwhile not only counted on the economic security offered by a massive home market, but had effected, within a few brief years, the artistic maturing of the cinema.

This was practically speaking the single-handed achievement of David Wark Griffith (1875–1948). His great disciple, Erich von Stroheim (1885–1957), wrote of him at his death, that he 'put beauty and poetry into a cheap and tawdry sort of amusement'. His achievement can hardly be paralleled in the history of art. From a popular mechanical entertainment he fashioned an autonomous art, giving it forms and laws that were to remain largely unchanged and unchallenged for the next fifty years.

In Griffith we find the same anomaly as in Méliès. Both were equipped by the nineteenth century to mould the art of the twentieth. D. W. Griffith was born in 1875 (though vanity often made him subtract five years from his age). He came from an impoverished Southern family, claimed that his father was a hero of the Civil War, 'Roaring Jake' Griffith, and always retained a passionate affection and loyalty for the South. He grew up in Louisville where, he said, the family had migrated after being forced out of their old lands and homestead. He worked as an errand boy, cash boy and theatre super before committing himself to the stage as a member of the Meffert Stock Company in 1897. For the next ten years engagements as a strolling actor alternated with a variety of menial fill-in jobs. Throughout his life, even when he had become the most honoured film artist in the world, Griffith cherished ambitions in literature. In these early years he occasionally managed to sell a short story or poem; and in 1907, he succeeded in selling his play *A Fool and A Girl* to the impresario James Hackett. But even with the great stage star Fannie Ward, the production failed; perhaps this disappointment helped drive Griffith, recently married, to the extreme step (for an established stage actor) of finding work in the movies. According to Griffith's first wife* – an entertaining but not always reliable authority – Griffith had never seen a movie when he first tried to sell a scenario (an adaptation of *Tosca*) to the Edison Studio. The scenario was rejected, but Edwin S. Porter hired Griffith as an actor in the short melodrama *Rescued from an Eagle's Nest* (1907). Griffith next succeeded in selling some scenarios to the American Biograph Company. His work proved superior to the general run of Biograph material and he stayed on. In the summer of 1908 he was allowed to direct a film, *The Adventures of Dollie*. In this action-filled nine-minute melodrama he began his collaboration with the cameraman G. W. (Billy) Bitzer, who was to photograph all Griffith's silent films and contribute largely to his artistic discoveries. Even in this first insignificant work Bitzer was surprised by the care Griffith took in casting his actors and choosing his locations.

*Mrs D. W. Griffith, *When The Movies Were Young* (New York, 1925 and 1969).

In the course of the next five years, Griffith made a vast number of films (upwards of five hundred) at Biograph. Turned out at such a rate, many of them must have been repetitive and stereotyped. Even so they seem to have been superior in content and technique to anything that had been seen in the American cinema before. Biograph's previously failing fortunes soared along with the popularity of its new films; and Griffith, long before the great works of his maturity, was acknowledged as the undisputed master of the craft.

'David buckled to the job like a true sport: It was *his job* and he would dignify it', wrote Mrs Griffith. It seems unlikely that during these years Griffith was directly conscious of the revolution he was creating in filmic expression. Primarily he must have regarded himself as a professional story-teller, in a new, strange and (for a literary and theatre man) inferior medium, simply striving to relate his narratives in the most effective possible way, in the light of his tastes and previous experience. And it was this discipline which controlled his film-making.

Griffith's tastes were rooted in his passion for the great Victorian writers, and dictated not only the subjects of his films, which maintained the tone of lofty moral idealism and the sense of social and universal order of the Victorian novel, but also his choice of players. Griffith's girls – the Gish Sisters, Mae Marsh, Blanche Sweet, Bessie Love, Mary Pickford – were for him the ideal heroines of the Victorian poets. Mrs Griffith has said that *ingénues* who particularly wanted to please her husband had only to moon about rather soulfully with a volume of Tennyson in their hands.

Griffith's instinctive mastery of narrative technique and *mise-en-scène* had been developed through contact with the nineteenth-century novel and the nineteenth-century theatre. In the course of directing hundreds of tiny films at American Biograph, he gradually but surely discovered the full expressive range of the cinema and the specific means to develop it. His fundamental discovery was to split up a scene into small fragments, isolated elements incomplete in themselves, out of which the whole was reassembled:

D. W. Griffith:
The Squaw's Love.
U.S.A., 1911.
Contemporary
poster.

Where Porter's camera had impartially recorded the action from a distance (i.e. in long shot) Griffith demonstrated that the camera could play a positive part in telling the story. By splitting an event into short fragments, and recording each from the most suitable camera position, he could vary the emphasis from shot to shot and thereby control the dramatic intensity of the events as the story progressed.*

Working in this way Griffith found himself possessed of a complex armoury of techniques to conduct his narrative and command its dramatic and emotional effect. He could provide emphasis through the composition and framing of his images; by the placing and the movement of the camera; and, most important, by the juxtaposition of the images and the speed and rhythm with which they were cut.

*Karel Reisz, op. cit.

Before Griffith, photography of dramatic films had not often gone beyond the concept of placing the players before the camera, and using the camera's field of vision as a kind of proscenium arch. The accepted convention was to show actors in full length, from head to foot. Griffith, from the start, with his love of Victorian painting, employed composition. He saw the image as having a foreground and a rearground as well as the middle distance; perspective as well as two-dimensional movement. By 1910 he was quite regularly using close-ups to reveal significant details of the scene or of an actor's playing, and extreme long shots to achieve a sense of spectacle and distance. Aided by the resourceful Bitzer, he devised effects of masking the screen to heighten visual emphasis. (The most famous example of this technique is in *The Birth of a Nation* in which an intimate shot of a little family group huddled on a hillside is shown framed in an iris mask, which then opens up to reveal a vast battle-scape in the far background). Before Griffith, cameramen had rarely been required to show any subtlety in the way they lit their shots. To indicate night or sunlight, it was generally sufficient simply to tint the film blue or gold (the practice continued long after Griffith). As early as 1909 Griffith achieved extremely realistic effects of light and shade (*Edgar Allen Poe; Pippa Passes*).

Porter, as we have seen in Chapter 2, demonstrated the idea of making a narrative out of a montage of scenes. Griffith's development of the principle of cutting within a scene seems to date from *After Many Years*, made in November 1908, only four months after his first film. The film was an adaptation of *Enoch Arden*; and Mrs Griffith describes the doubts of the directors of American Biograph:

> It was the first movie without a chase. That was something, for in those days, a movie without a chase was not a movie. How could a movie be made without a chase? How could there be suspense? How action? 'After Many Years' was also the first picture to have a *dramatic* close-up – the first picture to have a cut-back. When Mr Griffith suggested a scene showing Annie Lee waiting for her husband's return to be followed by a scene of Enoch cast away on a desert island, it was

altogether too distracting. 'How can you tell a story jumping about like that? The people won't know what it's about'.

'Well', said Mr Griffith, 'doesn't Dickens write that way?'

'Yes, but that's Dickens; that's novel writing; that's different.'

'Oh, not so much, these are picture stories; not so different.'

The cut from a close-up of Annie Lee to the subject of her thoughts represented a tremendous leap: the two images were linked not by concrete dramatic logic, but by a thought connection. Griffith's recognition, in 1908, of the similarity of montage to the methods of the novelist is especially interesting and it was to be taken up and developed much later by Sergei Eisenstein (1898–1948) in the U.S.S.R.

A film of 1909, *The Lonely Villa*, first employed a device which Griffith was to make famous – the 'last-minute rescue'; the use of cross-cutting between two parallel actions for the sake of suspense and drama. In *The Lonedale Operator* (1911) he still further developed the device, building up suspense and speed and excitement by the accelerated pace and rhythm of the cutting from shot to shot and between the two actions. The following year, in *The New York Hat* (the first scenario submitted by Anita Loos, then eighteen years old) Griffith was freely using the flash-back. The editing process had now achieved mastery of time as well as space.

Besides developing the cinema's language, Griffith immensely broadened its range of subjects. Although his output in the early years was cheerfully eclectic, including broad comedy (though in real life humour seems never to have been his strong point), melodrama, westerns, thrillers, sentimental romance and historical subjects, Griffith had startled his employers in the first months by offering the American public Browning and Tennyson as well as safe literary favourites like Dickens, Poe and Shakespeare. In *The Song of the Shirt* (1908) and *A Corner in Wheat* (1909; based on a novel by Frank Norris, whose *McTeague* was later to provide Stroheim with the subject of *Greed*) he essayed social subjects.* His ambitions grew, carrying the whole American cinema with them. When he came to remake *Enoch Arden* in 1911 he insisted, as we have seen, that a subject of such importance could not be made in the then conventional length of one reel. Griffith's introduction of the American-made multi-reel picture began an immense revolution. Two years later, in the summer of 1913, *Judith of Bethulia*, an elaborate historico-philosophical spectacle, reached the unprecedented length (for an American film) of four reels, or one hour's running time. After six decades the pretensions of this film, or such a work as *Man's Genesis* – 'a psychological study founded upon the Darwinian Theory of Evolution' – may seem a trifle ludicrous, but at the time they provoked endless debate and discussion, and gave a new intellectual status to the cinema.

In 1913, the undisputed master of the screen, Griffith left American Biograph for the Reliance Majestic Company, which released through the Mutual Company. He directed four preliminary films, but his whole energy was concentrated on creating 'the greatest picture ever made'. This, no more nor less, is what he did: *The Birth of a Nation* (1915) remains the most influential picture in film history. It was based on a novel of the Civil War by the Rev. Thomas Dixon, *The Clansman* (the title was only changed after the first showings). Griffith's fascination with American history had already been revealed in a number of short films, notably *The Massacre* (1912) in which he treated the Custer affair. The narrow Southern and racist prejudices which Griffith uncritically absorbed from Dixon cannot detract from the larger achievement of the film. All the skills, all the power over his medium and over the audience's emotions which Griffith had learned in the past seven years, were applied to this massive interpretation of the Civil War, in which the great historical events are seen parallel to their effects on individual human beings. *The Birth of a Nation* finally compelled unreserved recognition of the cinema's artistic possibilities.

*So, earlier, had Porter in *The Kleptomaniac* (1904) though at a much less sophisticated level.

The profits of *The Birth of a Nation* were immense (it cost about $110,000, and has proved one of the most profitable pictures in history); and Griffith poured all he had made from it into his next film *Intolerance* (1916). In this he 'conferred both magnitude and complexity as well as expressiveness on the motion picture'.* The initial thematic conception of the film could have been insupportably pretentious; the theme of intolerance as illustrated by four episodes from history, set in Ancient Babylon, Biblical Judaea, Mediaeval France and Modern America. Yet despite such demonstrations of Griffith's essential lack of humour as his touches of rank sentimentality and the pedantic if somewhat imprecise source references ('fashioned after the splendours of an Ancient Time') which he appends to the subtitles, it is a magnificent achievement. The four episodes are welded with immense complexity yet total control; the parallel dramatic climaxes are built up to a peak of excitement and passion such as film audiences had never seen before.

* Iris Barry, *D. W. Griffith – American Film Master* (New York, 1940).

D. W. Griffith directing Mae Marsh (foreground) in *Intolerance*. U.S.A., 1916. G. W. Bitzer on camera; behind, Dorothy Gish.

1

2

3

4

5

6

7

8

9

10

Cutting sequence from *Intolerance* showing
how Griffith builds up dramatic tension by
cutting between the scene of an execution,
the race against time of the party bringing
the Governor's pardon; and the boy's
despairing friends waiting in fading hope of
the pardon. At one point Griffith also
introduces a long-held, dramatic image of
the Crucifixion. *[footage]*.

11

1   [3] *Long shot:* Train enters station and stops.
2   [6] *Medium shot:* Side of train. A party of people
    rushes out.
3   [6] *Medium shot:* A car. The same people enter and
    drive off.
4   [17] ¾ *shot:* The execution procession at the prison.
    Camera tracks back with procession. Priest faulters
    and drops prayer book.
5   [36] *Extreme long shot:* The Crucifixion. Flashes of
    lightning.
6   [4] *Medium long shot:* Head on view of speeding car.
    Camera tracks.
7   [2½] *Long shot:* Gallows. The boy is led to steps.
8   [2½] *Medium shot:* A waiting room. Two women are
    summoned by prison guards.
9   [1] *Close up:* Man telephoning. He talks agitatedly.
10 [1] *Long shot:* Gallows. The boy is led up the steps.
11 [6] *Medium shot:* Top of gallows. The boy's ankles
    are strapped.
12 [1] *Medium close shot:* Boy with guards holding his
    arms. He sways into camera.
13 [4] *Close up:* Boy's anguished face. He stares and
    staggers backwards and forwards.
14 [1½] *As* 11: Men strap upper part of legs as priest
    reads.

12

13

14

In fact the audiences of 1916 seemed unable to grasp the film. Certainly it was not a commercial success; and for much of the rest of his career Griffith was painfully struggling to repay the debts the film had incurred.

Another architect of America's supremacy in the cinema after 1914 was Mack Sennett (1880–1960) the son of Irish immigrants to Canada. He joined Biograph as an actor when Griffith was making his first films there. In 1909 he took to writing (he provided the scenario of *The Lonely Villa*) and in 1910 he became a director. We have Sennett's own evidence that he took every opportunity to study Griffith's method of working, and used to hang about the studio doors at night so that he could walk home with the Master, and discuss their craft with him.

In 1912, with the financial backing of two bookmakers (his creditors, according to legend) he founded the Keystone Studio. At first he directed his own films; soon, as the studio came to employ a whole company of players and recruited new directors, Sennett became a supervising producer, overseeing the work of his strange establishment from a tower which he had built in the centre of the lot. The films which came from Keystone had elements of comic-strip, vaudeville, circus, pantomime, commedia dell'arte, and the old French comic films; yet the genre was distinct and unique. The setting of the Sennett comedies was the real world of America in the teens of the century – wide dusty streets with one-storey clapboard houses, grocery and hardware stores, angular automobiles just beginning to edge the horse and buggy off the roads, policemen, men in bowlers and large whiskers, ladies in harem skirts and huge hats. The films transformed this real and familiar world with happenings that were anarchic, surreal, orgiastic.

The Keystone comedies enriched the world's folklore with a universe of curious creatures who were in every possible way larger and wilder and more vivid than life. They might be gross or emaciated, giants or midgets, with obscene moustaches or tormented spectacles, clothes that were over-sized or under-sized. Sennett's earliest stars

Mack Sennett: The Keystone Kops in an unidentified film, c. 1915.

were the obese Fred Mace, the wry and goatee-bearded Ford Sterling (habitual superintendent of the redoubtable Keystone Kops) and Mabel Normand, the most graceful of lady clowns. Later *alumni* of the studio included Fatty Arbuckle, cross-eyed Ben Turpin, Charley Chase, Billy Bevan, Chester Conklin, Mack Swain, Edgar Kennedy, Louise Fazenda and Polly Moran. The Sennett studios were also an incomparable training ground for directors: among other subsequently distinguished directors of comedy were two Sennett gag writers, Malcolm St Clair and Frank Capra, and two Keystone Kops, Eddie Sutherland and Edward Cline.

The vast international popularity of the Keystone comedies and the imitators who soon followed in their wake did much to help America's commercial domination. Beyond this, however, (and quite incidentally to Sennett's personal aims, which were simply to turn comedy into a commercial commodity) the films made an invaluable contribution to film art by contributing new rhythm and fluidity to film editing, and new freedom to the camera, which had to develop the agility to catch the clowns where they fell, or to follow them into the depths of the endless landscapes whither their breakneck chases were liable to lead.

Late in 1913 Sennett engaged a 24-year-old English comedian who was touring the American vaudeville circuits with Fred Karno's 'Mumming Birds' company. When

The Karno Company, including Stan Laurel (left) and Charles Chaplin (in life-belt) on the way to America, 1913.

he saw the first films made with Charlie Chaplin, Sennett was inclined to feel that he had made a mistake; the young man's much more quiet and relaxed style of comedy tended to be at odds with the hectic mugging and leaping of the Sennett stock company. Within a year however Chaplin was world famous – the cinema's first universal legend. Curiously, Chaplin was in upbringing a Victorian. The child of struggling music hall artists – the father a drunkard and wastrel, the mother mentally delicate – as a small child he had known the miseries of a Victorian London of extreme poverty and institutions of Dickensian severity. This childhood made a lasting impression on him: the atmospheres, the perceptions, the morality, the sentiments, the vision of the world of the underprivileged which appear in his films are essentially Victorian. Though romanticised and transmuted into comedy, a hard core of truth and painful experience lies at the heart of Chaplin's best work.

His technique and style derived from his training in the English music halls. There he had learned his grasp of character and psychology, the polish, the versatility, and the expert *mise-en-scène* which a music-hall artist had to bring to his act. Instinctively he possessed the qualities of a fine actor: a gift for mimicry, remarkable grace and rhythmic sense, inexhaustible invention, and, in addition, a native poetic sense.

In his first film for Sennett Chaplin was dressed as a broken-down swell. In his second he had already adopted – almost casually, according to legend, picking out props and garments at random – the costume which became famous: too-tight jacket and too-loose pants held up with string; oversize boots and undersize bowler-hat; holey gloves, a little cane, a tie and wing collar all indicating vain aspirations to gentility.

In this little tramp audiences seemed to perceive a universal quality. Thus encouraged, Chaplin refined the character over the years: though the main lines are similar, the gentle, even melancholy hero of *City Lights* (1931) and *Modern Times* (1936) is very different from the larcenous little sprite of the first Sennett films, scuttling round corners on one leg, clutching his hat as he is chased by the Kops or by some angry, whiskered giant, whose gouty feet he has accidentally trampled. What remained, retaining the devotion of audiences throughout the world, was the supremely human fallibility and resilience and range of emotion, the originality and the perfection of the comic business. Chaplin's rise coincided with the first great boom of the star system. Wherever films were sold, Chaplin shorts were a major bargaining power. As Chaplin moved from Keystone to Essanay, and then in 1916 began to produce his own films for release by Mutual, his earnings shot up to more than a million dollars a year.

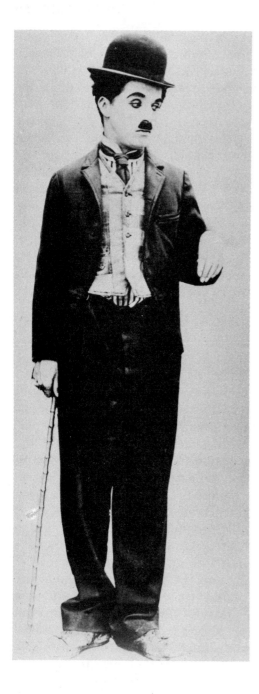

Charlie Chaplin, c. 1915.

Less popularly celebrated than Sennett, Griffith or Chaplin, Thomas Harper Ince (1882–1924) played no less a role in shaping the American film industry of the war and post-war years. On the stage from six years old, he became an actor with the I.M.P. Company in 1910, was directing pictures soon afterwards, and eventually opened his own studio. With characteristic flamboyance he hired the Miller Brothers' 101 Ranch Wild West Show, and rented 16,000 acres of land to shoot westerns. In 1915, with Griffith and Sennett, he became one of the guiding triumvirate of Triangle, and the same year built a big new studio at Culver City (it was later to become the MGM Studios). In 1916 he produced his answer to *Intolerance* entitled *Civilisation*, a massive allegory in support of Wilsonian pacifism.

Ince was dogged by a tiresome vanity which made him claim every film he produced as his own creative work as director. If anything this foible has obscured the very large contribution he made to the American cinema through his work as a brilliant creative producer. He had evidently an acute anticipation of audience tastes, in addition to a sophisticated appreciation of the nature of the film medium. Ince, who set his directors standards of well-made, tightly constructed films, is credited with the introduction of the film scenario, an organisational improvement which had far-reaching effects upon narrative form. John Ford, whose brother Frank Ford was one of Ince's directors, has said recently: 'Ince had a great influence on films, for he tried to make them move.'

The developments which these artists brought to film style did not long remain isolated and personal experiments. Other producers and directors were nervously watching every move which Griffith made; and each innovation was at once imitated and adopted as general practice. Standards in American film-making rose immeasurably in the years between 1910 and 1918. America took the artistic as well as the economic lead. As film making became a comparatively respectable occupation, doubtfully acknowledged in certain quarters as an art, there was a rapid rise in standards of screen writing, acting, direction, design and criticism.

Meanwhile economic organisation was changing. Movies were bigger and bigger business; and the slow but certain establishment of the long 'feature' film, finally forced on the industry by Zukor's powerful Paramount distribution organisation, helped bring about the collapse or withdrawal of many of the old pioneer companies – Edison, Biograph, Méliès and Kalem among them. The Motion Picture Patents Company faded away. Vitagraph, Lubin, Selig and Essanay merged as VLSE. Mutual, Kessell and Bauman merged into Triangle. Several smaller companies were absorbed into Carl Laemmle's Universal. Vast new studios – Inceville at Culver City, Fox, Universal City – sprang up in and around a new Hollywood which was mushrooming out of the quiet town of wide roads and one-storey houses that the first film-makers had found.

As salaries and production costs mounted, producers sought ways of standardising production methods, of discovering sure-fire values that could be injected into their films to guarantee success at the box office. Hence there came into being certain characteristics of American production which were to persist for several decades: the star system;* the formula picture (the repetition ad nauseam of a style or subject that was successful with the public); massive use of advertising and publicity.

It became increasingly clear that the key to success was the control of effective distribution outlets. Zukor's Paramount Corporation fought mercilessly to gain control of massive exhibition outlets and to exploit them by use of the 'block booking' system, whereby an exhibitor was obliged to agree to accept a whole series of programmes in order to get one especially attractive film. The system was clearly open to many abuses by the distributor, who could exploit it to unload any junk on the unfortunate exhibitor; and resentment led to the formation in 1917 of the First National Exhibitors' Circuit. First National did away with the block booking system; but the fight with Paramount was long and bitter, leaving many scars on the organism of the American cinema.

*The war years saw the first massive inflation of star salaries, with idols like Mary Pickford and Chaplin powerful enough to command million-dollar incomes and terrorise the moguls of the industry.

As pictures became bigger and more costly and more sophisticated in their technique and content, cinemas also acquired new economic and social status. In the years around the start of the European war, there was a huge boom in cinema building. Cinemas were no longer converted stores, but custom-built edifices, elegant 'Palaces' in high class districts. In 1914 the Vitagraph Theatre and the Strand invaded the Broadway district itself. In turn these more opulent cinemas attracted a new, middle-class audience and the changing clientele dictated still further change in the content of films.

Before the war the great audience was the poorer working class, and the films they apparently preferred were those of high moral values and didactic tone; the taste was a heritage of Victorian times. The films of the pre-war era favoured bible stories, morality dramas and melodramas in which virtue was rewarded and vice suitably punished (with poverty and virtue, riches and vice very often equated). The films were optimistic. America was depicted as the land of opportunity (for immigrant groups were eager supporters of this entertainment which put no strain on their limited grasp of the language of their adopted land). The films stressed the virtues of home life and the sanctity of marriage; they frowned on get-rich-quick schemes and people, or those who sought to rise above their natural station. For the bigger excitements there were subjects of military patriotism and the Westerns of Tom Mix, W. S. Hart and Broncho Billy Anderson. Occasionally social issues might be raised – female suffrage or white slavery perhaps – but as the historian Lewis Jacobs has shown stories involving political corruption, or capital-labour issues or racism, generally adopted strictly reactionary values. But Jacobs saw the start of a more liberal approach with the rise of Wilsonian progressivism.

Around the start of the European war however there was a marked change of attitude:

Having until now dealt mostly with the working man and his world, the camera turned toward the middle class. In the future it was to concentrate not on interpreting the working man's world, but on diverting him

from it by showing the problems of the economically
fortunate, which problems would interest him as entertainment rather than sermons. Henceforth the movies
were to return only sporadically to his milieu, and then
only during national economic crises.*

The new middle class audience demanded greater sophistication. The outbreak of the European war brought changes
in American life and outlook, a new self-confidence and
materialism. Mary Pickford and the Griffith girls con-
formed to the Pollyana ideals of the pre-war world. In 1916
quite a different idol made its appearance in Theda Bara
(1890–1955). In real life she was a quiet Cincinatti girl called
Theodosia Goodman; but William Fox's publicity built up
a great edifice of myth and mystery about her, giving her
an oriental background, a predatory quality of eroticism,
and the word 'vamp' to define her quality. Bara was the
glowering *femme fatale* in more than forty films, beginning
with the archetypal *A Fool There Was* (1916) directed by
Frank Powell and describing how a rich and distinguished
American casts aside family, fortune, health and finally
life for the sake of Bara's sultry and unattainable charms.
The Bara films definitively established sex as the *sine qua*

*Lewis Jacobs, op. cit.

J. Gordon
Edwards:
Cleopatra,
U.S.A., 1917.
Theda Bara.

non of American films, with domestic intrigue, marital infidelity and the triangle drama as dominant motifs. Bara was followed by a whole harem of women-of-the-world heroines, of which the Russian actress Alla Nazimova (whose first film was Herbert Brenon's *War Brides*, in 1916) was the most notable. With the new women came new heroes, more debonair than the solid, almost middle-aged leading men of pre-war films. The new styles were exemplified by Wallace Reid, J. Warren Kerrigan and the rapidly rising star Douglas Fairbanks.

All forms of cinema acquired sophistication to match. The genial buffooneries of the stout John Bunny (1863–1915) made between 1912 and 1915, now belonged very much to the past. Alongside the Sennett extravagances, which took a delight in parodying all the old film conventions (*East Lynne with Variations, Uncle Tom Without the Cabin*) there grew up a genre of comedy largely conceived at the expense of out-dated small-town manners. Typical of these were the endearing comedies starring Charles Ray and the early Harold Lloyd *Lonesome Luke* series. There was a vogue for a more sophisticated kind of parody than Sennett's: at least two early Fairbanks films – *Manhattan Madness* (1916) and *Wild and Woolly* (1917) – were light-hearted demolitions of the Western myth.

The cinema, previously so cautious with its precarious reputation, was now emboldened to tackle 'daring' subjects – divorce, birth control, sex in general. Undress, formerly restricted to French productions marketed for gentlemen's smoking concerts, became habitual, if by later standards fairly modest.

The new cinema demanded a new kind of director; and between 1912 and 1918 there was a large recruitment of new young artists to replace the old master-craftsmen of the primitive years and the film factories. Lewis Jacobs points out that in the first days there were three directors in America: by 1908 there were perhaps ten; by 1912 thirty. By 1918 the number of working film directors could not be assessed. The individual achievements of some of these newcomers will be considered in the next chapter.

The war inevitably provided an interlude in cinema production as it was to produce a watershed in national and social life which would have far-reaching effects on the nature of American films. Before the war there was a prevailing mood of pacifism; but by 1916 feeling had turned violently; and pictures like *Civilisation*, *War Brides* (which was actually suppressed) and *Intolerance* (whose commercial failure was probably as much as anything due to its discordance with the mood of the times) were markedly out of step with American feeling as a whole.

The United States entered the war on 5 April 1917; and a great flood of aggressive and propagandist films was released. There was a large-scale production of hate films, heroism films, battle films; films to shame the stay-at-homes, to stir the German immigrant population to hatred of their own land and people, to hearten the bereaved. As it happened this stage was reached at a time when the other combatant nations – France, England and Germany – had passed beyond the vogue for war subjects, and audiences were demanding escapism.

One branch of production which flourished in practically every film-making country during the war years, and which represented pure escapism, was the serial adventure. The style had originated in France in 1908 when Victorin Jasset, a former sculptor and expert in costume spectacles, made his phenomenally successful series of films about the adventures of *Nick Carter*, which he followed with *Zigomar* (1911) and *Protée* (1913). At this point Jasset himself died, but the serial had already become a rage. By 1909 Britain had the regular adventures of *Lieutenant Rose, R.N.* soon afterwards followed by *Lieutenant Daring*. In 1912 the Edison Company released the first American serial, *What Happened to Mary?* The following year the Selig Company began *The Adventures of Kathlyn*, starring Kathlyn Williams and assorted animals from the zoo which was a speciality of the particular company. From this point new serials came thick and fast, generally with female stars (Mary Fuller, Norma Phillips 'the Mutual Girl', Florence La Badie, Helen Holmes, Helen Gibson, Ruth Roland, Marguerite Courtot, Grace Cunard) though there was at least one notable male serial star, the athletic Eddie Polo, while in 1919 Harry Houdini, the famous escapologist, appeared in a series called *The Master Mystery*. The undisputed queen of the Hollywood serials (though in fact most of her films were made for the Pathé company and directed in New York or Paris by the French director Louis Gasnier) was Pearl White, star of the most celebrated of all the series *The Perils of Pauline* (1914) and *The Exploits of Elaine* (1915).

Every country had its native serials. Germany boasted *Homunculus*, the adventures of a man-made superman; Italy had *Tigris* and *Za-la-Mort*; Austria, *The Invisible Ones*; Britain, to follow *Lieutenant Daring*, George Pearson's *Ultus*. But in France the serial achieved the status of art, with the work of Louis Feuillade. For Alain Resnais, Feuillade was the peer of D. W. Griffith, with an 'instinct poétique prodigieuse qui lui permettait de faire du surréalisme comme on soupire'.

Such a judgment would have been startling to Feuillade, a prolific, efficient, dedicatedly commercial film-maker whose main ambition was to make enough money to retire in the sun (which he never did; he died at the age of 52 in 1925). He had no artistic pretensions and disapproved of cinema aesthetes (an opinion which the long view of history appears by and large to vindicate): 'Ce n'est pas grâce aux chercheurs que le cinéma gagnera sa place un jour, mais grâce aux ouvriers de mélodrame dont je me flatte d'être un des plus convaincus'. Seeing himself only as artisan, Feuillade's artistic achievements were, as it were, involuntary.

Born at Lunel in 1873, Feuillade joined Gaumont as a scenarist in 1906, having tried his hand at journalism and playwrighting. The following year he succeeded Alice Guy-Blaché, the world's first woman director, as head of production at the Gaumont studios. In the next few years he turned out hundreds of films of startling variety. In 1911 he made a virtue of Gaumont's necessity for economy in costumes and sets, by issuing a forceful manifesto in defence of cinema realism, to launch his series *La Vie telle qu'elle est*, which dealt with real-life subjects which could be largely shot on location. These films revealed for the first time Feuillade's unique gift for observing and evoking the contemporary scene.

It was this gift which gave his serials their special quality. The first of them was *Fantomas* (1913–14), based on

FANTOMAS

Louis Feuillade:
Fantomas.
France, 1913–14.
Contemporary
poster.

a popular pulp serial by Marcel Allain and Pierre Souvestre. *Fantomas* was followed by ten episodes of *Les Vampires* (1915), relating the battle between the French police and the lovely, villainous and anagrammatically named Irma Vep. The Paris *préfet* raised objections to the unflattering depiction of the police in this series; so Feuillade, as conformist in daily life as he was individual in his imagination, made his next hero the good and handsome *Judex* (1917). After this came twelve episodes of *La Nouvelle Mission de Judex* (1918), *Tih Minh* (1918) and *Barabas* (1920).

The unique quality of the Feuillade serials was their ability to create 'mystery and drama from the most everyday elements' (Alain Resnais). The tales are wildly extravagant, the heroes and villains alike indestructible, and as motivelessly demonic or angelic as characters from a fairy tale. The fantastic incidents of the films were often the first notions that came into Feuillade's remarkable imagination, and frequently the action was improvised during actual shooting. Yet with all this, the settings remain solidly and unmistakably the Paris of 1914, with its bowler-hatted men and long-skirted ladies, its elegant *salons* and grey *banlieues*, its angular gleaming brass and mahogany cars and *art nouveau* architecture. This contradiction – and the possibility that a cheerful nun will suddenly reveal herself a brutal kidnapper, that reality will at any moment turn to nightmare – gives Feuillade's films a characteristic poetic flavour which appealed enormously to the surrealists, who were the first to acknowledge the unique merit of Feuillade's films.

The playing is far in advance of the period. Feuillade's actors are expressive, restrained, natural, and manoeuvred with a balletic precision and deliberation so as constantly to maintain the composition of the image. The sheer plastic beauty of all Feuillade's films is striking. Of course the leotards and capes which his heroes and villains tend to wear help, but Feuillade had an astonishing sense of composition and atmosphere. He was as sensitive to the strangeness and beauty of a misty suburban wasteland as to the dramatic potential of a twist of stairs or a wooded roadside, the Paris sewers or rooftops. His approach to the visual aspect of his films was characteristically unpretentious: 'We wanted clear, luminous, pretty images . . . The best photography is that which is most pleasant to watch'.

Above all Feuillade was simply a great *metteur-en-scene*. Even in his own time he was strikingly conservative. Long after Griffith and *Intolerance* he still eschewed modern *montage* methods, clinging to the older style of building films in 'tableaux', scenes staged in theatrical form and played towards the audience as if within a stage proscenium. He told his story more by the content of the images than by the juxtaposition of shots. This of course goes far to explain his eclipse during the long post-Griffith period when *montage* predominated, and his rehabilitation in our own times when, as we shall see in subsequent chapters, the emphasis has returned to *mise-en-scène* and *mise-en-shot*. Feuillade planned his pictures with extraordinary accuracy. His images are full of precise, economical, informative detail, beautifully placed, perfectly timed. He knows exactly how to use the full dimensions of the frame, and how to set up a piece of action, the moment to reveal and the moment to conceal.

Elsewhere in Europe also there were artistic discoveries. In Russia for instance, as we shall see in the next chapter, the great theatrical *metteur-en-scène* Vsevolod Meyerhold was turning his attention to the cinema, with far-reaching results; while a young art director, Lev Kuleshov, was laying the foundations of film theory. But only the Scandinavian cinemas developed a sustained cinema tradition during the war period to rival the achievements of the American cinema.

The Swedish cinema and its early successes were very largely due to one man, Charles Magnusson (1878–1948). A pioneer cameraman, in 1909 he was hired as production manager to the Svenska Bio company of Kristianstad. There he soon acquired an important collaborator in Julius Jaenzon, who had also been an early news cameraman. Magnusson had the qualities of an outstanding producer, and above all a recognition of the need to give directors total creative freedom. His first production was *The People of Värmland* (1910), directed by Carl Engdahl, a well-known actor of the period, which inaugurated the fruitful tradition of films rooted in national and rural folklore. In 1912 Svenska Bio, prospering under Magnusson's artistic direction, moved to Stockholm.

The climax of Magnusson's achievement and of Swedish cinema however was reached during and immediately after the European war, when neutrality gave the country an advantage over her neighbours. In that brief golden age Swedish film-makers attempted themes of far greater sophistication than in any other country, and consistently took their cameras outside the limitations of painted studio sets. Working in natural locales induced other qualities: a lyrical sense hitherto undiscovered by the cinema; a feeling for the drama of the setting itself, for man seen against the background of natural forces with which he develops mystical relationships; and a restraint and realism in the work of players taken out of the context and associations of painted canvas scenery.

Apart from Magnusson's own highly imaginative approach to film creation, the Swedish achievement can be explained by the influence of a particular school of Swedish literature, especially the novels of Selma Lagerlof; the ready availability of exceptionally photogenic scenery and light; and above all Magnusson's happy discovery of two film-makers of outstanding talent.

Both Mauritz Stiller and Victor Sjöstrom began their careers in the theatre and were originally recruited to Svenska Bio as actors, in 1911 and 1912 respectively. Sjöstrom was born in 1879, and at nineteen was already an immensely popular actor throughout Scandinavia. 'The thing that brought me to film-making was a youthful desire for adventure and a curiosity to try this new medium of which I then did not have the slightest knowledge.' He had already acted in and directed a number of films when he made his first notable success, *Ingeborg Holm* (1913), a bitter and tragic attack upon the workings of the poor law system, but which barely hints at Sjöstrom's future achievements in liberating the screen from the stage and the studio. Little evidence remains of his next twenty or so films; but in *Terje Vigen* (1917) the epic and pantheistic quality of his best work is already evident. Perhaps indeed this film specifically marked Sjöstrom's self-discovery; for though he was at first very reluctant to attempt a screen version of Ibsen's poem, a sudden dramatic change of heart led him to undertake it after all. The mystical feeling for nature was still more apparent in the dramatic period piece *The Outlaw and His Wife* (1918).

Sjöstrom found his most congenial material however in the novels of Selma Lagerlof, whose 'predilection for dreams and supernatural events', wrote another Scandinavian director, Carl Dreyer, 'appealed to Sjöstrom's own somewhat sombre artistic mind'. Lagerlof's novels inspired *The Girl from Marsh Croft* (1917) and Sjöstrom's great trilogy, *The Sons of Ingmar* (1919), *Karin Ingmarsdotter* (1920) and *The Phantom Coach* (*Thy Soul Shall Bear Witness*) (1921).

Mauritz Stiller (1883–1928) perhaps lacked the sustained poetic gifts of Sjöstrom; but at his best this immigrant Russian Jew (his real name was Mowscha) produced films as fervently and characteristically national to Sweden as the elder director. On his first assignment for Magnusson (*Mother and Daughter*, 1912) Stiller was writer, director and actor. A second film, *The Black Masks* (1912), startled the industry with its technical virtuosity, for Stiller had been avidly absorbing the lessons of the Griffith shorts which were then reaching Sweden in great numbers.

In the course of the next six or seven years he established himself as a director of eclectic interests, but principally as a creator of witty and sophisticated social comedy – a field in which the sombrely gifted Sjöstrom was not likely to follow, though as an actor he could be deft in comedy as his performance in Stiller's brilliant and complexly struc- tured *Thomas Graal's First Film* (1917) reveals. So successful was this film that it was followed by a sequel, *Thomas Graal's First Child* (1918). The most famous of Stiller's comedies, if perhaps not as good as the *Graal* films or the earlier *Love and Journalism* (1916), is *Erotikon* (1920).

In 1919 Stiller for the first time attempted a Selma Lagerlof subject; and the taut, dramatic, richly atmos- pheric *Herr Arne's Treasure*, set in the sixteenth century, remains his masterpiece. Stiller returned to Lagerlof and the epic style in *Gunnar Hede's Saga* (1922) and *Gösta Ber- ling's Saga* (1924). In this last film an immensely long and complex narrative defied adaptation; and the sole reason why *Gösta Berling's Saga* is today Stiller's best-known work is that it introduced his remarkable discovery Greta Garbo. Before this role Garbo had played only in a publicity film and a slapstick short; but already the extraordinary stillness and interior quality of her playing distinguishes her.

The example of Sjöstrom and Stiller heartened others; and the wartime and immediate post-war years brought

Mauritz Stiller:
Gösta Berling's Saga. Sweden, 1924. Greta Garbo.

impressive works by John W. Brunius (1884–1937), and Gösta Molander (born 1888); but neither they nor any other directors of the period were to prove strong enough talents to support Sweden's position in the international cinema after the departure of Sjöstrom and Stiller to America in the early twenties.

Denmark had a film industry slightly earlier than Sweden. The showman (and former shepherd) Ole Olsen founded the Nordisk Film Company – today one of the oldest surviving production organisations in the world – in 1906. Within a few years Nordisk films were enjoying a remarkable popularity throughout all Europe. Partly no doubt this was due to such sensational subjects as prostitution and abortion, though much more to superior production and technical qualities. As in Sweden stories were carefully prepared; photographic standards were high; and films were very largely shot in natural surroundings, in which players developed, like the Swedes, naturalistic acting styles.

Two of these players were especially influential in winning overseas markets for Danish films. Valdemar

Psilander, a handsome and virile actor who seems to have
been a sort of prototype of Valentino, had built up an
immense international following by the time of his suicide
– a victim of melancholia – in 1917. Asta Neilsen was the
cinema's first true star. A fine and intelligent actress, with
unusually striking features – a pale, tragic mask in which
were set great expansive eyes – her popularity created a

vast international demand for Danish films in the immediate pre-war years. Her first film was *Afgrunden (The
Abyss)* (1910), directed by Urban Gad (1879–1947), who was
to become her husband and her regular director. By 1913
the English distributor Walturdaw advertised her as 'The
Queen of Picture Play Artists and the People's Favourite';
and her following was no less devoted in other countries.

Benjamin
Christensen:
*Witchcraft
Through the
Ages*. Denmark,
1922.

Other Danish actors too, like Clara Pontoppidan and
Olaf Fønss enjoyed almost comparable international
celebrity. While the Nordisk company continued to lead
Danish production – its films included the very sophisti-

cated science fiction spectacles *Atlantis* (1913) and *The Sky Ship* (1916) – other companies followed in the wake of Nordisk's success. For instance, it was the Dansk Biograf-kompagni which produced the first films of the remarkable Benjamin Christensen (1879–1959). Christensen was a medical student, opera singer, actor and wine merchant before starting to write films in 1912. The following year he became a successful film actor, and also directed his first picture, *The Mysterious X*, a melodrama remarkable in its day for its pictorial invention and lively montage. This was followed in 1915 by *Nights of Vengeance*, and in 1922 by his masterpiece, *Witchcraft Through the Ages* (made in Sweden), a recreation in spectacular documentary style of various historical and contemporary manifestations of witchcraft and witchhunting.

Other Danish directors of the period were August Blom, Hjalmar Davidson and Holger-Madsen; but the outstanding personality of the Danish cinema remains Carl Theodor Dreyer (1889–1968), whose silent films saved part at least of Denmark's former world market for several years after competition from Hollywood, Germany and Sweden, and the loss abroad of Neilsen, Gad and other artists had eclipsed Denmark's production.* Dreyer began to write scripts for Nordisk in 1912, but it was not until 1919 that he directed his first film, *The President*. He was a notable peripatetic and, failing to find consistently congenial conditions for production at home, made *The Parson's Widow* in Sweden in 1920, *Love One Another* and *Mikhail* in Germany in 1921 and 1924 respectively; *The Bride of Glomdal* in Norway in 1925 and *La Passion de Jeanne d'Arc* in France in 1928. But between work in other countries he made two more silent films in his native Denmark: *Leaves From Satan's Book* (1919), a Griffith-inspired, episodic adaptation from Marie Corelli; and *Master of the House* (1925), a remarkably delicate and acute study of character, the story of a wife's revolt against her tyrannical husband.

*Denmark's other continuing export at this time was the comedies of Carl Schenstrom and Harald Madsen, directed by Lau Lauritzen.

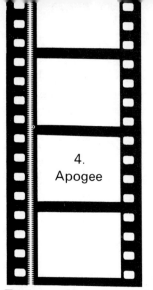

4.
Apogee

Even as the war ended however another country – the defeated Germany – was moving into the forefront of film production. This was one of the first of several instances in cinema history where the revival and triumph of a nation's cinema has been the deliberate result of official intervention. Rather surprisingly in view of her energetic interest in other mechanical innovations of the nineteenth century, and the pioneering work of the Skladanowsky brothers, Germany had made little progress in developing the cinema industry in the pre-war years. In the period of fairground exploitation (for the progress of cinema exhibition was exactly parallel to that of France and England and indeed most other European countries) Oskar Messter (1866–1943), who had been manufacturing cameras and projectors in Berlin since 1896, supplied showmen with topical films and two-minute buffooneries of his own manufacture and even carried out some experiments with sound films around 1908; but most of the films shown in Germany in the early years of the century were imported from France, Italy, America and later Denmark.

The cinema enjoyed a very poor reputation in Germany where the intelligentsia and socially respectable held themselves aloof from it far longer than in other countries. As late as May 1912 the Association of Berlin Theatre Directors refused to allow stage actors to work in films. Several events, however, contributed to change these attitudes. In 1911 the producer Paul Davidson persuaded Asta Neilsen and Urban Gad to work in Germany; and the actress's unique art of mime convinced many previous doubters of the artistic possibilities of the medium. Actors as distinguished as Albert Bassermann defied the rulings of the Theatre Directors' Association to work in pictures. In 1911 Davidson persuaded Max Reinhardt (1873–1943), already the leading figure in the German theatre, to interest himself in films; and a little later Hugo von Hofmanstahl was writing a 'dream play', *The Strange Girl*, produced as a film in 1913. Big new studios were built at Tempelhof and Neubabelsberg.

Asta Neilsen. English cinema poster, 1913.

The participation of distinguished stage people and the campaigns of the *Kinoreformbewegung* for the *Autorenfilm* tended to produce in Germany the worst effects of the literary *film d'art*; nevertheless it succeeded at the same time in giving artistic prestige to the cinema. The popular audience, for all that, resisted such artistic innovations and showed a marked preference for the detective films which made their appearance in 1913 (German film detectives always had English names like Henry Higgs and Stuart Webb). The one really singular pre-war German production, which succeeded in attacking intellectuals and popular audience alike, was Paul Wegener's *Der Student von Prag* (1912), a *doppelgänger* story treated with visual style considerably in advance of its time, and a significant harbinger of the taste which German film-makers would reveal in the twenties, for the macabre and supernatural.*

The war brought an enormous stimulus to production. While the audience became ever larger and more demanding, and new cinemas sprang up throughout the country, the pre-war sources of supply were cut off. The first flush of hate and propaganda films soon died down; and as in other countries, the public sought escapism. Yet even under such stimulation, the German cinema showed little capacity for innovation, or urge to create a national style. Among the most successful films of the war years were two-reel slapsticks made in imitation of the French pre-war comedies.

As the war progressed, the authorities became deeply conscious of the adverse effect of anti-German propaganda films abroad. Recognising the inadequacy of the home industry as it was then organised, therefore, industrialists set up Deulig (Deutsches Lichtbild Gesellschaft); and a year later in 1917 Bufa (Bild-und-Filmart) was established to provide offical documentaries and films for the front line theatres. In the same year General Ludendorff recommended the merging of the main film companies; and thus Ufa (Universum Film A.G.) came into being, with one third of its capital provided by the state. Ufa very deliberately

*Bassermann's first film appearance was in Max Mack's *Der Anderer* (1913) a much more banal treatment than Wegener's of a 'psychological' theme – a Jekyll and Hyde story.

set about the tasks of raising film standards and reorganising production and marketing methods. With Germany's defeat in November 1918 control of Ufa passed to the Deutsches Bank. It remained virtually unchanged, though there was now much more pressing compulsion to make the German cinema commercially viable, and to project a flattering image of a country which was the object of almost universal detestation.

To the stimulus provided by the organisation of Ufa was added the intellectual and artistic excitement – the 'Aufbruch' – which accompanied the political ferment of the end of the war. All the old prejudices were swept aside. Avant-garde forms of all kinds and in every field of art were enthusiastically cultivated, with 'Expressionism' the favourite watchword. Left-wing artists eager to communicate with the ordinary people in the most direct way possible seized upon the cinema as an ideal and exciting new medium. The sense of freedom, as Siegfried Kracauer points out in his celebrated study of the psychology of the German cinema,* was brief; the German revolution was illusory: a break-down rather than a revolution in the positive sense.

Following the abolition of censorship, there was a flood of sex films, the pioneer and most successful director of which was one Richard Oswald (b. 1880). With titles like *Hyaenas of Lust* and (for a film on homosexuality) *A Man's Girlhood*, their level of social responsibility was not especially high. Even before the resumption of censorship in May 1920 there had been strong reaction against such productions; though Kracauer seeks ulterior reasons – socialist propagandising perhaps or an excuse to attack Jewish producers – behind the public demonstrations against sex pictures.

Aiming to recapture Germany's place in world culture, Ufa for a beginning pursued the *Kolossal*, with massive historical and costume films. The style seems to have been set by Joe May's *Veritas Vincit* (1918), but Ernst Lubitsch (1892–1947), the former comic actor 'Meyer', made himself the undisputed king of the genre. He turned to the style

*English translation published by Secker and Warburg, London, 1971.

against his will, it seems, when Davidson asked him to direct his favourite, Pola Negri (a Polish actress originally called Apollonia Chaluperz), in two dramatic vehicles: *Die Augen der Mumie Ma* and *Carmen* (both 1918). These costume pictures led Lubitsch on to *Madame Dubarry* (1919), which established a new fashion for 'psychologically' realistic historical films; though its success at that particular point in German history was probably as much due to its innate opposition to revolutionary ideals as to any spectacular, aesthetic or psychological merits. Lubitsch pursued this formula with *Anna Boleyn* (1920) and *Das Weib des Pharao* (1921). He was enormously versatile however; and at the same time as these grandiose pageants he was developing a style of operetta film, with *Die Puppe* and *Die Austernprinzessin* (both 1919), in the latter of which he cruelly satirised American manners. He made screen

Ernst Lubitsch:
*Madame
Dubarry*.
Germany, 1919.
Pola Negri.

versions of *Rausch* (1919) and *Miss Julie* (1921), an adaptation of Reinhardt's fantasy-spectacle *Sumurun* (1920), a rather odd and unsuccessful satire with Pola Negri, *Die Bergkatze* (1921) and a film in the currently fashionable 'street' idiom, *Die Flamme* (1923). Between 1915 and his last German film, *Das Millardensouper* (1923), the indefatigable Lubitsch had made some three dozen films.

The historical genre, profiting from the lessons of Reinhardt in the handling of crowds and spectacle, prospered for several years. Among its most successful practitioners were Dmitri Buchowetski (*Danton*, 1921; *Othello*, 1922; *Sappho*, 1921; *Peter the Great*, 1922) and Richard Oswald, who turned, more or less, from his sex films to make a *Lady Hamilton* (1922) and a *Lucrezia Borgia* (1922). Alexander Korda (1893–1956), an *emigré* from Hungary after Horthy's crushing of the Republic of Councils, began the investigations of the 'Private Lives' of historical personages which were later to make him famous. A more sinister portent of Germany's future was Arsen von Cserepy's aggressively nationalist *Fridericus Rex* (1923), which was to have several sequels during the twenties and Nazi thirties.

In 1919 the new German cinema experienced its greatest triumph with *Das Cabinet des Dr Caligari*. The scenario was the joint effort of the Czech Hans Janowitz and the Austrian Carl Mayer; and was the outcome of shared memories and experiences of psychiatric clinics, fairgrounds, and sensational murders. The plot told how the mysterious Dr Caligari used a somnambulist, Cesare, to carry out his vengeful murders on the inhabitants of a little German town. The producer Erich Pommer insisted that the narrative be enclosed within a framing story which at the end reveals that Dr Caligari is in fact the head of a mental hospital and that the tale of the somnambulist and the murders is the fantasy and fabrication of one of his patients. Clearly this revision enfeebled the anti-authoritarian parable of the story (with the somnambulist representing the innocents sent out during wartime to commit murder in the name of the state). It was the plastic qualities of the picture which eventually attracted so much critical enthusiasm and established its place in film history.

Pommer originally asked the Austrian director Fritz

Robert Wiene:
*Das Cabinet
des Dr Caligari.*
Germany, 1919.

Hermann Warm:
design for the
same scene.

Lang to make the film; but when Lang refused, he engaged instead Robert Wiene (1881–1938). Wiene selected as designers three painters, Hermann Warm, Walter Röhrig and Walter Reimann. All three belonged to the Expressionist group which had been formed in Munich around 1910 in avant-garde reaction against impressionism and naturalism, and had had great influence on literature, music and architecture, as well as on painting. 'Films', said Warm, 'must be drawings brought to life'; and the idea was put into practice in *Caligari*. The playing of the actors (Conrad Veidt, Werner Krauss, Lil Dagover) complemented the strange, angular, distorted images presented by the decors; and all was used as an outward expression of the inward thoughts and activities of the characters.

The visual and formal extravagance of *Caligari* never had any direct successors: its far-reaching importance was in showing how expressionism of a limited kind was the cinema's natural method; how images could be used to reflect and interpret psychological states and interior action.

By the time of *Caligari* German films had set an example to the whole world by their use of a free-ranging camera, their ability to use significant visual detail for 'psychological' illumination, their Reinhardt-learned use of crowds (a lesson shared by the Nazis), the magnificence of their sets and the brilliance of their lighting and photography. *Caligari* in particular served, in supplementing the lessons of the Scandinavian cinema, to confirm the supremacy of the Studio film; and after 1920 German films moved into a period of almost hundred per cent studio production.

Wiene himself never succeeded in repeating the success of *Caligari*; and it fell to other directors to take up the artistic lead he had given in the application of expressionism to the cinema. Expressionism, and the German temperament, seemed to favour subjects of horror and fantasy; and *Caligari* set off what Kracauer defines as 'a Pageant of Tyrants' – all in films superbly designed, lit, photographed and acted according to more or less Expressionist principles. In *Das Wachs-figurenkabinett* (1924) Paul Leni, formerly a designer, brought to life Haroun-al-Raschid,

Ivan the Terrible and Jack the Ripper. Artur Robinson's *Schatten* (*Warning Shadows*) (1922) was a phantasmagoria of prophecy and crime. Paul Wegener's *Golem* (1920), the sequel to a film which he had made in 1914, introduced a tyrannical man-made monster.

The most distinguished directors to emerge from the Expressionist school were Friedrich Wilhelm Murnau and Fritz Lang; though the most influential creative figure of the era was the writer Carl Mayer (1894–1944). For a little while Mayer continued in the expressionist style; and elements of expressionism survived in all his work (notably in his mode of writing; see the chapter on 'Murnau and his Writers' in Lotte H. Eisner's *Murnau*). With *Hintertreppe* (1921; directed by Leopold Jessner and Paul Leni) Mayer inaugurated the *Kammerspielfilm*, of which he was to be the principal author and theoretician. The subjects of the *Kammerspiel* were set in everyday and contemporary life. They observed the three unities. Kracauer defines them as 'instinct' films and characteristically they dealt with the irresistible effects of social destiny. For the extravagance of the Expressionist style was substituted sober, realist, muted acting; though in a way it seemed an extension of Expressionist methods that objects and settings played a crucial dramatic role. After *Hintertreppe* (characterised by Kracauer as 'a veritable excess of simplicity') Mayer scripted a trilogy which brought the *Kammerspiel* to its apogee. *Scherben* (1921) the tragedy of a railwayman who murders his boss, the seducer of his child, and *Sylvester* (1923) in which the disharmony between his wife and mother drives a man to suicide, were both directed by Lupu Pick. *Der Letzte Mann* (1924) one of the greatest of silent films, the story of a hotel porter who loses with his job and uniform all his self-respect and pride, was directed by F. W. Murnau. After this Mayer passed to a new stage of his development. Identifying with the *Neue Sachlichheit* (New Objectivity) school of art, he attempted to eliminate all the acted elements in favour of the setting alone. The result was *Berlin, Symphonie einer gross Stadt* (1927), which was directed by Walter Ruttmann and was to spawn a whole line of montage documentary which thirty or more years later still breeds its 'city symphonies'.

Murnau (1888–1931) was one of the supremely creative figures of the cinema. Stage crazy from his childhood, he started writing for films after his release from a prison camp at the end of the First World War. In 1919 he directed his first film (now lost); and in 1920 first worked with a Carl Mayer script (*Der Bucklige und die Tänzerin*) and with a script by Janowitz, *Der Januskopf* an adaptation of *Dr Jekyll and Mr Hyde*. He continued to alternate almost purely commercial chores with experimental Mayer scripts; until in 1922 he made his first truly personal masterpiece, *Nosferatu*. Adapted remotely (and without permission) from *Dracula*, this demonstrated Murnau's uncompromisingly individual approach to expressionism; among other innovations he combined the angularity, elaborate lighting and stylisation of the manner with actual locations. Turning, along with Mayer, to the *Kammerspiel*, there too he made his individual contribution. In contrast to the austerity of the Lupu Pick films, *The Last Laugh (Der Letzte Mann)* is a work of enormous technical virtuosity. Murnau's apparently inexhaustible technical and pictorial invention was carried to still further limits in *Tartuffe* (1925), which emphasised the contemporary relevance of Molière's comedy; and the dazzling, virtuoso *Faust* (1926), Murnau's last German film.

F. W. Murnau:
Nosferatu.
Germany, 1922.
Max Schreck.

Fritz Lang (born Vienna, 1890) started his career as an architect. Invalided out of the army during the First World War, he began to write scripts for the DECLA Studios, specialising in detective thrillers with titles like *Hilda Warren and Death*. His first significant essay as a director was a serial thriller *Die Spinnen* (1919). Lang contributed a key work to the first doom-ridden period of expressionism, *Der Müde Tod* (*Destiny*) (1921), written by his wife and frequent collaborator, Thea von Harbou, and clearly marked with his majestic architectural sense. *Dr Mabuse der Spieler* (1922) combined expressionist techniques, a *Fantomas* style of thriller, and the growing German fascination with the superman (in this case the super-criminal). Lang contributed still more significantly to German twentieth-century mythology with his massive re-telling of the Siegfried legends in *Die Nibelungen* (1923 4) a diptych of incomparable plastic splendour, with marvellous, architectural, studio-built forests, fire-spitting dragons and a Siegfried (Paul Richter) of suitably ideal mould.

Next Von Harbou and Lang collaborated on a prophetic fantasy, *Metropolis* (1926), which envisaged the sky-scraper city of the twenty-first century, with a master race and a slave class who, in a not very convincing symbolic finale, were reconciled. Its philosophical pretensions are less impressive than its spectacular achievements. After *Metropolis* Lang's last silent films (*Spione*, 1928; *Frau im Mond*, 1929) were an anti-climax. Lang seemed to be infected by the general feeling of decline that settled on the German cinema after the triumphant years from 1920 to 1925.

Yet two films of 1925 seemed to mark an apogee of the post-war German cinema. E. A. Dupont's *Varieté*, which brought to a commonplace circus melodrama all the observation of *Kammerspiel* and virtuoso subjective camera-work, was hailed as a masterpiece throughout the world. A film of perhaps more substantial quality, *Die freudlose Gasse* (*Joyless Street*) revealed a new talent in Georg Wilhelm Pabst (1885–1967).

Pabst's social realism was quite different from the mannered, abstracted style of the *kammerspiel*. *Die freudlose Gasse*, despite certain melodramatic elements, showed the reality of inflation Germany in hard, documentary

Fritz Lang: *Metropolis*. Germany, 1926.

E. A. Dupont: *Varieté*. Germany, 1925. Emil Jannings.

terms, with its misery, prostitution, bread queues. 'What is the point of a romantic treatment' Pabst asked, 'when real life is romantic enough and horrible enough as it is?' Thus committing himself to the *neue Sachlichheit*, Pabst brilliantly visualised a psychoanalytical case in *Geheimnisse einer Seele* (1926), and in keeping with the rising vogue for 'street films', adapted Wedekind's play *Lulu* (*Der Büchse der Pandora*) (1928) with the beautiful, tragic-featured and intelligent American actress Louise Brooks. Ilya Ehrenburg's novel provided the subject of *Die Liebe der Jeanne Ney* (1927), which set a love affair between a French girl and a Soviet officer against a panorama of post-war Europe. In *Tagebuch einer Verlorene* (1929), Margarete Bohme's novel provided a more realistic, less melodramatic, and more socially critical story of the life of a prostitute than Wedekind's play had offered.

The *neue Sachlichheit* school, along with the vogue in montage documentary begun by Ruttman's *Berlin* (1927) and the influence of the new Soviet cinema, attracted other directors to films of objective realism. A group of film-makers, several of whom were later to become individually distinguished in the cinema – Eugen Shuftan, Billy Wilder, Fred Zinnemann, Moritz Seeler, Edgar Ullman and Robert Siodmak – made *Menschen am Sonntag* (1929), which sympathetically portrayed the lives and leisure of the humbler bourgeois, generally neglected by the German cinema. Karl Junghans borrowed the star of Pudovkin's *Mother*, Vera Baranovskaia, as well as the techniques of Soviet films, for *So ist das Leben* (1924), the wretched life and death of a Berlin washerwoman. Piel Jutzi's brilliant adaptation of a Heinrich Zille script, *Mutter Krausens Fahrt ins Glück* (1929) described a seedy tragedy of the slums in terms that would only reappear many years later in Italian neo-realist cinema. More avant-garde in techniques was Erno Metzner's *Überfall* (1929), an ironic anecdote about a street robbery.

Not all German films of the twenties belonged to the school of expressionist horror or the cheerless realism of the *Kammerspiel* and the *neue Sachlicheit*. Alongside the continuing production of commercial detective, comedy and (silent) operetta subjects, other film-makers pursued individual lines. Dr Ludwig Berger (1882–1969) made charm-

ing, escapist trifles of baroque elegance, such as *Der Verlorene Schuh* (1923) and *Eine Glas Wasser* (1923). More significant of Germany's future were the mountain films of Dr
Arnold Fanck (born 1889) and his followers and imitators.
(Among his collaborators, unexpectedly, was Pabst, who
co-directed *Die weisse Hölle Piz Palu* in 1929). Seizing on
a national enthusiasm for winter sports, these films carried
them to the point of a cult, an immature worship of physical
endeavour and achievement. 'The uninitiated' wrote
Kracauer 'could not help feeling irritated at the mixture
of sparkling ice-axes and inflated sentiments'. Closely
allied to the mountain films were such *Kulturfilms* as Ufa's
Wege zu Kraft und Schönheit (1925), whose promotion of the
concept of 'the regeneration of the human race' sinisterly
looks forward to Nazi aims; but which owed its large international success less to its ideology and callisthenics than
to its nudism.

The German films of the great period from 1920–25 – but
particularly *Madame Dubarry*, *Caligari*, *The Last Laugh* and
Varieté – made a tremendous impression in America, whose
passion for imported art was derided by a title in Will
Rogers' comedy *The Ropin' Fool* (1922): 'If you think this
picture's no good, I'll put on a beard and say it was made in
Germany: then you'll call it art'. Recognition of the
superiority of the product imported from Europe in the
immediate post-war years launched the American cinema
on a policy of conquest and annexation, which was to
maintain the domination of the American film whilst
effectively destroying the industries of smaller countries.

Germany was the first country to be despoiled in this
way. In 1923, with xenophobia and German-hating still
powerful in the states, Mary Pickford brought Lubitsch to
Hollywood to direct her in *Dorothy Vernon of Haddon Hall*.
On arrival he capriciously refused to do the film, and they
made *Rosita* (1923) together instead. The film was a failure;
but immediately after it Lubitsch directed *The Marriage
Circle* (1923) from a script by the German writer Hans Kraly.
This film launched both Lubitsch himself and a new style
of film-making. The German director seemed to sense with

peculiar accuracy the tone of the new morality; and introduced American audiences to a novel, sophisticated,
frivolous, 'continental', idea of sex which admirably suited
the emancipated mood of the times. In a series of films –
Three Women (1924), *Kiss Me Again* (1925) and *So This is Paris*
(1926) – Lubitsch introduced a new form of visual wit and a
new subtlety of comedy acting, exploiting and developing
players like Florence Vidor, Adolphe Menjou, Monte Blue
and Ronald Colman. It was a style which Lubitsch was to
pursue with still greater subtlety and success in the sound
period.

Though scores of German technicians, artists, writers
and actors settled in Hollywood, none of the other German
directors brought over at this time had the sustained
success of Lubitsch; and the importance of their recruitment seemed less the contribution they made to American
films than the extent to which their loss impoverished
their native cinema. Murnau and Mayer, hired by William
Fox, on the strength of *The Last Laugh*, made one masterpiece – in its way the apogee of the expressionist cinema –
in *Sunrise* (1927). After the honeymoon period with Hollywood however, Murnau found himself experiencing more
and more difficulties with his producers; and his first
sound films *The Four Devils* (1929) and *Our Daily Bread* (1930)
were both released in much compromised forms. After this,
breaking with Fox and producing independently, he made
Tabu (1931) an exotic tragedy shot on location in the South
Seas with native actors; but he was killed in a car crash
before its première and considerable commercial success.

Paul Leni (1885–1929) had directed some good comedy
thrillers – essentially parodies of the expressionist horror
films – before his early death. Ludwig Berger, E. A. Dupont
and the producer Erich Pommer stayed only briefly in
Hollywood. Dmitri Buchowetski directed half a dozen
indifferent costume vehicles for stars like Mae Marsh and
Pola Negri. Apart from Lubitsch, the most considerable
permanent enrichment of American films from the plunder
of Germany lay in actors like Conrad Veidt, Pola Negri and
Joseph Schildkraut.

The effect of MGM's raids on Sweden were still more
disastrous than the pillage of the German cinema; for

Victor Sjöstrom: *The Wind*. U.S.A., 1928. Lillian Gish, Lars Hanson.

Stiller and Sjöstrom *were*, effectively, the Swedish cinema. Sjöstrom's Hollywood career was as distinguished as his earlier work in Sweden. Arriving in 1923, his first notable success was an adaptation of the Andreyev play *He Who Gets Slapped* (1924). In the actress Lillian Gish, Sjöstrom (renamed Seastrom) found an ideal interpreter; and together they made two masterpieces *The Scarlet Letter* (1926) and *The Wind* (1928). Practically suppressed by studio politics, and rarely seen since its first release, *The Wind* was one of the most extraordinary of all silent films. Sjöstrom brought his unique sense of the communion of man and nature to the story of the destruction of a sensitive young woman brought about by alien circumstances. Throughout it seems to be the elements – specifically the wind – that condition as well as symbolise human destinies. Perhaps depressed by the studio's lack of interest in this film, as well as by the pressures under which in 1927 he directed Garbo in *The Divine Woman* (eight studio rewrites reduced a reasonably intelligent script based on the life of Bernhardt to novelette rubbish), Sjöstrom returned to Sweden after a single talking picture.

It was never clear whether MGM brought Mauritz Stiller to Hollywood in order to gain possession of his creature

and protegée, Greta Garbo; or whether Garbo was an un-
looked-for bonus which came with the director of the
admired *Gösta Berling* (1924). Whatever the facts, Stiller's
relations with MGM turned out to be unhappy and fruitless,
though he managed to make a couple of films – one of them
the distinguished *Hotel Imperial* (1926), with Pola Negri – for
Paramount. In 1928 he returned to Sweden, where he died
shortly afterwards.

A third distinguished Scandinavian director, the Dane
Benjamin Christensen having accepted a Ufa contract on
the strength of the success of his *Witchcraft Through the
Ages* (1922), came to Hollywood, and directed a group of
successful thrillers and comedy thrillers, before returning
home to give up the cinema for more than a decade.

Two Hungarians who had fled from Budapest to Austria
and Germany after the collapse of the Republic of Councils
in 1919 subsequently landed in Hollywood. Alexander Korda
(1893–1956) made a number of American films of which only
The Private Life of Helen of Troy (1927) predicted his successful career in England. Michael Curtiz (formerly Mihály
Kertész) (1888–1962) began a prolific and eclectic career
that lasted into the 1950s. Another Hungarian, Paul Fejös
(1898–1963) was a scientist in the States when he drifted into
theatre and cinema work. The most remarkable of his four
Hollywood films, *Lonesome* (1928), is a brilliant, funny,
charming, pathetic study of urban loneliness, filmed in a
precocious style of improvisation, location shooting and
informal hand-held camerawork which anticipates styles
of the 1960s.

These men and hundreds of lesser emigré film artists were
absorbed into American cinema at the zenith of a power and
prosperity which survived one of the most eventful decades
in American history – between the Armistice and the Wall
Street crash. It was a period of administrations of start-
lingly contrasted character: Wilson's austere idealism was
followed by the easy-going corruption of Harding's government; the worship of Big Business under chilly Calvin
Coolidge had suddenly to face the desertion of the Gods, in
the market crash of 1929.

It was a period of immense technological and social revolution. The motor car, radio, advertising – and the cinema – combined to change the pattern of American life. Returning servicemen, and women newly emancipated by both war service and the suffrage won in 1920, were no longer satisfied with Victorian ideas and ideals. Stimulated by literature and by the cinema, America conceived firm notions of the New Morality and the New Woman, and did its best to live up to them. The rise of the tabloid press and the other means of popular communication, gave enormous publicity to the activities of the post-Prohibition gangsters, to sex and sport and ballyhoo, to seven-day wonders and popular heroes. It was an era of sensation.

America followed up the mercantile advantages the war had given her with the aid of vast natural resources and Fordist streamlining of industry. Investment (as the Crash was to prove) was immense. Stimulated by new prosperity, salesmanship and advertising, America consumed as no society had ever consumed before. Economic self-confidence made itself felt in a cultural self-confidence that was quite new to America, which had always in the past imported its art from abroad. At the same time it resulted in a reaction of radical dissent, scepticism and disillusion, which set in most strongly in the last years of the twenties and reached its inevitable high point with the Crash; and which found its most influential voices in writers like H. L. Mencken, Theodore Dreiser, Sherwood Anderson and Sinclair Lewis.

All the change and tumult of American life found its reflection – albeit often somewhat distorted – in films. At the start of the twenties the cinema was the nation's fifth largest industry. By the time that talkies revolutionised Hollywood, it was the fourth.

By the end of the war, Hollywood had adopted its definitive industrial form, with monopolistic power in the hands of the great major distributors and studios, ruled over by moguls who with few exceptions had arrived in the States as poor immigrants and had learnt to fight for survival as proprietors of cheap nickelodeons at the start of the century – men like Carl Laemmle of Universal, William Fox, Louis B. Mayer of MGM, the Warner Brothers, Adolph Zukor. The monopoly of these 'majors' was confirmed by

the short but sharp slump which hit the movies in 1918 in
the wake of the war-time boom, as a result of the disastrous
Spanish 'flu epidemic and embargoes on American product
imposed by many European countries. The crisis was
sufficient to send all but the strongest to the wall.

Revival followed as dramatically as the slump had arrived, helped on by massive injections of capital from Wall
Street. This was the period of the first of America's perennial 'Red Scares'; and it appears that Big Business saw
the cinema not only as a potentially good investment, but
also as an effective way to combat Bolshevism, through the
sort of films which would unquestioningly celebrate the
American way of life. The increased participation of Wall
street aggravated still further those symptoms of capitalist
investment which were noted in the preceding chapter: the
search for predictable sales values (star names, best-
selling titles, costly and showy production values); the
development of formula pictures and assembly line
methods; the creation of the myth of 'giving the public
what it wants'. 'New men from Wall Street', wrote Lewis
Jacobs, 'educated in finance, became the overseers of the
motion picture business.' What is astonishing in these
circumstances is that so much of real worth came out of
this cinema and this era.

In the early twenties movie stock, financial as well as
moral, fell as a result of a number of notorious scandals,
eagerly taken up by moralists and by a public that delighted
to see Hollywood as the Twentieth Century Babylon. An
indifferent director called William Desmond Taylor was
murdered; and though the case was never solved, the names
of two actresses who had been associated with him – the
fine comedienne Mabel Normand and Mary Miles Minter –
were needlessly smirched. Wallace Reid, a star who had
embodied all the virtues of young American manhood, died
of an overdose of narcotics. The well-loved comedian
Fatty Arbuckle was charged with the manslaughter of a
girl who died in the course of a party in his hotel suite. The
industry sought to protect itself by the formation of the
Motion Picture Producers and Distributors of America
Inc., presided over by William Hays, formerly Harding's
Postmaster General. The Hays Office not only laid down

standards for screen morals which condemned American films to a kindergarten scope of discussion for the next forty years; but did useful public relations work when the industry came under criticism for its monopolistic structures.

The American film industry had moved definitively into the age of superlatives. The building of cinemas of ever greater size and splendour culminated in Rothapfel's stupendous Roxy, built in 1927 with 'Gothic form, renaissance detail and Moorish architecture'. The movies were now without doubt all America's favourite amusement.

Film content continued to widen in scope as the output – now definitely committed to the full-length 'feature' film – and consumption of movies grew. Production, however, still rarely departed from clearly defined patterns. Foremost were the films which declared, with self-conscious enthusiasm and narcissism, the new social and moral standards of the post-war era: the Jazz Age. The motives for social comedies and domestic dramas alike were found in the new, post-Freud fascination with sex, the emancipation of American women, the working girl, the discarding of old codes of manners and ethics, the slackening of marital ties. The cycle was begun by Cecil B. DeMille in 1918, with *Old Wives For New*. DeMille (1881–1959) and his successors and imitators followed this up with hundreds of other films with titillating titles and ultra-modern content, which introduced the whole of America to the world of night clubs, country clubs, speakeasies and the moral frivolity which went with them. Erich Von Stroheim's *Blind Husbands* (1919) and *Foolish Wives* (1921) injected a more brutal note: Ernst Lubitsch, as we have seen, brought delicacy and sophistication and continental wickedness to the form.

But the attitudes of the Jazz Age and the New Morality were not as deeply entrenched or so widely accepted as America – and particularly its films – liked to believe. Consequently the Jazz Age films almost invariably end up with dénouements firmly in accord with older tastes and standards. The activities of the Dancing Daughters and flappers and 'It' girls are seen as temporary aberrations, high-spirited excesses. The erring wives come back to patient husbands; the Dancing Daughters marry the boy next door who loved them all the time.

For there was still a place – and it would long remain – for plain, old-fashioned sentimentality. Two of the great successes of the immediate post-war were D. W. Griffith's *Way Down East* (1920) and *Broken Blossoms* (1919), both melodramas in the Victorian manner, though treated by Griffith with great style and sincerity. Marie Corelli and Hall Caine remained popular throughout the period; and the essence of Elinor Glyn's success was her ability to wed the old romanticism to the new morality in her novels and screenplays of the twenties.

There were tougher strata in American production. Gangster films which were to reach their notable peak in the sound period were already popular in the twenties, with the Von Sternberg series in 1927–28 (*Underworld*, *The Dragnet*, *The Docks of New York*) and Lewis Milestone's *The Racket*

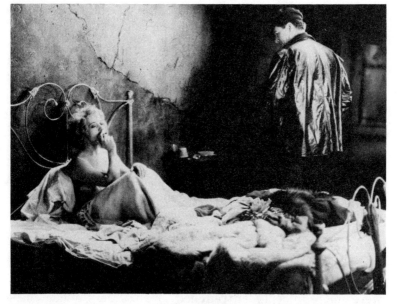

Josef von Sternberg: *Docks of New York*. U.S.A., 1928. Betty Compson, George Bancroft.

(1929) among the most distinguished. Reaction against war films (which did not however affect the popularity of Chaplin's great comic metamorphosis of the horrors of war, *Shoulder Arms*, or Griffith's touching *Hearts of the*

World, both made in 1918) lasted for several years; but with King Vidor's phenomenally successful *The Big Parade* (1925) and the change in attitude brought about after the Locarno Pact, there was a large-scale revival of interest in war, and particularly aviation battle films.

A more consistent source of action subjects was the Western. Parodies of the West, such as the Fairbanks films already mentioned, never succeeded in damaging the myth. The memory of the old West became even more important as it came to represent urban America's dream of lost innocence, of a pastoral freedom now sacrificed to hustle and the motor car. The twenties were a classic period, in which the perennial formulas were laid down; and the best Westerns of the time – King Baggot's *Tumbleweeds* (1925; starring W. S. Hart), James Cruze's *The Covered Wagon* (1923) and *The Pony Express* (1925), and above all the films of John Ford (*The Iron Horse*, 1924; *Three Bad Men*, 1926) – can still astonish with their epic grandeur.

John Ford: *The Iron Horse.* U.S.A., 1924. George O'Brien.

The frustrated romanticism of the materialistic and cynical Jazz Age found other outlets in the costume and spectacle film. With *The Mark of Zorro* (1921) Douglas Fairbanks began a phenomenally successful series of costume pictures which rivalled the earlier German productions in the taste and opulence of their design and their

George Melford: *The Sheik*. U.S.A. 1921. Rudolph Valentino, Agnes Ayres

Fred Niblo: *Ben Hur*. U.S.A., 1926. Shooting the battle of the galleys.

fast and witty action, and started endless imitations. Rudolph Valentino set a fashion for exotic romance with *The Sheik* (1921). Every age and land was explored to provide vehicles for the new generation of romantic stars such as Ramon Novarro and Antonio Moreno, Mary Astor and Vilma Banky.

DeMille, always sensitive to the drift of public taste, revived the biblical spectacle film with *The Ten Commandments* (1923) and *King of Kings* (1927); but even he was outdone by the most spectacular of all spectacles, *Ben Hur*, based on a late nineteenth-century theatrical success, and released in 1926. The outcome of fiasco upon fiasco, changes of location, director, cast, scrapping of sets and scripts, the cost ultimately soared to more than six million dollars. The fact that despite its cost the film quite quickly went into profitability helped permanently to change Hollywood's attitudes towards film budgeting.

Perhaps the vogue for anthropological and pseudo-anthropological documentary in the twenties indicates yet another direction of escapism for the motor-car age. The comparative success of Robert Flaherty's *Nanook of the North* (1924) undertaken with the backing of a fur trading company, encouraged William Fox to commission Flaherty to make *Moana* (1926) in the South Seas. Flaherty later

Robert J. Flaherty: *Moana*. U.S.A., 1926.

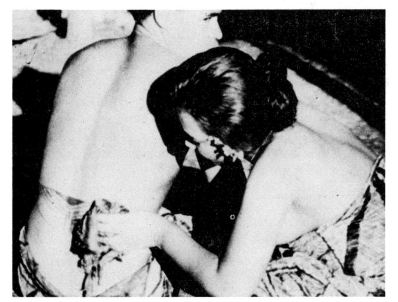

returned there in a short-lived partnership with Murnau, with whom he began *Tabu* (1931), finished by Murnau alone. Cooper and Schoedsack made *Grass* (1925) and *Chang* (1927). At a less scientific level, adaptations of Edgar Rice Burroughs' *Tarzan* remained popular from the early years of the century right up until recent times.

Comedy prospered and alongside the two-reelers there grew up a large production of comedy feature films. Chaplin's greatest pictures, notably *The Kid* (1921) and *The Gold Rush* (1925) were made during the period. It was an age of great comic stars: Harold Lloyd (1893–1971), with his spectacles and speciality of thrill-comedies; Buster Keaton (1895–1966) of the still features and acrobatic body; Harry Langdon, the elderly baby; Raymond Griffith, Gloria Swanson, Marion Davies. The comedians of these years by and large dealt with contemporary life and follies; and it is through the mirrors that they held up to nature that we see what it was like to be alive in America in the 20s.

The industry's quest for predictable sales values meant that a very large bulk of production consisted in adaptations of successful plays and novels of the day. Ninety per cent of this material was, of course, even less suitable for silent films than, later, plays and novels would be for talking pictures (for the habit has continued right to the present day). Occasionally the results could be triumphantly successful – *Greed* and *Way Down East* are only two examples; nor did Hollywood only seize upon the worthless; Sinclair Lewis and Scott Fitzgerald were adapted as well as Ethel M. Dell. But by and large it was as Elinor Glyn wrote:

> All authors, living or dead, famous or obscure, shared the same fate. Their stories were re-written and completely altered either by the stenographers and continuity girls of the scenario department, or by the Assistant Director and his lady-love, or by the leading lady, or by anyone else who happened to pass through the studio; and even when at last after infinite struggle a scene was shot which bore some resemblance to the original story it was certain to be left out in the cutting-room or pared away to such an extent that all meaning which it might once have had was lost.

It was of course exceptional for obviously leftist writers like Sinclair Lewis to reach the screen. Hollywood was (as the bankers had rightly observed) whole-heartedly committed to a reactionary line. The movies reflected the self-satisfaction of the Harding and Coolidge eras, of the new middle-class audience, the newly prosperous working class and the conservative business element of America. Films as a whole were concerned with a wholly imaginary leisured class, with lovely homes and lovely clothes and lovely cars and lovely manners. It was the great wish dream of (in Harding's memorable phrase) American 'normalcy'.

Occasionally reactionary sentiment was more militantly expressed in films. The Red Scare of the immediate post-war provoked a run of films, one of them, *Bolshevism on Trial* (1919) scripted by the same Thomas Dixon who wrote *The Clansman*, the book on which *The Birth of a Nation* was based. Closely related to these films too were those which depicted malcontent labour being brought to its senses and abandoning strikes in the face of capitalist paternalism.

The war had made newsreels an important and popular part of the cinema programme; and by the twenties each of the major film empires had its own news service. These were especially valuable in cementing the cinema's political connections. President Hoover showed lasting and valuable gratitude to MGM for the support the Hearst newsreels had given to his election campaign.

Another secondary but popular feature of cinema programmes was the animated cartoon, which had already become a regular element in supporting programmes even before the war. Mutt and Jeff, based on newspaper cartoon characters, originated in 1917 and continued throughout the silent period. Pat Sullivan's Felix the Cat, animated by Otto Mesmer, was as characteristic a personality of the twenties as Rudolph Valentino. Max Fleischer created Koko the Clown, whose speciality was appearances alongside human actors; and Walt Disney (1907–66) was at work from 1924, producing the *Alice in Cartoonland* series, the Oswald the Lucky Rabbit series and, on the eve of sound, Mortimer (later Mickey) Mouse.

Since Griffith and the Germans, the craft of film-making had become infinitely more complex than in the pre-war days when it was enough for a director to possess the talent of an amateur photographer and an amateur stage producer. The director, wrote Ince, 'must know life, but he must know too, how to project life, not in narrative form, but by selected dramatic moments, each of which builds towards a definite crisis or climax that will bring a burst of emotional response from every audience'. In these changed circumstances the writer had become a vital figure in the studios. The higher costs of production and the producers' eagerness to maintain control over every aspect of film-making made the element of pre-planning represented by a detailed shooting script essential. The big producers from time to time sought prestige by engaging distinguished authors (Maeterlinck, Blasco Ibañez and Somerset Maugham among them) to work in films; but the most successful writers were generally those who had grown up in Hollywood – Anita Loos, June Mathis who devised the best Valentino vehicles, Frances Marion who wrote *The Scarlet Letter* and *The Wind*, Jules Furthman and others. An important subsidiary writing craft, that of devising titles, was lost with the coming of sound pictures: at their best, film titles could be poetic in their brevity.* One of the imported writers who did, exceptionally, enjoy striking success in Hollywood, was the English novelist, Elinor Glyn who in 'It' devised one of the most successful sexual formulas of the period, and into the bargain taught Valentino to kiss the *palm* of a woman's hand. Indirectly Glyn's insistence on the accurate staging of the milieux she portrayed had its effect on film design, which was assuming much greater importance in the period. The art director made his appearance immediately after the war; and the best of the studio art departments, supervised by men like Cedric Gibbons of MGM, and Van Nest Polglase and the German Hans Dreier at Paramount, established consistently high standards of design. Allied to the art department

*It is worth noting too how the typography and layout could subtly convey the emphasis and stresses which an actor in a talking film could convey by speech.

was the work of the make-up artists, among whom the most influential was the veteran Max Factor.

The work of Hollywood cameraman in this period – combining the craft traditions of Victorian art photography with the new lessons of the German and Swedish cinema – reached standards rarely bettered since, despite improvements in equipment and stock. Silent film cameramen like Leon Shamroy, Lee Garmes and William Daniels (Garbo's favourite cameraman) were still in demand in Hollywood in the late 1960s. Along with the cameraman the importance of the cutter or editor, upon whose work the rhythm and effect of a film largely depended, increased with the elaboration of montage techniques.

It is impossible to discuss in any detail the men who as directors played the most important creative role in the films of this period of American silent cinema. Out of the hundreds of directors who came to Hollywood in the last decade before talking pictures, some achieved standards of artistry which would have made them outstanding in any period of cinema history less rich than this. Here it must be enough to mention briefly the activities of some dozen particularly influential figures.

Few of the directors who had made their names before the World War survived afterwards; 1919 seemed to be the start of an entirely new and gifted generation, most of whom had entered the cinema in some capacity or other in the years between 1910 and 1914. The greatest survivor of course was D. W. Griffith, whose standing was at its peak at the end of the War. In the course of the succeeding decade his career declined progressively and irretrievably. His great narrative power and creativity survived for a while, in *Broken Blossoms* (1919), *Way Down East* (1920), a costume spectacle, *Orphans of the Storm* (1921) that excelled the Germans, an extraordinary portent of neo-realism, *Isn't Life Wonderful* (1924), shot in Germany and examining the effect of the war's aftermath on humble lives. But Griffith was hopelessly in the thrall of debts incurred by *Intolerance*; and after Carol Dempster replaced Lillian Gish as his favourite leading actress, none of his films succeeded at the box office. Though he survived to make two sound pictures, *Abraham Lincoln* (1930) and *The Struggle* (1931), he spent the last seventeen years of his life inactive, an archaic and embarrassing survival of Hollywood's infancy.

Two earlier directors than Griffith, J. Stuart Blackton (1875–1941), who had made animated cartoons for the Vitascope in 1896, and Sidney Olcott (1873–1949), a Mutoscope actor from 1904, continued to work with success into the twenties; Olcott directing Valentino at the height of his fame, in *Monsieur Beaucaire* (1924). Two other directors who were established before the war also showed remarkable durability. Allan Dwan (born 1885) continued to make films into the 1960s, and Herbert Brenon (1870–1958) into the forties. Dwan was perhaps the most prolific director in the history of the cinema. His star rose with Douglas Fairbanks, and he made some of his best costume pictures (*Robin Hood*, 1922; *The Iron Mask*, 1929), though his most enduring and engaging work is the series of comedies he made with Gloria Swanson. Dublin-born, Herbert Brenon was early typed as a director of 'big films', works like *The Garden of Allah* (1925) and *Beau Geste* (1926) which promoted the Hollywood myth of the colossal. With equal facility he could turn to Scott Fitzgerald (*The Great Gatsby*, 1926), Sir James Barrie (*Peter Pan*, 1925; *A Kiss For Cinderella*, 1926) or films featuring the swimmer, Annette Kellermann.

Perhaps the most influential of all directors in the twenties was Cecil B. DeMille. There were many finer directors, but none who more accurately anticipated and more influentially moulded public taste. DeMille's career began in the theatre – specifically and significantly in David Belasco's nineteenth-century style of spectacular drama. In 1912 he formed a partnership with Jesse Lasky and Sam Goldfish (later Goldwyn) and went to Hollywood to shoot the company's first and spectacularly successful production *The Squaw Man* (1913). Though in his early years he clung to stage plays, players and methods, he showed a considerable flair for experiment in lighting and *mise-en-scène*. After having brilliantly reflected in his pictures the changing moods of the war period, he equally accurately anticipated the post-war temper with his cycle of socio-sexual comedies. They depicted lives of luxury and leisure, of moral freedom. More practically they offered people examples of 'how to go on'; instructed audiences in contemporary manners and etiquette. DeMille shaped, as much as he reflected, the life of the twenties, from the bath tub to the dinner table.

In 1923, as we have seen, DeMille's career took a different turn when he made the first of the biblical spectacles with which his name remains inseparably associated. Though he would continue to have a remarkably eclectic output, turning with facility to Westerns, musicals and social dramas, the epic was his destiny; and his last film was a spectacularly profitable remake of *The Ten Commandments*. In 1930 Paul Rotha could sum up DeMille's career: 'a pseudo-artist with a flair for the spectacular and the tremendous; a shrewd sense of the bad taste of the lower type of the general public, to which he panders and a fondness for the daring, vulgar, and pretentious'.*

Chaplin (born 1889) by the twenties was regarded as the greatest creative figure in the movies. In 1919, with Griffith, Mary Pickford and Douglas Fairbanks he had formed United Artists, to distribute the films of the artists whose salaries were so great that no studio could afford to employ them. This allowed Chaplin to work with infinite care and leisure on his films – taking up to three or four years on each – and his post-war films refined, and deepened the character of the little tramp-clown. A unique undertaking for Chaplin was *A Woman of Paris* (1923) which Chaplin directed but in which he played only a walk-on role – the main characters being taken by Edna Purviance and Adolphe Menjou. The film is a strange mixture of Victorian sentiments and Lubitsch urbanity; but its style and subtlety are quite individual. The gift for allusion and suggestion which Chaplin had developed and exploited in his own comedies was applied with brilliance to this drama: for instance in the scene where a masseuse is working on the body of a beautiful demi-mondaine (out of sight below the frame) and her face at once reflects the geography of her patient's body and the progress of the demi-mondaine's conversation. The visual methods of this film proved in-

*Paul Rotha, *The Film Till Now* (London, 1930, revised 1967).

The United Artists in 1919:
Douglas Fairbanks, D. W.
Griffith, Mary Pickford and
Charles Chaplin.

Charlie Chaplin: *The Gold Rush*.
U.S.A., 1925.

fluential as Chaplin's personal comedy could not; and it is significant that all of his assistants – Monta Bell, Henri d'Abbadie d'Arrast, Mal St Clair and Jean de Limur – later became directors of comedy in their own right, all continuing to evidence their debt to *A Woman of Paris*.

At this time the reputation of Buster Keaton (1895–1966) as director and comedian was overshadowed by that of Chaplin. In retrospect he appears comparable as a clown and superior as a director – for Chaplin had acquired his methods of cinematic *mise-en-scène* from Sennett in 1914, and never found it necessary to change methods that provided a perfectly adequate proscenium for his art. Keaton was characterised by a still, sad face attached to a frenetically active body. Trained in vaudeville, he came to the cinema with a highly developed comic technique and a rich invention that took advantage of his exceptional agility and athleticism. 'He performed miracles as easily as he breathed'. In addition to his other gifts he had extraordinary taste, restraint and structural sense, whether applied to the plotting of a film or the formation of a single visual gag. His mechanical ingenuity rapidly made him a master of the whole craft of film-making, from the optical trickery of Méliès to the subtleties of post-Griffith montage. The films in which he starred and which he largely directed himself – *Our Hospitality* (1923), *Sherlock Jr* (1924), *The Navigator* (1924), *Seven Chances* (1925), *The General* (1926) – today seem entirely undated, and their silence has more the appearance of choice than necessity.

Erich von Stroheim (1885–1957) remains one of Hollywood's most tragic figures: a creative genius who could never compromise with the industrial establishment. Arriving from Vienna in the early years of the century, he eventually drifted into films, was assistant and actor on *Birth of a Nation* and after various setbacks succeeded in interesting Carl Laemmle of Universal in his project for a film which became *Blind Husbands* (a novelettish title which Stroheim always detested) made in 1919. This was the first of a trilogy on adultery (the others were *The Devil's Passkey*, 1920, and *Foolish Wives*, 1921); and the exact psychological observation, unsparing realism and 'continental' morality were a thrillingly shocking revelation to

Buster Keaton: *Our Hospitality*. U.S.A., 1923.

Erich von Stroheim: *Greed*. U.S.A., 1924. Gibson Gowlan, Zasu Pitts.

American audiences. Working under increasing difficulties with studio bosses who were alarmed and outraged by his autocratic and uncompromising working methods, Stroheim embarked on another trilogy, this time set in the years of the decline of the Hapsburg Empire. Between the first of these* *Merry-Go-Round* (1923) and the later two, *The Merry Widow* (1925) and *The Wedding March* (1927) Stroheim embarked on a line-by-line, literal adaptation of Frank Norris's verist novel of working class life in pre-war San Francisco, *McTeague*. Despite MGM's merciless cutting of the film from Stroheim's twenty-four reels to barely one third of that length, the finished film, *Greed* (1924) remains a masterpiece of the silent cinema, in its unremitting, cruel psychological clarity, its faultless realism, its performance and its use of location.

Few of Stroheim's films were finished under his direction; after *Foolish Wives* practically all were released in versions more or less mutilated by their producers. His last silent film, *Queen Kelly* (1928) was abandoned when funds ran out and talkies threatened its commercial future, though it was later finished by the star, Gloria Swanson. Stroheim's single talking film, *Walking Down Broadway* (1933) was suppressed and partly remade as a result of internal strife in the studio.** Stroheim, who had brought to the silent film a sophistication and maturity the cinema was hardly to know again, and a unique, horrific vision of an old world in decay but still destructively lingering, was a houseless giant in the era of sound pictures. Intermittently he acted, in America and France, his performances as striking as his films had been. He left behind a sad trail of unrealised projects. Hollywood's failure to contain this trying genius is one of the tragedies of art.

Another 'von' (though unlike Stroheim he admitted that his 'von' was a fiction created by a Hollywood title-designer), Josef von Sternberg (1894–1968) was also born in

*The trilogic form of Stroheim's work appears to have been quite accidental: the Vienna films, for instance, were made for different producers.

**Rediscovered in 1970, the film, bore even in its mutilated form, Stroheim's unmistakable signature.

Vienna. He had been around Hollywood in various capacities for ten years before, in 1925, he and an English actor George K. Arthur raised the tiny budget for a dazzling, atmospheric film, *The Salvation Hunters.* The sophisticated visual effects of this film attracted much attention in Hollywood, but Sternberg's aggressive and unyielding personality resulted in several aborted projects before he achieved a large success with the public with *Underworld* (1927), the first of three gangster films (the others were *The Dragnet* and *The Docks of New York*, both 1928) which firmly established his reputation.

Of all Hollywood's great creative artists, John Ford (born 1895) seems to have most easily accommodated himself to the conditions imposed by the film industry. 'I have never thought about what I was doing in terms of art . . . To me it was simply a job of work – which I enjoyed immensely'. But Ford is an Irishman, full of contradictions and evasions. The son of an Irish immigrant, he is above all a story teller. Although able to turn his hand to anything from detective thrillers to expressionist melodrama (*The Informer*, 1935), Ford's main work has been in Westerns; and he is the supreme poet of the Western saga.

Other directors of outstanding gifts also managed to accommodate themselves to the realities of industrial Hollywood, and to produce works of singular merit. Henry King (born 1892) made a series of fine films, one of which, *Tol'able David* (1921), so masterfully put into practice the teachings of Griffith that it was to become a formative and much quoted influence in the Soviet cinema. King Vidor (born 1894) made the silent film into a highly expressive, articulate and personal medium which he used with great flexibility. His films include operatic melodrama (Lillian Gish in *La Bohème*, 1925), massive war spectacular (*The Big Parade*, 1925), and Marion Davies comedies, made to the order of her patron William Randolph Hearst (*Show People*, *The Patsy*, both 1928). But his greatest achievement in the silent cinema was *The Crowd* (1928), one of the most individual films to emerge from twenties Hollywood, comparable only to Fejös' *Lonesome*. Using unknown actors and camerawork of freedom unprecedented in the American cinema, dispensing with conventional story values and happy ending, the film traced the insignificant tragedies of a humble life, a small city clerk whose child dies, leaving him victim to psychological pressures which result in the loss of his job and livelihood.

Clarence Brown (born 1890) also, working at MGM, remained supremely a 'commercial' director without ever compromising his great talent and taste and very personal, romantic vision. He directed Valentino in the satirical-romantic *The Eagle* (1925), Louise Dresser in the gently melancholy *The Goose Woman* (1925) and Pauline Frederick in *Smouldering Fires* (1924). His best work however was with Greta Garbo, beginning with two outstanding silent films, *The Flesh and the Devil* (1927), adapted from Sudermann, and *A Woman of Affairs* (1928), a highly articulate, if somewhat emasculated version of *The Green Hat*.

Hollywood in the twenties could, however, also accommodate individualists: Rex Ingram (1892–1950) with his penchant for exotic pictorialism, seen at its best in *The Four Horsemen of the Apocalypse* (1921) which launched Valentino's starring career, and the series of romantic adventure films he made with Ramon Novarro; the French-born Maurice Tourneur (1876–1961), who had come to America for the Eclair company, and made some of the most visually stylish films of the early twenties; Frank Capra (born 1897), a Sicilian immigrant whose comedies with Harry Langdon were a foretaste of the comic vision of American society which he would apply to greater effect in the 1930s; James Cruze (1884–1942), prolific but capricious, who alternated commercial chores with films like *The Covered Wagon* (1923) and Hollywood's only significant contributions to the twenties avant-garde – *Hollywood* (1923) and *Beggars on Horseback* (1925); Tod Browning (1882–1962), with a unique line in the horrific and bizarre.

There were women directors too – Dorothy Arzner, Lois Weber, the scenarist Frances Marion, and even Lillian Gish, who directed one film, starring her sister, Dorothy. Other directors, like Sidney Franklin, W. S. Van Dyke, Frank Borzage, William Wellman, William Wyler and Howard Hawks, were to achieve their most notable work in the next decade and the sound film.

The stars, and the system which created and sustained

them, had become a vital economic factor and a significant artistic influence (for good as well as bad). By the early twenties, Pickford, Fairbanks and Chaplin were the most famous and the highest salaried people in the world; and it was their faces and their fame which assured the market for American films from Siberia to Africa, from London to Tokyo. As we have seen, the Griffith girls – the Gish sisters, Blanche Sweet, Mae Marsh, Bessie Love – representing Victorian ideals of sweetness and innocence, tended to be eclipsed by a more sophisticated style of star; though they were all professionals talented enough to maintain their careers at least to the end of the silent era. After Theda Bara came stars like Alice Terry, Norma Talmadge, Norma Shearer, Florence Vidor, and the legendary Gloria Swanson – women of a more cynical and frivolous world than the mystically sinful and torrid universe inhabited by the older star, whose career rapidly faded with the twenties. The era also brought the flapper girls; Joan Crawford, Colleen Moore, Constance Bennett, Marion Davies, and – with her unique quality of fatality – Louise Brooks. In 1927 Clara Bow starred in Clarence Badger's film of Elinor Glyn's It, and established, as 'The It Girl' a new, aggressive sexual symbol of the times.

Rudolph Valentino (1895–1926) who was 'the symbol of everything wild and wonderful and illicit in nature'* brought unprecedented dreams and visions to the women of the world in films like The Sheik and Monsieur Beaucaire; and started a whole line of successors. Ramon Novarro, Antonio Moreno, Rod la Rocque, Ricardo Cortez, Gilbert Roland, and the all-American John Gilbert, all offered varied erotic images of the Latin Lover. The lady exotics included Pola Negri, Vilma Banky, Nita Naldi, Lupe Velez and Dolores del Rio. An individual variety of exotic glamour was offered by Sessue Hayakawa, Hollywood's only oriental romantic star, who had made his name in De Mille's The Cheat (1915), in which he played a dastardly, fascinating role in the amorous fortunes of Fannie Ward.

By and large the male part of the American audience felt more at home with the identifiably virile qualities of the

*Life, 15 January 1950.

Western stars, like Tom Mix, William S. Hart and George O'Brien. But the twenties' appetite for stars seemed endless. Jackie Coogan's affecting and comic performance in *The Kid* won him universal adoration, and set off a fashion for child stars. The undisputed king of innumerable animal stars was Rin-Tin-Tin, the Alsatian hero, found as a puppy on the battle-fields of Flanders, who starred in a long series of canine dramas.

All, however, divas, dogs and babies alike, were eclipsed towards the end of the twenties by MGM's Swedish star, Greta Garbo (born 1905). Uniquely photogenic, so that her ungainliness and irregular features glowed with incomparable beauty on the screen; and possessing an extraordinary, radiant, indefinable talent, she metamorphosed anything in which she played (and MGM gave her some shamefully novelettish rubbish) into art; and made every other star seem faded and unreal. Her popularity on the Continent was to prove a vital economic factor in the next stage of Hollywood's imperialism, after the arrival of talking pictures.

The one country that the American cinema was unable to pillage, even though it provided a major artistic impetus to the cinema in the 1920s, was Soviet Russia. Before the war, a tremendous appetite for films throughout the Russian Empire had been fed with a monotonous diet of sentimental melodramas, costume pictures (which proved fairly safe from censorship), clownish farces in the French style, thrillers and detective stories, and a growing taste for 'decadent' pictures on mystical or satanic themes. There had been a few stirrings of more creative approaches before the Revolution however. In 1913 a group of futurist artists, including the poet Vladimir Mayakowsky, made a bizarre avant-garde film, *Drama in Futurist Cabaret 13*. Working within the commercial context of the Khanzhonkov studios, Yevgenii Bauer was attempting increasingly realistic and contemporary themes at the time of his death in 1917. In that year too Yakov Protazanov (1881–1945), already a veteran director at thirty-six, took advantage of the relaxation of censorship to make a version of

Tolstoy's *Father Sergius* which in maturity of acting, setting, psychology and narrative style went far beyond the general run of Russian production.

The work of two men was still more indicative of the direction films were to take in Soviet Russia. Vsevelod Meyerhold (1874–1940), the most creative and controversial figure of his time in the Russian theatre, suddenly recanted earlier declarations that the cinema could never be accounted an art, and undertook to make two films for the firm of Thiemann and Reinhardt. Both films, *Dorian Gray* (1915; in which Dorian was played by an actress, Varvara Yanova, while Meyerhold himself played Lord Henry) and *The Strong Man* (1915) are lost; but they were to exert a powerful influence upon the cinema, both through the effect of Meyerhold's highly individual conception of cinematic *mise-en-scène* upon the artists who saw them at the time; and, more important, because Meyerhold had brought to the cinema his ability for fundamental analysis of the nature and the problems of a medium – the gift for asking the right questions. The lessons which Meyerhold was to impart to the pupils of his theatre studio in the early twenties were to have far-reaching effects on the formation and progress of the Soviet cinema.

A little later, one of Bauer's assistants, a young designer barely eighteen years old, Lev Kuleshov (1899–1970) published a series of articles on film theory in the journal *Vestnik Kinematografia*. Kuleshov and his theory of cinema – far in advance of his time – were also to be formative within a very few years.

The October Revolution in 1917 gave the cinema an entirely new role as a massive socio-educational force. Lenin told Lunacharsky, the first Commissar for Education, around 1920: 'The cinema is for us the most important of all the arts'. This belief was positively demonstrated on 9 November 1917, when a special cinema sub-section was set up under the State Commission on Education, under Lenin's wife, Krupskaia. Film schools – the first in the world – were set up in the new Soviet Union. Short propaganda and agitational films (*agitki*) were produced; and film showing and film-making played an important role in the work of the agit-trains and the agit-steamer that

Vsevolod Meyerhold: *The Portrait of Dorian Gray*. Russia, 1915.
Varvara Yanova as Dorian and Meyerhold as Lord Henry.

were sent out to disseminate revolutionary propaganda throughout Soviet lands.

All this was accomplished despite the large-scale emigration of the old film people,* and the active non-cooperation of those that remained. The nationalisation of the film industry in August 1919 was inevitable.** 'The cinema', said Stalin, the Commissar for Nationalities, 'is the greatest medium of mass propaganda. We must take it in our hands.' The strongest impetus to the revival of production and the beginnings of a Soviet cinema came with Lenin's New Economic Plan (N.E.P.) in 1921. With this partial return to private enterprise, film stock and equipment which had vanished after 1917 returned to light; and feature production shot from eleven films in 1921 to 157 in 1924. Given only this soil to grow in, the climate was conducive to the creation of a revolutionary cinema. Sergei Yutkevitch, who was thirteen at the time of the revolution and was within a very few years to become one of the pioneers of this cinema, has written movingly of those enchanted years:

> They were astonishing and wonderful days, the debut of a revolutionary art. When we talk about the years when we began to work, people are always surprised by the birth-dates of almost all the directors and the important artists of those times. We were incredibly young! We were sixteen and seventeen-year-olds when we started into our artistic lives. The explanation is quite simple: the revolution had made way for the young. It has to be remembered that an entire genera-

*The first line of retreat was Odessa, where there were attempts to set up a new film-producing centre. From Odessa the old artists were scattered all over the world. Some, including Protazanov and the most celebrated Russian star, Ivan Mosjoukine, ended up in Paris; others (Grigori Khmara, Dmitri Buchowetski) went to Germany.

**This was not the first nationalised cinema in the world. Four months before, in April 1919, the short-lived Hungarian Republic of Councils had nationalised the Hungarian cinema, with an administrative board that included Sándor Korda (Alexander Korda), Mihály Kertesz (Michael Curtiz) Laszlo Vajda and Béla Lugosi.

tion had disappeared. Our elders had been dispersed throughout the country or had perished in the Civil War, or had even left Russia. Hence the Republic lacked a clear organisation, lacked people; and our way in was easy – the country wanted us to work; the country needed people in every department of culture. That is why our generation, then so young, began its artistic life so early.

The Revolutionary young felt an aggressive, religious duty to replace the past with the present. Old was bad and must be swept away; only new was good. Grigori Kozintsev, a contemporary and collaborator of Yutkevitch, has described how the young artists of his native Kiev would ride about the streets in lorries, yelling the latest Mayakowsky poems that had arrived from Petrograd:

Away with tuppenny truths!
Sweep the rubbish out of your heads!
The streets are our paint-brushes;
The squares are our palettes.*

Mayakowsky provided the most coherent ideological influence on the new cinema. Artistically the development of the revolutionary cinema is in great part due to Kuleshov and Meyerhold.

In 1920 Kuleshov was given a studio, or 'Workshop' to study film methods with a group of students barely younger than himself. (He had at first taught at the newly formed cinema institute; and it is probable that more conservative teachers preferred him to work outside the institute's formal curriculum). His work there was interrupted while he was sent to the front to shoot reportage of the interventionist wars; and on his return to Moscow, raw film stock was so short that the group had to exercise themselves on 'films without films' – improvisational acting studios. In 1922 however he was able to rake up enough film to make his experiments in montage which were to become famous as 'The Kuleshov Effect'. Sergei M. Eisenstein later

*Both the Yutkevitch and Kozintsev quotations are from *Cinema in Revolution*, an anthology translated and edited by David Robinson (London, 1972).

explained the respects in which Kuleshov's theory of montage went beyond that of D. W. Griffith's already very complex methods of film editing:

> Griffith's . . . close-ups create atmosphere, outline traits of characters, alternate in dialogues of leading characters, and close-ups of the chaser and the chased speed up the tempo of the chase. But Griffith at all times remains on a level of representation and objectivity and nowhere does he try through the juxtaposition of shots to shape import and image.*

In one experiment Kuleshov took shots made at different times at places as varied as Red Square and the White House, and assembled them in such a way as to suggest a single action in a single location:

> The scene demonstrated the incredible strength of montage that, apparently, was so powerful that it was able to alter the basic imagery of the material. We learned from this scene that the chief strength of cinema lies in montage, because with montage one can destroy, repair, or completely recast material.**

In a further experiment shots of various parts of the body of several girls were assembled to give the spectator the impression that he was seeing only one girl, making up in front of a mirror. The third and most famous experiment consisted in juxtaposing the same, negative close-up of the face of the actor Mosjoukine with shots of a plate of soup, a dead woman lying in her coffin, a little girl playing with a toy:

> When we showed the three combinations to an audience which had not been let into the secret the result was terrific. The public raved about the acting of the artist. They pointed out the heavy pensiveness of his mood over the forgotten soup, were touched and moved by the deep sorrow with which he looked on the dead woman, and admired the light, happy smile with which

---

*Sergei Eisenstein, *Collected Works* (Moscow, 1965–1970).
**Film Form* (London: Dobson, 1951).

he surveyed the girl at play. But we knew that in all three cases the face was exactly the same.*

Briefly, Griffith's discovery had been to use editing to assemble individual elements into a continuous story. Kuleshov had gone further, to show how the juxtaposition of shots can alter the intrinsic meaning of each shot. Another example given by Pudovkin in illustration of Kuleshov's idea, was to join a shot of a smiling actor to a close-up of a revolver and follow this with a second shot of the actor, looking frightened. Formed in this way the sequence would give the impression that the actor was a coward. The simple process of reversing the two shots of the actor would give exactly the reverse meaning: the audience would see the actor's behaviour as bravery. Thus different emotional effect may be achieved simply by changing the order of the shots.**

In 1923 the Kuleshov collective were able to put their ideas into practice in a satirical comedy about the adventures of an American in the country of which he has heard only horror tales: *The Strange Adventures of Mr West in the Land of the Bolsheviks*. Following a mystery film, *The Death Ray* (1925), which was much criticised for its extravagance and social irrelevance, the collective made its best silent film, *By The Law* (1926), based on a story by Jack London, and shot with an almost geometrical stylisation of performance and form.

Kuleshov's theories were however most notably vindicated in the work of his pupil Vsevelod Pudovkin (1893–1953), who had given them wide circulation in his influential books *Film Technique* and *Film Acting*. Trained as a scientist, he drifted to the Kuleshov workshop after release from a prisoner of war camp. His first independent work as a director was a full-length documentary of Pavlov's experiments in conditioned reflexes, *Mechanics of the*

*Pudovkin's account of the experiment in *Film Technique* (London, 1929). Kuleshov himself on various occasions gave varied accounts of it, all different from Pudovkin's version. The essential point however remains valid.

**Griffith could not of course have remained unaware of this possibility. The Russians, however, were the first to deduce a theoretical basis for what he had achieved instinctively.

Brain (1926); but whilst working on this he put together an
amusing demonstration of the Kuleshov Effect, by combining actuality material of Capablanca at an international
chess match with specially shot acted material, to create
a fiction film, *Chess Fever* (1925).*

Lev Kuleshov:
Dura Lex.
U.S.S.R. 1926.

Undoubtedly the Kuleshov-Pudovkin group exaggerated
the importance of montage ('. . . film art does not begin
when the artists act and the various scenes are shot – this
is only the preparation of the material. Film art begins
from the moment when the director begins to combine and
join together the various pieces of the films.'), which may
be the reason why these two very talented directors never
really came to grips with sound film technique. Still, the
accomplishment of Pudovkin's silent films was self-evident.
His classic work is the adaptation of *Mother* which he made
in 1926 with the collaboration of the scenarist Nathan
Zarkhi and the cameraman Anatoli Golovnya, who was
always to photograph Pudovkin's films. After this the
same team made the monumental *End of St Petersburg*

*Another Kuleshov disciple used the effect even more ingeniously
by fabricating a new film 'starring' Mary Pickford and Douglas
Fairbanks, which was in fact a combination of acted material (with
other players) juxtaposed with news shots of the American stars on
their Soviet tour.

(1927) to commemorate the tenth anniversary of the October Revolution and *Storm Over Asia* (1928), a story of a simple Mongolian trapper who comes into unsought conflict with colonialist powers.

Kuleshov's other pupils included the directors Boris Barnet (formerly a boxer) and Leonid Obolensky (whose most important contribution to Soviet cinema was to be as a sound expert in the early days of talking films); and the actors Alexandra Khoklova (Kuleshov's wife), Vladimir Fogel, Valeri Inkidzhinov, the star of *Storm Over Asia*, and Mikhail Doller, Pudovkin's assistant throughout his career.

A second line of artistic descent in the Soviet cinema can be traced from Vsevolod Meyerhold.* In that period when no extravagance was too great in the theatre, and all the young artists were dedicated to the overthrow of the old and traditional (even the Moscow Art Theatre, so recently revolutionary itself, had now become a bastion of reaction in their view), Meyerhold was a god. As early as 1900 he had revolted aggressively against Stanislavskian 'naturalism'. After the Revolution he reappeared in a striking semimilitary uniform, preaching new forms, new ideas, new theories, adapting to the theatre all the most avant-garde ideals of revolutionary art (in particular, Constructivism which was closely allied to Meyerhold's system of 'biomechanics').

Despite various projects to work in the cinema, apart from brief acting appearances, Meyerhold himself never worked in cinema after his two pre-Revolutionary films. Yet in 1936 Kozintsev declared that 'the Soviet cinema has learned much more from Meyerhold than the Soviet theatre.' The young people who fought for a place in his studio in Moscow in the early twenties included many who were to become celebrated in the Soviet cinema – the actors Ilinsky, Martinson and Straukh, the future directors Nikolai Ekk, Nikolai Okhlopkov, Sergei Yutkevitch, Lev Arnstam; and above all Sergei Mikhailovitch Eisenstein

---

*Perhaps the two lines were not entirely distinct. The form and phraseology of Kuleshov's pre-Revolutionary articles suggest that he was not unaware of Meyerhold's writings at the time of *Dorian Gray* and *The Strong Man*.

(1898–1948). In fact Eisenstein rather quickly became impatient with the work at the Meyerhold studio; though in later years – even when Meyerhold had been discredited and executed on false charges of treason – he acknowledged him as his 'artistic father'. Eisenstein's principal debt to Meyerhold was his gift for analysing the fundamentals of his art.

Eisenstein, the son of a bourgeois Jewish family from Riga, trained as an engineer and, recently returned from work as an artist in a front-line agit-train, joined Meyerhold's studio on the same day as Sergei Yutkevitch; and the two young men worked together on their earliest theatrical projects. In 1923 Eisenstein made a short film sequence to use in his stage production of Ostrovsky's *Enough Simplicity in Every Wise Man*. The same year, with extravagance characteristic of the times, he staged Tretyakov's play *Gas Masks* in an actual gas works. (It was not a commercial success: the public made clear their preference for seeing plays in theatres, by simply staying away). Next Eisenstein made a feature film; and this, *Strike* (1924), marks the real beginning of the classic period of Soviet silent cinema. The theme was industrial oppression and industrial revolt in pre-Revolutionary Russia. In it, Eisenstein abandoned conventional narrative structure in favour of a chronicle form; abandoned the conventional hero in order to make the 'mass' the protagonist. Alongside extravagances imported from the theatre, he used elements of actuality – the factory, the streets, the workers' tenements, the workers themselves.

Following *Strike* Eisenstein had already begun work on a story of the Civil War when he was commissioned to make a film to celebrate the twentieth anniversary of the 1905 Revolution. The script by Nina Agadjanova-Shutko was a massive panorama of the events of that year; but a single episode, *The Battleship Potemkin* (1925), grew in scope till it became the entire film. It was edited in considerable haste (there is a legend that when the first reel went on at the premiere, Eisenstein and his assistants were still cutting the last one); but the energy and power and accomplishment of the film were totally new; and were to have a tremendous impact on film-makers wherever it was shown.

Eisenstein's theories of montage, which he developed
theoretically only after having already put them into
practice, diverged from those of Kuleshov and Pudovkin;
and their contemporaries delighted in fanning the debate,
which became particularly colourful when both directors
were making their films for the tenth anniversary of the
October Revolution. Pudovkin was making *The End of St
Petersburg* and Eisenstein *October* at the same time, on the
same locations and with the same essential themes.

Pudovkin, in his theory of constructive editing, claimed
that a scene is most effectively presented by linking
together a series of specially chosen details of the
scene's action. Eisenstein emphatically opposed this
view. He believed that to build up an impression by

simply adding together a series of details was only the most elementary application of film editing. Instead of linking shots in a smooth sequence, Eisenstein held that a proper film's continuity should proceed by a series of shocks; that each cut should give rise to a conflict between the two shots being spliced and thereby create a fresh impression in the spectator's mind. 'If montage is to be compared with something', he wrote, 'then a phalanx of montage pieces, of shots, should be compared to the series of explosions of an internal combustion engine, driving forward its automobile or tractor; for, similarly, the dynamics of montage serve as impulses driving forward the total film.'*

Eisenstein himself described a sequence in *October* to illustrate his thesis. The only narrative action is Kerensky climbing a flight of stairs to his office in the Winter Palace. Eisenstein however uses this simple piece of action as the basis for a whole series of intellectual comments:

Kerensky's rise to power and dictatorship after the July uprising of 1917. A comic effect was gained by subtitles indicating regular ascending ranks ('Dictator', 'Generalissimo', 'Minister of Navy and of Army', etc.) climbing higher and higher – cut into five or six shots of Kerensky, climbing the stairs of the Winter Palace, all with exactly the *same* pace. Here a conflict between the flummery of the ascending ranks and the hero's trotting up the same unchanging flight of stairs yields an intellectual result: Kerensky's essential nonentity is shown satirically. We have the counterpart of a literally expressed conventional idea with the *pictured* action of a particular person who is unequal to his swiftly increasing duties. The incongruence of these two factors results in the spectator's purely *intellectual* derision at the expense of this particular person.**

The danger of this method is obscurity. When *October* appeared in 1927 – but particularly after his next film, *The*

*Karel Reisz, op. cit.
**Sergei M. Eisenstein, *Film Form* (London: Dobson, 1951).

Sergei M. Eisenstein:
October, U.S.S.R., 1927.
Series of stills
illustrating Eisenstein's
editing method.

5

1

6

2

7

ГЛАВКОВЕРХ -

3

ДИКТАТОР

8

4

9

10

11

12

13

14

15

16

17

18

19

October: The Staircase Sequence [*footage*].

1 [4] *Medium long shot:* Rear view of Kerensky and two aides going down corridor.

2 [3] *Medium long shot:* Front view of Kerensky and aides mounting stairs.

3 [2] *Title:* DICTATOR.

4 [3] *Medium shot:* Staircase. Close up of Kerensky's legs as figure moves into camera.

5 [6] *Long shot:* Staircase. Kerensky coming into view at turn.

6 [2] *Long shot:* Kerensky mounting stairs.

7 [2] *Title:* COMMANDER IN CHIEF.

8 [9] *Long shot:* Kerensky mounts staircase . . . *Jump cut*

9 [12] *Long shot:* . . . . . followed by aides.

10 [3] *Title:* MINISTER OF WAR.

11 [8] *Long shot:* Kerensky mounting stairs . . . . *Jump cut*

12 [10] *Long shot:* . . . . followed by aides.

13 [3] *Title:* PRIME MINISTER

14 [4½] *Long shot:* Kerensky mounting stairs.

15 [3½] *Extreme long shot:* Longer view of all three mounting stairs.

16 [3] *Title:* AND SO ON AND SO ON AND SO ON

17 [3] *Long shot:* All three mounting stairs.

18 [2] *Close up:* Marble statue with wreath (hand and arm only).

19 [3] *Close up:* Torso of statue.

20 [1] *Close up:* Statue.

21 [4] *Title:* THE HOPE OF THE PEOPLE AND THE REVOLUTION.

22 [3] *Medium close up:* Low view of statue.

23 [3] *Title:* A. P. KERENSKY.

24 [4] *Extreme close up:* Kerensky's face. He smiles.

20

23

А. Ф. КЕРЕНСКИЙ.

21

НАДЕЖДА РОДИНЫ И РЕВОЛЮЦИИ-

24

22

Old and the New (1929) – audiences, and worse, the Soviet authorities, made it clear that they preferred stories to complex ideas. Eisenstein never pursued his ideas of intellectual montage further than in these films but for the rest of his career he was constantly dogged by official criticism for his 'intellectualism' and 'formalism'.

Eisenstein's fellow-student at the Meyerhold Studio, Sergei Yutkevitch, joined up with two other boys of his own age in Petrograd – Grigori Kozintsev and Leonid Trauberg. Like Eisenstein they tried to break away from traditional theatre forms with new styles created out of elements of circus, vaudeville, puppet and exotic theatres. Eccentricism was a watchword of the times, and they called their theatre the Factory of the Eccentric Actor (FEKS). Carrying their eccentricism into films, from 1924 they made a lively series of pictures, some which they had to admit were totally chaotic, but all invigorating in their invention and youthful exuberance: *The Adventures of Octyabrina* (1924), and *Mishka and Yudenich* (1925), a brilliant expressionist adaptation of Gogol's *The Overcoat* which was in aggressive reaction against the old, upholstered forms of Russian costume cinema. After this the various members of the group pursued independent careers, though Kozintsev and Trauberg remained as a team for some years, and in 1929 made a dazzling, sophisticated, sardonic recreation and interpretation of the Paris Commune, *New Babylon.**

There were many roads to the Revolutionary cinema.** Eisenstein and FEKS were formed by a distinctly theatrical tradition. Dziga Vertov (1896–1954) rejected all theatricality and artificiality in favour of an uncompromised actuality, films which should pass 'right over the heads of

*The film had a score specially composed by Shostakovitch – his first work for films. It was not always a success with the audience, who were inclined to complain that the orchestra conductor appeared to be drunk.

**The gifted Friedrich Ermler (1898–1969) whose films all proclaimed the faith of an unswerving but humanely idealistic Communist Party member, began his career in the early twenties by establishing a group called KEM, to oppose the idea of revolutionary *form* proclaimed by FEKS, with revolutionary *content*.

actors and over the roofs of the studios, directly into life and truth, multi-dramatic and multi-detective reality'. Applying to cinema the ideals of Constructivist art, he aggressively condemned the un-revolutionary falsity of the feature film makers. They in turn retaliated with equal hostility. Audiences however appeared to like his newsreel, *Kinopravda* which began to appear in 1922. Put in charge of a studio, he embarked on *Kino Eye* (1924), 'the

Dziga Vertov: *Kino Eye*. U.S.S.R., 1924. Poster by Rodchenko.

organisation of the seen world', which was a prototype of modern *cinéma vérité* methods. The fallacy of Vertov's arguments about the superiority of actuality unadulter-ated by *mise-en-scène* and artistic interposition, is that his own films – in particular the highly emotional *Lenin Kinopravda* (1924) and *October Without Ilyich* (1924) derive their power not from the inherent quality of the documents, but from Vertov's own participation and personality.

Another revolutionary documentary approach was indicated by the editor Esther Shub (1894–1959), who was a pioneer of the creative compilation of old archive documents. Bringing to light thousands of feet of old, forgotten, mouldering news films, she assembled three brilliant, deeply committed historical chronicles: *The Fall of the Romanov Dynasty* (1927), *The Great Road* (1927) and *The Russia of Nikolai II and Leo Tolstoi* (1928)–at once establishing a new genre and asserting the need for film archives to preserve the film documents of the past.

With Eisenstein, Pudovkin and Vertov, the fourth of the giants of the Soviet silent cinema was the Ukrainian Alexander Dovzhenko (1894–1956), who began work for the Ukrainian Film Studios in 1926. (Thanks to Stalin's interest, the cinema industries of the Soviet Republics had become very active; one of the earliest successful Soviet feature films, *Little Red Devils*, had been made in the Georgian Studios, while another artist working in the Ukrainian Studios was the former Meyerhold actor Okhlopkov). Dovzhenko had been a teacher, a diplomat and a painter before joining the Odessa Studios at the age of thirty-two,·an extremely advanced age for a debutant in the Soviet cinema of those years. He wanted to direct comedy, and his first effort was a two-reel slapstick, *The Fruits of Love* (1926). After a foolish adventure film, distinguished none the less by visual style and romantic ennobling of the proletariat, he revealed his true talent with *Zvenigora* (1927), a wild and wonderful *mélange* of legend, folk-lore and magic. The praise of Eisenstein and Pudovkin overcame the alarm of the Studio heads in the face of this film; and Dovzhenko went on to make *Arsenal* (1928). Describing the revolutionary struggles of 1918, this was his most intense and concentrated film, a fiery assembly of drama, caricature, and folklore, welded into a unified lyrical vision. In 1930 Dovzhenko made his greatest film, *Earth*. It is a story of small, banal happenings: an old man dies, the collective buys a tractor, the young farm chairman is shot by a resentful Kulak and is buried. But Dovzhenko invests these events with poetic grandeur, generating through the images and their juxtaposition an impression of vast energy and inevitability.

Alexander P.
Dovzhenko:
Arsenal, U.S.S.R.,
1929.

The achievements of Eisenstein, Pudovkin, Dovzhenko and the rest were not isolated. The revolutionary excitement inspired dozens of artists and dozens of productions. Some pre-revolutionary directors continued to work, among them Olga Preobrazhenskaia, one of the few women directors of the period, who made *The Peasant Women of Riazan* in 1927. Yakov Protazanov returned from exile to resume his film-making activity; and created a science fiction fantasy, *Aelita* (1924), which was principally distinguished as the only film designed in Constructivist style. Yutkevitch was designer for Abram Room's brilliant comedy-drama *Bed and Sofa* (1927), which treated the theme of a *ménage à trois* produced by the housing shortage with outstanding social and psychological observation. Subsequently Room made an equally dazzling adaptation of a Barbusse subject, *The Ghost that Never Returns* (1930). A Kuleshov pupil, Boris Barnet, made two excellent dramatic comedies, *The Girl With the Hatbox* (1927) and *The House on Trubnaia Square* (1928). Viktor Turin created a dynamic documentary, *Turksib* (1929) on the building of the Siberian Turkestan railway; while Mikhail Kalatozov, depicting the other side of the coin, documented the lives of a poor and backward community in *Salt of Svanetia* (1930). Kalatozov was greatly criticised for 'negativism', and it was to be very many years before he next came to prominence with *The Cranes are Flying* (1957). Such attacks, like the growing criticism of Eisenstein, were symptomatic of what the next decade would bring. Mayakowsky's thundering accusations after various frustrations involved in submitting scripts to the authorities seemed to have progressively less effect; and were silenced altogether in 1930, when he committed suicide. Already in 1928 a Congress on Film Matters, timed to coincide with the first Five Year Plan, made very apparent a narrowing of ideological outlooks, a growing suspicion of anything that smacked of 'formalism'. The first heady flush of freedom and revolutionary excitement, which had produced such a notable flowering of art and artists, was over.

At the very moment when France's film empire was in collapse – and indeed largely as a result of that collapse – France gave the cinema its first true aesthetic theorist, Louis Delluc (1890–1924). Delluc rejected all previous French cinema tradition – except perhaps Lumière and Linder (Méliès was at that time so completely forgotten that it is possible Delluc may hardly have known his work at all). In particular he abhorred the practise of 'adaptation' which had been predominant in the French cinema since the heyday of the *film d'art*. While agitating for a truly national cinema, Dellux pointed, for examples, to the American cinema of Ince, Griffith and Chaplin, to the Scandinavian schools, to the German expressionists. The school of enthusiastic young cinéastes which gathered around Delluc and his revue, *Cinéma*, acquiring the name of 'Impressionists'. Delluc's own first scenario *La Fête espagnole* (1919), directed by Germaine Dulac (1882–1942) principally showed the influence of the well-constructed Ince westerns;

but the films he directed himself, *Fièvre* (1921) and *La Femme de nulle part* (1924), with their psychological observation and powerful atmosphere, reveal rather the influence of the *Kammerspiel* and the Swedish cinema.

Marcel L'Herbier (born 1890), a former symbolist poet, was Delluc's most loyal follower, and in his earlier films (*Rose France*, 1919; *L'Homme du large*, 1920) justified the group's name by seeking pictorial effects comparable to those of the impressionist painters of the preceding generation. In his search for distinction he later adopted other visual styles – cubism in *Don Juan and Faust* (1923), for example; while *L'Inhumaine* (1924), his best work, an extravaganza about a super-vamp, was designed by Fernand Léger and Mallet Stevens.

L'Herbier's chill aesthetic refinement was in contrast to the work of Abel Gance (born 1889), whose enthusiastic self-education is evident throughout the ebullient and inventive work of his immensely long career. He tried his hand as poet, dramatist and actor before playing in Léonce Perret's film *Molière*, at the age of twenty. Acquiring a passion for the medium, he acted in Linder comedies, and in 1910 was already writing for films. By 1911 he had his own production company. He was always his own *avant-garde*. In 1915, in *La Folie du Dr Tube* he used a subjective camera to convey the impressions of a madman's vision, four years before *Caligari*. In his spectacular anti-war documentary, *J'accuse* (1919) he used scenes shot on the front in 1918 in the context of a symbolic narrative. The rapid cutting of *La Roue* (1921–4) was unique in its time, anticipating Eisenstein in the emotional and metaphorical effects it achieved. It is known that *La Roue* was widely studied in the U.S.S.R. in the early twenties, and may well have had a profound effect upon the developments of Soviet film theory which have been discussed earlier in this chapter.

Napoléon (1925–7) remains Gance's greatest monument. As historical interpretation it is sometimes dubious, though as reconstruction it is hard to fault. In technique it was truly revolutionary – so much so that some of its innovations are only now being assimilated into film practice. Gance gave the camera a mobility and freedom it had not known before. He used dozens of cameras, whole batteries at once. He put cameras on automatic stands, on tracks, on dollies, on lifts, on guillotines, on special elevators, on stairways. He had cameras mounted on bicycles, on pendulums, on horseback; and he had little trucks like out-size roller skates. At a time when cameras were almost too heavy to lift, he introduced hand-held camera techniques. It was well over a quarter of a century before the camera was used again with such freedom; which explains why the French *nouvelle vague* (pp. 284–91) was so exhilarated at the rediscovery of *Napoléon* when it was re-issued in Paris in the late fifties.

Gance above all thought in images. He shattered the senses of his audience with pictures. Pictures already remarkable in themselves were hurled in torrents. They were cut with unprecedented rapidity, many shots lasting only a frame or two.* They were superimposed and multiplied. And finally Gance's compulsion to enlarge visual experience led to Polyvision, a system in which three images were projected side by side on a giant panoramic screen. Sometimes the pictures on the screens would be different, and complementary in their intellectual imagery; at other times they would join to form a single vast panorama.

The Impressionist school attracted other directors – Germaine Dulac and the young journalist Jean Epstein (1897–1953), whose *Coeur fidèle* (1923) asserted a *populisme* (the treatment of subjects involving real life and real people in distinction from the unreal world generally concocted in the American studios) which has always remained characteristic of French cinema at its best. Although the impressionist movement virtually ended with the death of Delluc in 1924, its legacies included the idea of the film society (Delluc's *Ciné-Club*) and the specialised cinema:

---

*In the early days of the cinema, projection speeds were in the region of 16 frames per second. Towards the end of the twenties films were being shot and projected at 24 frames per second, which was adopted as the standard shooting and projection speed on the introduction of sound films. Thus a shot of two frames' length would appear on the screen for only one twelfth of a second.

This group of men was the first in Europe to assert the stature of the film as an art – the equal (or even the superior) of music, literature and the theatre – and to obtain recognition for it as such. With the creation of independent film criticism they gave body and substance to their claim . . . Henceforward the cinema became a subject of dinner-table conversation like the novel or the play, and there emerged a group among the intellectual élite for whom it was a major artistic preoccupation.*

The Impressionist movement is often called the First Avant-Garde to distinguish it from the Second Avant-Garde which grew out of the cinema's contact with the literary and artistic *avant-gardes* of the twenties, deriving from the Cubist and Futurist movements, and taking in Dada and Surrealism. Dada had already made some impact on the cinema in Germany, through the work of Viking Eggeling (1880–1925), continued by Hans Richter and Walther Ruttman. In France the American photographer Man Ray made his ironically titled *Le Retour à la raison* (1923), which was premiered at the celebrated Dadaist assembly, 'La cour à la barbe'. The abstract images of this film were followed up by Fernand Léger and Dudley Murphy in their *Ballet mécanique*. In 1924 René Clair (born 1898), then a journalist and film actor, was commissioned to direct a film insert for the ballet *Relâche*, devised by the Dadaist Francis Picabia for Rolf de Mare's Ballets Suédois. Set to a musical score by Erik Satie, (who plays in the film alongside leading members of the Dada group in Paris) *Entr'acte* mingled elements of the pre-war French slapstick comedy, Feuillade mysteries and sheer nonsense in order to provoke surprise, shock and laughter. Dadaist elements persist, though less aggressively, in the film which Clair had begun before *Entr'acte*, *Paris qui dort* (also 1924), which speculated comically on the results of the sudden immobilisation of Paris by a magic ray.

Entr'acte was one of the last true manifestations of Dada, which was usurped by the Surrealist movement which had

*Georges Sadoul, *French Cinema* (London, 1953).

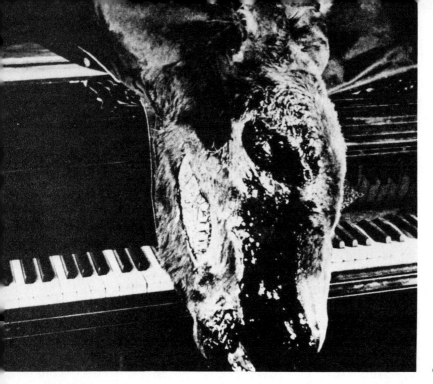

Luis Buñuel and Salvador Dali: *Un Chien andalou*. France, 1928.

emerged as an offshoot at the Cour à la Barbe assembly. Germaine Dulac's *La Coquille et le Clergyman* (1928) from a scenario by Antonin Artaud, was rejected by the British Board of Film Censors on the grounds that it was 'so cryptic as to be almost meaningless. If there is a meaning it is doubtless objectionable.' In fact the psychoanalytical symbols of the dream world of a repressed priest – too conscious for true surrealism – have worn much less well than *Un Chien andalou* (1928), written by the two Spaniards, Luis Buñuel (born 1900) and Salvador Dali, but apparently directed by Buñuel alone. 'A desperate passionate call to murder', as the opening title calls the film, it is a picture of comedy, brutality and tragedy, with images authentically dredged from the subconscious – an eye slashed with a razor, a severed hand, an ants' nest in the palm of a living hand.

The surrealist cinema survived into sound films. Alone, Buñuel made *L'Age d'or* (1930), full of potent and personal images – Christ in the image of the Marquis de Sade – and an exultant celebration of the surrealists' 'L'amour fou'. Throughout the next forty years, Buñuel was never completely to abandon the surrealist impulse. Jean Cocteau (1889–1963) added cinema to the wide range of arts in which he worked, and, also in 1930, made the richly atmospheric *Le Sang d'un poète* (financed, like *L'Age d'or*, by the Vicomte de Noailles): an assembly of personal and conscious poetic symbols, not in any real sense aligned with surrealist principle.

While a number of film-makers – Man Ray, Dulac, Marcel Duchamp and Jean Gremillon among them – continued to pursue the abstract cinema, the interest of the Second Avant-Garde moved in new and quite distinct directions. The interest in documentary was perhaps influenced by the Soviet films which were just reaching Paris, with their emphasis on images of real life and ordinary folk. The Brazilian Alberto Cavalcanti (who had worked as a designer on L'Herbier's *L'Inhumaine*) made *Rien que les heures* (1926), images of a day in the life of Paris, clearly influenced by Mayer and Ruttmann's *Berlin*. Other documentaries like Marcel Carné's *Nogent, Eldorado du dimanche* (1929) and Georges Lacombe's *La Zone* were more human in their interests, nearer to the sympathies of *Menschen am Sonntag* (see page 98). Jean Painlevé pursued scientific documentary, discovering geometric and abstract forms in the phenomena of nature.

This documentary phase of the *avant-garde* however produced two masterpieces of permanent value: *A propos de Nice* (1930) in which the young Jean Vigo (1905–34) combined social satire, surrealism and the sinew of Dziga Vertov (whose brother Boris Kaufman photographed the film); and *Las Hurdes* (a sound film of 1932 shot in Spain) in which with merciless irony Luis Buñuel surveyed the miseries of the people of Las Hurdes, in a land in which the only rich buildings were the churches and where the hopelessness of the natives' plight was symbolised by the folk-medicine with which they treated the bites of vipers: the wound was not fatal, but the herbs with which they treated them were.

These experimental activities, whose reputation and influence on the international cinema were quite disproportionate to the slender financial means with which most of the film-makers worked, went on alongside a commercial cinema at generally low ebb, and largely committed to a sterile policy of literary adaptation.* Exceptions were the work of Abel Gance, Jacques Feyder and René Clair. Although he had been directing films since 1916, Feyder (1888–1948) only achieved prominence with his adaptation of Benoît's *L'Atlantide* (1921), for which he shot all the exteriors in the desert. In *Crainquebille* (1922), a touching adaptation of Anatole France's novel, he combined ingenious expressionist effects with vivid realism. Of his later work, Feyder wrote that the formula was 'a setting, an atmosphere, and a popular plot with a little melodrama'; and these were the ingredients of his attractive *Visages d'enfants* (1925), an authentically Zolaesque *Thérèse Raquin* (1928; shot in Germany) and the light comedy, *Les Nouveaux Messieurs* (1929). When this last film was banned for its (extremely light-hearted) political satire, Feyder left for Hollywood, where he directed Garbo in *The Kiss* (1930) and the German-language version of *Anna Christie* (1932); and Ramon Novarro in *The Son of India* and *Daybreak* (both 1931).

Clair abandoned the ivory towers of the *avant-garde* for the commercial cinema; and after tentative beginnings (*Le Fantôme du Moulin-Rouge*, 1925; *Le Voyage imaginaire*, 1925; *La Proie de vent*, 1926) achieved one of his most brilliant successes with *Un Chapeau de paille d'Italie* (1927), in which he succeeded in creating visual equivalents to the verbal comedy of the celebrated stage farce by Labiche and Michel, giving it a rhythm that could almost be *heard* in musical terms. In *Les Deux Timides* (1928) Clair attempted to repeat the formula, with only limited success.

In Britain, where economic weakness was closely followed by technical weakness, it was reckoned that by 1925 ninety-five per cent of screen time was taken up by

*There were some successes in this field nonetheless, generally in the work of Jacques de Baroncelli (*Pêcheurs d'Islande*, 1924, *Père Goriot*, 1921), Léon Poirier (*La Brière*, 1924) and Henri Fescourt (*Les Misérables*, 1925). The young Julien Duvivier (1896–1967) made a notable feature debut with *Poil de carotte* (1925).

René Clair: *Un Chapeau de paille d'Italie.* France, 1927.

American films. There were long periods in which no films at all were being produced in British studios. Most of the production companies that were still in existence at the end of the World War had ceased to exist by 1924. Cecil Hepworth, a pioneer from the earliest years, closed his studios in 1923; prior to that they had been largely given over to the production of gentle romantic literary adaptations, the best of them directed by Henry Edwards. Other promising post-war companies like Broadwest and Alliance also closed down. Only a handful of directors succeeded in producing work of better than mediocre standards in the early twenties: Maurice Elvey and Victor Saville at Gaumont British; George Pearson (born 1875), working with his own company Welsh-Pearson for which he directed the excellent series of 'Squibs' comedies; Walter Summers and Geoffrey Barkas making their reconstructions of First World War battles; the eclectic and craftsmanlike Herbert Wilcox (born 1891) and Graham Cutts (born 1885).

A distinct revival however coincided with the Cinematograph Films Act of 1927. The outcome of agitation from all sections of the British film industry, this aimed at suppressing block booking and, most important, imposed a quota of British productions upon exhibitors. Even before this however, Michael Balcon (born 1896), who had produced Graham Cutts' *Woman to Woman* in 1924, had begun to show himself a producer of exceptional taste and intelligence. He established Gainsborough Pictures in 1924; launched, with Cutts' *The Rat* (1925), the film career of Ivor Novello who was to become one of Britain's very few silent stars of international stature (another was the comedienne Betty Balfour); and developed, at Gainsborough Pictures, a director of outstanding ability in Alfred Hitchcock (born 1899).* Already in *The Lodger* (1926) Hitchcock revealed his mastery of narrative and atmosphere, particularly when working in the thriller genre which he was afterwards to make peculiarly his own.

The Lodger was followed by adaptations of Novello's own implausible play *Downhill* (1927) and Noel Coward's *Easy Virtue* (1927); after which Hitchcock was put under contract by the newly formed British International Pictures whose big new studios at Elstree were intended to become the British Hollywood. There he made four silent films of uneven quality. *The Ring* (1927), his first film from an original screenplay was an unglamourised, atmospheric film of the rise of a boxer from a fairground booth to the Albert Hall; *The Farmer's Wife* (1928) adapting a play by Eden Philpotts, was set firmly in a sensitively recorded rural England; *Champagne* (1928) was a silly society comedy though with an endearing performance by the admirable Betty Balfour! and *The Manxman* (1929) was a no less absurd triangle drama, from a Hall Caine novel, unconvincingly played by its foreign stars, Carl Brisson and Anny Ondra. Sound films were to realise Hitchcock's full potential.

*Trained as an engineer, Hitchcock had become interested in art and gone to Islington Studios in charge of the Art Title Department of the British branch of Famous Players-Lasky. In 1922 he began an independent feature production, *Number Thirteen*, which remained unfinished. When Islington Studios were taken over by Balcon, in the same year, Hitchcock was kept on and worked as assistant director to Graham Cutts. In 1925 Balcon gave him his chance to direct on two films made in Germany (because of the British distributors' reluctance to try out a new director): *The Pleasure Garden* (1925) and *The Mountain Eagle* (1926).

Another outstanding director appeared in British films at the close of the silent era. As Hitchcock had learned his craft with Graham Cutts, Anthony Asquith (1902-68) worked with Sinclair Hill, an able craftsman of silent films, at British Instructional. (Among the 'prentice jobs he did at this period was doubling for Phyllis Neilson-Terry in dangerous scenes in *Boadicaea*). Asquith himself suggested to the studio the story for his first film, *Shooting Stars* (1928) which he made under the supervision of an experienced but not unduly talented director, A. V. Bramble. The film was an extremely witty and deft comedy about life in a film studio. His next silent film, *Underground* (1929), was a rarity among British films of the period in showing recognisable and realistic working-class characters – an electrician and a porter on the underground, both in love with the same shop girl. Neither this film nor *The Runaway Princess* (1930), a piece of Ruritanian nonsense made in Germany, was very successful; but *A Cottage on Dartmoor* (1930) confirmed all the promise of *Shooting Stars*. A tense and tragic story of an emotional triangle, it was conceived as a silent film, but in the craze following the introduction of sound, the producers required Asquith to add sound sequences. He chose to introduce sound only into a sequence where the hero and heroine go to the cinema; and the only sound is that of the film within the film. This witty device served at once to introduce light relief into an essentially dark story; to echo the state of mind of the characters in the film; and incidentally to present a rather cruel parody of some of the talking films which at that time were being imported from America.

In the face of American imperialism, it was all that other national cinemas could to to survive at all; and countries which had not established film traditions before the close of the First World War had now still less chance of creating authentic national cinemas. It is, however, worth mentioning parenthetically the progress, almost independent of what was happening in the rest of the world's cinema, made by the film industries of India and Japan. It is reckoned that the studios of Calcutta and Bombay had produced upwards of 1500 films between 1912 and the coming of sound – without leaving one title to be remembered. The Indian cinema was developed as a crude folk-craft of story-telling, which achieved immense popularity among the uneducated audiences whose taste was for familiar tales with recognisable stock plots and characters, and of inordinate length. These tastes were to dictate the form of a large proportion of Indian production for many years to come.

Japan on the other hand early developed a cinema of great sophistication, which was only to make its impact on international film activity after the 1950s, when there was a deliberate effort to infiltrate Western markets: earlier there had been a conviction – often found with Japanese art – that foreign audiences could not possibly understand or appreciate Japanese films.

At the time of the invention of the cinema, the Japanese were enthusiastically absorbing Western techniques. The Kinetoscope reached Tokyo in 1896, and the Lumière Cinématographe in February 1897. About the same time the first films were shot in Japan, and by 1899 brief but ambitious records of geisha dances and the greatest Kabuki artists were being made. For a long time the cinema was to retain its links with Kabuki; and the first narrative film made in Japan, *Momijigari* (*Let Us Walk Beneath the Maple Leaves*, 1902) was adapted from a Kabuki play. A curious effect of the Kabuki tradition was that for many years female parts in Japanese films were played by men; and at one point of his career the great Japanese actor Kasuo Hasegawa was concurrently the most popular male star and the most popular female star.

In 1908 the first studio was opened by the Yoshizawa Company, which the following year carried out experiments with talking films. A crisis occurred in 1910, when the Kabuki theatres refused to let their actors play in films. This shocked the cinema into sudden revolution, encouraged also by the impact of Western films imported to fill the gap left by reduced home product. Among other reforms was the admission of female actresses into films. Towards the end of the crisis, the four existing film companies combined as Nikkatsu, and set up new studios at

Tokyo and Kyoto, thus establishing the traditional division in the Japanese cinema between the historical films (*jidai geki*) made in Kyoto with the advantages of the availability of ancient sites and temples, and contemporary subjects (*gendai geki*) generally produced in Tokyo. From this time also, following the introduction of modern actors and acting styles, the Japanese cinema showed considerable enthusiasm for experiment: around 1914, for instance, there were experiments with sound and with colour films,* and with a remarkable *genre* called 'Rensageki' in which live actors performed alongside moving pictures. Foreign literary works, including Tolstoy, were freely adapted; the French *Zigomar* detective serials were extensively imitated.

After 1918, when *Cabiria* and *Intolerance* and foreign serials reached Japan, the cinema entered on a new period, absorbing post-Griffith techniques, and abolishing such reactionary traditions as the *benshi*, commentators originally employed simply to describe the action of the films, but who had gradually usurped greater and greater importance, often completely overshadowing the screen images with their chatter, song, dance and general entertainment.

Dating from the establishment in 1919 of the Art Film Association by the young director Norimasa Kaeriyama (born 1893), there was a notable artistic revival, and large numbers of new production companies were set up. Directors like Thomas Kurihawa, who had worked with Ince, and Henry Kotani, who had been a cameraman with Paramount, returned from the States, still further to impress Western methods on Japanese films. Kotani worked for the newly formed Shochiku company, whose competition and success spurred on the Nikkatsu studios – which had the good fortune to employ one of the greatest of Japanese directors, Kenji Mizoguchi (1898–1956) – to raise the quality of their work.

*Using the Kinemacolor process, an ingenious additive system developed by the British pioneer George Albert Smith (see page 32) with Charles Urban. The film ran at twice the normal speed, and was exposed and later projected through blue and red filters which rapidly alternated from frame to frame.

The earthquake of 1923 destroyed all the studios except Nikkatsu's at Kyoto, on which fell the task of meeting a dramatically increased demand for films. With an output of 875 films in the year 1924 alone, quality inevitably fell abysmally, although one or two directors – Minoru Murata (1894–1937) and Yutaka Abe (born 1898), who trained in America–succeeded in rising above the general level. A more deliberate and concerted effort to raise standards followed the formation of a film company by Shozo Makino, which produced the second classic master of Japanese film, Teinosuke Kinugasa (born 1896). A number of other directors who rose to reach their creative peak in the sound period and especially after the Second World War made their appearance at the end of the silent era, among them Heinosuke Gosho (born 1902), Mikio Naruse (born 1905), Yasujiro Shimazu and above all Yasujiro Ozu (1903–63), one of the most individual artists ever produced in the cinema – all directors who leaned strongly towards contemporary and social subjects.

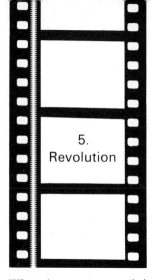

5.
Revolution

What is most surprising about the revolution which struck the cinema at the end of the twenties is that it had not happened earlier. Edison had first conceived moving pictures as an extension of his phonograph; and some of his early Kinetoscopes were equipped with sound reproducing attachments and earphones. The Lumière Brothers themselves took a patent on a purely theoretical proposal to synchronise the *cinématographe* with a phonograph in 1896; and about the same time Auguste Baron took out patents for more practicable equipment to produce talking films. At the time of the Exposition of 1900 there were at least three competing systems on show in Paris, of which the most successful, Phono-Cinéma-Théâtre, which presented talking images of such theatrical celebrities as Bernhardt, Coquelin Ainé, Réjane, Cléo de Mérode and Little Tich, enjoyed a profitable life of several years. In 1900 also, Henri Joly, the former associate of Charles Pathé, patented a system of synchronising sound and image, while Léon Gaumont gave the earliest demonstrations of the Chronophone which he was to exploit successfully practically up to the War.

Experiments continued in France and elsewhere for the next decade. In Germany Oscar Messter, in Sweden Paulsen and Magnusson, in Japan the Yoshizawa Company, in America the Actophone Company and Edison himself, and in Britain James Williamson and Cecil Hepworth, who successfully exploited his Vivaphone Pictures in 1909–10, all developed workable sound systems.

Cecil Hepworth:
Vivaphone
Pictures,
Britain, c. 1909.
Poster.

Not that the cinema was ever in the strict sense silent.
Long before the Lumières, Reynaud's *Pantomimes Lumi-
neuses* had a special musical score by Gaston Paulin. The
Lumières advertised that a saxophone quartet accom-

panied the films at their Boulevard St Denis theatre in 1897, while Méliès personally played the piano at his 'trade show' of *Voyage dans la lune* in 1902. For *L'Assassinat du Duc de Guise* (1908) a specially commissioned score was composed by Saint-Saëns; and throughout the rest of the silent period every important film would have at least a specially *compiled*, if not a composed score. We have seen that Shostakovich wrote an accompaniment for *New Babylon*. Honegger provided accompaniments for Gance's *La Roue* and *Napoléon*; and there is a legend, which may have an element of truth in it, that the musical score which Edmund Meisel composed for the Berlin showing of Eisenstein's *The Battleship Potemkin* was banned in some countries where the film itself was permitted. Such fully scored orchestral accompaniments had of course disadvantages as the film had to be shown in many different cinemas, with widely varying instrumental groups, ranging from a single piano and violin to a whole pit orchestra. In general, therefore, it was more convenient for distributors to accompany each film with a cue-sheet of suggested musical selections chosen from special publications of musical themes for moving pictures. Occasionally singers might also be engaged to accompany the pictures; the great comedian Oliver Hardy made his first acquaintance with the cinema as part of a male voice quartet which sang behind the screen of a nickelodeon in Atlanta, Georgia.

Sound effects were at first provided by rather haphazard means. A writer of 1912 recalled:

> The first attempts to introduce sound effects provoked humorous situations. The boy deputed to the task enjoyed the chance to make a noise, and applied himself with a vigour of enthusiasm which overstepped the bounds of common sense.*

The writer was able to report however that:

> Nowadays such effects are employed with all the care and discrimination expended on the pictures themselves, and the result is harmonious and pleasing.

*F. A. Talbot: *Moving Pictures: How They are Made and Worked*, 1912.

Sound effects machine for use in cinemas, 1912.

Pointing out that 'within the past two or three years the idea has come into vogue of accompanying movements in the pictures with characteristic sound effects', he offered the arguments in favour and against sound accompaniments:

> Some more cultivated motion photography lovers are opposed to it, on the ground that unless every motion is given its distinctive sound, none at all should be audible; others contend that sound imparts an additional realism to the scene. . . .

He concludes however that 'sound effects are perfectly justifiable in moving pictures, provided they are judiciously managed'. To aid this judicious management, exhibitors could instal a remarkable machine called the Allefex, invented by a Mr A. H. Moorhouse which was capable of producing upwards of fifty sound effects from storm noises, bird-song, and barking dogs to gun-fire, escaping steam and the rattle of pots and pans.

The desire for sound in films was, then, apparent and continuous. It was clear from the start that sounds, and especially music, intensified the effect of the images. An eloquent appeal for a medium which should add sound and speech to vision was one of the last great European silent films, Carl Theodore Dreyer's *La Passion de Jeanne d'Arc* (1928). Concentrating upon the last twenty-four hours of Joan's life and the final stages of the hearing against her as recorded by Bishop Dubois, Dreyer aimed at psychological realism within a setting that would recreate convincingly the physical nature of the time and place. He constructed the castle of Rouen after mediaeval miniatures. Costumes and properties were designed functionally, without the heavy self-conscious padding of historical films of the times. Taking advantage of the sensitivity of the new panchromatic film stock, Dreyer dispensed with make-up, and captured in the close-ups which predominate in the film the naked, revealing features of his actors. When Joan's head was to be shaved, the actress Falconetti had to submit to an actual razor. Working under Dreyer's unsparing direction, Falconetti (1893 or 1901–1946) – a highly esteemed stage actress whose career was compromised by her unmanageable temperament and whose only film performance this was – produced one of the greatest screen interpretations ever, completely internalised, totally true, totally expressive, with no relation or concession to theatrical traditions.

The film was begun in autumn 1926 and released in 1928; and Dreyer declared strongly his regret at being unable to use sound techniques. Structurally the film is largely dependent on the form of the inquisition; and for most of its length must rely upon the titles to represent the exchanges – the sophisticated questions of the judges and Joan's ingenous but ingenious replies. The alternation of close-ups with dialogue titles severely disrupts the film's natural rhythm. At the time this deficiency was not necessarily identified with the need for sound which Dreyer himself acknowledged. Paul Rotha, one of the most outspoken critics of those days, admired the film but felt it lacked 'the central aim of the cinema, in which each individual image is inconsequential in itself, being but a part of the whole vibrating pattern. . . . *It was not a full exposition of real filmic properties.*' The lacking element was sound.

The perfection of the sound film, like that of the moving image itself in 1895, depended on the combination of several techniques. It was necessary to record sound; to synchronise it with the image; to reproduce it with amplification sufficient to fill large cinema auditoria. Edison's phonograph and Berliner's disc gramophone had made recording practicable at the very time of the cinema's birth; but the apparatus for acoustical recording – the massive horns that had to be close to a performer's face – were hardly practical for use before the camera. An early solution to this problem was to record the sound in advance, and then subsequently fit the acted image to it. Only with the general introduction of electrical recording in the twenties was synchronous recording really practicable.

From the very first years of the cinema and the experiments of Auguste Baron there were devices to synchronise mechanically the projector and phonograph, which became more practical as hand-cranked cameras and projectors gave way to motorised machines whose speed was more readily regulated. The first sound film presented by Warner's Vitaphone system in 1926 was achieved by a synchronised disc reproducing system; but it was clear that the best synchronous effects were likely to be obtained when the sound could be recorded on the same strip of film as the image. The possibility of converting light impulses into sound was already known in the 1880s; and Eugene Lauste's experiments with recording sound on film by means of a selenium cell date back to 1906. The practical difficulties of making a projector which could reproduce images (which depended on a violently intermittent motion of the film) and sound (which required an absolutely smooth progression of the film) was a purely mechanical problem which presented fewer difficulties than the task of improving sound quality to the point where spoken words were recognisable. It was only in the twenties that Lee De Forest succeeded in achieving a record of his voice on which 'I was clearly able to determine whether or not it was being run backwards!' De Forest was the inventor of the audion amplifier, in 1906; and it was this which ultimately made possible a magnification of sound sufficient for practical theatre use. (Gaumont's Chronophone apparatus had made use of clumsy giant acoustic horns).

Research accelerated after the First World War, alongside the rapid development of radio.* The great and growing electrical and radio companies gathered in the patents. By 1920 General Electric were working on a sound-on-film system, and a year or so later Western Electric and Bell Telephone were both demonstrating disc systems. Meanwhile in Germany a group of scientists were developing the 'Tri-Ergon' system, which was to be acquired by Tobis-Klangfilm.

Sound films were actually shown in the theatres in the early twenties without causing much stir. De Forest

---

*The first regular transmissions by a private station in America began in 1920. By late 1922 there were 220 stations on the air.

demonstrated his system at the Rivoli Theatre, and soon had a repertory of two dozen or more short subjects of politicians and vaudeville artists. In 1925 his Photophone system was seen and heard at the British Empire Exhibition at Wembley; and a handful of American cinemas installed his equipment. Within a short time however William Fox had Photophone torn out of the six Fox theatres which had installed it.

The American film industry's reluctance to adopt sound films was not difficult to understand. The great expensive studios would at once become obsolete; new equipment and sound-proof stages would have to be installed. The home market would depend on the installation of costly equipment in thousands of cinemas; and the problem was aggravated by the incompatibility of the different systems. Even if foreign exhibitors were prepared to re-equip their cinemas for sound, the vast overseas market would surely collapse overnight when the international language of screen mime* gave place to films in which everyone spoke *American*.** In any case the companies had large backlogs of silent pictures which they could not afford to allow to become obsolescent. Moreover the stars who had been carefully groomed and publicised and deified so that their names and faces sold American films in every part of the globe, were trained and equipped to the art of mime. No one could know how they would cope with the difficulties of spoken drama.

The Western Electric Company, having received only discouragement from the bankers and the other film companies they had approached to exploit their synchronous disc system, finally addressed themselves to Warner Brothers. Warners had allowed themselves to fall behind in the race to gain control of the exhibition end of the industry in the earlier part of the decade, and were fighting for survival. So precarious was their position that in the midst of the craze for mergers, not even Columbia Pictures,

*Foreign language sub-titles were quickly and easily inserted into silent films.
**This fear was to a large extent proved true. Even in Britain the first experience of American speaking voices caused resentment, laughter, and even incomprehension.

then struggling up from Hollywood's 'Poverty Row', would consider a tie-up with the older firm.

Nevertheless the company had succeeded in getting backing from the finance house of Goldman Sachs; and had built a million-and-a-half dollar cinema in Hollywood, the huge Broadway Warner, and acquired the old Vitagraph Company, with its fifteen theatres and the remainder of a contract with Famous Players-Lasky. Thereupon, with this small guaranteed exhibition outlet, they gambled on sound, agreeing with Western Electric to introduce sound pictures in exchange for a royalty on every Western Electric sound apparatus sold.

On 6 August 1926 they presented at the 'Refrigerated Warner Theatre' at Broadway and 52nd, a programme whose centrepiece was *Don Juan*, starring John Barrymore and Mary Astor, and with a synchronised musical score and sound effects. In addition there was a group of shorts, mostly rather classy subjects like Anna Case, Mischa Elman, Martinelli, and Marion Talley, with a drab little filmed speech by Will Hays in which he introduced Warner's Vitaphone as an innovation which would revolutionize the cinema.

He was, as it happened, correct. The success of Warner's show was enough to force a *volte-face* on the cunning William Fox, who had acquired rights in a system (sound on film) developed by Theodore W. Case and Earl I. Sponable in irregular association with Lee De Forest, and now re-named Fox Movietone. Fox's first shorts were ready in January 1927, and in May 1927 he presented the first dialogue film, a comic short with the monologuist Chic Sale (*They're Coming to Get Me*). By the autumn of 1927 Fox had launched his Movietone News. Meanwhile Warners had been encouraged to hire the Broadway star Al Jolson to appear in *The Jazz Singer* (1927; directed by Alan Crosland), basically a silent film but with synchronised musical numbers and a line or two of dialogue, including a Jolson catch phrase: 'You ain't heard nothin' yet'. After this the race was on. In 1928 Warners presented the first all-dialogue feature film, *The Lights of New York*; and Paramount broke into sound with *Interference*. By 1929 three quarters of the feature films made in Hollywood had at least some sound

sequences; and practically every sizeable cinema in the
United States had installed equipment – though as late as
1930 most sound films were made in silent versions also.
The politics of the competing systems and the industry
giants which backed them involved an elaborate jockeying
which only was resolved by an international agreement on
standardisation of sound equipment in July 1930.

The introduction of sound brought great changes to the
economic organisation of Hollywood. From their faltering
state in 1926, Warners rapidly became a major power,
gaining control of a distribution outlet of 500 theatres by
the acquisition of the great Stanley chain of theatres and
the First National circuit. Fox built a splendid new studio,
and for a while gained control of the vast Loew entertainment empire. The Rockefeller group's RCA bought out the
old FBO production group to set up a new major company,
RKO. Box office takings shot up by fifty per cent between
1927 and 1930 as a result of the revived enthusiasm stimulated by sound pictures. This in large part explains the

Alan Crosland:
The Jazz Singer.
U.S.A., 1927.
Al Jolson.

success with which the film industry rode the storms of the great Crash and Depression with which the twenties closed.* Only Warner's timing of the introduction of sound films, perhaps, had saved an industry which by 1926 was showing clear signs of decline, as a result of too great reliance on old production formulas.

Artistically the new medium brought problems and doubts. To many it seemed catastrophic that a new art, unique in its means and disciplines, should be annihilated overnight. Richard Griffith wrote movingly of the loss the cineastes and intellectuals felt at the time:

> Whatever improvements it might have developed if it had survived a few years longer, the silent film at its best had by 1928 attained singular completeness as a human experience. To walk into a darkened theatre, to focus upon a bright rectangle of moving light, to listen somewhat below the level of consciousness to music which was no longer good or bad in itself but merely in relation to what was on the screen, and above all to watch, in a kind of charmed, hypnotic trance a pattern of images which appeared and disappeared as capriciously as those pictures which involuntarily present themselves to the mind as it is dropping off to sleep – but which, also like those of the mind, gradually mount to a meaning of their own – this was an experience complete and unique, radically unlike that provided by the older arts or by the other new media of mass communication. It bade fair to become the characteristic art-experience of our time.**

The film-makers of the late twenties were torn between excitement at the potential of the new medium, and terror. Pudovkin considered that:

> the sound film is a new medium which can be used in entirely new ways. Sounds and human speech should

*It must, at the same time, be recognised that the cinema has always seemed to provide a needed opiate in depressed societies.
**Paul Rotha, op. cit.

be used by the director not as a literal accomplishment but to amplify and enrich the visual image on the screen. Under such conditions could the sound film become a new form of art whose future development has no predictable limits.

Along with Eisenstein and Alexandrov, Pudovkin published a famous manifesto on the use of sound, in which they welcomed it with enthusiasm, whilst trying to establish theoretical principles for its use. They shared with many film-makers a rooted suspicion of the film of natural dialogue:

> A first period of sensations does not injure the development of a new art, but it is the second period that is fearful in this case, a second period that will take the place of the fading purity of a first perception of new technical possibilities, and will assert an epoch of its automatic utilization for 'highly cultured dramas' and other photographed performances of a theatrical sort.

In Britain the young Paul Rotha condemned dialogue films even more vehemently:

> It may be concluded that a film in which the speech and sound effects are perfectly synchronised and coincide with their visual images on the screen is absolutely contrary to the aim of the cinema. It is a degenerate and misguided attempt to destroy the real use of the film and cannot be accepted as coming within the true boundaries of the cinema. Not only are dialogue films wasting the time of intelligent directors, but they are harmful and detrimental to the culture of the public. The sole aim of their producers is financial gain, and for this reason they are to be resented.**

The first Hollywood all-talking pictures must have confirmed the worst fears of Rotha and the many who were in agreement with him. Sound equipment was clumsy; and cameras, together with their cameramen, had to be enclosed in enormous sound-proof booths. Thus camera movement

*Pudovkin, *Film Acting and Film Technique*.
**Paul Rotha, op. cit.

which had been used so inventively during the twenties, was practically abandoned. Recording techniques were elementary, and the boom-supported microphone had not been invented, so that actors had to be anchored within the range of microphones hidden inside prop bunches of flowers, or strapped onto the backs of conveniently large and un-speaking extras. Editing, too was minimised. In consequence the early talking pictures had often a static quality which is nowadays eerily soporific.

Following the immediate change-over period, when desperate attempts were made to salvage silent films already on the shelves by tacking on to them synchronised scores and talking interludes, however irrelevant they might be, the producers' first reaction was to bring Broadway to Hollywood. Plays were transferred to the screen word by word and scene by scene. Stage players were rushed to Hollywood; and though many of them proved unadaptable to the more intimate medium of the screen others stayed, to produce a striking new generation of Hollywood actors, among them Fredric March, George Arliss, Leslie Howard, Clark Gable, Frank Morgan, Fred Astaire, Paul Muni, Edward G. Robinson, James Cagney, Katharine Hepburn and Spencer Tracy. A proportion of the old Hollywood silent actors, particularly those who had orginally come from the stage, made the transition without pain; some, like Marie Dressler, Norma Shearer, Ronald Colman, Janet Gaynor, William Powell and the Barrymore family, found their careers taking a promising new turn. Others however found it harder; and some of the old giants like Fairbanks and Pickford never managed to regain the momentum which their careers had had before the sound revolution. John Gilbert is the most often quoted instance of a star who was unable to make the transition; yet his perfectly satisfactory talkie performances do not provide an adequate explanation for the decline of his career in the early thirties; and it seems likely he fell victim to the company politics which were inclined to make talking pictures in one way or another the excuse for disembarrassing the studios of artists no longer *persona grata*. Garbo rode the storm triumphantly, making her first talking appearance in *Anna Christie* (1930).

Among the directors brought from Broadway – they included Richard Boleslavsky and George Cukor – one at least, Rouben Mamoulian (born 1898) brought striking innovations into the creative use of sound. In *Applause*, made in 1929 in Paramount's New York Studios, he restored mobility to the camera by putting the whole booth on wheels, used two cameras, and introduced the super-imposition of sound tracks. In *City Streets* (1931) he used sound non-realistically – as soliloquy, heard over a close-up of the heroine's face; and in impressionist montages of aural sensations.

Of the older Hollywood directors, the best were able to adapt, often with brilliance. Lewis Milestone (born 1895), who had started his career with Mack Sennett after emi-grating from Russia, and had directed feature films since 1925, adapted Erich Maria Remarques' *All Quiet on the Western Front* (1930) into one of the greatest of all war films, ranging freely from the great blasted battlescapes of the French front line to intimate scenes of delicate psycho-logical observation. After this he lifted the stage play, *The Front Page* (1931) clear of its theatrical origins. King Vidor's *Hallelujah!* (1929), an all-negro drama enriched with black American folk music, despite its conventional story elements and racial attitudes, made brilliant use of sound *and silence*; while using the camera with complete freedom. Lubitsch was delighted with the new medium and demon-strated that sound could be used with as much wit as the image, in *The Love Parade* (1929).

Sound was to shape the American cinema into new patterns. Some staple silent *genres* began to disappear. With the loss of the silent film's technical flexibility, the freedom it allowed for improvisation and the possibility of detailed revision of the film in accordance with audience reactions, the slapstick comedy tended to decline sharply. Sennett never regained his commanding position in the industry. Great figures like Harry Langdon and Buster Keaton (a victim of politics rather than sound) disappeared from view. Chaplin approached the new medium with great caution; and did not risk a full talking film till 1940. *City Lights* (1931) and *Modern Times* (1936) are really silent films with a greater or less degree of synchronised sound effects

Rouben Mamoulian: *Applause*. U.S.A., 1929. Helen Morgan.

Lewis Milestone: *All Quiet on the Western Front*. U.S.A., 1930. Pen Alexander, Lew Ayres.

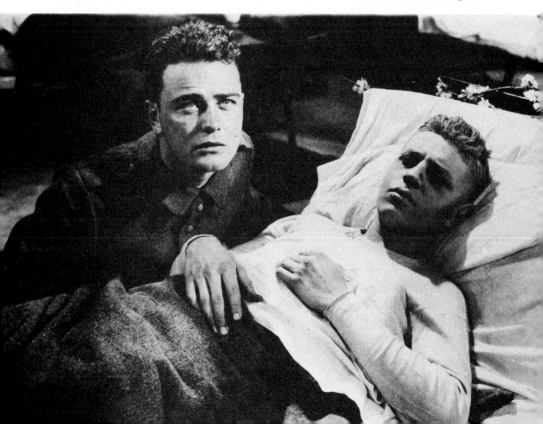

and music. Other styles of comedy came to the fore however. Laurel and Hardy, who were just establishing themselves as a team at the end of the silent era (though both
were already veterans before they joined forces) turned
sound to their advantage, with their admirably foolish
dialogue exchanges, Stan's whimpers and Oliver's howls of
rage and pain, and their celebrated signature tune 'The
Dance of the Cuckoos'. Comedians imported from Broadway – Mae West, W. C. Fields, Eddie Cantor, Burns and
Allen, Jack Benny, Jimmy Durante, the Marx Brothers –
settled permanently in Hollywood.

Other new *genres* flourished. Walt Disney's Silly Symphonies showed new roads to the creative use of sound. The
gangster film came to vivid life when audiences could for
the first time hear the blast of gun-shots and the speech
idioms of the thrilling underworld they had previously
only seen. With *Broadway Melody* (1929) MGM introduced
a new kind of film, the musical, which during the next
forty years was to prove one of Hollywood's most significant contributions to screen art.

Hollywood had now to fight to maintain world domination. Its principal strength was that, apart from those of
the German Tobis Klangfilm, most of the world patent
rights in sound film equipment were held by its studios.
France, for instance, had to pay crippling royalties in order
to embark on sound film production. With this upper hand
Hollywood exercised varying tactics to retain its foreign
markets. For several years films were shot in different
language versions, generally made on the same stages and
concurrently, with different directors and different stars
waiting their turn to go through the same scenes. This
naturally gave special value to stars like Garbo, Lili
Bamita and Lillian Harvey, who could play in several
different languages. A number of foreign directors – Jacques
Feyder, as we have seen, among them – were kept employed in Hollywood for a while on these alternative
language versions. The artistic results of this multiple
production were predictably not often very happy; though
two of the most famous films made in this manner were

the German productions *Der Blaue Engel* (1930) and *Die Dreigroschenoper* (1931). As an alternative to this method some studios made tentative experiments in dubbing foreign and alien voices onto their actors. In countries such as Britain and Hungary where quotas had been levied to restrict the import of American product in the late twenties, Hollywood companies began a policy of production abroad, in the countries themselves – a policy that has persisted until very recent times.

The patents owned by Tobis-Klangfilm permitted Germany a brief Indian summer before the onset of the Third Reich. G. W. Pabst made two films of passionate pacifist tendencies and great technical accomplishment: *Westfront 1918* (1930) an adaptation of Johanssen's harrowing *Four from the Infantry*, and *Kameradschaft* (1931), a highly drama-

G. W. Pabst: *Kameradschaft.* Germany, 1931.

. tic but humanely observed account of a mine disaster near the Franco-German border, and the bonds of fraternity it reveals between the traditionally alienated nationalities. Between these films he made *Die Dreigroschenoper*, a brilliant, stylishly staged adaptation which Brecht himself repudiated of Brecht's own free adaptation of *The Beggars' Opera*. Fritz Lang's *M* (1931) was an altogether new approach to the psychological thriller, with inventive use of sound montage and effects (for instance the little Grieg *leitmotif* which eerily indicates the proximity of the murderer). Lang was to make only one more film before leaving Germany for America: a sequel to his arch-criminal film of 1922 – *Der Testament des Dr Mabuse. Der Blaue Engel* was directed by Josef von Sternberg, who returned to his native Germany with a reputation (for temperament as well as artistic accomplishment) acquired in the United States. Adapted from a novel by Heinrich Mann, its story of the degradation and destruction of a middle-aged schoolteacher (Emil Jannings) by his infatuation for a cabaret singer (Marlene Dietrich) it was in direct line of descent from the 'street' films of the earlier German silent cinema.

Two directors who were later to work with distinction in America made auspicious debuts in sound films – Anatole Litvak with *Dover-Calais* (1931) and Robert Siodmak with an adaptation of Stefan Zweig's *The Burning Secret (Brennendes Geheimnis,* 1933). Two of Germany's big international successes of the period were Gerhardt Lamprecht's *Emil und die Detektive* (1931) and Leontine Sagan's celebrated study of tensions and lesbianism in a girl's school, *Mädchen in Uniform* (1931).

The mountain film (see page 99) survived, discovering a new heroine in Leni Riefenstahl (born 1902), who was to play a key role in Nazi cinema in the next decade. The operetta film came into its own, and discovered its favourite heroine in the English girl Lillian Harvey (*Drei von der Tankstelle*, 1930; *Der Kongress tanzt*, 1931).*

Britain opened the sound period auspiciously. Alfred Hitchcock had already completed his thriller *Blackmail* (1929), adapted from a play by Charles Bennett, when the industry was thrown into panic by the arrival of sound. The producers took the boldly desperate decision to re-shoot the bulk of the film with sound, retaining only those parts which could be dubbed with effects. In addition to the difficulties created by the unreadiness of equipment and technicians was the problem that the German star, Anny Ondra, spoke little English, so that the heroine's role had to be wholly dubbed – at that time an exceedingly taxing process.** Nevertheless Hitchcock used sound with an inventiveness that remains impressive even today; he used natural noises in an impressionistic way – a shop bell reverberating endlessly and painfully in the mind of the

*Austria, which had already made important contributions of personnel to the cinema – including Lang, Stroheim, Mayer and Robert Wiene – enjoyed a brief period of international success with its first sound films, but notably with Willy Forst's society drama *Maskerad* (1934) which established Anton Walbrook as an international star.

**The actress who dubbed Miss Ondra, Joan Barry, became a notable British star in her own right in the 1930s.

heroine, a continuing conversation which fades from her consciousness leaving only the repetition of the word 'knife' clearly audible among an otherwise incomprehensible murmur of talk. Apart from *Blackmail*, however, and a striking German co-production *Atlantic* (1930), made at Elstree Studios by E. A. Dupont, the director of *Varieté*, British producers on the whole settled into a timid policy of adaptation. Even Hitchcock directed a signally static version of *Juno and the Paycock* (1930), while the principal box-office successes of 1930–31 were screen versions of recent stage hits like *Young Woodley*, *Journey's End* and the popular farces in which the Aldwych Theatre specialised.

France, with its own industry at low ebb, was a particular victim of the new directions of American imperialism. Paramount aimed to make Paris the centre of multilingual production. In their large new studios at Joinville, films were made in as many as fourteen or fifteen different language versions, the same scenes being played successively on the same sets by different groups of actors. Such a factory process imposed inevitable restrictions on subjects; these had to be without national identity, adaptable for sets (mostly interiors) which could be quickly and effectively built and managed in the studio; and with conveniently small casts. Although Paramount hired some of the best directors then available in France, including Alexander Korda and Alberto Cavalcanti, the results were generally disastrous in terms of art.

The German Tobis company made a more intelligent invasion of Paris, building a large new studio at Epinay, where they aimed at quality production, making use of the best native talent and aiming at a distinctive national character in their French productions. The first French Tobis film was René Clair's *Sous les toits de Paris* (1930), which remains the freshest and most attractive of all early sound films. A comedy of humble life in a Paris *faubourg*, with music, it used sound techniques with a remarkable fluency and virtuosity. Musical numbers were staged with great verve and mobility. Sound effects were used with humour – for example a glass door which slams shut on a group of characters just when they are about to speak, so that we *see*, but do not hear their conversation.

The Soviet Union predictably followed its own individual path, having two Soviet-developed sound systems of which the Tager system, first demonstrated in 1927, was eventually adopted generally in the Soviet cinema. The U.S.S.R.'s late start in sound helped Soviet directors to avoid some of the mistakes made elsewhere (and in any event pointed out in the manifesto of the Eisenstein group); and Soviet directors showed no nervousness in face of the new medium. The first Soviet sound film was Abram Room's *Plan of Great Works* (1930), a documentary with sound accompaniment; and the first Soviet dramatic sound film was Yuli Raisman's *The Earth Thirsts* (1930), a visually rich but conventionally conceived story about the construction of a canal. The Soviet cinema pioneered sound reportage: a very early sound film was a direct record of an actual trial of some industrial saboteurs; while another film simply recorded the daily activities of a collective farm.

More obviously creative uses of sound were developed by Dziga Vertov with the exhilarating sound montages of his *Enthusiasm, or Donbas Symphony* (1930); by Sergei Yutkevitch in *The Golden Mountains* (1931) and *Counterplan* (1932; co-directed with Friedrich Ermler, the old enemy of the FEKS group); and Nikolai Ekk in *The Road to Life* (1931), a study of the plight of the abandoned children of the Revolution, which managed to be at once humane, realistic and inventive in its use of sound.

Among the great directors of the silent era, Kuleshov made a disappointing debut in the sound period with *Horizon* (1933), though he was rapidly to reassert his intense originality in *The Great Consoler* (1933), an elaborate interweaving of O. Henry's actual life story, his fictional creations and their historical originals. Pudovkin was obliged for technical reasons to abandon his idea of making *A Simple Case* (1930–32) with sound. His first experiment with the medium was *Deserter* (1931–3) which was perhaps *too* experimental, too much a theoretical demonstration, for its elaborate editing and sound techniques attracted charges of 'intellectualism'; and it is from this time, and especially after the death of his constant collaborator, the scenarist Nathan Zarkhi, that Pudovkin's work appreciably declined into a conventionality calculated to please the establishment.

Dovzhenko's *Ivan* (1932) used sound and dialogue with masterly fluidity. In this film Dovzhenko, characteristically, discovered lyrical exhilaration in something so improbable and mundane as the Dnieper hydroelectric project. Montages of the construction work had a powerful sensuous effect, and the characterisation of the workers – even of the slacker, played by Stepan Shkurat – possessed a warmth and geniality notable even for Dovzhenko.

Only the greatest Soviet director, Eisenstein, had no part in the experimental fever of the early days of sound. His activities at this time were a curious side-track of the industrial revolution at the end of the twenties. Eisenstein, along with Alexandrov and Tisse, was sent abroad ostensibly to study sound techniques in other countries, but with various secondary motives such as collecting research material for one of Eisenstein's innumerable never-to-be-realised projects, an adaptation of *Das Kapital*. The trip was eventually prolonged for more than eighteen months. Having travelled in Germany, Switzerland, France and Britain, lecturing, participating in film-making activities, inspiring hundreds of young enthusiasts and students, and occasionally being moved on by the police, the three eventually passed to Hollywood, where they were invited by Paramount to put up a project for a film. Several ideas and two finished scripts – for *Sutter's Gold* and *An American Tragedy* – eventually came to nothing. Next they moved on to Mexico to make a film produced by the novelist Upton Sinclair. After a year and the shooting of many thousands of feet of film this project too had to be abandoned because of muddle, misunderstanding and exhaustion of funds. Eisenstein was obliged to return to the U.S.S.R., and never again saw, or had the chance to edit, the marvellous material he had filmed in Mexico. In the Soviet Union too he had his difficulties and it was not until 1938 that he was able to complete another feature film.

6.
On the Eve

The boom in cinema attendances in America effected by the opportune arrival of the sound film was only temporary. Having leapt from 57 million admissions a week in 1927 to an average of 110 million admissions a week in 1930, the figures began to drop rapidly, to 75 million in 1931 and 60 million in 1932. This delayed depression, in addition to the vastly increased costs of sound film production and the capital costs that had been involved in the changeover to sound, was a considerable economic shock to the industry; it served to confirm and consolidate the grouping of industrial power into the hands of a small number of producer-distributor-exhibitor organisations. Something like 95 per cent of American production was now in the hands of eight organisations, the five 'Majors' (Loew-MGM, Paramount, Warner Brothers, 20th Century-Fox and RKO), and three 'minors' (Columbia, Universal and United Artists which was concerned only with distributing the products of independent producers and artists.) The relative importance of these big companies can be gauged by a breakdown of production in 1930:

Paramount	64 feature films	Columbia	29
20th Century-Fox	48	Tiffany	27
MGM	47	Sono-Art	20
Warner Brothers	39	United Artists	16
First National	37	Pathé	14
Universal	36	Other companies about	50
RKO Radio	32		

In the course of the 1930s these eight organisations themselves came under the control of the two great financial groups which dominated the States: Morgan and Rockefeller. Wall Street had been impressed by the film industry's apparent proof against depression in 1929–30, and set about getting total control in the first instance by controlling the all-important sound patents. This they achieved, by the mid-thirties, after bitter fights and litigation, whose victims included the veteran William Fox himself, forced out of the industry in which at the close of the twenties he had been one of the most powerful figures. By 1939 Lewis Jacobs could write:

> The peak figures in American finance, Morgan and Rockefeller, either indirectly through sound-equipment control or directly by financial control or backing, now own the motion picture industry.
>
> Competition in the motion picture industry today has narrowed down to a fight between the two major financial interests of the country for the balance of power within the eight major studios and their affiliated theatre and distribution interests.*

Despite the rivalry, he added, 'it must be pointed out that both Morgan and Rockefeller have interests in each other's enterprises'.

This domination by Wall Street had radical effects on the organisation of the industry and consequently upon the artistic form and the content of American films in the period from sound to the Second World War. Depression in the industry which reached its peak in 1933, when a third of the nation's cinemas were closed down, only served to tighten the financiers' control over the organisation of film production. There was even less place for imponderables. Emphasis was laid upon achieving the highest possible standards in those aspects of film-making which could be controlled: quality of equipment, techniques, photography, staging and costuming. Every step was taken to eliminate those unpredictable elements which are of the nature of art. Writers had acquired a paramount

*Lewis Jacobs, op. cit.

importance with the arrival of sound, but in the thirties producers sought to overcome the possible dangers of idiosyncracy by employing teams of as many as fifty writers on each film. The director's role was subordinated to that of the organiser, the associate producer. Individual producers such as Hal Wallis, Samuel Goldwyn and Albert Lewin often imposed their own personality upon a film; and individual directors continued to leave the signature of authority on their work, but for the most part 'the director's part in the execution of the film has been minimized'. John Ford, continued Lewis Jacobs writing in 1939:

> has declared that the director is ordered to do a picture, having been neither consulted about the script nor asked how he feels about it. On arriving at the studio, he is given a few pages of straight dialogue or final calculated action; often he does not know any more about the full story than the players know. Everything has been made ready for the shooting; he has little to say, no opportunity for choice. Allowed an hour to study his day's job, he then proceeds to stage the scene. When it is over, he goes home with little or no idea of what he will do the next day. Under such circumstances direction has become depersonalised and synthetic.*

John Ford, it should be observed, was one of the rare directors who did succeed in imposing his personality on practically every film he made. For the most part, however, the films made in Hollywood during the thirties and forties took their style from the studio which produced them – a style which was formed by the taste and temperament of the studio executives, the particular talents of their contract personnel, the special skills of their designers and dressers, cameramen and carpenters. It was often possible to identify the product of a particular studio from a few seconds only of one of their films. It is common to condemn this elimination of the artist's role. Yet the incontrovertible evidence is that a very large number of

*Lewis Jacobs, op. cit.

films of this period remain impressive tributes to organisation and craftsmanship, still retaining their validity as entertainment of high quality.

MGM, founded in 1924 by the merger of Metro Pictures, the Goldwyn Company and Louis B. Mayer Pictures, became in the thirties the symbol of all that was most glamorous and opulent in moving pictures. Its large capital, backed by the Chase National Bank, gave it command of all the finest talent that was to be bought. It boasted 'More Stars Than There Are in Heaven'; and they included Garbo, Jean Harlow, Norma Shearer, Joan Crawford, Myrna Loy, Clark Gable, Spencer Tracy, the Barrymores, Marie Dressler, Wallace Berry, William Powell, Robert Taylor, Nelson Eddy and Jeannette MacDonald; and later Judy Garland and Mickey Rooney. Its contract directors included Clarence Brown, King Vidor, George Cukor, Sidney Franklin, W. S. Van Dyke; its cameramen, the German master Karl Freund, William Daniels, Harold Rossen and others developed an impeccable pictorial quality, while MGM's designers were second to none. The extravagance and quality of MGM's costumes and properties was demonstrated when twenty thousand lots, the accumulation of fifty years, was sold by auction in 1970.

Throughout its great years MGM was ruled by Louis B. Mayer, one of the most universally detested men, it seems, ever to work in films. Notwithstanding his own evident vulgarity and defensive detestation of artists, Mayer seems to have been an astute businessman, deeply conscious of the value of MGM's reputation for incomparable gloss. In the later twenties and early thirties, however the style of MGM was very much formed by the young production manager Irving Thalberg (1899–1937). A cultivated and civilised man by the standards of the Hollywood tycoons of those days, Thalberg acquired a legendary reputation as a creative producer, responsible for MGM's greatest successes. The predominant style of MGM films was glamorously escapist: musicals, romantic melodramas, adaptations of period or prestige novels, all translated into terms of opulence and optimism. Experimental and controversial subjects like *Hallelujah!* (1929), *The Big House* (1930) or Fritz Lang's *Fury* (1936) became rarer at MGM as the

thirties progressed; and after Thalberg's death the company's films tended more and more to reflect Mayer's own sentimental beliefs in the sanctity of a particularly rose-tinted view of America and the American family. MGM's most celebrated film of the thirties was made after Thalberg's death. *Gone With The Wind* (1939), produced for MGM release by David O. Selznick, was the apogee of all the virtues of the studio system. Essentially anonymous in terms of direction (it seemed almost immaterial whether the credited director was ultimately Victor Fleming or any of the other candidates* there had been for the job) it is a tribute to the art of the producer in assembling the necessary talents, and to the impeccable craftsmanship of the times. Even now its quality as sheer entertainment remains unimpaired.

Paramount's origins traced back to 1912 when the Famous-Players company was formed by Adolph Zukor, who ruled the company for over forty years, and in 1972,

Fritz Lang: *Fury*. U.S.A., 1936. Helen Flint.

*George Cukor is known to have directed some scenes before being replaced.

at the age of 99, still retained an office at the studios. More than the other studios, the character of Paramount's production reflected the character of its star directors. For Paramount release, De Mille continued in a line of flamboyant, vulgar spectacles – *The Sign of the Cross* (1932), *Cleopatra* (1934), *The Crusades* (1935), *The Buccaneer* (1938) – interspersed with westerns. Josef von Sternberg created a repertory of exotic subjects, ever more visually elaborate and generally starring his discovery Marlene Dietrich: *Dishonoured* (1931), *Blonde Venus* (1932), *Shanghai Express* (1932), *The Scarlet Empress* (1934). The Georgian-born Armenian, Rouben Mamoulian, and the Berlin-born Jew Ernst Lubitsch (who was in charge of production for a period in the mid-thirties) brought to Paramount production a sophisticated 'continental' style. Paramount had financial ties with UFA, which probably explains the large number of German artists who were engaged by the studio, notably

Victor Fleming: *Gone With the Wind.* U.S.A., 1939.

the art director Hans Dreier, whose department gave a characteristic pictorial style to all Paramount pictures of the period: 'a glow', an enthusiastic recent critic has said; 'The best of them seemed gilded, luminous, as rich and brocaded as Renaissance tapestry.'* Due perhaps to the predominating influence of Lubitsch, Paramount excelled in light comedy in all genres, ranging from the sophisticated brand of Lubitsch himself to the broader comedy of the Marx Brothers, W. C. Fields and Mae West, all of whom worked at the studios. Other Paramount stars included George Raft, Ray Milland, Fredric March, Claudette Colbert, Miriam Hopkins, Herbert Marshall, Sylvia Sidney, Cary Grant, Nancy Carroll, Bing Crosby, Dorothy Lamour and one of the most gifted of sophisticated comediennes, Carole Lombard.

The Warner Brothers Studio was notorious for its iron discipline. The Warners' memories of their early struggles and of the hard times before their lucky gamble on sound, died hard. The studio worked on the principle of the maximum economy of production consistent with quality – a principle which, with producers like Hal Wallis and Henry Blanke to apply it, had happy results in the well-made scenarios, the spareness and drive of Warner films. The sinewy structural quality of the best Warner production reflected a tough virility in the subjects chosen. Warner musicals reached perhaps their finest flowering in the highlit and surreal choreographic fantasies created by Busby Berkeley. *42nd Street* (1933) was a fierce and funny depiction of back-stage anxieties and jealousies; one of the earlier *Gold Diggers* series, *Gold Diggers of 1933*, included among its musical numbers 'My Forgotten Man', a moving, passionate statement of Depression resentment. Warners pioneered the gangster films of the sound period (*Little Caesar*, 1930; *Public Enemy*, 1931); risked social subjects like the agricultural depression (*Cabin in the Cotton*, 1932) and lynch law (*They Won't Forget*, 1937). When they embarked on a series of historical biographies – *The Story of Louis Pasteur* (1936), *The Life of Emile Zola* (1937), *Juarez* (1939) – they were not the apotheoses that MGM biographies were,

*John Baxter, *Hollywood in the Thirties* (London, 1968).

Mervyn Le Roy: *Gold Diggers of 1933*. U.S.A., 1933. Contemporary sheet music cover.

but realistic and literate, conceived with relevance to contemporary political and social preoccupations. Warners were not even above the occasional foray into artistic experiment, like Max Reinhardt's *A Midsummer Night's Dream* (1935), with Mickey Rooney as Puck. The studio's top stars were Bette Davis – outstandingly – Paul Muni, James Cagney, Humphrey Bogart, Edward G. Robinson, all artists with the same quality of tough intelligence that the pictures themselves revealed. Warner's directors – Mervyn LeRoy, the Hungarian pioneer film artist Michael Curtiz, and the former German actor William Dieterle – were astonishingly eclectic in their output, all able to turn without difficulty from broad comedy or romantic swash-buckler to gangster films.

Fox was merged with Twentieth Century in 1935, but both before and after that date the company's most important assets were the director John Ford (born 1895), who pro-duced his films independently but generally released through Fox, and the child star Shirley Temple who was America's top box office attraction between 1935 and 1938. Apart from Ford's westerns and Shirley Temple's sac-charine vehicles, Fox production showed a preference for musical revues, items of old Americana like *Lillian Russell* and *In Old Chicago* and particularly for remakes of such former romantic successes as *Under Two Flags*, and *Seventh Heaven*. Fox stars also included Will Rogers (an old vaude-ville player who became America's favourite popular philosopher and starred in two of Ford's best early talkies, *Judge Priest*, 1934; and *Steamboat 'Round the Bend*, 1935), George O'Brien, Janet Gaynor, Victor McLaglen, Spencer Tracy, John Wayne and Joan Bennett.

Between 1935 and 1937 Ford deserted Fox to release three films through RKO, presumably because their literary content was found too highbrow by the other studio: *The Informer* (1935), a strange, post-expressionist adaptation of Liam O'Flaherty's novel about the I.R.A., which was one of the most admired and most prize-honoured films of the whole decade; an adaptation of Maxwell Anderson's *Mary of Scotland* (1936); and an adaptation of Sean O'Casey's *The Plough and the Stars* (1936). RKO seemed to alternate such assaults on culture (others included *Of Human Bondage*,

1934 which starred Bette Davis and later, more significantly, the early films of Orson Welles) with programme
pictures; though the possession of Katharine Hepburn
resulted in some stylish literary adaptations (*Little Women*,
Morning Glory), while the dancing team of Fred Astaire and
Ginger Rogers led RKO to make some highly individual
musicals, whose staging remains a beautiful apogee of
thirties decoration. From 1937 with *Snow White and the
Seven Dwarfs*, RKO took over from Columbia the distribution of Walt Disney's enormously successful output. (See
page 351).

Columbia Pictures was ruled by its redoubtable founder
Harry Cohn (1891–1958), and through the thirties was
struggling for survival. Cohn, the archetypal Hollywood
autocrat and vulgarian, built up Columbia by a policy of
borrowing from other studios talent temporarily out of
favour and so available at advantageous prices. Later in the
thirties he was able to engage on one-picture deals, star
directors like Rouben Mamoulian (for *Golden Boy* in 1939,
a project which Mamoulian accepted when Cohn turned
down an idea for *Porgy and Bess*, which Mamoulian had
directed on the stage) and Howard Hawks (*Only Angels
Have Wings*, 1939). Columbia's most significant director
however was Frank Capra (born 1897) upon whose work
between 1928 and 1939 the studio's fortunes were largely
founded. At the time Capra's whimsical ('daffy' in the
parlance of the thirties) comedy and his shrewdly calculated flattery of American values, earned him a critical
reputation of the first rank. Latterly a distaste for his too
conscious sentimentality has brought an eclipse. His
characteristic style was established with *It Happened One
Night* (1934), a brisk comedy about a journalist in professional and amorous pursuit of a runaway heiress, which
still retains its attraction; and which established the
direction of American comedy in the thirties. The simul-
taneous success of this film and *One Night of Love* (directed,
1934, by Victor Schertzinger) which established the singer
Grace Moore as a star, launched Columbia on its rise to becoming a major studio by the forties, and particularly
after the discovery of its biggest star, Rita Hayworth.

Universal was until 1936 still controlled by its founder

Frank Capra:
Platinum Blonde.
U.S.A., 1931.
Jean Harlow,
Robert
Williams.

Erich von
Stroheim:
*Walking Down
Broadway*,
U.S.A., 1933.

Carl Laemmle; and into the start of the thirties still
retained its old reputation for bold experiment (for instance Milestone's *All Quiet on the Western Front*). However,
it was the great popularity of *Dracula* and *Frankenstein*,
both made in 1931 respectively by Tod Browning and James
Whale, the two most distinguished directors ever to work
in the field of gothic horror, which determined the trend of
Universal's production during the next decade. Horror
films mostly alternated with women's matinée pictures
(*Back Street, Only Yesterday*). In 1936 however, with *Three
Smart Girls*, Universal discovered their singing star, Deanna
Durbin, upon whom the studio's fortunes were based for
several years.

Even taking into account the 'social' subjects attempted
by Warners, the American cinema in the thirties was
characterised by the bland, optimistic, essentially unreal
and reactionary virtues its films, overtly or more subtly,
preached. It is too easy to assume that this kind of escapism
was the response to a massive public demand. Rather
it must be seen as the outcome of the general interests of
the big capitalist organisations which ultimately controlled the cinema. In a period of constant and violent
political and economic upheaval, the cinema fulfilled its
periodic function as the opiate of the masses. No film seems
to have acknowledged the Depression at all until around
1933. At best, and then extremely rarely, the great events
of the time – the Spanish war, the war in China, the rise of
fascism, the march of events within the U.S.S.R. under
Stalin – were only employed as exotic background material.

Sometimes capitalist values and reactionary attitudes
were more positively asserted in Hollywood productions.
In the early thirties the studios were at considerable pains
to help restore the confidence in banks and bankers which
had been severely shaken in 1929. Apart from biographical
films like *The House of Rothschild* (1935) and *Lloyds of
London* (1937), the crusty millionaire, usually played by
Charles Coburn or Edward Arnold, who proves at the last
moment to have a heart of gold thus providing a convenient
deus ex machina, became a stock fairy-tale figure in late

thirties comedies. If on the other hand films touched upon capital-labour disputes, sympathy was always firmly turned against the malcontent proletariat, who were depicted at worst as villains, at best as dupes.

Where contemporary abuses were discussed and 'exposed' it was patently more for sensation's sake than out of any very deep social concern; the abuses depicted were so indisputably antisocial as to be quite unsupportable and therefore hardly topics of provocative controversy. The gangster cycle began in 1930 with Mervyn Le Roy's excellent *Little Caesar*, which was followed by a succession of no less high quality films: *the Public Enemy* (1931), Mamoulian's *City Streets* (1931), Roland Brown's *Quick Millions* (1931), Howard Hawk's *Scarface* (1932), which was based sufficiently closely

Howard Hawks: *Scarface*. U.S.A., 1932. Paul Muni, Ann Dvorak.

on the exploits of Al Capone as to attract undesirable interest on the part of the underworld itself. Such films as these uncompromisingly depicted the gangster in an un-favourable light; but it was largely due to less scrupulous imitations which more or less glamourised the gangster figure, the get-rich-quick spirit and the use of force – coinciding with a number of real-life gangster outrages – that led to the formation in 1934 of the League of Decency, a reinforcement of censorship which only made more difficult the production of films which treated adult themes in adult terms. The revival of the gangster film in the later part of the decade showed a more unambiguous condemnation of crime (*The Petrified Forest*, 1936), and a concern, albeit generally fairly superficial, to show the social conditions which could produce gangsters (Wyler's fine adaptation of Lillian Hellman's *Dead End*, 1937).

It would be mistaken to doubt the truth and concern of all the films of this period. Inevitably among all the great productions of Hollywood there were directors and writers who found it possible to deal honestly with subjects of weight. A handful of films dealt forcefully with the treatment of criminals (*The Big House, I Was a Fugitive*), with press corruption (*Front Page*), with the dangers of lynch law (Lang's *Fury*: Le Roy's *They Won't Forget*), even with specific cases of public concern, for instance in Arthur Santell's adaptation of Maxwell Anderson's *Winterset* (1936), which commented, however obliquely, on the notorious Sacco and Vanzetti affair.

Certain genres remained staple. The musical, as we have seen, took different forms at different studios: Busby Berkeley's extraordinary use of chorus lines as plastic material for abstract art-deco structures, Warner's social realism, the suave light comedy of Astaire and Rogers. Comedy enjoyed a revival thanks to the recruitment of artists from vaudeville: Jack Benny with his characterisation of 'the meanest man on earth', pop-eyed Eddie Cantor, Joe E. Brown, Jimmie Durante, Wheeler and Woolsey, Bob Hope, and a host of supporting players. W. C. Fields brought a totally personal iconoclasm and the Marx Brothers a style which seemed a natural outcome of dada and surrealism. Laurel and Hardy possessed something of an older style, derived from the character comedy of vaudeville and the silent traditions of slapstick, which they translated from silent to sound films, and then from two-reel shorts to feature-length films.

Alongside the sophisticated comedy of Lubitsch grew up a more distinctively native style* mainly inspired by the

*It is an interesting sidelight on Lubitsch's comedy that he more often than not set the stories of his films in foreign countries.

Ernst Lubitsch:
Ninotchka.
U.S.A., 1939.
Greta Garbo,
Melvyn Douglas.

J. M. Anderson
King of Jazz.
U.S.A., 1930.

'daffy' comedies of Capra, which were widely imitated. Lewis Jacobs defined the style:

> Here the genteel tradition is 'knocked for a loop'; heroes and heroines are neither lady-like and gentlemanly. They hit each other, throw each other down, mock each other, play with each other. *It Happened One Night* (1934) was the first successful example of this school. *20th Century* (1934), *My Man Godfrey* (1936) and *Theodora Goes Wild*, *Topper*, *True Confessions*, *Live*, *Love and Learn*, and *The Awful Truth* (all 1937) similarly lampooned the dignified and accepted. These films were all sophisticated, mature, full of violence – hitting, falling, throwing, acrobatics – bright dialogue, slapstick action – all imbued with terrific energy.*

These comedies above all reflected a totally changed attitude to sex. The relations of men and women, married or not, were weighed down neither by guilt nor responsibilities. The sexual relation was fun; girls were no longer creatures of menace or mystery, but good companions. Claudette Colbert, Katharine Hepburn and Carole Lombard represented a new kind of girl altogether different from the old-time vamp of Theda Bara's day or the newer jazz babies of Clara Bow's generation. A still more aggressive image of womanhood was projected by Jean Harlow, the original Platinum Blonde – a masterpiece of art deco, with her sleek curves, sculpted hair and shimmering, clinging gowns. Mae West for over half a century used her mock-voluptuous physique, face and voice to ridicule the old mystiques of sexuality.

Some directors accommodated themselves all too easily to the dominance of the studio style. King Vidor, so great an individualist in the twenties, became a high-class commercial craftsman during the thirties, achieving his principal prestige success with *The Citadel* (1938). Directors like Warners' Mervyn Le Roy and Michael Curtiz (with an output that ranged from *Cabin in the Cotton*, 1932, and *20,000 Years in Sing Sing*, 1933, to *The Walking Dead* and *The Charge of the Light Brigade*, both 1936) managed, at least in

*Lewis Jacobs, op. cit.

James Whale: *Frankenstein*. U.S.A., 1931. Boris Karloff.

the earlier part of the decade to put clear signatures on work in vastly varied fields. Howard Hawks perfectly defined his own accommodation to the system and his ability to produce work of the highest craftsmanship within it: 'A good director is someone who doesn't annoy you.'

Apart from Chaplin, who followed the highly sentimental yet brilliant *City Lights* (1931) with *Modern Times* (1936), a very personal comment upon industrialised society, the outstanding figures of the period were: Capra; Ford, whose majestic Westerns have tended to outlast his more pretentious experiments like *The Informer*; James Whale, trained in the English theatre (he was the original director of the phenomenally successful London production of *Journey's End*) and Universal's master of horror; George Cukor, a former Broadway director who made some of MGM's most sophisticated and civilised films (*David Copperfield*, 1935; *Camille*, 1936); Lewis Milestone (*Front Page*, 1931; *Hallelujah I'm a Bum*, 1933; *The General Died at Dawn*, 1936; *Of Mice and Men*, 1939); Josef von Sternberg; Clarence Brown; W. S. Van Dyke; Sidney Franklin.

With the introduction of talking films, and the impoverishment of the European cinema, there was less plundering of foreign artists than in the previous decades, though a fair number of directors, artists and actors fled from Hitler's Germany. Fritz Lang voluntarily left Germany following *The Testament of Dr Mabuse*; and after making a film in France, directed his masterly *Fury* (1936) and *You Only Live Once* (1937) in Hollywood. William Dieterle, before giving his name to the best of Warners' biographical films, made the cinema's most coherent summing up of Scott Fitzgerald's 'lost generation', *The Last Flight* (1932).

One factor that had contributed to the depression in the American cinema in 1933 was the unexpected competition that suddenly came from Britain, whose cinema had experienced a startling recovery following the Cinematograph Films Act of 1927 and the arrival of sound. The Act stimulated production and investment. Studios were built, cinemas re-equipped, the public's enthusiasm for the pictures revived. The number of production companies more than doubled, from 26 in 1927 to 59 in 1928. The output of films during the same period rose even more sharply, from 26 to 128. For the first time strong production-distribution-exhibition organisations were created; and the thirties were a period of industrial empire-building.

If organisationally the revival can be credited directly to the Cinematograph Films Act and the imposition of quotas on imported programme material, creatively it was largely due to four men: two directors, a producer and a producer-director. This last was Alexander Korda (1893–1956), a man who enjoyed several careers. Originally a journalist and film critic he turned to film direction in 1914 in his native Hungary and, as Sándor Korda, rapidly became the leading figure in the cinema there. When the Hungarian film industry was briefly nationalised in 1919 Korda was inevitably one of its leaders. Fleeing after the overthrow of the Hungarian Republic of Councils, he moved to Vienna and then Berlin; and finally in 1926 found himself in Hollywood, where his *Private Life of Helen of Troy* (1927) developed the style of historical biography created in post-war Germany by Ernst Lubitsch.

The arrival of sound films found Korda working for Paramount in Paris, where he directed *Marius* (1931), part of the popular trilogy of films based on Marcel Pagnol's plays of Marseilles life. He came to London for Paramount, but soon afterwards formed a company of his own, London Films. For this company he made *The Private Life of Henry VIII* (1933) a witty, humanising of history which went much further than the Lubitsch costume films in its sophistication. Finely designed by Robert Armstrong, splendidly photographed by Georges Perinal, and boasting above all an aggressively showy performance by Charles Laughton, the film was an immediate and overwhelming success both in Britain and abroad. Korda succeeded, as relatively few other British producers have done, in conquering the United States market; and *Henry VIII* launched a boom for the British cinema whose production rose to 225 films in 1937, to become the second largest in the world.*

---

*This figure inevitably included a very large proportion of second-rate material. The quota encouraged the production of cheap and

Alexander Korda: *The Private Life of Henry VIII*. Great Britain, 1933. Charles Laughton, Elsa Lanchester.

Korda, armed with this success and the resulting capital backing, embarked upon an ambitious and highly successful production policy. He himself directed two more period films, *The Private Life of Don Juan* (the last film role of Douglas Fairbanks) in 1934 and *Rembrandt* (again starring Laughton) in 1936. It is interesting that though he made excellent use of British studios, actors and technicians, Korda seemed unable to find English directors to his taste, and followed a policy throughout the thirties of bringing to Britain distinguished foreign film makers. Thus Leontine Sagan directed *Men of Tomorrow* (1932), Paul Czinner, *As You Like It* (1936), René Clair, *The Ghost Goes West* (1936), William Cameron Menzies *Things to Come* (1936), William K. Howard *Fire Over England* (1937), Robert Flaherty *Elephant Boy* (1937) Korda's brother Zoltan *The Four Feathers* (1939) and Jacques Feyder *Knight Without Armour* (1937). In 1936

undesirable films familiarly classified in the trade as 'quota quickies'.

Josef von Sternberg was brought over to England to film Robert Graves' novel of *I, Claudius*, but tensions between Sternberg and his actors and eventually an automobile accident (providentially perhaps) involving the star Merle Oberon, frustrated the production, from which only fragments remain as a strange monument to the Korda era and the intractibly proud von Sternberg.

Michael Balcon added to his other high qualities as a producer a modesty and honesty almost unknown among film tycoons. Summing up the difference between himself and Korda, he wrote:

> He possessed so many of the qualities which I lack. He took many chances. I am much more canny. He had, I suppose, a brilliant if unconventional financial flair. I tend to orthodoxy in matters of finance. He was cosmopolitan in his outlook while I retain some of the influences of my provincial upbringing. He spoke and thought in four or five languages and altogether was a much more sophisticated character than I.*

As it happened, in the most important period of Balcon's career, which followed the Second World War, it was the very Englishness of his tastes which proved his greatest strength.

Accepting responsibility for a major miscalculation in British films of the thirties, Balcon has said also:

> I admit that during the thirties I supported the mistaken policy of importing stars from Hollywood in order to make our product more saleable in the Americas . . .**

Nevertheless very much of the best that came out of British studios in the thirties was produced by Balcon as Head of Production at Gaumont British and Gainsborough between 1930 and 1936, when he moved for a brief unsatisfactory period to MGM who were then attempting production in

---

*Sir Michael Balcon, *A Lifetime of Films*, (London, 1969).
**Among these artists were Richard Dix, Edmund Lowe, Constance Bennett, Sylvia Sidney, George Arliss (British in origin but by this time settled in Hollywood), Madge Evans, Robert Young, and most significantly Paul Robeson.

Britain. Among the films for which he was responsible the most courageous was certainly *Man of Aran* (1934) Robert Flaherty's ethnographical poem of the struggle for life on a barren, treeless rock island off the Galway coast of Ireland. In quite a different field Balcon skilfully developed the cinema possibilities of native comedy and musical talents such as Jack Hulbert, Cicely Courtneidge, Tom Walls, Jessie Matthews and the North Country comedian George Formby.

In retrospect this essentially popular tradition of British cinema in the thirties, disdained by the critics of the time, has often survived better than more prestigious, more consciously 'artistic' work. Much later than Hollywood (which had developed many British comedians, Chaplin and Stan Laurel among them), the British cinema, having failed to create a tradition of silent comedy, drew upon a rich music hall tradition at the very moment when it was already becoming extinct in the theatres. The Crazy Gang, a knockabout troupe of rare verve and vulgarity were starred in a highly successful series of low budget films. Gracie Fields and George Formby, with their character-isations of the Lancashire working class, had remarkable appeal in a cinema which had otherwise not generally acknowledged regional cultures. Other music hall comedians who were brought into films at this time included the unjustly neglected Sydney Howard, Tommy Trinder, Arthur Askey, Norman Evans. The most original and enduring of the group however were Will Hay, who seemed always to personify figures of authority – schoolmasters, station masters, policemen, prison governors – to whom he imparted an air of seediness and ineffectual corruption; and Arthur Lucan whose character of Old Mother Riley – a belligerent, vulgar, comic, fantastic and yet completely truthful creation of an old Irish washerwoman – appeared in innumerable films made on tiny budgets and distributed generally only in cinemas in the sort of working class districts which a quarter of a century before had provided the patrons of the music halls.

The high craftsmanship of directors of the period like Victor Saville, Herbert Wilcox (who specialised in tasteful costume pieces starring his wife, Anna Neagle) George

Pearson, Tim Whelan and the special talents as directors of comedy of Walter Forde and Marcel Varnel, cannot be ignored; nor can the emergence of new directors like Carol Reed (*Bank Holiday*, 1938) and Michael Powell (*The Edge of the World*, 1938) who were to become major figures in the next decade. But the outstanding directors of the period remain Hitchcock and Asquith. Apart from his surprisingly tentative adaptations of *Juno and the Paycock* (1930), a better one of Galsworthy's *The Skin Game* (1931), a bizarre musical biography *Waltzes From Vienna* (1933), a peculiar little women's magazine romance, *Richard Strange* (1932), and the last film he made before departing definitively for America, *Jamaica Inn* (1939), a melodramatic adaptation from Daphne du Maurier, Hitchcock dedicated himself to a series of thrillers of progressively growing brilliance and personality. He combined a unique gift for suspense narrative with a quirky observation of character and a gift for discovering strange and sinister qualities in the most ordinary places, objects and people. *Murder* (1930) and *Number Seventeen* (1932) were made at British International studios at Elstree; but the best of the series were directed for Balcon at Gaumont British and Gainsborough: *The Man Who Knew Too Much* (1934), *The Thirty Nine Steps* (1935), *Secret Agent* (1936), *Sabotage* (1936), *Young and Innocent* (1937) and the supreme *The Lady Vanishes* (1938).

Asquith's career during the same period was uneven. He began triumphantly with *Tell England* (1931) whose archaic caste attitudes (derived from Ernest Raymond's original book) have dated it badly, though in its day it was enormously admired for its spectacular stagings of the Gallipoli fighting. *Dance Pretty Lady* (1931) was an endearing, nostalgic adaptation of Compton Mackenzie's *Carnival*. For Balcon he made a Clair-esque comedy about a footballer and a sweepstake ticket, *Lucky Number* (1933). After a bad patch with an Anglo-German musical biography, *The Unfinished Symphony* (1934) and a spy drama for Korda, *Moscow Nights* (1935), Asquith made the most successful film of his career, a marvellously elegant and stylish adaptation of *Pygmalion* (1938), produced by Gabriel Pascal who had persuaded Bernard Shaw to allow him to make film adaptations of his plays. Asquith's last pre-war film was an adaptation of Terence Rattigan's *French Without Tears* (1939) which launched the director on a collaboration with Terence Rattigan and a general preference for play adaptation which were to last for the remainder of his career.

Like Britain the French film industry sought means to protect itself from continued American domination at the start of the sound period. Strict limits were set upon the number of dubbed and subtitled films that could be imported. The Paramount production experiment at the Joinville studios soon put a stop to itself by the sustained low quality of its production. When Paramount productions became so notorious that first nights were the signal for public protests, the studios were turned into a dubbing plant.

A year or so of prosperity brought by the coming of sound was followed by crippling economic depression, around 1934. Artistically however the thirties proved an outstanding era in French films. It may indeed be that the collapse of the old production companies and the consequent scope for independent production made possible the flowering of an extraordinary generation of film-makers, most of whom had made tentative debuts in the silent period, and were to continue in dominant creative positions throughout the war and early post-war period.

René Clair followed the joyous musical burlesque *Le Million* (1931) with its parade of extravagant Parisian characters, with *A nous la liberté* in the following year. This fantasy about industrialised society had obvious affinities with Chaplin's later *Modern Times* (1936); indeed the film's German producers, Tobis, attempted to persuade Clair to sue Chaplin for plagiarism. Clair failed to sustain his run of successes with either *Le Quatorze Juillet* (1933) or *Le Dernier Milliardaire* (1935), a comic satire on political economics; and having accepted Korda's invitation to make *The Ghost Goes West* (1936) in England, passed to the United States where he was to work throughout the war.

Two talents were outstanding. Jean Vigo (1905–34) was the son of a well-known anarchist who died in mysterious circumstances while under arrest during the First World War. A wretched orphan upbringing in second-rate provincial schools was followed by a manhood spent fighting the tuberculosis which resulted in his early death at the age of twenty-nine. His few films are absolutely individual. Following *A propos de Nice* (see page 147) and another documentary, *Taris, roi de l'eau* (1932) in which Méliès tricks were applied to the filming of a champion swimmer, to produce thoroughly surrealist effects, Vigo made his strange masterpiece *Zéro de conduite* (1933). Comedy, fantasy, surrealism, music and the powerful rhythms and unique poetical sense of all Vigo's work are combined in an anarchical memory of his own unhappy schooldays. The film is ostensibly a comedy, but the ending, with a revolt by the oppressed boys against their midget headmaster and the grown-up establishment who are depicted as straw dummies, was powerful enough to bring the film under a ban which lasted for many years after Vigo's death.

Vigo left behind a single feature film, *L'Atalante* (1934). The script – about the life of a young newly-wed couple aboard a canal barge – was imposed on Vigo by the studio, but he made it into his own, with touching and lyrical observations of humble life, an affectionate feeling for naive young love, and the memorable and extremely bizarre portrait of the eccentric old sailor played by Michel Simon. In Vigo, as in Delluc ten years before, the French cinema mourned an artist of exceptional promise.

The greatest of all French directors, Jean Renoir (born 1894) was the son of the painter Auguste Renoir. As a child he was deeply impressed by Méliès' *Le Voyage dans la lune*. Following war service he developed a passion for the work of Chaplin and for Pearl White serials; and in 1923, after seeing *Le Brasier ardent* – a film made by the emigré Russian actor-director Ivan Mosjoukine which made use of formal effects derived from the *avant-garde* – resolved to make the cinema his career. He proved to be strikingly prolific and uneven in the silent period, during which the best of his half dozen or so films was a spectacularly beautiful adaptation of Zola's *Nana* (1926), a delicate fairy-tale *La Petite Marchande d'allumettes* (1928), and a farcical comedy *Tire-au-flanc* (1928).

Renoir's first encounter with sound was an adaptation of a one-act Feydeau comedy, *On purge bébé* (1931) not especially memorable even for Renoir's use of the sound of a flushing W.C. for comic effect. After this he adapted a fatalistic novel by Georges de la Fouchardière, *La chienne* (1931) whose subject – a middle-aged clerk forced by his sensual young wife into becoming an embezzler – was clearly attractive to distributors following the success of Sternberg's *Der Blaue Engel*. In contrast Renoir then directed *Boudu sauvé des eaux* (1932), an anarchic comedy about a humane bookseller who takes into his home a dreadful old tramp (Michel Simon again), with the disastrous results to be expected from the collision of bourgeois and anarchist values. Each new film seemed to reveal different aspects of Renoir's richly varied imagination. After an indifferent adaptation of *Madame Bovary* (1934) he made the extraordinary *Toni* (1934), a drama of passion set in the Marseilles region, whose use of unknown actors, location shooting and a supporting cast of real workpeople seen at their own jobs, both looked back to the Soviet silent cinema and foreshadowed the Italian neo-realist cinema of the forties and fifties. *Le crime de Monsieur Lange* (1935), scripted by Charles Spaak, belonged to the period of populist enthusiasm and the Front Populaire. To a story about the inhabitants of a little faubourg who form a cooperative to defeat the wiles of a capitalist crook, Renoir added some genial studies of Parisian life and character. *La Vie est à nous* (1936) was commissioned by the French Communist Party as an election manifesto. This film was of several episodes on which Renoir's assistants included Henri Cartier-Bresson, Jacques Becker and Jacques B. Brunius (a distinguished actor, writer, documentary director and member of the surrealist group), seen again in 1971 after over 30 years' hiding in the vaults, it proved a touching period piece, a mixture of frustrated anger and optimism that was to prove unfounded. Dated though the film now is, its alternation of actuality and dramatic sequences was boldly innovatory in its time. The same year Renoir made a brilliant adaptation of Gorki's *The Lower Depths*, as *Les Bas Fonds*, removing its setting from identifiable place and time.

Renoir was to make four more films before his war-time emigration to America, two of them masterpieces. *La Grande Illusion* (1937) is one of the richest films in the cinema. A group of French officers are imprisoned in a German fortress. We observe particularly the relationships of the camp commandant, a member of the traditional officer caste, one of the prisoners, from the same aristo-cratic class, and another, a clever engineer who has risen from the ranks. Played with extreme subtlety – particu-larly by Erich von Stroheim as the camp commandant – it becomes a profound philosophical study of a moment in mankind's history, the end of an era, the collapse of old structures and the uncertainty of the new ones. The same sense of social break-up informs *La Règle du jeu* (1939). A film of troubled history (several times cut by its distribu-tors and suppressed on the outbreak of war since its heroine, Nora Gregor, had a German accent, it was only restored to a form approximating to Renoir's original a quarter of a century after is first appearance.) Here Renoir sets an elaborate Musset-like comedy in an opulent château; the amorous antics of the servants and masters are observed in parallel, and followed to a tragic dénouement. Between these two films Renoir made *La Marseillaise* (1938) a recon-struction of some incidents of the French Revolution which

Jean Renoir:
La Règle du jeu.
France, 1939.
Jean Renoir,
Carette.

after more than thirty years has worn decidedly thin; and
La Bête humaine (1938), a modernisation of Zola, transferring Zolaesque naturalism, as well as the story, into
modern cinema terms.

One last pre-war work by Renoir has a strange history.
He had shot only the exteriors for a film of a Maupassant
story when he was obliged to abandon the project. The
material was subsequently assembled by Jacques Prévert
into the ravishingly atmospheric *Une Partie de campagne*
(1936), which reveals in Renoir – as *Déjeuner sur l'Herbe*
(1960) was to do much later – Auguste Renoir's feeling for
light and landscape. In 1939 Renoir was invited to conduct
a course at the Centro Sperimentale del Cinema in Rome,
and to direct *Tosca* at Cinecittà Studios. Before the project
could be accomplished however, the war broke out, and
Renoir left for America, early in 1941.

The critic Georges Sadoul characterises the prevailing tone of the French cinema after 1934 as 'poetic realism'; in which

> can be traced the influence of literary naturalism, of Zola, certain traditions of Zecca, Feuillade and Delluc, certain lessons also from René Clair and Jean Vigo. But, like it or not, poetic realism also owes something to a man of the theatre, at that time very much looked down on by cinema people, Marcel Pagnol.*

Pagnol's early adaptations of his own plays of Marseilles life (*Marius* directed by Korda; *Fanny* directed by Marc Allegret) were as eagerly received by the public as they were condemned by the critics, as not being 'true cinema'. Turning to direction himself, Pagnol (born 1895) progressed from these early essays in filmed theatre to work which could even satisfy the critics that it was truly 'cinematic'; and moreover distinguished by the authenticity of the films' setting (generally they were shot on location), characters and dialogue: *Merlusse* (1935) *César* (1936; the third of the Marseilles trilogy), *Regain* (1937) and above all *La femme du boulanger* (1938) which, with the great comic actor Raimu, did more than any other film to establish the French cinema in English-speaking countries.

Other adherents of the poetic realist school included Jacques Feyder, who returned from America in 1933 to direct a distinguished series of films: *Le grand jeu* (1934), *Pensions Mimosas* (1935) and *La Kermesse héroique* (1935) a return to the costume *genre*, sumptuously designed by Lazare Meerson, photographed by Harry Stradling, and with a dazzlingly witty central performance by the director's wife, Françoise Rosay.

Julien Duvivier (1896–1967), working in the cinema from 1915, had directed a score of successful commercial silent films. In the early sound period he proved himself a serviceable director, with a feeling for atmosphere and an ability to get the best out of his actors. In *La belle équipe* (1936), with its script by Charles Spaak, he contributed another to the little group of films that promoted the Front Populaire

*Georges Sadoul, *Histoire du Cinéma Mondial* (Paris, 1949, new edition 1963).

Marcel Pagnol: *La Femme du boulanger*. France, 1938. Raimu (in centre).

mood: a story of a group of working people who form their own cooperative. After this however Duvivier found his happiest métier in a series of films of powerfully romantic atmosphere and the fatalistic tone which seemed to dominate all the most popular French films on the eve of the Second World War. As Georges Sadoul writes:

> The influence of Feyder combines in these films with that of the kammerspiel, of Expressionism, of Murnau, of Sternberg . . . And French pessimism derives, to a large degree, from American models.

The prototype of the group is *Pépé le moko* (1937) in which Duvivier carried the conventions of the Hollywood gangster films into the Casbah of Algiers. Pépé, played by Jean Gabin, the archetypal hero of this series of films, is a gangster doomed by his destiny. Duvivier enjoyed an even greater commercial success with *Un Carnet de bal* (1937), a film of ambivalent nostalgia in which a woman seeks out all the men whose names appear on a *carnet de bal* of her youth, to discover what fate has brought them, what has become of their hopes and ambitions. *La Fin de jour* (1939) tells of the pitiful attempts of a group of forgotten and aged actors and actresses to make a comeback.

While Duvivier's usual scenarist was Charles Spaak, Marcel Carné (born 1909) generally worked with the gifted writer Jacques Prévert. After a melodrama *Jenny* (1936) and an eccentric fantastic comedy *Drôle de drame* (1937), the collaborators eagerly adopted the prevailing romantic-pessimist mood. Their *Quai des brumes* (1938), adapted from a novel by Pierre Mac Orlan was the story of a deserter whose *grand amour* lasts for only one day before he is shot. *Hotel du nord* (1938) recounts the adventures of two suicide lovers in a Paris hotel; *Le Jour se lève* (1939), the masterpiece of the school, has Gabin as a gangster besieged and eventually shot in his hideout by the police.

The old guard – Gance, L'Herbier, Raymond Bernard, Léon Poirier, Jacques de Baroncelli – were mostly concerned with commercial chores. Foreign directors came and went in this unsettled period – Pabst to make a fine *Don Quixote* (1933) with Chaliapin in the leading role; Anatole Litvak to direct *Mayerling* (1936); the Austrian Max Ophuls *Werther* (1938). Sacha Guitry (1885–1957) made a series of strange but fascinating homages to himself, in which he was inclined to play all, or most, of the leading roles. And meanwhile a new generation was forming: Pierre Chenal, Jean Benoît-Levy, Marc Allegret. Claude Autant-Lara; while the novelist André Malraux made a unique film, another portent of neo-realism, *L'Espoir* (1938), filmed in Civil War Spain.

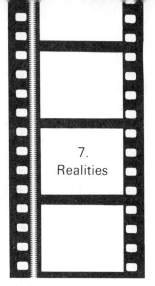

7.
Realities

'My final thought on this part of my life', wrote Sir Michael Balcon, recalling the later thirties,

> is one that has nagged at me for a long time. I realise that the preceding chapters of this personal story have been played against a shadowy background of world events – some world-shattering. Alongside them, the then important seeming struggle and internal conflicts for the control of Gaumont British . . . were relatively trivial. Those were, for example, the days of Mussolini's Abyssinian War, the Civil War in Spain, with all its implications for the future, and now that events can be seen in their historical perspective, one cannot escape the conclusion that in our own work we could have been more profitably engaged. Hardly a single film of the period reflects the agony of those times.*

Balcon's regret is touching and credible. The British studios were not alone however in their ostrich attitude to the real world of the thirties. The American studios, as we have seen, were dedicated to the manufacture of dreams to keep the nation content through stressful times. The French were seeking refuge in the bitter-sweet fatalism of Duvivier and Carné. Even in Germany and the U.S.S.R., with determinedly political cinemas, there was operetta.

Yet throughout the thirties there were stirrings outside the regular commercial cinema of new approaches to reality

*A Lifetime of Films, London, 1969.

and new recognition on the part of the film-maker of the affairs of his time. The most significant influence in this direction had been the Soviet silent cinema; and we have noted also the growing interest of the Second French Avant-Garde in documentary, towards the close of the twenties. It was in Britain however that the documentary film reached a peak which was to have world-wide influence; and it was due very largely to the singlehanded efforts of one man, John Grierson (1898–1972).

The American critic Richard Griffith wrote in 1949:

> The record of British film achievement is a documentary record. I risk repetition when I emphasise that this is because these films have something to do with life in Britain as it is lived, and that British fiction films by and large seldom have anything to do with significant life anywhere.*

If there is a certain cruel justice in the second part of this judgment, the first is also true. From the very beginning, British film-makers had seemed to excel in recording actuality: the pioneers with their fascinated observations of high seas at Brighton or traffic in the streets of Liverpool or Leeds or Manchester or anywhere else; Herbert Ponting's stirring film record of Captain Scott's expeditions to the South Pole (1912); above all the records of the First World War made by J. B. MacDowall and Geoffrey Malins for the British Topical Committee and the War Office. Completely innocent of any artistic intentions or pretensions, these last films have a quality that serves to make them the British cinema's first true masterworks. Long before Vertov, in these films truth and feeling and the monstrous nature of the events they described took hold and gave them qualities far beyond those of simple reportage.

These films had no direct successors (the battle reconstructions made in the late twenties were indeed pathetic in contrast to them); and the strongest influence on Grierson, who had been trained as a public relations man in the States, were Soviet films like *Turksib* (1929) and

*In: Paul Rotha, *The Film Till Now* (London, new edition, 1967).

The Old and the New (1929). His definitions of the nature and ends of documentary still stand. Broadly and conveniently he described 'documentary' (the term was derived from the French *documentaire*) as 'the creative treatment of reality'; more precisely he said

> The documentary idea, after all, demands no more than that the affairs of our time shall be brought to the screen in any fashion which strikes the imagination and makes observation a little richer than it was. At one level the vision may be journalistic; at another it may rise to poetry and drama. At another level again its artistic quality may lie in the mere lucidity of its exposition.*

Grierson's own first film was a piece of public relations for the Empire Marketing Board, promoting the principle of 'The Projection of Britain', which had been propounded by the Board's chief, Sir Stephen Tallents. It is hard, seeing *Drifters* (1929) today, with its undue length, formlessness and repetitions, to appreciate the extent of its initial impact, the exciting novelty in describing the daily routine of ordinary British working people, and seeking out the drama and dignity inherent in it. The film led the Empire Marketing Board to form a regular film unit under Grierson; and when that came to an end in 1932, Grierson went

Grierson on Documentary (London, 1946).

John Grierson:
Drifters. Britain,
1929.

on to establish the G.P.O. Film Unit. At the G.P.O. Grierson put a very wide interpretation on the Unit's concern with 'communications', and by the end of the thirties it had become a central government film agency.

Grierson developed a singularly able group of young film-makers, most of whom could be identified (privately, if not in their official professional capacity) with the progressive intellectual Left. They were clear where they stood over Spain and Hitler and the U.S.S.R.; over housing and hunger and education.

> They came to regard their immediate task as not merely to describe and dramatise industry and labour and the everyday world, but to present a cross-section of modern society in this country, exploring its weaknesses, reporting progress, dramatising issues,

wrote Grierson; and, in a phrase worthy of Vertov himself:

> a mirror held up to nature is not so important in a dynamic and fast-changing society as the hammer which shapes it.

The documentarists informed and campaigned. Comparatively few of the three hundred or more films that they made between 1929 and 1939 have now great artistic interest; but as a whole they are a remarkable record of the social concerns of Britain in those years.

Moreover the Grierson school did number among its members some of the most distinguished film talent of the period. Basil Wright's (born 1907) lyrical gifts were seen at their highest in the very sophisticated *Song of Ceylon* (1934). The film adopts a 'symphonic' form, arranging its material in four 'movements' of quite distinct character and tone. With considerable daring, instead of a conventional commentary Wright used the words of a seventeenth century traveller in Ceylon. This kind of experimentalism became characteristic of the G.P.O. Film Unit, which was Britain's true *avante-garde. Night Mail* (1936) directed by Wright with Harry Watt (born 1906), employed a verse commentary by W. H. Auden, while *Coal Face* (1936), supervised by Alberto Cavalcanti, was

Basil Wright:
Song of Ceylon.
Britain, 1934.

presented as a new experiment in sound. A very simple visual band was taken and an attempt made to build up, by use of natural sound, music and chorus, a film oratorio . . .*

Such experiments, and the G.P.O. Film Unit's flirtations with other fields of art, were sometimes naive or self-conscious; but they were of inestimable value for the morale of the cinema in a country where film had generally been held in low regard by the intellectuals.

Among other British documentarists, Paul Rotha's (born 1907) forceful critical writings, constantly pleading for a cinema of social purpose more linked to real life, have tended to distract attention from his achievements as a director, in developing a style of powerful visual journalism. Such a film as *The Face of Britain* (1935) did not forbear to draw attention to the economic and social inequalities at the heart of our democracy. Harry Watt's interesting experiments in story-documentary and the use of non-

*London Film Society, programme note, 1936.

professional actors in pre-organised fictional narratives, were to prove their value in the wartime period. Arthur Elton (born 1906) was fascinated by the wonder and beauty and poetry of technology (*Aero Engine*, 1934; *Transfer of Power*, 1935); though he was also associated with one of the most human films produced by the Grierson school. *Housing Problems* (1935), which he co-directed with Edgar Anstey (born 1907), is still the most vital documentary of the period. Overcoming enormous technical difficulties the film-makers shot interviews with slum dwellers, using synchronous sound, and techniques that pre-date by twenty-five years modern methods of television reportage. Anstey's most significant work after this time was as a producer, notably on the British section of the *March of Time* series. Under Grierson's aegis Len Lye (born 1901) and Norman MacLaren (born 1914) pursued individual paths in animation and graphics.

Grierson also brought distinguished artists from abroad. Robert Flaherty (1894–1957) directed *Industrial Britain* (1932) for the G.P.O. before making his British feature films, *Man of Aran* (1934) for Balcon and the seriously compromised *Elephant Boy* (1937), co-directed with Zoltan Korda for Alexander Korda. The Brazilian Alberto Cavalcanti (born 1897) brought to the G.P.O. Film Unit the benefit of his years of association with the *avant-garde* in France.

Not the least important aspect of Grierson's work was that he devised entirely new economic and producing organisations for his new kind of film-making. 'I do not think there is much use discussing what to do with a medium unless we are talking about it in terms of access to the means of production', he wrote. The system of sponsorship was something quite new in the economics of film-making in the West. In Britain, government film production was a significant recognition of the importance of the medium. After persuading the British Government to sponsor an organised programme of public relations film-making, Grierson began to sell the idea to private sponsors like the British Commercial Gas Company (who made *Housing Problems*), Imperial Airways and so on. In 1933 Shell was the first commercial organisation to set up its own self-contained film unit. Independent companies like

Edgar Anstey
and Arthur
Elton: *Housing
Problems*.
Britain, 1935.

Robert Flaherty:
Man of Aran.
Britain, 1934.

Strand (1935) and Realist (1937) began to grow up; and with them organisational and promotion bodies like the Association of Realist Film Producers and Film Centre.

From the artistic point of view what was most important in this organisation of the documentary movement was the tendency of documentary film-makers to form themselves into regular units. This meant not only that artists were working together in teams and in steady employment (never a common feature of British film making) but that there was a possibility of regular training for recruits such as had never existed before in the British cinema. This organisational aspect of the British documentary movement was to be of especial importance when documentary came to be geared to the needs of war.

Towards the end of the thirties, and parallel with – perhaps to some degree consequent upon – the most rapid period of growth of the documentary movement, it is possible to discern a slight but distinct trend towards conscious realism in the choice and treatment of feature subjects. Pen Tennyson made *There Ain't No Justice* (1939), about boxing rackets, and *Proud Valley* (1939), about the reaction of Welsh miners to a coloured worker. The young Carol Reed (born 1906) also dealt with a mining subject (*The Stars Look Down*, 1938) and with Londoners at the seaside (*Bank Holiday*, 1938). Other directors travelled to what had been for the metropolitan-bound cinema remote parts of the country – Norman Walker to Yorkshire for *The Turn of the Tide* (1935), Michael Powell (born 1905) to the Shetland Isles for *Edge of the World* (1937), Victor Saville to Yorkshire also for *South Riding* (1938). One of the most interesting of all the films of this period was by Arthur Woods (1904–42), a very promising young director who was killed in the war: *They Drive By Night* (1939), a thriller set against the true-to-life background of the work of long-distance lorry drivers. More often than not the 'realist' settings of these films were compromised by conventional story elements; but they mark the beginning of a feature film tradition which was to acquire great importance with the war.

When the war began the future looked singularly in-auspicious for the British cinema, with studios requisi-tioned, cinemas closed, artists and technicians drafted into the services, and a films division of the Ministry of Inform-ation without any clear aims. By mid-1940 however the G.P.O. Film Unit became the Crown Film Unit, with a studio at Pinewood; and a Colonial Film Unit was also formed. Rapidly a first-class machine for information and propaganda was developed, producing everything from spectacular feature films to little two-minute trailers urging people to save fuel or to use their handkerchiefs when they sneezed – a genre of film-making which dis-covered one of the British Cinema's true originals, the writer-director-clown, Richard Massingham (1898–1953).

The earliest successes of the wartime documentaries were *The First Days* in which Cavalcanti and Humphrey Jennings endeavoured to capture the feeling of London at the close of 1939; and Cavalcanti and Watt's *Squadron 992*, an account of the work of the barrage balloons, which was already considered outdated on its appearance in 1940. Watt went on to direct feature-length documentaries, the first really important one being *Target for Tonight* (1941), the record of a bombing raid on Germany, which was a singularly effective stimulus to morale at home and rela-tions abroad. Less successful with the public, his *Nine Men* (1943), telling of a group of soldiers stranded in the Libyan desert, nevertheless gave a documentary conviction to a fictional subject.* J. B. Holmes' *Merchant Seamen* (1941) and *Coastal Command* (1942) are recalled as quiet, understated records of the activities of individual fighting services. Pat Jackson's *Western Approaches* (1944), filmed in colour, was perhaps the most ambitious film ever produced by the Crown Film Unit.

The most remarkable figure of this period was, however, Humphrey Jennings (1907–50). He is, indeed, an artist unique in the British cinema. Lindsay Anderson has called him 'the only real poet the British cinema has yet pro-duced'; and he brought an entirely new impulse and totally

*The theme and treatment were close to Ford's *The Lost Patrol* (1934) and Mikhail Romm's *The Thirteen* (1937).

personal vision to the documentary. Jennings was able to bring to film making a wide-ranging culture, an exceptional intellect, an abnormal perception. He was a sound literary critic, a poet and a historian. He was also a painter, in the thirties associated with the British surrealist group. He was recruited to the G.P.O. Film Unit in 1935; but it was not until the war that his gifts were able to flower. The poet Kathleen Raine wrote of Jennings:

> In the tradition of Chaucer and Blake, Humphrey Jennings had a sense of the organic whole of the English culture . . . What counted for Humphrey was the expression, by certain people, of the ever-growing spirit of man; and, in particular, of the spirit of England. He sought, therefore, for a public imagery, a public poetry. He addressed himself, in much the same spirit as Blake, to 'the British public', not expecting the mass to understand him, but because he was seeking to discover and activate the collective symbols of England.*

In his best films – *Words for Battle* (1941), *Listen to Britain* (1941), *A Diary for Timothy* (1945) and in a different way in

Humphrey Jennings: A Tribute (London, 1950).

Humphrey Jennings: *Fires Were Started*. Britain, 1943.

Fires Were Started (1943) which was a dramatic reconstruction of the work of the Auxiliary Fire Service – he composed films exactly like a poet. Images and sounds are juxtaposed in such a way that the whole is infinitely richer in its significance than the sum of the individual parts that compose it; so that there is something like a chemical reaction about the meeting of the elements.

Meanwhile as documentary film-makers became more ambitious in the production of feature-length films, wartime feature producers seemed to draw much nearer to the documentary style. Some of the biggest successes, commercially as well as critically, of the war years, were in a directly realist idiom. In the earliest films, like Asquith's *Freedom Radio* (1940) about an anti-Nazi underground in Germany, and Pen Tennyson's *Convoy* (1940), the war itself had not become a reality; while the extreme violence which characterised Michael Powell's *49th Parallel* (1940) weakens its impact in the cooler consideration of thirty years after. Other films of the war, however, dramatising the work of the fighting services or of civilians at war, still seem truthfully to record a way of life and a period: Charles Frend's *The Foreman Went to France* (1942), Michael Powell's *One of Our Aircraft is Missing* (1941), Thorold Dickinson's *Next of Kin* (1942), Asquith's *We Dive at Dawn* (1943), Leslie Howard's *The First of the Few* (1942), Noel Coward and David Lean's *In Which We Serve* (1942).

As the war went on, realist feature films seemed to maintain their popularity with audiences as well as filmmakers, though a distinct change of emphasis is discernible in the pictures made towards the end of the war. By 1944–45 the concentration is much less on action, adventure and heroism as a generalised concept than on the psychological effects of war experience upon individuals. Seeing these films again (so far as is now possible) they have survived the intervening years better than the earlier and more extraverted pictures. Launder and Gilliatt's *Millions Like Us* (1943) was about workers in a munitions factory. Carol Reed's humane, humorous and sensitive *The Way Ahead* (1944) showed seven civilian individualists turned into a fighting unit. Asquith's *The Way to the Stars* (1945), despite a quality of sentimental romanticism in Terence Rattigan's script, treated tellingly the themes of comradeship and of the waste of war.

The war years confirmed a number of significant new talents in the British film industry, among them Thorold Dickinson (born 1903), noted before the war for a documentary about the Spanish Civil War, who attracted attention with a stylish adaptation of *Gaslight* (1940); David Lean (born 1908), who had worked as an editor on Asquith's films; the Boulting twins (born 1913) (*Pastor Hall*, 1939 and *Thunder Rock*, 1942) and the actor, Laurence Olivier (born 1907) who embarked on direction late in the war with *Henry V* (1945). Predictably, the outstanding productions of the war years which did not adhere to the realist movement tended to stress a certain nostalgia, an affection for old traditions of British life and values: Dickinson's *Gaslight*; Reed's *Kipps* (1941), John Baxter's *Love on the Dole* (1941), Michael Powell and Emeric Pressburgers' spectacular pageant of British history in the twentieth century, *The Life and Death of Colonel Blimp* (1942), Asquith's *Fanny by Gaslight* (1944), David Lean's *This Happy Breed* (1943; adapted from Noel Coward) and Olivier's *Henry V*.

From the very beginning of the Third Reich the most important instrument of Goebbel's Reich Ministry of Public Enlightenment and Propaganda had been the Reich Film Chamber, which exercised almost total control over independent as well as state film-making by centralising film finance, vetting all scripts before production, and enforcing upon all film workers membership of affiliated party organisations. By the start of the war, the German cinema had been brought virtually under a nationalised monopoly, incorporating not only the old German companies but also those of annexed Austria and occupied Czechoslovakia. As the war progressed and Germany occupied more territories, generally banning or at least severely restricting authentic national production, the market for German films became bigger and bigger, with audiences rising, it was reckoned, from 250 million per year in 1933 to 1,000 million per year in 1942.

Before the war escapist pictures – operettas and detective melodramas – alternated with more obviously propagandist films: on the one hand nationalist historical pageants like *Operation Michael* and the revived *Fridericus* series; on the other films which glorified the rise and early history of the Nazi movement: *Blütendes Deutschland*, *Hans Westman* (based on the Horst Wessel myth), *S. A. Mann Brandt*, *Hitler Jugend Quex*. The most brilliant of these pre-war propaganda films however were those made by Leni Riefenstahl (born 1902) who, having started her career as an actress, notably in 'mountain films', now proved herself a film-maker of outstanding gifts particularly in the field of montage. *Der Triumph des Willens* (1936) the record of the Nürnberg party rally of 1934 and *Olympia* (1938) a massive documentary on the Olympic Games of 1936, were extraordinary pageants, metamorphosing the Nazi leaders into a glorious pantheon.

Leni Riefenstahl: *Olympia*. Germany, 1936–8.

With the outbreak of the war, the propaganda machine moved into still more vigorous action. The distinction between the films aimed at pure escapism and generally maintaining the morale of a people at war, and those instilling Nazi principles, became still stronger. For home consumption there were inevitably documentaries glorifying the work of the fighting forces (*Crew Dora*, *Fighter Squadron Lutzow*), attacking the Soviet Union and the other allies; justifying the oppression of Jews (*The Eternal Jew*). The newsreel acquired a paramount importance.

Fiction films included 'historical' biographies which flattered the Nazi Aryan image, preferably at the expense of the Allies or the Jews: Rembrandt, Menzel, Bach and Schiller (improbably) were all so honoured. *The Rothschilds* offered a field-day for attacking the Jews; and *The Heart of a Queen* and *Ohm Kruger* provided scope for anti-British propaganda. The most celebrated (or notorious) of the anti-semitic films however was *Jude Süss* (1940), directed by Veit Harlan (1899–1964), one of the most successful of Nazi directors. Nationalist subjects included yet another *Fridericus* trilogy and an aggressive biography of *Bismarck*. Other films treated social 'problems': justifying euthanasia (*I Accuse*) or unmarried child-bearing to provide new citizens for the Reich.

Films intended for use abroad were of two main kinds. Some aimed simply to terrorise nations into submission by depicting the horrors inflicted by German campaigns against reluctant satellites (*Feuertaufe*, *Sieg im Westen*). Another group, which must have carried much less conviction, were intended to improve the world image of Nazism. Especially notorious was a notably repellent piece of hypocrisy, *The Führer Presents a Town to the Jews* (1943–4), made under duress by Kurt Gerron, a well-known UFA actor in pre-war days.

In the Soviet Union the arrival of sound films had coincided with the start of a radically changed attitude to the arts. The experimental and revolutionary fervour of the twenties, the heroic age of socialist art, was no longer in fashion, 'no longer required by the People' in the phrase of those times. The new cry was 'Socialist Realism'. Abstraction, formalism and intellectualism were condemned; art must be immediately available to The People, must indeed conform to a lowest common denominator of comprehension. Symbolically, it seemed, Mayakowsky, having delivered a ferocious, hopeless blow at the new attitudes in his play *The Bathhouse*, committed suicide in 1930. Symbolic too was the fact that Eisenstein was unable to realise any film project between 1928 and 1938. His *Bezhin Meadow* was begun, reshot to suit changed ideologies, and finally abandoned for ever. The known antipathy of the Head of Soviet Cinematography, Boris Shumyatsky, only partially explained Eisenstein's situation.

The Soviet cinema which so short a time before had been the most vital, contemporary and militant in the world, had retreated into forms of escapism as complete if not always as apparent as those of Hollywood. Eisenstein's former collaborator, Grigori Alexandrov, pioneered a gay, hollow genre of musical comedy (*Jazz Comedy*, 1934; *Circus*, 1936; *Volga-Volga*, 1938), in which his followers included Ivan Pyriev. There was a vogue for historical spectacles, which culminated happily in Eisenstein's *Alexander Nevsky* (1938) and *Ivan the Terrible* (1944–6). Safe topics and safe heroes of recent revolutionary history were brought to the screen after the success of the Vassiliev Brothers' *Chapaev* (1934), though few of them attained the humanity of this prototype or of Zarkhi and Heifets' *Baltic Deputy* (1936). Lenin himself began to be represented, deified, in feature films, the best of them being made by Mikhail Romm (*Lenin in October*, 1937; *Lenin in 1918*, 1939) and the former FEKS director Sergei Yutkevitch (*The Man With the Gun*, 1938; *Yakov Sverdlov*, 1940).* These films of recent history also began to introduce a glorified figure of Stalin, generally clad in seraphic white and played by Mikhail Gelovani, a fellow Georgian.

Occasionally, when politically desirable, film-makers might treat contemporary subjects. A group of films (to

*Yutkevitch was to return to the figure of Lenin, with even more distinction more than twenty years later, in *Stories of Lenin* (1957) and *Lenin in Poland* (1966), using the same Lenin – Maxim Straukh, a former collaborator of Eisenstein – as in the pre-war films.

Sergei M. Eisenstein
during the shooting of *Bezhin Meadow*. U.S.S.R., 1935–7.

which Eisenstein's *Bezhin Meadow* was intended to belong) justified official agricultural policy and the liquidation of the Kulaks (Ermler's *Peasants*, 1932). Ermler's *The Great Citizen* (1939) presented the official version of the assassination of Kirov, which had led to the notorious political trials of 1934.

Yet there were a few bright spots in these pre-war years. Kozintsev and Trauberg, the other survivors of FEKS, made a trilogy about a fictional revolutionary hero Maxim (*The Youth of Maxim*, 1934; *The Return of Maxim*, 1937; *The Vyborg Side*, 1939). Like Yuli Raisman's *The Last Night* (1937) these films succeeded in giving new life and humanity to traditional revolutionary themes. Dziga Vertov, who otherwise became less and less prominent in the atmosphere of the thirties, created his finest film, the monumental *Three Songs of Lenin*, in 1934. In the darkest days of the immediate pre-war period, Mark Donskoi made a trilogy of films, based on the memoirs and early life of Maxim Gorki, which still today retain their vast humanity and optimism, and remain the best-loved of all Soviet films. And finally in 1938, Eisenstein at last returned to film work, with *Alexander Nevsky*, co-directed with Dmitri Vassiliev. His first association with the composer Prokoviev and the remarkable use of music and symphonic structure in this (in other respects uncharacteristic) Eisenstein film, make the years of enforced silence only more tragic.

In 1939 the U.S.S.R. was reluctantly forced into a non-aggression pact with her traditional enemy, Nazi Germany, with the result that a group of anti-Nazi films which had been made in 1938–9 (and among which was included *Alexander Nevsky*, so delicate was the political situation) were rapidly suppressed, to be succeeded by a spate of pro-German films, to which Dovzhenko contributed a documentary, titled with unintentional irony, *Liberation* (1940). The war gave a tremendous impetus to documentary, which until this time had signally failed to follow the lead given by Vertov and Shub. War films included grandiose efforts like *A Day in the New World* (1940), shot simultaneously in different parts of the Soviet Union by dozens of cameramen. News films suddenly became of vital importance, and newsreel production occupied the Mosfilm studios after all feature film activities had been evacuated. Among the many documentary and reportage films of this time, one above all is memorable. Though credited to his wife Yulia Solntseva, with Dovzhenko only as supervisor, *Battle for the Ukraine* (1943) proved to be the last of the director's great personal film poems.* The material was shot by twenty-four cameramen at different parts of the front, though Dovzhenko is said to have given each of them detailed advance instructions, and even drawings of what he wanted. In the finished film the images sweep forward with the inevitability of a musical structure; and the harrowing images of actuality recall in their forms and juxtapositions the great dramatic films, *Arsenal* (1928) and *Earth* (1930).

The feature film studios too were mobilised, and put under the artistic control of feature film-makers including Eisenstein, who was put in charge of Mosfilm, and Dovzhenko, at the Kiev studios. Following the German invasion in the summer of 1941, the studios were evacuated to the Eastern republics. All the leading film-makers contributed to monthly *Fighting Film Albums* which consisted of short, quickly made sketch films aimed at propaganda or morale.

Feature films proper did not in the main reflect the war directly, though there were pictures about the Finnish war (Eisiment's *The Girl from Leningrad*, 1941), about the role and sacrifice of women and children in the war (Donskoi's *The Rainbow*, 1941; Romm's *Girl No 217*, 1944), about the Resistance (Ermler's *She Defends Her Country*, 1943; Pudovkin's *In the Name of the Fatherland*, 1942–3), about the home front (Kozintsev and Trauberg's *Plain People*, 1945). But the output of musicals (Pyriev even made a war musical, *At 6 p.m. After the War*, 1944) and historical films (Pudovkin's *Admiral Nakhimov*, 1944–6 and *Suvorov*, 1950, among them) continued as before.

The most distinguished of the historical films was Eisenstein's *Ivan the Terrible* (1944–6), a magnificent panorama of sixteenth-century Russia, of incomparable plastic qualities and with a superb score by Prokoviev. This was

*Dovzhenko had lost official favour, apparently after his biographical film about the revolutionary hero *Schors* (1939).

to be Eisenstein's final conflict with authority. The first part of the intended trilogy was released; but the second was criticised and suppressed as being historically, psychologically and artistically in error. Eisenstein collapsed with a heart attack on the day he finished editing this second part. The controversy continued throughout his illness, obliging him to publish an abject disclaimer and 'confession'. He never recovered sufficiently to resume work on the required revisions before his death two years later, in 1948.

In 1944 the studios were brought back from evacuation, and a new artistic council was set up to regulate the affairs of the industry. An interesting experiment in giving documentary assignments, related to the Allied victory, to feature directors like Raisman (*Berlin*, 1945), Yutkevitch (*Liberated France*, 1944) and Zarkhi and Heifets (*The Defeat of Japan*, 1946) prompted an enthusiastic declaration from Eisenstein: 'Documentary was once the leading branch of our cinema and feature films were influenced by it. Twenty years later we see the process reversed. Feature film makers have renewed links with documentary . . . The collaboration will be fruitful for both.' In fact however the Soviet cinema was about to enter the most unproductive era of its history, coinciding with the most negative period of communism.

Alone among the territories occupied during the war, France maintained a strongly individual production. The declaration of war had brought cinema activities to a standstill as studios were requisitioned and personnel drafted; but with the Occupation production was rapidly resumed. At first Goebbels, having succeeded in appropriating as German property at least 30 per cent of French film concerns, attempted to impose German production on French cinemas, but the spontaneous boycott of the low quality German productions, leading to a very appreciable slump in box office takings, forced the occupying power to encourage native production. Inevitably, with every film having to pass both the Vichy and the German censorship at both script and completion stages, producers tended to steer clear of dangerously contemporary themes; and out of the poetic realism of the immediate pre-war period there developed a new vein of poetic romanticism. Directors sought escape into any place and period but Paris 1941; and the results included some of the most glittering fantasies in the history of the cinema. Marcel L'Herbier's *La Nuit fantastique* (1942) was a tribute both to Méliès and to the old Impressionist School of the twenties. Marcel Carné, departing completely from the style of his fatalist dramas, made *Les Visiteurs du soir* (1942), a superbly decorated fantasy which tells how the devil comes to earth in a fairytale castle of the sixteenth century. The story of true love which cannot in the end be defeated by the powers of darkness was fairly clearly intended by Carné and his writer Jacques Prévert as a symbol of occupied France. An even more sumptuous essay in style, *Les Enfants du paradis* (1945) was a pageant of good and evil, love and jealousy in the theatre of the great mime of the 1840s, Debureau (memorably played by Jean-Louis Barrault).

Jean Cocteau returned to the cinema, ten years after the isolated experiment of *Le Sang d'un poète* (1930). He wrote the dialogues for L'Herbier's *La Comédie du bonheur* (1939) and Serge de Poligny's *Le Baron fantôme* (1942); but his creative presence was more evident in, indeed dominated, every image of *L'Eternel Retour* (1943), directed by Jean Delannoy (born 1908), an adaptation of the Tristan and Iseult legend which was naïvely taken in Britain after the war as an example of French collaboration. (The legend in fact has a Breton, not a German, origin).

Another Cocteau script of the wartime period resulted in Robert Bresson's *Les Dames du Bois de Boulogne* (1945), a modernisation of an episode from Diderot's *Jacques le fataliste*. This brilliant stylistic exercise and the preceding *Les Anges du péché* (1944) confirmed Bresson's austere, uncompromisingly perfectionist talent. Other new directors also emerged during the war. Jacques Becker (1906–60), formerly Jean Renoir's assistant, after a fairly conventional detective subject, *Le Dernier Atout* (1942) made *Goupi mains-rouges* (1943), a bizarre mystery story set in and around a French country inn whose geography and characters were brilliantly sketched, and *Falbalas* (1945) in which with similar certainty he evoked the atmospheres of the backstage of the fashion world.

Marcel Carné: *Les Enfants du paradis*. France, 1942–5.

Jean Gremillon (1910–59), most of whose work had been confined to short films, made two of his finest features during the war period. *Lumière d'été* (1943) was from a Prévert script, a morality play involving a conflict of the decadent aristocracy and the virile working world. The occupants of the aristocrats' castle seem to prefigure the world of Fellini. For his next film *Le Ciel est à vous* (1944) he turned to the other leading scenarist of the war and pre-war era, Charles Spaak. Henri-Georges Clouzot (born 1907) achieved celebrity with his second feature film, *Le Corbeau* (1943), a brilliant study of demonic malice in a small provincial town. Its use as anti-French propaganda by the German authorities however led to unfortunate repercussions after the war both for the director and his scenarist Louis Chavance. One of the few entirely realist films of distinction at this period (though based on a safely pre-war book) was Louis Daquin's (born 1908) debutant work, *Nous les gosses* (1940), a touching film of suburban childhood.

In the inauspicious climate of the last years of Mussolini's régime, and through a rediscovery of realism, the Italian cinema experienced a startling renaissance. Despite strenuous efforts by the Fascists – the building of the great Cinecittà studios; the boosting of production from seven to eighty-four films between 1930 and 1939; and the creation of a notable film school, the Centro Sperimentale in Rome – the Italian cinema had never recovered the artistic distinction it had held briefly in the years immediately before the First World War. One or two film-makers of evident ability emerged during the decade: Alessandro Blasetti (born 1900) who specialised in historical reconstructions, of which outstandingly the best was *1860* (1934) and Mario Camerini (born 1895) with comedies of middle-class life such as *Il capello a tre punte* (1934); but their successes were limited and isolated. Much more characteristic of the period were the grandiose costume and operatic spectacles of Carmine Gallone (born 1886) whose career spanned the period from 1914–60; and vapid social dramas and comedies which earned the categorisation of 'telefono bianco', from the style of their décors, and which frequently starred a handsome young juvenile actor called Vittorio de Sica.

Soon after 1940 however a revolution was in the making in the film schools, the cine clubs, among progressive critics, historians and short film makers. By 1942 the revue *Cinema* was vociferously pleading for a cinema that should be realist, popular, national. The most ardent theoreticians of the movement were Giuseppe di Santis and Umberto Barbaro, who christened the movement 'neo-realist'. Conveniently the neo-realist movement in Italian cinema may be dated from 1945 and Roberto Rossellini's *Roma, città aperta*; but firm and varied roots can be traced back to the realist experiments of *Sperduti del buio* (1914) or de Robertis' *Uomini sul fondo* (1941) which used non-professional actors and was shot on the actual locations of its story – a submarine rescue drama; or in Blasetti's gentle realist

comedy *Quattri passi fra le nuvole* (1942) whose scenarist, Cesare Zavattini was to be one of the key theorists and practitioners of neo-realism. More generally accepted as the true prototype is Luchino Visconti's *Ossessione* (1942), on which the scenarist was de Santis himself. Although the film was adapted from an American thriller, James Cain's *The Postman Always Rings Twice*, and although its plot tended to melodrama, the setting (a roadside cafe in a remote country district of Ferrara), the characters and the treatment were far removed from the current airless styles of studio film-making.

Cesare Zavattini (born 1902), the Marxist writer whose first scenario had been for Mario Camerini's *Daro un milione* (1935), conceived an ideal of neo-realism as a cinema that would be all truth, abolishing the artificially plotted story, the falsehood of the actor, and transferring the whole

Luchino Visconti: *Ossessione*. Italy, 1942.

reality of life directly to the screen. Its subjects must be entirely contemporary and must give people a consciousness of their own dignity as human beings. Ideally real people would play their own real-life roles in their own real-life settings. Of the emergence of neo-realism he wrote 'The reality buried under the myths slowly reflowered. The cinema began its creation of the world. Here was a tree; here an old man; here a house; here a man eating, a man sleeping, a man crying' The critic Penelope Houston has written:

> The cinema had been liberated from its studios; the film-makers were out in the streets and the fields, bringing together professional and non-professional actors, putting their country's experience on record. Affectionately (as in Luigi Zampa's *Vivere in Pace*, an undistinguished film which enjoyed a great vogue), luridly (as in Giuseppe de Santis's *Caccia Tragica*), energetically, (as in Renato Castellani's *Sotto il Sole di Roma*) they built a national cinema out of their own recent history.*

Inevitably Zavattini's total ideal of the neo-realist cinema had to be compromised, not least in many of the films which he wrote himself and which always betrayed an inescapable fondness for sentimental and dramatic conventions. Nevertheless this conscious return to reality was to have a deep and far-reaching effect upon the post-war cinema. Zavattini formed a fruitful collaboration with the former *jeune premier* Vittorio de Sica (born 1907), beginning with *I bambini ci guardano* (1943) which used professional star actors, but dealt with problems of family life with an honesty and frankness which provoked strong disapproval from the fascist regime. In succeeding films they were able to move closer to Zavattini's stated ideals, improvising action on location, in the actual streets of Rome: *La porta del cielo* (1946), and *Sciuscia* (1946), a cruel account of the persecuted lives of child shoeblacks struggling for survival in the streets of post-war Rome. Their finest work together was *Ladri di biciclette* (1948) which

*Quoted in Penelope Houston, *The Contemporary Cinema* (London, 1963).

came nearest to Zavattini's ideal of creating films out of the natural drama of real life. The crux of the story is the disaster that the simple theft of a bicycle can bring to a man whose hard-won job and livelihood depend upon it. *Miracolo a Milano* (1951) introduced an element of Clairesque fantasy into the neo-realist setting; but *Umberto D* (1952) was the last major film in the pure classic form of neo-realism – an intimate observation of the minor tragedies which loneliness inflicts upon an aged pensioner – acted, like *Ladri di biciclette*, entirely by non-professionals.

The first film of the neo-realist school to make an international impact was *Roma, città aperta* (1945), directed by Roberto Rossellini (born 1906) who had previously directed a variety of documentaries and features, including works of fascist propaganda. Shot on the streets of Rome, with minimal resources, the film reconstructed incidents of the

Vittorio de Sica: *Ladri di biciclette*. Italy, 1948. Enzo Stailoa, Lamberto Maggiorani.

resistance with a harsh vividness which made audiences
feel that they were seeing actuality. In *Paisà* (1946)
Rossellini abandoned the use of actors (Anna Magnani and
Aldo Fabrizi had led the cast of *Roma, città aperta*) for his
six episodes of life in Italy at the close of the war. In *Germania, anno zero* (1947), with less success, Rossellini
attempted to transplant the neo-realist experiment to
defeated Germany. In *Francesco, guillare di Dio* (1950) he
applied neo-realist techniques to a period subject.

After *Ossessione* Luchino Visconti (born 1906) did not
make another solo feature film until 1948 and *La terra
trema*. Intending a trilogy, he was able to make only the
first part, *L'episodio del mare*. This film, comparatively
little shown both because of its uncompromisingly anti-
commercial values and the difficulties for Italian audiences
of the Sicilian dialect in which the original version was
shot, is one of the great peaks of the neo-realist era. Its
subject is a family of fisher folk fighting – hopelessly, for

Visconti spurns easy solutions – against an oppressive system and impeded by fate. The people, the setting and the tragedy are totally intertwined and totally self-contained. The audience is entitled to watch, as it might watch real events, but not to enjoy the easy satisfaction or catharsis that comes from pathos or identification.

Visconti's next film was a complete contrast, but still, with its observation of the small tragi-comedies of common life, true to the Zavattini principles: *Bellissima* (1951) is the story of an ordinary woman whose ambition to see her child win a Cinecittà talent contest drives her to the point where she is prepared to sacrifice everything – herself, her marriage, and, worse, the child.

Twelve years after *La terra trema* in *Rocco e i suoi fratelli* (1960) Visconti returned to neo-realist themes (between he had made *Senso*, 1953, and *Le notte bianche*, 1957, both richly decorative romantic costume pieces), but by now he applied to the story of Southern peasants migrating to the industrial north of Italy a grand operatic treatment.

Older directors had affected the neo-realist manner at the end of the war: Blasetti in *Un giorno nella vita* (1946), Camerini in *Due lettere anonime* (1945), Aldo Vergano (1894–1957) in the excellent *Il sole sorge anche* (1947). New talents emerged also. Apart from *Caccia tragica* (1948), the former critic De Santis (born 1917) made *Riso amaro* (1949), whose images of Silvano Mangano waist-deep in the waters of the rice-fields won international celebrity whilst initiating the decline of neo-realism into the old star and glamour values, and *Roma ore 11* (1951). Carlo Lizzani (born 1922) made *Achtung Banditi!* (1951) and *Cronaca di poveri amanti* (1954), Luigi Zampa (born 1905) *Vivere in pace* (1946), *Anni difficile* (1948), Alberto Lattuada (born 1914), *Senza pietà* (1948). The next generation too was preparing. Federico Fellini (born 1920) was a writer on *Roma, città aperta* and a number of Rossellini's films as well as Alberto Lattuada's *Il delitto di Giovanni Episcopo* (1947), *Senza pietà* and *Il mulino del Po* (1949), and Pietro Germi's *In nome delle legge* (1948) and *Il cammino della speranza* (1950) – all films in the mainstream of neo-realism. A former critic, Michaelangelo Antonioni (born 1912) was a writer on *Caccia tragica*, and directed many documentaries between 1943 and 1950.

Perhaps neo-realism in the pure ideal concept of Zavattini never existed: *Roma, città aperta* employed virtuoso acting performances; *Ladri di biciclette* is shot through with sentimentality of a kind perfectly honourable but produced by the same conscious dramatic devices as in theatrical films. In any event by 1950 the first powerful impulse of the immediate post-war was ended, or at least largely compromised. Still the influence of Italian neo-realism was to have a profound effect on world cinema during the succeeding two decades.

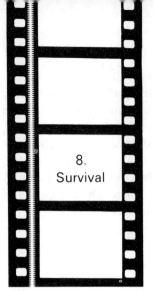

8.
Survival

The war as such did not basically affect the American cinema. The stars had joined up, or washed up at the Hollywood Canteen or entertained men in the front line, or raised money for charities and war loans. But the old studios and the studio systems survived untouched; the staple genres like crime thriller, musical, western, womens' romances continued with only minor modifications and concessions due to the passage of time. Even the loss of European markets was only a temporary setback since it coincided with a boom in cinema attendances at home.*

The war, it is true produced scores of commonplace adventure films in which Nazi uniforms and resistance heroes refurbished old cops and robbers formulas. There was a spate of films aimed to bolster enthusiasm for America's allies. William Wyler's *Mrs Miniver* (1942) presented a peculiar never-never land of Britain at war but nevertheless aroused a good deal of enthusiasm in America for the English. Lewis Milestone's *North Star* (1943), scripted by Lillian Hellman, was seriously intended to introduce the Soviet Union to the American public. Only towards the end of the war however did a group of more sober films emerge, treating in more human terms the effects of war upon ordinary men and women: John Ford's *They Were Expendable* (1945), the story of the Navy's P.T. boats in the

*It is significant in this respect that after the outbreak of war, MGM never made another film with Greta Garbo who formerly had been immensely valuable to the company in attracting a large European following.

Philippines, Milestone's *A Walk in the Sun* (1946) which endeavoured to do for the Second World War what his *All Quiet on the Western Front* had done for the First; William Wellman's *The Story of G.I. Joe* (1945); and after the war, William Wyler's sincere, if commercially calculated *The Best Years of our Lives* (1946).

These films had a degree of realism about them which probably owed something to the American documentary example. Documentary had found more difficulty in striking root than in the sympathetic English soil. Pare Lorentz (born 1905) had managed to get government sponsorship for *The Plow That Broke the Plains* (1936) and *The River* (1937), on soil erosion and land conservation; and so had Robert Flaherty (*The Land*, 1942) and the Dutch documentarist Joris Ivens (*Power and the Land*, 1940). But Government sponsorship came to an end after a few such efforts; and private industry at that time showed little enthusiasm for financing films. Meanwhile from 1934 the Time-Life Organisation had been producing its periodical *March of Time* series, whose aggressive style in news commentary exerted a powerful influence on cinema and ultimately television documentary. The immediate influence of *March of Time* was seen in Anatole Litvak's *Confessions of a Nazi Spy* (1939), a film which did much to awaken the American public to the dangers of Fascism.

The war mobilised the documentary cinema. Frank Capra was put in charge of Army Educational Film Programmes and produced the *Why We Fight* series, for which he employed directors like John Huston, William Wyler and Litvak. The application of Hollywood expertise to propaganda, instructional and realist subjects, and the assembly by feature directors of actuality film material, produced some new and invigorating results that in certain respects seemed to continue on from the Soviet experiments of the twenties. The same techniques were applied to battle records for home consumption and to the *Army-Navy Screen Magazine*.

The war and immediate pre-war period also saw the rise of a new generation, of which the most spectacular and perhaps in the long term the most influential was Orson Welles (born 1915). Coming from the theatre and radio (he

had achieved national notoriety for the alarm caused by a too realistic adaptation of H. G. Wells's *The War of the Worlds*), Welles, at twenty-four, was given complete freedom by RKO on his first film *Citizen Kane* (1941). Both in content and technique the film was audacious. Its story of the meteoric rise and tyrannical old age of a newspaper tycoon was taken to refer directly to William Randolph Hearst, who was incited by his columnist Louella Parsons to pursue a vendetta against the film and against Hollywood in general. Loyal to his sometime partner, Louis B. Mayer offered to buy the negative of the film at full production cost so that he might destroy it; but the gesture was happily refused by the producers. (Hearst much later saw the film and professed himself very pleased with it, even as a portrayal of himself).

Few of the technical devices employed by Welles were entirely without precedent: revealing ceilings in the framing of interior shots; chiaroscuro camerawork and deliberate, expressionist distortion; the use of long-focus lenses so that action might be conducted in parallel in foreground and background of the shot; a story told by means of flashbacks; even the employment of a narrative device whereby different people gave their different ver-

Orson Welles:
Citizen Kane.
U.S.A., 1941.
Orson Welles,
Ruth Warwick.

sions of the same character or action; a camera which moved with all the extravagance of Abel Gance. What was new was that Welles used all these devices, recklessly, together, and yet managed to integrate them into an aggressively personal style. Added to the visual novelty of the film was the inventive use of sound Welles brought from his radio experience, and entirely new standards of ensemble acting by a group of players, hitherto unknown in the cinema, from his Mercury Theatre. Even twenty-five years afterwards the full effect of the film's influence was being felt.* At the time there were plenty of critics to condemn his excesses, his extravagant use of camera movement as a means of overthrowing the classical, post-Griffith and post-Eisenstein dominance of montage.

The film was an immense critical success; but not a commercial one; and this fact, added to Welles's rush to finish his next film before embarking on subsequent projects, may have heartened the studio to mutilate *The Magnificent Ambersons* (1942), cutting Welles' original 148 minutes to a mere 88. Even so, this adaptation of Booth Tarkington's novel about the decline of a rich, conservative bourgeois family with the rise of modern industrial America remains a powerful and stylish narrative. After that Welles' career was erratic: from time to time he returned to direction with films from which the original brilliance was never absent, albeit intermittent: *Journey Into Fear* (1943), *The Stranger* (1946), *The Lady from Shanghai* (1947), *Confidential Report* (1955), *Touch of Evil* (1957), *The Trial* (1962, in France), *L'Histoire immortelle* (1968; for French television) and three arrogant, individualist essays in adapting Shakespeare: *Macbeth* (1948), *Othello* (1952) and *Chimes at Midnight* (1966), a composite of the Falstaff scenes from the Histories.

Other directors were recruited from the theatre. Elia Kazan (born Constantinople 1909) began his film career as a director of moderately non-controversial problem pictures like *A Tree Grows in Brooklyn* (1945), *Gentlemen's Agreement* (1948) and *Pinky* (1949). His theatrical background was to

*In a international poll of critics, organised by *Sight and Sound* (winter 1971–2) *Citizen Kane* was voted the best film of all time.

Orson Welles:
*L'Histoire
immortelle*.
France, 1968.
Jeanne Moreau,
Norman Eshley.

have a profound influence upon American acting styles, when the Stanislavski Method acting of Kazan's Actors' Studio was spectacularly publicised by the work in Kazan's films of Marlon Brando (*A Streetcar Named Desire*, 1951; *Viva Zapata!*, 1952; *On the Waterfront*, 1954) and James Dean (*East of Eden*, 1955). Among Kazan's later neglected films the most notable was the part-autobiographical *America! America! (The Anatolian Smile*, 1963), the experiences of a young immigrant in early twentieth century America. Kazan's assistant on *A Tree Grows in Brooklyn* was Nicholas Ray (born 1911), who made his debut as a director with *They Live By Night* (1948) an excellent drama, reminiscent of Lang's *You Only Live Once*, on the theme of a criminal's attempts to escape the pursuits of fate. After this Ray's career moved from highly efficient thrillers, sober sociological films (*Knock on Any Door*, 1949) and the film which

made James Dean the hero and symbol of a whole generation, *Rebel Without a Cause* (1955) to grandiose spectacles
like *King of Kings*, (1961) and *55 Days in Peking* (1963).
Formerly an actor, Jules Dassin (born 1911) made a short,
The Tell-Tale Heart (1941) in consequence of which he was
promoted to feature direction, achieving success in the
forties with his realist gangster films *Brute Force* (1947) and
Naked City (1948), which re-introduced Hollywood to the
possibility of shooting films on actual locations.

The majority of this new generation however had grown
up within the industry during the great days of the studio
system which, whatever its demerits, did provide place and
opportunity for young men to learn their crafts on shorts
direction, writing, editing or assistant direction. John
Huston (born 1906), after a swashbuckling youth as a
boxer, cavalry man and painter, became a writer at Warners
and Universal before making his stylish and brilliant debut
with *The Maltese Falcon* (1941). This adaptation of a Dashiell
Hammett thriller was the prototype of a whole cycle of
taut, tough, witty gangster pictures, the best of which
generally starred Humphrey Bogart along with distinctive
character players of the calibre of Sydney Greenstreet and
Peter Lorre. Before Huston, like Ray, was caught up in

John Huston:
*The Maltese
Falcon*. U.S.A.,
1941. Barton
Maclane, Ward
Bond and
Humphrey Bogart.

multi-million-dollar blockbusters, culminating in *The Bible* (1966) he established himself as one of the American cinema's most compelling story-tellers (*The Treasure of the Sierra Madre*, 1947; *Key Largo*, 1948; *The Asphalt Jungle*, 1950; *The Red Badge of Courage*, 1951, a sensitive and sober adaptation of Stephen Crane's Civil War story; *The African Queen*, 1951).

Fred Zinnemann (who had co-directed *Menschen am Sonntag* in Germany in 1930 and made a feature, *Redes*, in Mexico in 1934–6), and Joseph Losey were both apprenticed on the MGM series of short subjects *Crime Does Not Pay*. Zinnemann (born 1907) arrived at MGM in 1936 and established himself in the forties as a director of violent thrillers; he was later to prove a reliable and always honourable commercial director. The films of his best period were *The Men* (1950) and *High Noon* (1952), both scripted by Carl Foreman. Later he spent his talents, like so many of his generation on huge, anonymous commercial films like *The Nun's Story* (1959) and *Hawaii* (1966), though enjoying his biggest prestige success with *A Man For All Seasons* (1966). Joseph Losey (born 1909), who was to prove one of the best and most durable directors of this generation made his first feature film, a modern parable, *The Boy With Green Hair* in 1948; then went on to a series of highly efficient thrillers, including a remake of Fritz Lang's *M* (1950).*

Joseph L. Mankiewicz (born 1909) was a screenwriter for many years before directing *Dragonwyck* (1946), which launched a career as writer-director whose most notable works were *A Letter to Three Wives* (1949), *All About Eve* (1950), *Julius Caesar* (1953), *The Barefoot Contessa* (1954), *Suddnely, Last Summer* (1959) and the notorious *Cleopatra* (1963). Robert Rossen (1908–66) had also been a writer. Edward Dmytryk (born 1908) had done every job around the studio in the fifteen years before he made his first film, *Television Spy*, a second-feature, in 1939; after which he gradually worked up through a run of indifferent war thrillers to *Crossfire* (1947), a powerful and authentic tract on anti-semitism.

---

*For Losey's subsequent career in Europe, see pp. 299–300.

Billy Wilder (born 1906) had for years been a writer, first in Germany and then in the United States, where he provided some of Lubitsch's best scripts; and had directed a feature, *La Mauvaise Graine* (1933), in France. In 1942 he began his long, successful American career as a director with a comedy, *The Major and the Minor*. From *Double Indemnity* (1944) his characteristic tone of ironical disenchantment was clear; though from *Sabrina Fair* (1954) and *The Seven Year Itch* (1955) a new vein – still sardonic, but with a reckless gaiety reminiscent of Lubitsch – entered his work, to be most fully realised in *Some Like it Hot* (1959). Another immigrant, the Viennese Otto Preminger (born 1906) made his first film in Austria in 1932 and began to direct in the United States four years later; but all his biggest successes, from *A Royal Scandal* (1945) to the run of large-scale pictures he made in the sixties (*Anatomy of a Murder*, *Exodus*, *Advise and Consent*, *The Cardinal*) belong to the post-war period.

Other new directors of the forties and early fifties who came from within the industry were Robert Aldrich (born 1918), an assistant director to Wellman, Milestone, Losey, Renoir and Chaplin before making his first film *The Big Leaguer* in 1953 (later he was to achieve notable success with horror-comedies like *Whatever Happened to Baby Jane?* 1963); Stanley Kramer (born 1913), a former producer who made his first film, *Not as a Stranger*, in 1955, and later made a speciality of somewhat grandiose 'problem' pictures like *On the Beach* (1959), *Judgment at Nuremburg* (1961), *Guess Who's Coming to Dinner* (1967); the Hungarian born Laszlo Benedek (born 1907), formerly a cameraman with UFA, a Hollywood editor and a writer in Mexico, whose best films were *Death of a Salesman* (1951) and *The Wild One* (1953), a curious amalgam of fatalist romance and leather-and-motor-cycle delinquency. Don Siegel (born 1912), a former editor, became a specialist in crime thrillers, generally choosing to work with the comparative freedom offered by low budgets, as did Samuel Fuller (born 1911) who was usually the producer and writer of his tense, structured, violent melodramas.

This recruitment took place in boom years; 1946 was the most profitable year in the history of Hollywood. But it was the swansong of the movie capital of the great old days. From 1945 the industry had been suffering increasingly serious labour troubles. That year saw an eight-month strike; and in 1946 the studios had to add to costs that were already soaring a 25 per cent pay rise for studio employees. In 1947 Britain, America's major overseas market, announced a 75 per cent tax on foreign film earnings, to which America retaliated with a total boycott of the British market which lasted eight months. By late 1948 the Warner and Eagle studios were both temporarily closed down. Stringent new economies were inevitable. There was new emphasis on script values and pre-planning; and film content tended towards the kind of subject that could be shot with small casts and on small sets or – a totally new departure for studio-oriented Hollywood – on locations. Dassin's *Naked City* (1948), as we have seen, was a prototype. A large part of Hollywood production was now devoted to sociological and psychological dramas, and realistically-treated crime subjects. Costume films and spectacles were quite out of fashion. In the long term the effects of this period on artistic quality – the new economy which was transmitted to narrative method, the return from escapist subjects – were wholly beneficial; and emphasised by the considerable advances in technical development, in equipment, film stock, recording techniques, studio materials, which took place incidentally in the immediate post-war period.

The sombreness of many of these films may in part also be a reflection of the disaster which struck the film industry around the same time. The immense publicity potential of Hollywood and its inhabitants made it a natural target for the great Red-hunts of the end of the forties. In October 1947 the House Committee on Un-American Activities began an 'investigation of communism in motion pictures'. As a result of the hearings ten witnesses who pleaded the Fifth Amendment were imprisoned on charges of contempt of Congress; and the Association of Motion Picture Producers declared that since their action had 'impaired their usefulness to the industry' they would not be employed again until they had purged themselves of the contempt and declared under oath that they were not communists. This was only the beginning of a blacklist that was to grow larger and larger as new hearings continued until 1951, and artist after artist was invited to cleanse himself by naming names, and impugning his colleagues. By the time this witch-hunt, on authentic mediaeval models, was over, more than three hundred persons named by 'co-operative witnesses' were exiled from the studios.

Thus at a crucial moment Hollywood's vital talent was disastrously depleted. People like Joseph Losey, Jules Dassin and Carl Foreman went to Europe. Writers like Arthur Miller and Lillian Hellman and scenarists like Dalton Trumbo and Michael Wilson were forbidden to write for films. Others bought the right to work at the price of 'naming names', a sacrifice of self-respect that must have been as disastrous for some as exile was for others. Inevitably panic spread over what was left of an industry in which the most half-hearted invocation of the ideal of democracy had come to be looked on as dangerous subversion. Hollywood was never to recover completely from the self-evisceration of this moment.

The studio system was undergoing severe attack from another quarter also. Since 1945 actions under anti-trust laws had been in process against MGM and Paramount; and by the end of the forties the big studios had been obliged to divorce their production from their distribution operations. The result was a total reorganisation of methods of production, and the rise of independent producers, distributing their films through the old, big distributors, who would finance them with an advance against eventual box office takings.

A significant illustration of the parallel decline of the studios and the rise of the independent producers – who were often the stars and star directors themselves – are comparative figures for the numbers of actors, writers and directors under contract to the big studios: in 1940 the figures were reckoned respectively as 458, 375 and 117; by 1960, 139, 48 and 24. Independence, of course, was only a relative term. Films had still to be sold to the same distributors and the same audiences; so in the short term this change did not have a profound influence upon film content.

The next blow came from television. The competition of television reduced audiences in the United States from 90 million in 1948 to 70 million in 1949 and 60 million in 1950. Between 1946 and 1956 the figures halved. The closure of thousands of cinemas was only partly offset by the development of the 'drive-in' in the late forties. Production dropped by over one third.

Hollywood's first solution was to fight the small, flat, (then) black-and-white-screen with big, deep and coloured screens. From the early fifties colour, which had developed strikingly in quality since the war, became more and more widespread. In 1952 Cinerama was developed, adapting the idea of the triptych screen which Abel Gance had used in *Napoléon*, twenty-six years before, Cinerama was not used with the flair or imagination of Gance however; and it was ten years before anyone risked a feature film in the process instead of the side-show series of novelty views which recalled film styles of the 1890s. Moreover the three-projector process was never technically perfect, and the elaborate equipment necessary anchored Cinerama to specially fitted big-city cinemas. By the mid-sixties the three-projector method had been abandoned in favour of a more conventional large-film, large screen process.

There had been intermittent experiments with stereoscopy (developed for still photography a century before) throughout most of the cinema's sixty years; and indeed some of the earliest nineteenth century inventors had conceived notions of stereoscopic animated photographs long before 1896. During the war the Soviet inventor Semeon Ivanov (born 1906) had perfected a system of stereoscopy which dispensed with the need for special spectacles;* but all the Western systems required audiences to adopt such appendages, which presumably explained the very brief popularity of the 3D experiment. Before it expired however one or two films had seriously attempted to exploit the dramatic, as against the novelty value of the medium, notably

---

*The system is comparable to the process currently (1973) used for apparently stereoscopic picture postcards.

It puts **YOU** in the picture!

See the greatest entertainment event of the century . . .

For the first time a motion picture reacnes out to bring you into the story. In seconds you are lifted out of your theatre seat, moving breathlessly with the picture, surrounded by adventure, spectacle and thrills. CINERAMA is the only entertainment that really puts you in the picture.

YOU become part of the WORLD'S GREATEST Theatrical Attraction!..

THIS IS

CINERAMA

Cinerama poster, 1952.

A Lowell Thomas-Merian C. Cooper Presentation. **Print by TECHNICOLOR**

Alfred Hitchcock's *Dial M for Murder* (1954), which was never, however, released in the stereoscopic version.

The lasting revolution was the wide screen, first introduced with Cinemascope and *The Robe* (1955). Again it was a fairly old technique and, like sound films, had been offered unsuccessfully to producers years before they eventually adopted it under the pressure of special anxieties. The anamorphic lens which squeezed the image by distortion onto conventional 35 mm film frames and then expanded it again during projection to the characteristic 'wide-screen' shape, had its origins in the seventeenth century, and had been developed by Professor Henri Chrétien (1879–1956) for use in tank sights during the First World War.* In place of the 4 × 3 screen ratio that had been standard since Edison and Lumière, Cinemascope offered a 2.5:1 oblong. Cinema-Scope was followed by various systems using varying screen ratios, varying technical systems, varying film sizes and with a variety of colourful, pseudo-scientific trade names. 70 mm film, used by Demenÿ in 1896, was revived by several of the systems, all of which aimed to produce the biggest, clearest screen image possible. The old screen ratio became so unfashionable that in all cinemas the top and bottom of the picture was masked off even if the film had been shot in the 'Academy' ratio of 4:3. Since then it has become practice to shoot even conventional 35 mm films 'wide-screen', that is allowing for cutting off top and bottom of the frame in projection. As we shall see (p. 281) the new screen shapes and sizes had quite unforeseen effects upon screen aesthetics.

Still in pursuit of paths which television could not follow, there started a vogue for massive, multi-million dollar 'blockbuster' productions. It was not by and large a very fruitful policy. Very occasionally a film like Stanley Kubrick's *Spartacus* (1959) might be vigorous and intelligent, but more often than not there were so many people and committees nervously supervising the expenditure of so much money that the creative part of the undertaking was nullified. Contributing also to the fashion for big spectacles was the growing habit of shooting abroad – in Italy or Spain – where blocked capital could be used and labour was cheaper than at home. For a decade or more these 'runaway' productions were a feature of American film production. Commercially speaking, when they were good they were very very good (*The Ten Commandments* grossed between thirty and forty million dollars; *Around the World in Eighty Days* twenty-two million); but a failed blockbuster could be a crippling loss, as studios like Twentieth Century Fox were to find as a result of the great unrecouped cost of films like *Hello, Dolly!* and *Star* in the 1960s.

*Chrétien's anamorphic lens had in fact been used in 1929 for Claude Autant-Lara's *Pour construire un feu*.

Eighteenth-century 'anamorphic' painting. The distortion can be corrected by placing a reflecting cylinder of the same diameter, on the circle marked. The principle is the same as is employed in Cinemascope.

By the end of the fifties it was clear that the cinema was going to come off worst in the battle with television; and must find some means of truce. Old films were sold to television; studios were let out for television production. Meanwhile television had begun to make its aesthetic contribution to cinema. Delbert Mann's *Marty* (1955), from a script by Paddy Chayevsky, a television writer, attracted what might seem in retrospect disproportionate attention (partly stimulated, it is true, by a massive promotional effort after the lead actor Ernest Borgnine was nominated for an 'Oscar'). The story of two ordinary and modest people – a shy butcher who courts an equally shy school-teacher – it reintroduced from television the lesson that audiences can be interested in contemporary characters and stories of ordinary, unglamorous life. A spate of films, all made in 1957 – Robert Mulligan's *Fear Strikes Out*, Sidney Lumet's *Twelve Angry Men*, John Frankenheimer's *The Young Stranger* – introduced at once new styles of film-making and, more important, a new generation of directors and writers, trained in television and bringing from that training different approaches and insights.

Through the revolutions certain genres survived in-destructibly. The musical, one of Hollywood's major con-tributions to popular art, had undergone significant revival in the forties, largely due to the talents of Vincente Minelli (born 1913), Gene Kelly (born 1912) and Stanley Donen (born 1920) and the availability of a generation of admirable musical stars, but most notably Judy Garland. The characteristics of the films by these new directors were a closer integration of story and musical numbers, more sophisticated design and balletically inspired choreo-graphy. The beautiful mechanical inconsequence of Busby Berkeley's chorus numbers was outdated, though there was to be a nostalgic revival of interest in his work in the seventies. The blockbuster period of production was un-happily inimical to the new style; and after the late fifties the quiet, civilised values of the Minelli-Kelly-Donen musicals (*Meet Me in St Louis*, 1944; *On the Town*, 1949) was usurped by a spate of massive films which endeavoured to reproduce the effect of magnified stage productions.

Comedy was prolific but at a low ebb. The great music hall and vaudeville generation was dying out; and the newcomers from radio and a declining burlesque tradition were not their equals. The top box-office comedians of the forties were Abbott and Costello, poor shadows of the fat-and-thin combination of Laurel and Hardy. The films of Bob Hope and Danny Kaye provided more sophisticated

values, however; and Dean Martin and Jerry Lewis, especially in the films directed by Frank Tashlin (born 1913) – a former animated cartoon maker, Laurel and Hardy gagman, and director of the best Bob Hope vehicles – indicated new styles of comedy. Adaptation continued to be a staple of American prestige production. There was a spate of anti-Red films – most notorious, because most effective, William Wellman's *Iron Curtain* (1948) – designed less to please the public than to protest political respectability on behalf of the witchhunters. The Western tended to grow more sophisticated in these years: and one outstanding example, Fred Zinnemann's *High Noon* (1952), written by Carl Foreman, offered a remarkable allegory on McCarthyism.

Of the veterans, Chaplin, who in 1940 had made his timely satire on the Axis leaders, *The Great Dictator*, made two last American films. In *Monsieur Verdoux* (1947) he departed forever from his famous tramp character to play a modern Bluebeard. The film, with its caustic comparisons between the morality of private murder and the mass slaughter licensed by war, was very unpopular in the United States, and began the Red hunt after Chaplin which culminated in his departure from America after the completion of *Limelight* (1952), a richly nostalgic remembrance of London and the music halls of his youth before the First World War. Alfred Hitchcock produced a continuous series of brilliant suspense thrillers, one of which, *Rope* (1948) – an adaptation of Patrick Hamilton's play based remotely on the Leopold-Loeb murder case – was novel in its use of a ten-minute take, a characteristically audacious demonstration against the old montage ideal. John Ford made some of his finest tributes to the Western legend – *My Darling Clementine* (1946), *She Wore a Yellow Ribbon* (1949), *Wagonmaster* (1950), *The Sun Shines Bright* (1953). And Hollywood still continued to produce its stars, even though they were fewer than in the great old days. Some of the new talent was outstanding. Of the biggest of those who emerged in the early fifties – James Dean, Marlon Brando, Elizabeth Taylor, Marilyn Monroe – two died young, victims perhaps of their own myths.

Britain emerged from the war in a state of high optimism. Artistically her stock was as high as at any time, with directors like Asquith, Lean, Reed, Cavalcanti, Olivier, Thorold Dickinson, Michael Powell, Emeric Pressburger and the Boulting brothers at the height of their creative powers. Cinema attendances had reached an unprecedented peak; the home industry was protected by a 40 per cent quota; and production rose from 83 feature films in 1945–6 to 170 in 1947–8. But the optimism was illusory; already the British film industry was nearer trouble than anyone could guess. The efforts of the powerful Rank organisation to break into the American market during 1948 were disastrously unsuccessful, and left some costly productions, aimed at the transatlantic market, to become embarrassing white elephants.

Meanwhile the 75 per cent tax levied on foreign film profits in 1947, in an effort to meet balance of payment deficits, spurred America to retaliate with an embargo on film imports to Britain. Instead of stimulating the home industry in a healthy way, this only led to the rapid production of low-quality material (which probably represents a good proportion of the high 1947–8 production figures) which only contributed to the large production losses that the film industry began to show. At this stage the Government was obliged to step in to assist production with the creation of the National Film Finance Corporation, a kind of Government film bank, in 1949; and by the 'Eady' levy through which a proportion of box-office earnings was (and in 1972, still is) channelled back directly to the producers.

This financial instability, added to a sudden rapid drop in production and consequent high unemployment, coincided with the growing competition of television. The late forties saw a decline of audiences similar to that experienced in the States. The depths of depression seemed to have been reached just ten years after the hopeful auguries of the end of the war; and was symbolised by the coincident death of Korda and the sale of Ealing Studios to television in 1956, soon after the opening of commercial television in Britain.

The rise and fall in artistic quality of British films followed very closely the path of this optimism and defeat. The few years following the war saw some very notable British films. Literary adaptation – always characteristic of British film-making – enjoyed a new lease of life. David Lean made beautiful period-piece adaptations of *Great Expectations* (1946), and *Oliver Twist* (1947); Laurence Olivier followed his wartime *Henry V* (1945) with an elegant *Hamlet* (1948). Anthony Asquith adapted the Rattigan plays *The Winslow Boy* (1948) and *The Browning Version* (1950) and Wilde's *The Importance of Being Earnest* (1951); and Thorold Dickinson *The Queen of Spades* (1949). Carol Reed adapted a novel by F. L. Green for *Odd Man Out* (1946), a stylish film which recalled at once German Expressionism and the Carné style of French fatalism. Grahame Greene stories inspired *Fallen Idol* (1948) and *The Third Man* (1949, Reed's

most celebrated picture, which created a haunting vision of corrupt post-war Vienna and a memorable Cold War character, 'Harry Lime', played by Orson Welles.

Side by side with these prestige works there was a strange area of popular cinema which generally appeared under the rubric of Gainsborough Pictures: novelette stories, favouring the Regency period and generally starring the young James Mason, Stewart Granger, Margaret Lockwood and Phyllis Calvert as highwaymen or rakes or Wicked Ladies. It is hard too to know how to place two 'cultural' exploits of Powell and Pressburger: *The Red Shoes* (1947) did a good deal to popularise ballet in Britain in the late forties; *The Tales of Hoffmann* (1951) was a more vulgar and less successful attempt to do the same for operetta.

Far and away the most important films of the period were the comedies produced at Ealing under Michael Balcon. They had in common their peculiarly national

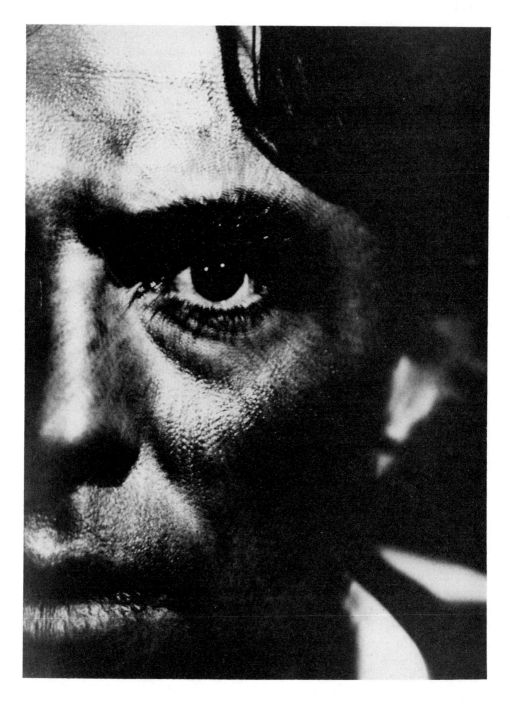

Carol Reed: *Odd Man Out*. Britain, 1946. James Mason.

settings and characters and situations; they were written with intelligence and with the logic and seriousness due to comedy; and were played with the extended skills of a generation of fine British character actors, led by the versatile Alec Guinness. Ealing developed some richly talented directors: Alexander Mackendrick (*Whisky Galore*, 1947; *The Lady Killers*, 1955); Robert Hamer (*Kind Hearts and Coronets*, 1949); Charles Crichton (*Hue and Cry*, 1947; *The Lavender Hill Mob*, 1951); and Henry Cornelius, who wrote *Hue and Cry* and directed the irresistible *Passport to Pimlico* (1949). The quirky, local, human comedy of Ealing marked a peak in British films.

Their noticeable decline in the early fifties was less significant than the mechanisation of their formulas in the films of other people: for instance in the series directed by Ralph Thomas which began with *Doctor in the House* (1954). The depression of British cinema seemed reflected also by a retreat into heroic Second World War subjects like *The Cruel Sea* (1953), *The Colditz Story* (1955), *The Divided Heart* (1954), *The Dambusters* (1955) illustrating, it seemed, that phenomenon which Arnold Toynbee called 'archaism', and which consists in a retreat from a disagreeable or uninspiring present to the recollection of past achievement.

France ended the war with more justified optimism. Industrial organisation was stronger than at any time since the great days before 1912, thanks to steps taken by the Government to assist production. These measures were strengthened by the Loi d'Aide à l'Industrie Cinématographique of 1949, and a Loi de Développement de l'Industrie Cinématographique of 1953, which set up a national aid fund. Production rose from 72 films in 1945 to 126 in 1953, despite the introduction of television between those years. Moreover France earned immense prestige from the films produced during the occupation, which were now launched all at once upon the international market.

The high morale thus produced and augmented by successes in the first post-war international film festivals helped sustain the French cinema at a high level of achievement for several more years. One reason for the French

Robert Hamer: *Kind Hearts and Coronets*. Britain, 1949. Alec Guinness.

cinema's apparent ability constantly to renew itself, so that it is the only national industry with a practically unbroken record of high creative achievement despite serious economic ups and downs, may lie in its resistance – at least since the dismantling of the Pathé empire – to monopolistic structures. In 1953 for instance, with a production of slightly more than one hundred feature films, there were 323 registered production organisations in business.

Clair and Renoir returned from America at the height of their power. Clair's *Le Silence est d'or* (1947), a touching study of the onset of age, evoked with pleasant nostalgia the cinema of his childhood. *La Beauté du Diable* (1950), an updating of the Faust legend, was less successful. *Belles-de-nuit* (1952), which the director characterised as 'a comic *Intolerance*', told of a provincial music teacher's dreams of other epochs; while *Les Grandes Manoeuvres* (1956) was a bitter-sweet comedy aimed to undermine the myth of the *belle époque*. Clair's best post-war film however was *Porte des Lilas* (1957), a melancholy comedy which returned to Clair's mythic low-life Paris as the setting for a story of the friendship between a drunkard and a mendicant musician. Clair was never to better this, or to return to the form of his prime.

Jean Renoir remained in the U.S.A. throughout the forties (*The Southerner*, *Diary of a Chambermaid*, *Woman on the Beach* and, directed in India, *The River*); then in 1952 he went to Italy to make a glittering comedy about the travails of a company of *commedia* players, *La carozza d'oro* (1952). Back in France he made two more costume pictures, the exquisite recollection of the early years of the Moulin Rouge, *French Can-Can* (1955), and the romantic *Eléna et les hommes* (1956). After a film for television, *Le Testament du Dr Cordelier* (1959) he paid tribute to his father Auguste Renoir, and, nostalgically, to his own *Une Partie de campagne*, with *Le Déjeuner sur l'herbe* (1959), a philosophical, pantheistic fantasy, set in sunlit impressionist landscapes. In *Le Caporal epinglé* (1962), forsaking colour, which he had used in his recent films, he made a comedy of army and prison-camp life which recalled his silent *Tire-au-flanc*.

Julien Duvivier never regained his earlier form, even in

Panique (1946) his best film of post-war years, with a virtuoso performance by Michel Simon as an eccentric persecuted by a suspicious community. Nor for that matter did Carné, though he showed himself adept at keeping up with the current fashion; in his 'youth' film, *Les Tricheurs* (1958) he even seemed to be in step with the mood and preoccupations of the coming *nouvelle vague*.

Claude Autant-Lara (born 1903), who had directed his first feature film in 1933, seemed the outstanding talent of the immediate post-war, with a remarkable run of prestige successes: *Le Diable au corps* (1947) sensitively adapted Raymond Radiguet's delicate novel of schoolboy love; *Occupe-toi d'Amélie!* (1949) was a dazzling Feydeau adaptation; *L'Auberge rouge* (1951) gave vent to Autant-Lara's vigorous anti-bourgeois sentiments; in *Le Blé en herbe* (1954) he adapted Colette as delicately as he had adapted Radiguet; *La Traversée de Paris* (1956) was a resistance subject, treated with taut dramatic effect.

The most durable talents however were to prove those of Robert Bresson and Jean Cocteau. Bresson (born 1907) revealed himself as one of the most uncompromisingly individualist of directors, making films whose means – settings, dialogue, acting method – were reduced to a classical austerity, while never losing the human quality of his heroes, most of whom were characters gripped by

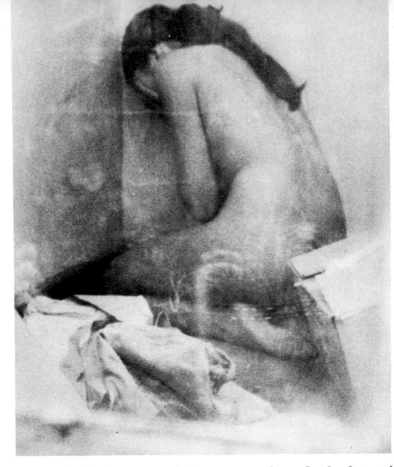

Robert Bresson:
Au hasard,
Balthasar.
France, 1966.
Anne
Wiazemsky.

some private fervour – religious or profane. In *Le Journal d'un curé de campagne* (1950) from a novel by Bernanos, he told of the lonely agony of a young priest in a remote unwelcoming parish. All Bresson heroes seem to be in quest of some kind of grace – the resistance prisoner of *Un Condamné à mort s'est échappé* (1956); the pickpocket in *Pickpocket* (1959); Joan, in *Le Procès de Jeanne d'Arc* (1961), an even more austere rehearsal of the actual words of Joan's trial than Dreyer's (pp. 159–60); the unloved children of *Au hasard, Balthasar* (1966) and *Mouchette* (1966). *Une Femme douce* (1969), an adaptation of a Dostoievsky story of a man of mean spirit who tries vainly to rise to the love of a generous gentle girl, showed a distinct elaboration of style, emphasised perhaps by the use, for the first time in a Bresson film, of colour. In 1971, with *Quatre nuits d'un rêveur*, an adaptation of *White Nights*, he again transposed a Dostoievsky story into a purely Bressonian world.

Cocteau (1889–1963) succeeded uniquely in creating a cinema that was integrated to his total *oeuvre* in literature, poetry, painting, the theatre and his personal existence. The exquisite *La Belle et la Bête* (1946), with its fine design by Christian Bérard, Cocteau's own surrealist inventions and the performances of Jean Marais and Josette Day, did much to reopen foreign markets after the war. *Les Parents terribles* (1948) defied all the conventions of play adaptation by refusing to broaden the scene from the claustrophobic confines of the theatrical setting. The result was perhaps his best film: an extraordinarily concentrated psychological study of the mutual torments of an intimate family group. Later, in 1950, Jean-Pierre Melville directed Cocteau's *Les Enfants terribles*, in which the contribution of the author was unmistakeable. *Les Enfants terribles* touched upon the personal and poetic mythology which Cocteau had first brought to the screen in *Le Sang d'un poète* (1930), and which he elaborated in the memorable *Orphée* (1950) with its surrealist dream atmospheres, its symbols, its uniquely Cocteauesque poetry. All these were taken up yet again in *Le Testament d'Orphée* (1960) which Cocteau

Jean Cocteau:
*Le Testament
d'Orphée.*
France, 1960.
Edouard Demit.
Jean Cocteau.

Jacques Becker:
Le Trou. France,
1960.

deliberately intended as his artistic testament, and which was, significantly, in part financed by the young new generation to whom the uncompromising idiosyncracy of Cocteau's work had been an essential inspiration.

There were other originals in post-war France. Jacques Becker's fascination with character and his fanatical truthfulness in every detail of psychology or setting gave several interesting turns to his post-war activity. From directing psychological comedies (*Antoine et Antoinette*, 1947; *Rendez-vous de Juillet*, 1949; *Edouard et Caroline*, 1951), Becker (1906–60) moved to elegant period reconstruction of Paris of the Feuillade era in *Casque d'or* (1952); the gangster film *Touchez-pas au grisbi* (1954); the period comedy-thrills of *Arsène Lupin* (1957) and the psychological drama of his

Jacques Tati
Mon oncl
France, 195
Jacques Tat

last and best film, *Le Trou* (1960) which described tensions and betrayals among a group of prisoners.

Jacques Tati (born 1908) metamorphosed his experiences as a sportsman into music hall comedy; and then brought his music hall experience to the cinema, establishing himself as the most complete and original screen comedian since the classic silent days. After several short comedies he made a feature, *Jour de fête* (1947) in which he created the character of the supremely abstracted post man of a self-important French village, who unwittingly spread disaster wherever he moved. In *Les Vacances de M. Hulot* (1953) he created a new character whose innocent individualism was opposed, with still more anarchically comic consequences, to the new world of automation, in *Mon oncle* (1958), *Playtime* (1967) and *Trafic* (1971). Tati, for all his carefully

restricted output, is one of the truly great comic creators, who has made the modern world a comic wonderland in which he lovingly, cruelly, indulgently, uncomprehendingly watches the antics of the people who have made it and now scuttle about in their plastic miracle with the pride of White Rabbits. Other comedians – Pierre Etaix (born 1928) and Robert Dhéry (born 1921) – applied their circus and music hall experience to films with intermittent success, but without ever equalling the comic genius of Tati.

Other French directors of the post-war decade tended towards darker themes. Henri-George Clouzot's (born 1907) most successful films were *Le Salaire de la peur* (1952) a tense thriller about a group of men from the colonial underworld driving a lorry of dangerous explosives; and *Les Diaboliques* (1956) a horror murder mystery. René Clément (born 1913) returned to the fatalist themes of the pre-war with *Au-delà des grilles* (1949), though he also made the tender *Jeux interdits* (1953) and, in England, a dazzling light comedy, *Monsieur Ripois* (1954), which starred Gérard Philipe, the most popular male star of the post-war French cinema. André Cayatte, (born 1909) with *Justice est faite* (1950) and *Nous sommes tous des assassins* (1952) made a speciality of court-room dramas. Other directors who emerged in the post-war decade were Jean Delannoy (born 1908); Jacqueline Audry (born 1908), with her sensitive observations of the sentiments of women, as in *Gigi* (1949) and *Mitsou* (1956); Jean-Paul Le Chanois (born 1909), Louis Daquin (born 1908), Yves Allegret (born 1907) and Georges Rouquier (born 1909), who made a fine lyrical study of the land through the changing seasons, *Farrébique* (1947).

A notable transient in Paris in these post-war years was Max Ophuls (1902–57). A peripatetic, Ophuls made twenty-one films in six different countries in the course of his career. These tended towards operetta themes and settings – ideally, Vienna at the end of the nineteenth century; and they were generally about women in love. But it was particularly his film style, his preference for moving his camera, for *mise-en-shot*, over classical methods of editing, that made him influential on the generation that followed his death. His film career began in 1930 in Germany, where his best work was an already characteristic and very stylish adaptation of Schnitzler's *Liebelei* in 1932. After Hitler, he worked in France, Italy, Holland, Switzerland and the U.S.A., where his best film was *Letter From an Unknown Woman* (1948). Back in France, in 1950 Ophuls returned to Schnitzler – the play *Reigen* – for *La Ronde*, a

Max Ophuls: *La Ronde*. France, 1951. Anton Walbrook.

witty episodic satire on love and infidelity, which enjoyed an overwhelming international success. He was slightly less at ease with the three Maupassant short stories of *Le Plaisir* (1951) and Louise de Vilmorin's *Madame de . . .* (1953). His masterpiece – whose mutilation by the distributors certainly hastened Ophuls's early death – was *Lola Montès* (1955) a rich kaleidoscopic impression of the career of the great courtesan, enriched with extravagant rococo decoration and Ophuls' unique camera style.

The nations of the socialist bloc had also entered the post-war world with high optimism. Few of the new socialist countries had managed to support substantial capitalist film industries before the war – Albania, for instance, had no film industry at all. Now however they found themselves with the possibility of organising state controlled and subsidised cinemas, with all the wonder of a new, ideal socialism to be celebrated in their films. In Albania, Bulgaria, Rumania, Yugoslavia and Czechoslovakia results were slow; but the countries with strong existing film traditions – East Germany, Hungary and Poland – began the post-war era promisingly. In the DEFA studios (the former Althoff Studios in Dresden) Wolfgang Staudte (born 1906) made *Die Mörder sind unter uns* (1946) and Erich Engel (1891–1966), a well-known stage director before the war, made *The Blum Affair* (1948) – both militant anti-fascist films. In Poland, production was limited by the lack of studio facilities; but of the seven films made between 1947 and 1950 at least three – *The Last Stage* (1948) by Wanda Jakubowska (born 1907); *Border Street* (1948) by Alexander Ford (born 1908) already an outstanding director before the war; and *The Treasure* (1949) by Leonard Buczkowski (1900–1966), who had directed the first post-war feature, *Forbidden Songs* two years earlier, were memorable.

In Hungary Béla Balász (1884–1949) the great film theorist, returned from a long exile to teach at the newly founded Academy of Dramatic and Film Art. The classic Soviet films were shown in Hungary for the first time. American distributors tried to recapture the market, so that film-makers had a chance to see large numbers of Hollywood films. Under such varied artistic stimuli, a few films were made by private enterprise; but from 1947 permits to produce films were given only to the leading political parties. Two notable films resulted from this attempt to revive the industry: Istvan Szöt's *Song of the Cornfields* (1947) and Géza Radványi's *Somewhere in Europe* (1947), scripted by Béla Balász himself, a touching, idealistic fantasy about the reclamation of delinquent war orphans, strongly influenced by Nikolai Ekk's *The Road to Life*.

In March 1948 the Hungarian film industry was nationalised for the second time (see page 196); and the first films produced by the state film industry were auspicious: Frigyes Bán's *The Soil Beneath Your Feet* (1948), Imre Jeney's

Géza Radványi: *Somewhere in Europe.* Hungary, 1947. Artur Somlay.

A Woman Makes a New Start (1949), and the newcomer, Félix Máriássy's *Anna Szábó* (1949) which dealt with profound humanity with the problems of adjustment in the new socialist world.

Rapidly however the policies of the Soviet Union began to spread over much of the rest of the Soviet bloc. Soviet films had entered on the most barren phase of their history, coinciding with the most negative period of communism. The mystique of socialist realism inhibited all artistic activity; and there was a relentless witch-hunt against everything that smacked of 'formalism'. Films were banned, including Eisenstein's *Ivan the Terrible, Part II* (1946), Lukov's *A Great Life* (1946) and Yutkevitch's *Light from Russia* (1947). Others – including Pudovkin's *Admiral Nakhimov* (1946) and Gerassimov's *The Young Guard* (1948) – were only released after extensive revisions. Dovzhenko's biography of *Michurin* (1948) lingered through three years of changes and revisions after the scientist's work had become a political issue. The approved directors tended to dedicate themselves to approved official tasks, such as vicious Cold War propagandist subjects like Alexandrov's *Meeting on the Elbe* (1947). Other directors sought escape in filming theatrical productions – plays, ballets and operas – or comparatively safe 'historical' subjects.

Film-makers in the other socialist countries also found their work forced into the worst schematic moulds of 'socialist realism'. The script tended to become paramount, with any deviation from what was safely set down and approved in advance frowned on as opening the door to 'formalism'. The pressures were felt most keenly perhaps in Hungary, where the leader Rákosi loyally carried out repressive Stalinist policies. Béla Balász was removed from his post at the Academy of Dramatic and Film Art. Pudovkin was sent from Moscow to Budapest as 'adviser' on film affairs; and Hungary, along with the rest of the socialist world, moved into the most sterile period of her film history.

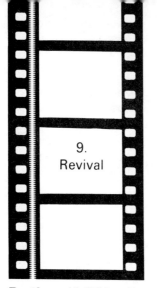

9.
Revival

By the mid-fifties it was very apparent that the old structures were breaking up. In America a whole generation had
been scattered or demoralised. Elsewhere in the West – in
Britain and France for instance – the generations that had
dominated the cinema in the years before the war, and
survived it while younger film-makers had been occupied
in war employment, were dying out. With the universal
challenge of television, the diminishing audience, the
rapidly rising costs of production, the old industrial organ-
isms had become obsolete.

At the same time there were quite new possibilities of
cross-fertilisation in the art. The cinema had become much
more international, though in a different way from the
silent period when there had been a fairly free exchange of
commercial products between the major producing countries. The first cineclub had been formed in France in the
twenties by Delluc, and the London Film Society had
followed only a little later; the first film archives had been
established in New York, London and Paris in the mid
thirties. Neither the film society movement nor the film
archive movement really came into their own however
until after the war, when they began energetically introducing audiences to films from all parts of the world. Still
more important was the growth in the forties and fifties of
international film festivals. The Venice Biennale had held
regular film exhibitions since 1932; and there had been a big
Soviet festival in Moscow in 1935; but again it was only
after 1946 that festivals flourished widely. Both commer-

cially and artistically, the chance to see the best production of other countries was of inestimable value. Again, as
blocked capital more and more encouraged the habit
of 'runaway' productions in the American cinema, American film artists came increasingly in contact, mutually
beneficial, with artists and technicians of other countries.

The value of festivals was spectacularly demonstrated in
1951 when Akira Kurosawa's *Rashomon* won the Grand Prix
at Venice, and at once opened up markets in Europe and
America where Japanese films had hitherto been unknown.
Since the coming of sound, the Japanese cinema had
continued to produce a vast output of commercially
oriented formula pictures, among which was always a
handful of works of real worth, generally the products of a
group of outstanding artists who had established themselves at the end of the silent period – Kenji Mizoguchi,
Teinosuke Kinugasa, Heinosuke Gosho, Yasujiro Ozu,
Yomu Uchida, Mikio Naruse. All these directors revealed
an initial preference for realist and socially critical films
of a kind which found less and less ready acceptance in the
climate of war-fevered Japan in the thirties and forties. In
the war period some of the best directors chose to go into
temporary retirement. This was not difficult to do, since
war difficulties decimated output between 1940 and 1944.
   The occupying Americans took over the studios; and at
Toho – whose former management had been most strongly
committed to the wartime regime – there was a renaissance
of Japanese cinema, which even managed to survive, more
or less, the return to power of the old reactionary heads of
Toho, in 1948. Kinugasa (born 1896) brought Japan another
big international success when his *Gate of Hell* won the
Grand Prix at the Cannes Festival in 1954. Mizoguchi
(1898–1956) was, wrote Penelope Houston, 'A poet who
thought like a painter . . . To the Japanese . . . essentially
the painter of women'. Best known to European audiences
for his mediaeval tales of ghosts and fair women (*The Life
of O Haru*, 1952; *Ugetsu Monogatari*, 1953; *Chikkamatsu
Monogatari*, 1954) Mizoguchi could as well deal with the
prostitutes of Yoshiwara in *Street of Shame* (1956). Ozu

Yasujiro Ozu:
Tokyo Story.
Japan, 1953.
Setsuko Hara,
Chishu Ryu.

(1903–63) specialised in gentle, lyrical celebrations of traditional family life. Another veteran, Heinosuke Gosho (born 1902) was one of the victims of Japan's post-1948 blacklist; and joining the ranks of other outcast left-wing independents, made a touching account of the urban poor in *Four Chimneys* (1953).

Of the generation which came to the fore during and after the war the most gifted was clearly Akira Kurosawa (born 1910), regarded by Japanese as the most 'Western' of their directors, though only perhaps because he refused to be tied to a particular category of production in the accepted custom of Japanese directors. He made traditional historical subjects, like *They Who Step on the Tiger's Tail* (1945) and *Rashomon* (1950); and also parodies of the genre (*Yojimbo*, 1961). He confronted modern themes (*Living*, 1952), philosophical crime stories (*High and Low*, 1963), free adaptations of Dostoievski (*The Idiot*, 1951), of Shakespeare's *Macbeth* (*Cobweb Castle*, 1957), of Gorki (*The Lower Depths*, 1957; *Dodeska Den*, 1970, seemed to be a still more personal gloss on the play.) All his work is characterised by the same deep intelligence and masterly sense of narrative which clearly owe much to his admiration for John Ford. The work of other Japanese directors also reached the west in the fifties and sixties, following the *Rashomon* breakthrough: Tadashi Imai (born 1912), Keisuke Kinoshita (born 1912),

Satsuo Yamamoto (born 1912); and the remarkable Kon Ichikawa (born 1915) who passed from light comedy to the mortal ferocity of *The Burmese Harp* (1956) and *Fires on the Plain* (1959), both of which dealt with the extremities to which the experiences of war can drive the human spirit; *Conflagration* (1958) from the novel by Yukio Mishima; *Odd Obsessions* (1960), a remarkable study of an ageing man's terror of impotence; and thence to the endearing record of an idiotic lone Atlantic voyage, *Alone in the Pacific* (1962), and a rich, lyrical and comic record of the 1964 Olympiad.

Akira Kurosawa: *Yojimbo*. Japan, 1961. Tatsuya Nakadai, Toshiro Mifune.

The Indian cinema with its vast and on the whole indifferent annual output remains (perhaps understandably) unexplored in the west;* but the Grand Prix awarded at the

*Though in the early fifties one or two films shown in Europe, notably Bimal Roy's *Two Acres of Land* and K. Abbas's *Munna* revealed the influence of Italian new-realism upon certain younger directors.

1956 Cannes Film Festival to Satyajit Ray's *Pather Panchali* launched a director of classic stature. *Pather Panchali* had been made with little money and under grave difficulties. Together with the succeeding two parts of the 'Apu' trilogy it forms one of the cinema's masterworks: the story of a Bengali life from childhood to maturity, related with an appearance of gentle, direct, casual simplicity which belies the highly complex intellect and attitudes behind it. Ray's subsequent films, including *Three Daughters* (1961), *Kanchenjunga* (1962), *Mahaganar* (1963), *Charulata* (1964), *Kapurush* (1965), *Days and Nights in the forest* (1969–70) all show the same ability to tell stories in direct and human terms, with comedy and pathos freely intermingled; and yet always to imply much more about the quality of life than is directly stated in the stories. It is a measure of his quality that while the films remain completely Bengali in setting and atmosphere, the spectator sees Ray's characters not as characters, or simply Indians, but as ordinary, sympathetic immediately recognisable people. Around Ray has grown up in Calcutta a school of directors some of whose work

Satyajit Ray: *The World of Apu*. Bengal, 1959.

reached Europe in the late sixties, notably the films of the American James Ivory (*The Householder*, 1962; *Shakespeare Wallah*, 1964; *Bombay Talkie*, 1970).

The films of Ingmar Bergman (born 1918) enjoyed a much wider and more sustained circulation throughout Europe than those of either Kurosawa or Ray. Paradoxically the films of this Swedish director seemed to become more marketable as they became more personal and elusive in content and imagery. Bergman entered films in 1944 as a writer on *Frenzy*, directed by Alf Sjöberg, a director who had continued the tradition of Sjöstrom and Stiller. Bergman's earliest films combined social observation with an expressionist manner (*Crisis*, 1946; *Prison*, 1949). Then came a whole group which dealt with the difficulties of erotic and marital relationships. Later films, from *The Seventh Seal* (1956) onwards, were more metaphysical in their examination of different aspects of psychological and spiritual suffering. He set his stories in the past (*The Seventh Seal, The Face*, 1958; *The Virgin Spring*, 1959) and the present (*The Silence*, 1963; *Persona*, 1966); in mediaeval Sweden, modern Stockholm or in the strange, isolated Bergman-land he invented on the lonely island of Faro (*Hour of the Wolf*, 1968; *Shame*, 1968; *A Passion*, 1969). But always his films have been distinguished by the same virtuoso visual style. His greatness, wrote Jan Dawson,* 'lies in his ability to express the obsessions of his age in the language of that age'. Bergman has always however acknowledged the older Swedish tradition, to which he seemed to pay a tribute in his use of Victor Sjöstrom as the star of one of his most successful films, *Wild Strawberries* (1957).

Luis Buñuel (born 1900) had virtually vanished after *Las Hurdes* (1932). He had returned to his native Spain to supervise, and in some cases direct, low-budget comedies. He had undertaken modest jobs in Hollywood and at the Museum of Modern Art in New York (he was dismissed, the victim of an early witch-hunt, for being the director of *L'Age d'Or*). In 1950 *Los Olvidados*, made in Mexico where he

The Sunday Times, 20 September 1970.

Ingmar
Bergman:
The Silence.
Sweden, 1963.
Gunnel
Lindblom.

had already directed a couple of minor comedies, dramatically renewed his international reputation. In this unsparing study of urchins brutalised by the slums of Mexico
City, the brilliance, the preoccupations and the surrealist
perceptions were still evident. Throughout the next two
decades Buñuel sustained an output of works all of which
bore his unmistakable signature, even when they were
made in the restricting economy of the Mexican commercial cinema. There were light comedies like *Susana* (1951),
black ones like *La vida criminal de Archibaldo de la Cruz* (1955),
psychological dramas (*El bruto*, 1952), exotic melodramas
(*La Fièvre monte à El Pao*, made in France in 1959), adaptations of Defoe (*Robinson Crusoe*, 1952) and of Emily Brontë

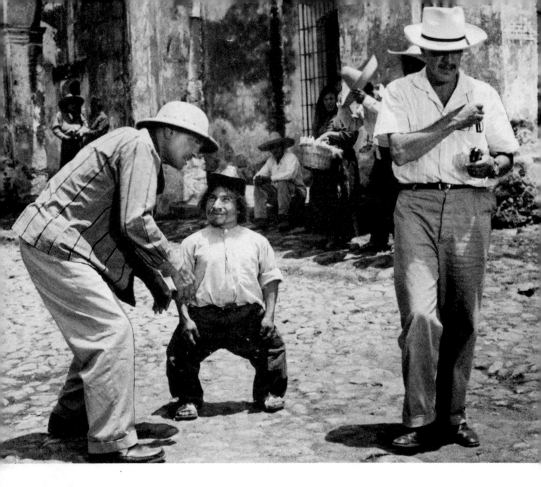

(*Abismos de passion*, 1953; remotely based on *Wuthering Heights*). All of them were marked by Buñuel's total assurance as a craftsman and illuminated by his personal and surreal imagery. His great period, returning to the full creative and anarchic force of *L'Age d'or*, began with *Nazarin* (1958). This film and *Viridiana* (1961), which was made – and rapidly banned – in his native Spain, examined in terms of comedy, horror and the surreal the impossibility of living a truly Christian life in the circumstances of the modern world. *El angel exterminador* (1962) was a pure surrealist exercise; *Simon del deserto* (1965) a hardly less surreal examination of St Simeon Stylites in the terms of modern society. Buñuel next made three films in France, transforming Mirbeau's *Journal d'une femme de chambre** (1964)

Luis Buñuel directing Jesus Fernandez in *Nazarin*. Mexico, 1959.

*Renoir also, had made an adaptation of this book in the U.S.A. in 1945.

and an indifferent novel by Joseph Kessel, *Belle de Jour* (1966), into works belonging purely to his own mythology; while *La Voie lactée* (1969) was a Buñuelian enquiry into the great heresies of the Catholic church. In 1970 he returned to Spain to direct *Tristana*, from a novel by Benito Perez Caldos.

Although Spain had produced Buñuel and had been making films since 1896, no Spanish film for almost six decades – excluding always *Las Hurdes* and some films of the Civil War period made by foreigners – merited serious critical attention. With the Franco regime, severe censorship and ideological pressures were added to apparent artistic bankruptcy. The early fifties however saw the beginning of a revival. This was largely due to the conscious effort of Juan Antonio Bardem (born 1922) and Luis Garcia Berlanga (born 1921) and to the success of their collaboration on *Benvenido, Mr Marshall* (1952) a satirical comedy about the reaction of a little village to the unexpected prosperity brought to it by Marshall Aid. Bardem wrote in 1955: 'After sixty years the Spanish cinema is politically ineffective, socially false, intellectually abysmal, aesthetically null, industrially bankrupt. Now we wish to struggle for a national cinema with love, sincerity and honour.' Bardem went on to make *Muerte di un ciclista* (1955) and *Calle mayor* (1956). Berlanga, working most successfully in a style of extreme black comedy, owing very much to Buñuel, made *Placido* (1962) and *El verdugo* (1964).

In 1955 the Spanish cinema took heart from the big commercial success of *Marcellino Pan y Vino*, a clever mixture of comedy, pathos and religion, directed by Ladislao Vajda, the expatriate son of the Hungarian Laszlo Vajda who had written Pabst's best films of the late twenties and early thirties. The end of the fifties saw the debut of a group of young Spanish directors of whom the most interesting was outstandingly Carlos Saura (born 1932). Saura's first film, *Los golfos* (1960) was a study of young delinquents, strongly influenced by neo-realism; *La caza* (1966) was more adventurous, a symbolic denunciation of Spanish society through the device of a hunting party. The Italian director Mario Ferreri (born 1928) discovered an entirely Spanish vein of black comedy in *El cochecito* (1959), the story of an old gentleman who is sound-limbed, but desires a wheelchair like the rest of his old friends.

Greece also revealed a new generation of film-makers, though the promise indicated by the first works of George Tzavellas, the American-trained Greg Talas, Nikos Kondouros and above all Michael Cacoyannis (born 1922) was not sustained after the fifties. Cacoyannis, who had trained with the British documentary group in London during the war, and whose best films were *Windfall in Athens* (1953), *Stella* (1954) and *The Girl in Black* (1957) nevertheless enjoyed a considerable success in the next decade with the ebullient Greco-American production *Zorba the Greek* (1966).

Such then were a few of the artists – and there were many lesser ones also – who appeared on the international scene out of national cinemas which had hitherto barely crossed their own borders. But apart from the enrichment of cinematic experience due to these new personal influences, together with a rediscovery and revaluation by the young of the cinema's past culture, another revolution was being effected in the medium, largely as a result of the new techniques adopted in the commercial cinema in the fight with television.

Suddenly, it became clear that the huge, wide screens made the old styles of rapid, rhythmic editing an obtrusive, awkward process. The kind of montage sequence Eisenstein had used with such striking effect in *October* was unthinkable on the Cinerama screen, or even on CinemaScope. The immediate reaction was fear that the cinema's basic tool had been taken away from it. Lewis Milestone mourned that the director 'is forced to throw away the "screen" for the "stage" technique. He loses the use of the close-up, the rhythmic cutting, and many other advantages of the "old" for the gain of width of the "new".' Others perceived however that the gain might be more than width; and that the particular kind of montage cinema that had been derived from Griffith and Eisenstein represented only one, not the only, approach to cinema. King Vidor wrote that 'the director was always conscious in the older methods of having to eliminate much of the benefit to either side of the aperture that he could not bring into his camera range'. With remarkable perception the veteran Henry King, one of the great masters of the silent montage style, whose work had been an important model for the Soviets, wrote:

This lens enables the director . . . for the first time to show on the screen cause and effect in the same shot, whereas before we used to have to cut from cause to effect in a story, which in a great measure slowed down the pace and prevented the actors from playing long scenes and really feeling the characterisations, as they do on the stage . . . We need fewer camera set-ups with this new lens and it brings to the screen a measure of three-dimensional illusion which adds tremendously to the realism of any story we are projecting.*

The classical concept of montage had also been questioned by television technique: directors, unable in the conditions of television to aspire to any very sophisticated montage method, had found other means of producing their dramatic effects.

Henry King's feeling was almost exactly echoed, though rationalised in more sophisticated terms, three or four years later by André Bazin (1918–58) in a series of extremely influential critical writings, published in collected form as *Que'est-ce que le Cinéma?* (Paris, 1958). Bazin questioned the kind of cinema in which

> The story was told by a succession of shots, which varied very little in number (around six hundred per film). The characteristic technique of this type of narrative was cross-cutting, which, in a dialogue for instance, consists of alternate shots of either speaker according to the logic of the text.

He expressed his mistrust of the manipulations of editing:

> When the essence of an event is dependent on the simultaneous presence of two or more factors in the action, cutting is forbidden.

Tracing a historical tradition of directors who had rejected the montage principle, he had especial praise for Murnau and for Stroheim, in whose films

> reality admits its meaning like a suspect who is being grilled by an indefatigable police inspector. The principle of his direction, a simple one, is to look at the world from so close and with such insistence that it ends up by revealing its cruelty and its ugliness. One can well imagine, in theory, a Stroheim film composed of a single shot, which would be as long and as close up as one liked.

*These statements were all made in answer to a questionnaire on *The Big Screens*, published in *Sight and Sound*, Spring 1955.

In the thirties Renoir had developed the travelling camera, and composition in depth, which had enabled him to employ long takes in preference to classical montage. Renoir' had written after *La Grande Illusion*:

> The longer I work in my profession, the more I am drawn to *mise-en-scène* in depth in relation to the screen: the more I do that, the more I am able to avoid the confrontation of two actors who stand like good boys in front of the camera as if they were at the photographer's.

Especially Bazin admired the *mise-en-scène* of Orson Welles and William Wyler:

> The reputation of *Citizen Kane* is no exaggeration. Thanks to composition in depth, whole scenes are filmed in a single shot (a device known as the sequence-shot), sometimes even without the camera moving. The dramatic effects which used to depend on the editing are all obtained here by the movements of the actors within a chosen framing. Welles did not of course 'invent' composition in depth, any more than Griffith did the close-up . . .

As further authority for the employment of *mise-en-scène* in preference to *montage* Bazin might have pointed to the (then) recent work of Buñuel, or to Hitchcock's famous ten-minute take in *Rope*.

Bazin was a founder and editor of *Cahiers du Cinéma*, a magazine whose influence was to prove crucial to the subsequent development of French cinema. Along with the rejection of the Pudovkin notion that 'film art begins when the director begins to combine and join together the various pieces of the film', the writers of *Cahiers* pleaded for the *authority* of the director (as early as 1948 a young critic, Alexandre Astruc, had preached the ideal of 'Le Caméra Stylo', arguing that the cinema should be a means of expression as personal, 'as supple and subtle as the written word'.). The militancy of *Cahiers* was most strongly reflected in its *politique des auteurs*, which raised a pantheon of directors – mostly in the Hollywood cinema – whose work was to be admired unquestioningly.

The position of *Cahiers* was often extreme; but its critics – Claude Chabrol, François Truffaut, Jean-Luc Godard, Eric Rohmer, Jacques Doniol-Valcroze – gave substance to their ideals by becoming film-makers themselves. They were encouraged in their undertaking by the very great success of the twenty-eight-year-old Roger Vadim's first film, *Et Dieu créa la femme* (1956) which launched a new sex image in Brigitte Bardot, and the more modest commercial but sizeable critical success of a twenty-five-year-old former assistant of Robert Bresson, Louis Malle, with *Ascenseur pour l'échafaud* (1957). Alexander Astruc (born 1923) had already made the transition from critic to director (*Le Rideau cramoisi*, 1952; *Les Mauvaises rencontres*, 1954). The possibility of independent film-making had been indicated also by the work of Jean-Pierre Melville (born 1917), a determined individualist who had made a series of outstanding films outside the commercial cinema, and eventually declared his allegiance to the classic Hollywood school in *Bob le flambeur* (1956).*

François Truffaut made a short, *Les Mistons* (1958), which was a tribute to Lumière, Méliès and all the cinema culture the *Cahiers* generation had lovingly acquired at the daily showings of the Cinémathèque Française, whose director Henri Langlois they acknowledged as their spiritual father. Chabrol made a feature, *Le Beau Serge* (1959), which was shortly followed by Truffaut's *Les Quatre Cents Coups* (1959). At the Cannes Festival of 1959 France walked off with all the major prizes, won with films by new directors: the Grand Prix to Marcel Camus' *Orfeu Negro*; the Direction Prize to *Les Quatre Cents Coups*; the International Critics' Prize to Alain Resnais' *Hiroshima mon amour*. Although Resnais was already well known as a director of short films, while Marcel Camus was almost forty and neither belonged directly to the *Cahiers* group, all the new directors were lumped together under the journalists' handy formula of *nouvelle vague*.

*Melville has revealed the immense effect made upon him by *Citizen Kane* which he saw innumerable times at the Classic Cinema, Baker Street, whilst serving in London as a member of the Free French forces during the war.

There was a certain justice in linking them in this way, however; they had all found their chance to make feature films in the same mood and moment – an atmosphere which permitted no less than sixty-seven new directors to make their first feature films in the course of the next two years. They all showed a greater or less determination to break with the economic, aesthetic and thematic conventions of the old commercial cinema, shooting in the streets, with hand-held cameras, employing improvisational acting, working cheaply and off the cuff, all paying homage to the recently deceased Bazin, all endeavouring to make the film an author's medium.

The Vadim-Bardot films which followed *Et Dieu créa la femme* were immense box-office successes, as were the first films of the *Cahiers* group, but in particular Jean-Luc Godard's *A bout de souffle* (1959) which at once introduced an altogether new style of film-making, and characters which seemed to chime with the mood of the times. The film's hero, Jean-Paul Belmondo, was one of a group of new stars of the *nouvelle vague* who were as different from the old idols as their films were from the conventional commercial product. Distributors were enthusiastic to back work by new directors. Of the 24 debutants in 1959 and the 43 in 1960 few got beyond their first film (and some did not even finish that); but the survivors were to shape the French cinema in the coming decade: Godard, Truffaut, Chabrol, Jean-Pierre Mocky, Jean-Daniel Pollet, Eric Rohmer, Jacques Doniol-Valcroze, Gabriel Albicocco, Henri Colpi, Jacques Demy, Armand Gatti, Claude Lelouch, Gerard Oury, who as a successful director of big commercial comedies only belongs by chronological accident with the *nouvelle vague*. Other directors – Agnès Varda, the wife of Demy, and Jacques Rivette – were to make their feature debuts in the course of the next year or so.

Godard (born 1930) was clearly the most innovatory of all the *nouvelle vague*. From his first film he audaciously rejected every convention of the narrative film, using jump-cuts to abridge a shot or a scene that bored him, or introducing philosophical dissertation regardless of the state of the action. In *A bout de souffle* he paid homage to the American gangster film. *Le Petit Soldat* (1960), Godard's statement on the Algerian war, was so strongly committed in its position that it was banned. *Vivre sa vie* (1962) was a series of impressions of a young prostitute, interspersed with sociological documentation. In *Les Carabiniers* (1963) Godard returned to the theme of war, but this time in the form of an allegory, a kind of modern military pilgrim's progress. Up to *Alphaville* and *Pierrot le fou* (both 1965) Godard's films often looked like stylistic firework displays; but from *Deux ou trois choses que je sais d'elle* (1966) his films become more and more aggressive in their political orientation, their faith in Chinese communism and despair in the U.S.-dominated decadence of the capitalist West. He used symbols, slogans, philosophical discourse, jokes, calligraphic tricks and lessons absorbed from Vertov and the agit-propaganda of the early Soviet revolution. By the end of the sixties, Godard had rejected narrative structure altogether, and with it the whole machinery of the commercial cinema, making his films on 16 mm and 8 mm.

Almost the entire *oeuvre* of Claude Chabrol (born 1930)
was a homage to Alfred Hitchcock, though at the same time
marked by his very personal bucolic humour. After *Le
Beau Serge* and *Les Cousins* (1959) he seemed for a while the
least interesting of the new French directors, with a string
of indifferent thrillers to his credit; but *Les Biches* (1967)
was a startling return to form, which was sustained with
La Femme infidèle (1969), *Que la bête meurt* (1969), *Le Boucher*
(1970) and *La Rupture* (1970)–all brilliantly stylish psychological studies of murder and its reverberations in families
and communities.

François Truffaut (born 1932), whose work showed more consistency, seemed to owe much more to Renoir than to Hitchcock (about whom both Truffaut and Chabrol had written books). His work revealed a quality of unsentimental tenderness and a special flavour of humour, seen most strongly in the trilogy of films he made about the character 'Antoine Doinel' (played by the actor Jean-Pierre Léaud) as he grew from the childhood of *Les Quatre Cents Coups* to manhood in *Baisers volés*, 1968 and *Domicile Conjugale* (1970); and in *L'Enfant sauvage* (1970). Truffaut's biggest success came however with *Jules et Jim* (1961). In England he made *Fahrenheit 451* (1966), from the novel by Ray Bradbury.

The output of Alain Resnais (born 1922) was much slighter than these younger directors – only five features in twelve years. He began his career as a director of outstanding documentary films, notably *Nuit et Brouillard* (1956) a horrific revisiting of Auschwitz. To a greater or less degree all his feature films – *Hiroshima mon amour* (1959), *L'Année dernière à Marienbad* (1961), *Muriel* (1963), *La Guerre est finie* (1966) and *Je t'aime, je t'aime* (1970) were experiments with memory and time.

The striking feature of this generation of the sixties was their individuality: Philippe de Broca (born 1933) with quirky, ironic vaudevilles like *Les Jeux de l'amour* (1960) and *Le Farceur* (1962); Jacques Demy (born 1931) with the bitter-sweet nostalgia of *Lola* (1961) and *Les Parapluies de Cherbourg* (1963); his wife, Agnès Varda (born 1928) ranging from the cool and elegant portrait of *Cléo de 5 à 7* (1962) to the freewheeling improvisations of *Lion's Love* (1969), made in decaying Hollywood; Jean-Pierre Mocky (born 1929), specialising in the iconoclastic vulgarity of *Snobs* (1962) or *Les Vierges* (1963); Eric Rohmer (*Le Signe du lion*, 1959; *La Collectioneuse*, 1967; *Ma nuit chez Maud*, 1969; *Le Genou de Claire*, 1971), Jacques Doniol-Valcroze (*L'Eau à la bouche*, 1960) and Jacques Rivette (*Paris nous appartient*, 1960; *La Religieuse*, 1965; *L'Amour Fou*, 1968) with small but highly personal and valued *oeuvres*. Claude Lelouch enjoyed an enormous international success with the sentimental kitsch of *Un Homme et une femme* (1966), whose showy technical effects had a singularly unfortunate effect upon the

work of innumerable impressionable young film-makers all over the world in the years that followed.

Not all the new directors were young. Georges Franju (born 1912) had been a co-founder with Henri Langlois of the Cinémathèque Française in 1934. From 1949 he made a series of distinguished documentaries, including *Le Sang des bêtes*, 1949; *Hôtel des Invalides* (1952; though commissioned by the Quai d'Orsay it turned out to be a violent denunciation of war and the military mind) and a touching tribute to *Le Grand Méliès* (1952). As a director of features he displayed a style that was at once classical and highly personal, an ability to combine great elegance with Méliès' magic and an expressionist *frisson*. *La Tête contre les murs* (1958) was the nightmare drama of a man mistakenly held in a lunatic asylum; *Les Yeux sans visage* (1960) was a gothic horror story; *Thérèse Desqueyroux* (1962) was a finely conceived adaptation of Mauriac's novel; while Franju's adaptation of *Thomas l'imposteur* (1965) was authentically Cocteauesque – as sincere a homage to a fellow film-maker as *Judex* (1964), an exquisite remaking of Feuillade's most famous serial.

The documentarists of the *nouvelle vague* – notably Jean Rouch and Chris Marker – found their watch-cry, in the early sixties, in '*cinéma-vérité*.' They returned to the principles of Dziga Vertov, the insistence that the camera should record life as it is found, without manipulation, without interposition of the artist's personality. Vertov's ideals seemed now at least more practicable with the technical developments in cameras and recording apparatus of the fifties. Concurrently with the development of the transistor, much more portable sound and photographic equipment had been developed, notably the Swiss Nagra tape recorder and the French Coutant camera. With highly sensitive film stock and easily portable light sources, film-makers found that they could shoot in places and under conditions that would have previously been impossible.

The flaw, of course, in the purist ideal of *cinéma-vérité*, as in Vertov's Kino-Eye, is that the camera *always* lies. As soon as there is any relationship between the subject and the camera, there is artifice. As soon as the angle of the camera is selected, as soon as the film and the sound are cut and edited, as soon as one piece of film material is juxtaposed with another, there must be an element of subjective interpretation. The *vérité* becomes the truth of the artist: there is no such thing as absolute truth, revealed only to the cine camera.

The American documentarists, led by Richard Leacock (see page 313) represented one school of *cinéma-vérité*; Rouch and Marker another. Jean Rouch (born 1917) began by using the camera as an ethnographical tool, and made a series of fine anthropological studies of primitive peoples between 1947 and 1959. From 1961 and *La Pyramide humaine* he turned his attention to Western society with a series of socio-psychological *enquêtes* and '*psychodrames*' – *Chronique d'un été* (1961), *La Punition* (1963), *Rose et Landry* (1963) and *Petit à petit* (1970), in which he used comedy to study the collision of a developing black society and a decaying white one. Chris Marker (born 1921) was too conscious an artist ever to claim any very strong adherence to the idea of *cinéma-vérité*: image and sound, content and form were constructed with unobtrusive sophistication in his films all of which revealed a passionately insatiable curiosity, and the ability to capture vivid impressions of a particular place and time as reflected by his highly individual and sensitive personality. His career began as co-director with Alain Resnais on *Les Statues meurent aussi* (1952) a study of primitive art which represented so vigorous an attack on decadent colonialist attitudes that it was promptly banned by the French censorship. After a series of shorts – *Dimanche à Pekin* (1956), *Lettre de Sibérie* (1958), *Description d'un combat* (1960), *Cuba, si!* (1961) he made the full-length *Le Joli Mai* (1963), a record of the life and thought of some of the people who were in Paris in the eventful month of May 1962 when the Evian agreement was signed, and the Madison was introduced to Paris. In the fictional short *La Jetée* (1963) Marker surprisingly departed from his documentary path to make a haunting fantasy exploration of time.

Most of the French directors, at least in 1959–60, revealed a primary preoccupation with form. The spirit which evinced itself in the British cinema a year or so earlier had a primary concern with content. Again the new movement had begun with a magazine, *Sequence*, which produced fourteen issues, against hopeless economic odds, between 1947 and 1952. It began as an Oxford university magazine. Its editors, Lindsay Anderson and Gavin Lambert, and later Karel Reisz and Penelope Houston, vigorously attacked the British cinema in which they felt 'fidelity to background, good acting, or sensitive direction palliated rather than atoned for sentimental falsification of character and atmosphere'. They found that British cinema persistently ignored regional cultures, and was dedicated to an image of a pre-1914 bourgeoisie:

> For the failure of Britain to achieve, in fifty years of picture making, any considerable tradition of cinema – at least as far as fictional films go – many and varied

reasons have been suggested. One seldom stressed but surely among the most relevant, is the influence of Class. The British commercial cinema has been a bourgeois rather than a revolutionary growth; and it is not a middle-class trait to examine oneself with the strictest objectivity, or to be able to represent higher or lower levels of society with sympathy and respect – limitations which account for the ultimate failure of even so exceptional an attempt as *Brief Encounter*. Whether from lack of ability among our film-makers or from fear of provoking controversy, it has been the function of the working-classes to provide 'comic relief' to the sufferings of their social superiors, or to nip in here and there with Dramatic Cameos; at any rate to support self-consciously rather than spontaneously to pre-figure . . .

During *Sequence*'s lifetime the Crown Film Unit was closed down; and with it the British cinema's last hold on reality seemed gone. Even before that, though, the heart seemed to have gone out of documentary. It seemed as if the particular tasks to which the Grierson school had applied themselves were done. 'In the best days', wrote Dilys Powell, 'the British documentary was an attacking cinema; something, it said again and again, had got to be done. We have the Welfare State – and the belligerent documentary-makers have lost their subject. It is no longer quite so obvious that something has got to be done in this country'.

It was no longer quite so obvious, perhaps, because the problems and disquiet were of a different order now. The sense of disorientation of the post-war generation was most articulately expressed in John Osborne's *Look Back in Anger*:

I suppose people of our generation aren't able to die for good causes any longer. We had all that done for us, in the thirties and forties, when we were still kids. There aren't any good, brave causes left. If the big bang does come, and we all get killed off, it won't be in aid of the old-fashioned grand design, it will just be for the Brave New Nothing-very-much thank-you. About as inglorious as stepping in front of a bus . . .

A new school of novelists, many of them provincial in origins and in themes, had already given expression to the sense of disillusion. A remarkable renaissance in the British theatre can be dated from the first production of *Look Back in Anger* in May 1956. The success this play brought to the Royal Court Theatre opened the way for new directors, new plays, new modes of drama, a new recognition of the importance and the problems of the lives of ordinary people, in a theatre which had traditionally become as far removed from everyday reality as was the cinema of which *Sequence* complained.

The renaissance in the cinema actually predated *Look Back in Anger* by a few months. In February 1956 the first of a series of programmes called collectively 'Free Cinema'

'Free Cinema'. Programme of the third show, which included Lindsay Anderson's *Every Day Except Christmas*, Britain, 1957. Even the handwriting used in the programme design is Anderson's own.

was presented at the National Film Theatre. Alongside a short story film *Together* by an Italian, Lorenza Mazetti, the programme included two documentaries, both made on derisory budgets: *O Dreamland*, in which Lindsay Anderson assaulted the spiritual and cultural impoverishment of the British working class, through impressions of a seaside amusement park; and *Momma Don't Allow* in which Karel Reisz and Tony Richardson – both making their first film – looked at dancers in a North London jazz club. The aggressive, manifesto manner of the programme notes was clearly the voice of *Sequence*, more specifically of Lindsay Anderson who was the prime inspiration behind 'Free Cinema'. Of the first programme Anderson wrote:

> The film-makers of 'Free Cinema' prefer to call their work 'free' rather than 'experimental'. It is neither introverted nor esoteric. Nor is the concern primarily with technique. These films are free in the sense that their statements are entirely personal. Though their moods and subjects differ, the concern of each of them is with some aspect of life as it is lived in this country today . . .
> Implicit in our attitudes is a belief in freedom, in the importance of people and in the significance of the everyday.

After this Karel Reisz persuaded the Ford Motor Company to embark on a programme of prestige sponsorship, and himself directed *We Are the Lambeth Boys* (1958), an intimate, human study of the teenagers of a South London youth club, while Lindsay Anderson made *Every Day Except Christmas* (1959), about the work of Covent Garden fruit and vegetable market. The two films together marked a significant revival and humanisation of British documentary. Now clearly looking towards the feature cinema, the Free Cinema programme which introduced Anderson's film declared:

> This programme is not put before you as an achievement but as an aim. We ask you to view it not as critics, nor as a diversion, but in direct relation to a British cinema still obstinately class-bound, still rejecting the

stimulus of contemporary life, as well as the responsibility to criticise; still reflecting a metropolitan, Southern English culture which excludes the rich diversity of tradition and personality which is the whole of Britain.

As it happened the first step in the British cinema's rebirth and return to reality was taken within the established industry, when Jack Clayton (born 1921), formerly a film editor, directed an adaptation of John Braine's novel *Room at the Top* (1959). Only a few weeks afterwards Tony Richardson's adaptation of *Look Back in Anger* (which he had also directed on the stage) was released. Karel Reisz's first film was an adaptation of Alan Sillitoe's novel *Saturday Night and Sunday Morning* (1961). Lindsay Anderson's *This Sporting Life* (1963), from a novel by David Storey with whom Anderson was later to have a fruitful association in

Tony Richardson: *Look Back in Anger*. Britain, 1958. Mary Ure, Richard Burton, Alan Bates.

the theatre, followed in 1962. In this way, borrowing the titles and subjects of successful new novels and the new drama, the British cinema treated – for the first time it seemed – subjects of authentic regional and working class life. These first films were a success; and inevitably there was a rush to imitate them. For a year or so practically every director took his turn at what were dubbed 'kitchen sink' films; but for all the cheapening of the new spirit into a commercial *genre*, the revolution had been accomplished.

Clearly the most gifted and the most influential of the whole generation was Lindsay Anderson (born 1923) whose activities in the sixties were divided between cinema and theatre. He waited seven years before making his second feature film, *If . . .* (1963) in which the humanist preoccupation and the anger of *This Sporting Life* and the earlier short films were if anything intensified; but his method had progressed from literal realism to an epic (in the Brechtian sense of the word) and poetic style, which, in a narrative set in an English public school, moved easily and im-

Jack Clayton:
Room at the Top.
Britain, 1959.
Simone
Signoret,
Laurence
Harvey.

perceptibly from direct and recognisable reality to fantasy. The short films he made between the features – *One, Two, Three* (1967) and *The Singing Lesson* (both in Poland) and *The White Bus* (1967) – as well as much of his theatre work of the same period looked in retrospect like preparation for *If . . .*

Tony Richardson's output after *Look Back in Anger* was large and erratic, revealing his fearlessness in experimenting with new subjects and new styles. From an organisational point of view Richardson (born 1928) was of immense importance to the new cinema. Indeed, the British renaissance of the early sixties might very well not have been achieved at all but for his organising genius, which was also mainly responsible for the creation and survival of the Royal Court Theatre's New English Stage Company, and later helped bring to fruition the projects of other young film-makers – including Kevin Brownlow's *It Happened Here* (1966) and Kenneth Loach's *Kes* (1969). English subjects seemed to suit Richardson's own temperament best. None of his foreign-made films – *Sanctuary* (1961) and an inventive adaptation of Evelyn Waugh's *The Loved One*

(1965) in America or *Mademoiselle* (1966) and *Sailor from Gibraltar* (1966) in France – seemed altogether successful. His best work was done in Britain: intelligent adaptations of John Osborne's *The Entertainer* (1960), Shelagh Delaney's *A Taste of Honey* (1961), Alan Sillitoe's *The Loneliness of the Long Distance Runner* (1963), and *Tom Jones* (1963) whose immense and sustained verve brought Richardson a very considerable box office success. In 1968 he turned to spectacular historical reconstruction, in *The Charge of the Light Brigade*.

Karel Reisz and Jack Clayton, after their first successes, seemed alike to suffer from their too limited outputs, and the consequent inhibiting feeling that the maximum was staked on each new film they made. Reisz (born in Czechoslovakia in 1926) made a rather unexpected adaptation of a hoary theatre thriller, *Night Must Fall* (1963); an excellent adaptation of David Mercer's *Morgan – a suitable case for treatment* (1966) and *Isadora* (1968), which was never seen in the director's original version, having been extensively cut at the request of the distributors. Clayton (born 1921) directed an elegant atmospheric adaptation of Henry James's *The Turn of the Screw*, *The Innocents* (1962) and disappointing adaptations of two novels *The Pumpkin Eater* (1963) and *Our Mother's House* (1967).

Other directors were given chances to make their first films following the success of this English 'New Wave'. John Schlesinger (born 1926), coming from television, was nearest in feeling to the Free Cinema group in *A Kind of Loving* (1962) from a novel by Stan Barstow, and *Billy Liar* (1963), from a Willis Hall and Keith Waterhouse play which had been directed on stage by Lindsay Anderson. *Darling* (1965) was an attempt to isolate a different kind of *malaise* of the sixties, personified by an aspiring model girl. After a critical failure with *Far From the Madding Crowd* (1967) Schlesinger went to America to make what proved to be a major international success, *Midnight Cowboy* (1970); but returned to Britain for *Sunday, Bloody Sunday* (1971). Bryan Forbes (born 1926), an actor turned screenwriter, proved to be a versatile commercial director; and from 1969 became for a year or so a powerful political force in the industry as production chief of Associated British Pictures. A talented stage director, Peter Brook (born 1925) proved uneven as a film director, his best works being *Moderato Cantabile* (1960), made in France in the context of the *nouvelle vague*, and *Lord of the Flies* (1963), from the allegorical novel by William Golding.

For some years after the Hollywood blacklist, Joseph Losey worked in England under pseudonyms, until in 1956 the producer Leon Clore – who had given important practical support to all the original Free Cinema group, and produced *Every Day Except Christmas* and *We Are the Lambeth Boys* – employed him in his own name as director of the thriller *Time Without Pity*. From this point Losey resumed the career that had begun so promisingly in the United States with *The Boy With Green Hair* (1948), *The Lawless* (1949) and *The Prowler* (1951). Despite individual setbacks –

Modesty Blaise (1966), *Boom* (1968), *Secret Ceremony* (1968) and *Figures in a Landscape* (1970) were not critical successes; and *Eva* (1962), made in France, was distributed only in a mutilated form – Losey made some of the most distinguished British films of the decade: *The Servant* (1963), *King and Country* (1964), *Accident* (1967), and *The Go-Between* (1971).

Richard Lester (born 1932), a Canadian, created a new and personal style of comedy out of his association as a television director with Spike Milligan and the television 'Goon' shows and later, in films, with the Beatles, who starred in *A Hard Day's Night* (1964) and *Help!* (1965). His outstanding success was *The Knack* (1965), from the play by Ann Jellicoe, which won the Grand Prix at the Cannes Festival. To the success of Lester's first films and the consequent rush to imitate them must be credited a period of reaction in the British cinema in the mid-sixties, co-

John Schlesinger: *Midnight Cowboy*. U.S.A., 1969. Jon Voight, Dustin Hoffman.

Joseph Losey: *King and Country*. Britain, 1964. Vivian Matalon, Tom Courtenay.
Joseph Losey: *The Go-Between*. Britain, 1971. Dominic Guard, Margaret Leighton, Julie Christie.

incident with the myth, created by the ad-men and Time-Life, of a new, 'Swinging Britain' culture. Writing in 1968, the present writer summed up the genre which resulted* and the subsequent disillusion:

> ... a style of cinema had been developed appropriate to the popular mythology. The influences which produced it were various: the popularisation (!) of pop art; the graphic adventures of the colour supplements and TV commercials; the arrival of new directors from television who had rediscovered the devices which Méliès had used with charm and discretion but which they wielded like bludgeons; uncritical and unassimilated admirations for Godard; the slackened reins of censorship; the wilder excesses of Fellini; the post-Resnais taste for mystification; self-confidence bred by the export market in British pop-music and pop-fashions; sheer bedazzlement in the end with the whole swinging vision of a Britain of boutiques and Beatles and dolly girls and Carnaby Street. Somewhere along the way the baleful influence of Claude Lelouch was added to the rest. The results – the disregard of form and structure, the visual extravagance, the devices used like purple phrases and exclamation marks in schoolgirl prose, the tourist fantasies of a colour-supplement Britain – were predictable more often than they were exhilarating.
>
> For a time all went well. Not all the films were bad, and there were enough commercial successes – the Beatles films, *Darling*, *Georgy Girl*, *Blow-up* – to convince producers in the States that here was a goldmine, an endless supply of new talent and ideas. For a while it seemed that every young British television director or theatre director with a success to his credit, or even without, was wooed to make films with American money. Perhaps at no time in the remembered history of the cinema had the money-men been so receptive to

*Some archetypes were Peter Watkin's *Privilege* (1967), Clive Donner's *What's New, Pussycat* (1965), Silvio Narizzano's *Georgy Girl* (1966), Desmond Davis's *Smashing Time* (1967).

new people and new ideas. It was a brief Utopia. Inevitably distributors' enthusiasm outran their judgment. Inevitably a lot of the new talent proved no
talent at all. More than one American company must
be paying the price of the adventure with an expensive
little cache of unmentionable films that have still to
see the light of day and will look pretty jaded if they
ever do.

The trouble is that now the cost is being passed on in
terms of greater caution on the part of the distributors,
a mass withdrawal from adventure . . .*

A few directors of obvious worth nevertheless emerged
in this period and survived it: Kenneth Loach (*Poor Cow*,
1967; *Kes*, 1969; *Family Life*, 1971), John Boorman (*Point
Blank*, 1967 and *Hell in the Pacific*, 1968, in America; *Leo the
Last*, 1970, in Britain), Jack Gold (*The Bofors Gun*, 1968, *The
Reckoning*, 1969), Kevin Billington (*Interlude*, 1968), Waris
Hussein (*A Touch of Love*, 1969) all came from television.
Anthony Harvey was for some years a distinguished film
editor before making *Dutchman* (1966), a low-budget adaptation of LeRoi Jones' play, after which he directed a big and
successful prestige production, *The Lion in Winter* (1968).
An actor very much associated with the renascence of
1958–60, Albert Finney directed a sensitive and mature
first film, *Charlie Bubbles* (1967). In Michael Reeves (1944–69)
the British cinema lost a young director of outstanding
promise. His three low-budget, uncompromisingly commercial films—*Sorelle di Satana* (Italy, 1965), *The Sorcerers*
(1967) and *Witchfinder General* (1968) – revealed a gift, rare
among British directors, of using cinema in Astruc's sense
of *caméra-stylo*.

In Italy, as we have seen, the pure neo-realist impulse did
not long outlast the forties. The hardship and poverty
which the neo-realists characteristically depicted was no
longer interesting to an Italy on the eve of an economic
miracle. Moreover the success of the films had developed,
in despite of neo-realism's most cherished ideals, a new

Sight and Sound, Winter 1968–9.

generation of big international stars – Sophia Loren, Gina Lollobrigida, Marcello Mastroianni, Anna Magnani, and De Sica himself. In particular the success of the Italian films in the United States and the investment of American money in the Italian industry produced commercialised and degraded imitations of neo-realism, which used Roman or Neapolitan backstreets and rural Italy as an arena for mildly risqué comedy, in which De Sica might play a policeman and Lollobrigida or Loren the nubile golden-hearted more-or-less whore. Neo-realism met the *telefono bianco*.

With the commercial revival came a renewal of the favourite old genres. The spectacle films which had always fascinated Italy now were made in Italo-American versions with American stars. Later, in the sixties American stars and directors (or Italian actors and directors given Anglo-Saxon names) were exploited in Italian adaptations of the old-style Hollywood horror genre, the best of them made by Mario Bava (born 1914), and the 'spaghetti westerns' whose most successful director was Sergio Leone (born 1921).

Nevertheless in the later fifties new directors were starting to develop the neo-realist experience in new individual directions. The first clear evidence of a new generation was the appearance of Federico Fellini (born 1920). Fellini had been a newspaper cartoonist before working as a writer on some of the most notable early neo-realist films, including *Roma, città aperta*, and his first two films oddly revealed the influence of both experiences: *Luci del varietà* (1951) was a comic and melancholy account of the life of a tatty touring revue company; and *Lo sciecco bianco* (1952), a comedy about the making of *fumetti* (photographic strip stories).

I vitelloni (1953) was perhaps an even more crucial film, both in Fellini's career and the subsequent development of cinema, than might be supposed from the fashion it set among film-makers in every country of the world, for films about little groups of youths restlessly and purposelessly wandering the streets of provincial towns. Set in Fellini's boyhood Rimini, it was novel in its genuine freedom from plot conventions and its observation of a class then quite new to the cinema, the unsettled bourgeois young, materially secure, but spiritually disoriented.

Federico Fellini:
Satyricon. Italy,
1969. Max Born,
Fanfulla.

Fellini's next film, *La strada* (1954), an artificial morality about travelling circus performers, was a major international success, as all Fellini's films have been since, with the comparative exception of *Il bidone* (1955), a bitter fable about small-time crooks. *Le notte di Cabiria* (1956) like *La strada* starred the director's wife Giulietta Masina, this time as a quixotic prostitute. With *La dolce vita* (1960) Fellini's activities took a new direction: all his films since this have been massive, apocalyptic pageants commenting fiercely, acidly, comically, obliquely upon contemporary society. *La dolce vita* was a fresco of modern Rome; *Otto e mezzo* (1963) was a surreal impression of the loneliness and neurosis of a creative artist in the modern world; *Giulietta degli spiriti* (1965) was another fantasy vision of sixties society; *Fellini-Satyricon* (1969) sought, in a highly decorated adaptation of Petronius, direct reflections of our own days and decadence. Fellini's great gifts as a metteur-en-scène seemed most completely realised in the films he made in the 1970s. *I Clowns* (1970)–a non-narrative essay on circus folk, made modestly for Italian television–was a preliminary exploration of the style of *Roma* (1972), which combined a portrait of the eternal city with nostalgic memories of Fellini's youth in the war and immediate pre-war period. *Roma* built its series of loosely-linked impressionist sequences into a spectacle of sustained and dazzling virtuosity. The film owed much to the resourceful photography of Giuseppe Rotunno, the decoration and costumes of Danilo Donati and the brilliant sound track based upon the musical score of Nino Rota, a veteran and prolific composer of Italian film music.

Michaelangelo Antonioni (born 1912) the other major Italian influence of the fifties and sixties, was a critic on the revue *Cinema*, a documentarist and an assistant to Carné on *Les Visiteurs du soir* before making his first feature film, *Cronaca di un amore* in 1950. This and the films that followed – *I vinti* (1952), a peculiar episode film made in three different countries; *La signora senza camelie* (1953) and *Le amiche* (1955) all dealt with middle-class *malaises*. *Il grido* (1957) returned to a style and to *milieux* much nearer to neo-realism, to tell a story of a man estranged from his wife and wandering the roads of the Po valley.

These films already revealed Antonioni's acute perception of individual sentiments; but only with *L'avventura* (1960) were his characteristic and highly personal style and his particular preoccupation with the fragility and impermanence of the basic human sentiments in a modern world fully realised. These interests were pursued in

Michaelangelo Antonioni: *L'avventura*. Italy, 1960. Monica Vitti.

succeeding films: *La notte* (1961), *L'eclisse* (1962) and *Il deserto rosso* (1964), in which the settings and geographical surroundings were always used to reflect and counterpoint the action; setting up

> a tension between setting and characters, so that what happens seems to be in part conditioned by where it happens. The island search in *L'Avventura*, one of the most brilliantly sustained passages in the whole of modern cinema, gives us his technique at full stretch. Every encounter, every shot of rock and sea and barren terrain, every oblique, edged fragment of dialogue, every intrusion from without . . . pushes forward this exploration of the landscape of the mind. 'I need to follow my characters beyond the moments conventionally considered important', he has said, 'to show them even when everything appears to have been said'.*

In later years Antonioni enlarged the field of his commentary on contemporary society and contemporary sentiment. In Britain he made *Blow-up* (1966) which examined the boredom and unease of the socially and culturally dominant new young. In 1969 he was in America, creating an apocalyptic vision of the rifts and decay in American society, named after the location which provided his most significant arena, *Zabriskie Point*.

Pier Paolo Pasolini (born 1922), a Marxist poet, had worked as a writer with Mauro Bolognini before making *Accattone* (1961). This and *Mamma Roma* (1962) showed strong neo-realist survivals in their treatment of the life of young men doomed by deprived social backgrounds to delinquency. *Ill vangelo secondo Matteo* (1964) was a startling contrast: an attempt to recreate the passion of Christ in naturalistic terms, which incidentally examined the relationships of Marxism and the Catholic Church. In the fable *Uccellacci e Uccellini* (1966) he employed comic allegory to assess the crisis of Italian Marxism. In *Edipo Re* (1967) and *Medea* (1970) he placed his own poetic and visual interpretations on classical stories. In *Teorema* (1968), perhaps

*Penelope Houston: *The Contemporary Cinema* (London, 1963).

his best film, he described the effects of the irruption into a rich bourgeois family of a Christ or devil figure, irresistibly seductive. *Porcile* (1969) was again a political fable, conceived in images of bestiality and cannibalism. Always unpredictable, Pasolini went on to make adaptations of mediaeval story cycles in *Decamerone* (1971) and *I Racconti di Canterbury* (1972).

Visconti seemed to be renewed in the sixties, withdrawing altogether from his neo-realist past to make a series of richly-decorated films of operatic splendour and tone: *Il gattopardo* (from Lampedusa's novel, 1963), *Vaghe stelle dell'Orsa* (1965), *The Damned* (1970), a pageant of the decadence of the Third Reich, and *Death in Venice* (1971). Between, he made a strange, literal, intermittently compelling adaptation of Camus' *L'Etranger*, *Lo Straniero* (1967).

The Italian cinema of the sixties seemed able to accommodate surprisingly varied styles and talents. The films of Ermanno Olmi (born 1931) characteristically observe the working lives of ordinary people, with a mixture of documentary perception and affectionate, warm comic vision. *Il posto* (1961) described the debuts of a Keatonesque innocent into the world of commercial office life; *I fidanzati* (1963), the disruption caused to an engaged couple by the young man's seeking promotion in a different part of Italy; *Un certo giorno* (1970) the stress of executive life; *I ricuperanti* (1970) the conflict between the restrictions of settled life and the freedom of more vagrant existences, as seen in the bizarre occupation of scavengers on the old battlefields of immediately post-war Italy. Francesco Rosi (born 1922) had been an assistant to Visconti before emerging as a director with *La sfida* in 1957. His hard documentary style was seen at its best in *Salvatore Giuliano* (1961) a reconstruction of the life and death of a celebrated Sicilian bandit, *Le mani sulla città* (1963), a vigorous condemnation of speculative building and the corruption in local politics which protects it; and *Il momento della verita* (1965), a story of the behind-the-scenes politics of bull-fighting, made in

Ermanno Olmi:
Il posto. Italy,
1961. Sandro
Panzeri.

Francesco Rosi:
*Salvatore
Giuliano*. Italy,
1961.

Spain. In 1967, in complete contrast to all his previous work, he made a charming, satirical fairy tale, *C'erà una volta*; and in 1970 *Uomini contro*, a highly critical examination of the role of Italy in the First World War. *Il caso Mattei* (1972) was, like *Salvatore Giuliano*, an inquiry into a historic event, this time the mysterious death of a prominent industrialist. Here, however, he combined dramatic reconstruction with actuality interview material. Other talents revealed in the late fifties were Mauro Bolognini (born 1923), Franco Rossi (born 1919), who never repeated the success of his *Amici per la pelle* (1955), Pietro Germi (born 1914) who won international acclaim with his didactic comedy *Divorzio all'italiana* (1962), Elio Petri (born 1929), Valerio Zurlini (born 1926) and the novelist Giuseppe Patroni Griffi (born 1924).

Outstandingly the most interesting new directors to emerge in the sixties was Bernardo Bertolucci (born 1941) whose first film *La commare secca* was made at the age of twenty. *Prima della rivoluzione* (1964) was an original and authentically poetic impression of the political and sentimental education of a middle-class provincial boy. After a rather unsatisfactory tribute to Godard, *Partner* (1969), Bertolucci made a startling recovery with two films of brilliance, *La strategia del Ragno* (1970) and *Il conformista* (1970) both stylish, caustic, highly personal investigations of the Fascist thirties.

An interesting aspect of Italian film-making at this period was the extensive participation of Radiotelevisione Italiana (RAI) in the production of feature films by distin-

Bernardo Bertolucci: *Il conformista*. Italy, 1970. Jean Louis Trintignant.

guished directors. Fellini's *I Clowns* (1970), Bertolucci's *La strategia del Ragno*, Rossellini's *The Acts of the Apostles* (1968) and *Socrate* (1970), Olmi's *I Ricuperanti* (1970), Nelo Risi's *Diary of a Schizophrenic* (1969), Liliana Cavani's first film *Francesco di Assissi* (1969) and first films by the film critics Giovanni Amico (*The Inquiry*, 1970) and Adriano Apra (*Olympia to her Friends*, 1969) were all produced by RAI, often in co-production with foreign television organisations, always with budgets that were sufficient, but modest enough to give their directors freedom from excessive producer supervision. 'Television', wrote Bertolucci, 'has no need to sell tickets. There is a much greater possibility for formal experiment'. Thus film-makers were finding in television opportunities which the commercial cinema seemed rarely able to afford them.

In America, perhaps because of the size and diffusion of cinema activities, there was no clearly defined New Wave as in other countries. Since the forties there had been an identifiable *avant-garde* – people like James Broughton, Marie Mencken, Maya Deren, the precocious Kenneth Anger (born 1930) – but their films, mostly made in 16 mm, mostly deliberately obscure in content, circulated little outside the most advanced film societies, and were only to have a large effect through their direct descendants – the 'underground' cinema, which arrived at its most aggressive and influential period in the middle and late sixties.

There were optimistic attempts to discern a rebirth, or at least a 'movement' in the so-called New York School – a handful of directors who succeeded in making films on location, away from the restrictive methods and conventions of the studios. The origin of the New York School also goes back to the late forties, when Irving Lerner (born 1909) made an ironic short, *Muscle Beach* (1948) and Sidney Meyer (born 1894) directed a story film about a lost child, *The Quiet One* (1948), both works distinguished by a scrupulous documentary vision and an intensely human attitude. Lionel Rogosin (born 1923) produced and directed a horrifying study of alcoholics, *On the Bowery* (1957); and in 1959 explored aspects of *apartheid* in *Come Back Africa*. Shirley

Clarke (born 1925) gave a documentary veracity to her adaptation of Jack Gelber's play *The Connection* (1960). Frank Perry filmed a sentimental story of love between two psychiatric patients in *David and Lisa* (1962).

None of these individual works was as widely influential as the first film of the actor John Cassavetes (born 1929), *Shadows* (1960), or the work of the group which formed around Richard Leacock (born 1921). *Shadows* was created entirely out of improvisational acting by the players; and though still within the technical framework of feature film-making – with the fragmentation of the acting and the method of multiple takes turning improvisation into rehearsal – it did indicate new methods and new potentialities in acting for the screen.* Richard Leacock, born 1921 in London, had been a cameraman on Flaherty's last film,

*Cassavetes was employed in Hollywood to make *Too Late Blues* (1961) and *A Child is. Waiting* (1962), in which the methods he had developed were rather uneasily compromised with more conventional Hollywood techniques. From time to time however he returned to independent, experimental, improvisational productions: *Faces* (1968) and *Husbands* (1970).

Louisiana Story (1948). Moving to television, he made impressive use of the new portable and adaptable photographic and sound equipment which had become available in the late fifties, developing a very individual approach to *cinéma-vérité*. Generally he chose to record events whose outcome was still in doubt – a pianoforte contest (*Susan Starr*, 1963), the agonised wait of a condemned man for the result of his appeal against the death sentence (*The Chair*, 1963), a primary election (*Primary*, 1962) – so that the significance of his actuality record only became fully apparent as the shooting came to an end. The effect was to give the films a tension and suspense which were new to documentary. Later Fred Wiseman (born 1930), a former lawyer, brought cinéma-vérité techniques and critical scrutiny to bear on basic American institutions, in *Titticutt Follies* (1967), *High School* (1968), *Basic Training* (1971), *Law and Order* (1969), *Hospital* (1970) and *Essene* (1972).

With the sixties, the Hollywood feature cinema, for the first time since the rise of Griffith, seemed to have fallen behind. Both in subjects and techniques, the general run of American commercial films looked archaic compared with the work that was coming out of Europe. Hollywood still turned out its comedies of manners, its musicals, its spectacles (bigger and blander than ever), its westerns, its crime thrillers. The new fashions which came and went – for instance the vogue for sexy, sophisticated, quip-filled crime and espionage thrillers on the model of the successful James Bond series – rapidly appeared as tired as the old ones. In production gloss and classic editing styles, the general run of films had changed little since the thirties, apart from the adoption of colour and wide-screen techniques.

A very few Hollywood directors of the fifties and sixties would have been outstanding in any cinema for their talent and originality. The vigour and invention of John Frankenheimer (born 1930) seemed to have been compromised by the end of the sixties in big commercial productions like *Grand Prix* (1966) and *The Fixer* (1969). Stanley Kubrick (born 1928) was a leading photographer before he made a couple of documentary films in the early fifties, which were followed by two efficient, taut dramas, *Killer's Kiss*

(1955) and *The Killing* (1956). *Paths of Glory* (1957), a sardonic anti-war film set in First World War France, established him as a major talent. Kubrick proved himself able to give personality to the traditional spectacle (*Spartacus*, 1959) and to big prestige productions like *Lolita* (1962. In *Dr Strangelove* (1964), *2001: A Space Odyssey* (1968) and *A Clock-*

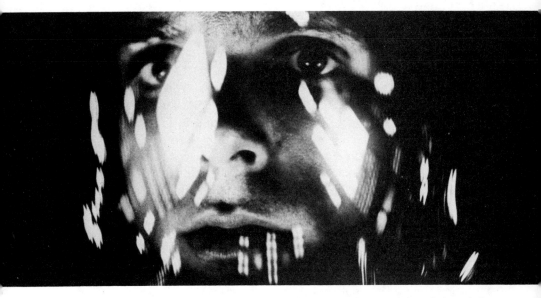

Stanley Kubrick: *2001, A Space Odyssey*. Britain, 1968.

work Orange (1972) Kubrick seemed committed to visions of an apocalyptic near-future, exploring with irony the ultimate implications of political, scientific and social development. In contrast, Roger Corman (born 1926), a director of great competence and panache, has generally preferred the assured independence of low budget productions. Between 1954 and 1964 he made sixty second-feature films, some shot in a matter of a few days (one reputedly in two days). He created his own special genus of comic-gothic horror in a series of free Poe adaptations (*The Fall of the House of Usher*, 1960; *The Raven*, 1963; *The Masque of the Red Death*, 1964), but with rather less limiting budgets made vivid, intelligent films on youth subjects (*The Wild Angels*, 1966; *The Trip*, 1967); and reconstructions of the lives of notorious gangsters, *The St Valentine's Day Massacre* (1967) and *Bloody Mamma* (1970) both of which showed a notable sensitivity to period.

Arthur Penn (born 1922) came from the New York Theatre to direct an account of the life and death of Billy the Kid, *The Left-Handed Gun* (1957). Subsequently he made a group of uneven films, *The Miracle Worker* (1962), *Mickey One* (1964) and *The Chase* (1965) before achieving great success with *Bonnie and Clyde* (1967), which did much to revive the gangster genre and thirties styles in clothes and design throughout a good deal of the cinemagoing world. In *Little Big Man* (1971) he brilliantly adapted Thomas Berger's novel about an Indian hero who has survived the Custer massacre and 121 years of uneasy relations between the red man and the white. The playwright George Axelrod made two admirable comedies, *Lord Love a Duck* (1967) and *The Secret Life of an American Wife* (1968), both of which were welcomed more generously by critical opinion than by the larger public in America and Britain. The erratic Sam Peckinpah (born 1926) acquired a cult reputation (which tended to incite him to excesses of 'artistic' display) with a series of Westerns, among which the most notable were *Major Dundee* (1964) and *The Wild Bunch* (1969). The taste for gratuitous violence evinced in this film was developed still further in Peckinpah's British film, *Straw Dogs* (1971). Mike Nichols (born 1931), an *avante-garde* entertainer in the fifties, emerged as a resourceful director with *Who's Afraid of Virginia Woolf* (1966), the commercially calculated *The Graduate* (1967) and *Carnal Knowledge* (1971), and a much better and more innovatory adaptation of Joseph Heller's best-selling anti-war novel *Catch 22* (1970).

It is hard to know where, geographically, to place Roman Polanski (born 1933) who was an actor in his native Poland, where he made his first experimental shorts and an arresting feature film, *Knife in the Water* (1962). He directed more shorts in France and three features – *Repulsion* (1964), *Cul-de-Sac* (1965), *Dance of the Vampires* (1967), in Britain. Polanski then went to Hollywood to achieve his biggest success with a macabre tale of satanism in contemporary New York, *Rosemary's Baby* (1969). Returning to Britain he made an undistinguished adaptation of *Macbeth* (1971).

Roger Corman: *The Trip*. U.S.A., 1967. Peter Fonda.

Arthur Penn: *Bonnie and Clyde*. U.S.A., 1967. Warren Beatty.

The Japanese cinema industry, dominated by the big
five companies (Daiei, Toei, Toho, Nikkatsu and Shochiku)
reached the peak of its power and confidence in the late
1950s. After that, with the competition of television, production became more aggressively, and defensively, commercial; and the production of work of outstanding artistic
quality dwindled, along with the rise of pure exploitation
films. (By the early seventies, Japan had the largest output
of 'Eroduction' pictures, cheaply-made sex films of short
feature length). The general atmosphere, and the apparent
impossibility of producing serious work within the studio
set-up, resulted in a striking rise of independent production
in the early sixties. New directors emerged from television,
advertising, documentary (notably Susumi Hani and
Hiroshi Teshigahara); others, like Tadashi Imai, Kaneto
Shindo, Nagisa Oshima, Shohei Imamura, Yoshishige
Yoshida and Masahiro Shinoda left the major studios to
work for small independent production units: Yamamoto's
own Yamamoto Productions, Shindo's Kindai Eikyo,
Ogawa Productions, and the Art Theatre Guild, which
moved from distribution to production.

Of the directors who emerged in this climate, the most
interesting was clearly Nagisa Oshima (born 1932), who
made no less than twenty-five films in the years between
1959 and 1969. Very many of Oshima's films are rooted in
contemporary actuality, often current news stories. Thus
Violence at Noon (1966) was about a gang of delinquent
youths; *Death by Hanging* (1968), a mixture of documentary,
fantasy and absurd comedy, was based on the actual case
of a young man, otherwise gentle and sensitive, who raped
and murdered his girl friend; *Boy* (1969), Oshima's best film,
was about the sufferings of the son of a family who lived by
staging automobile accidents and then blackmailing the
unfortunate drivers involved.

An older director, Kaneto Shindo (born 1912) first attracted attention with *The Naked Island* (1961), essentially a
silent film in its techniques, and the savage period drama
Onibaba (1964). Masahiro Shinoda's *Double Suicide* (1969)
turned to traditional historical settings; but other directors, like Oshima and Susumu Hani (*He and She*, 1963) have
preferred urgent and contemporary subjects.

Nagisa Oshima directing *Boy*. Japan, 1969.

Cinema had flourished at a commercial level for many years in Latin America. Production began in Mexico in 1896, in Cuba in 1897, in Argentina and Brazil in 1908, in Chile in 1917. In the peak year of 1950, Mexico's production of feature films reach 118; Brazil's 20, Argentina's 57. On the whole however production was aimed at strictly local markets. Films were produced cheaply and rarely aspired to any artistic quality.

Perhaps a new artistic self-confidence was brought to Latin America by the re-emergence of Luis Buñuel in Mexico in the 1950s. In 1957 *La Casa del Angel* revealed the very individual talent of Leopoldo Torre-Nilsson (born 1924) the son of a veteran Argentine director, Leopoldo Torres Rios (1899–1960), with whom he had co-directed his first feature, *El crimen de Oribe* (1950). His brilliant, mannered and atmospheric tales of a decaying bourgeois society, generally scripted by his wife Beatriz Guido, established him as a major talent, and provided encouragement for a minor new wave in Argentina.

To artistic reassurance was added political necessity. In Cuba, on the example of the Soviet Revolution and Lenin's order of priorities, the first law relating to a cultural-ideological activity promulgated by the Revolutionary Government referred to the cinema. 'El Cine es un arte', the preamble began, challengingly for a country

Leopoldo Torre-
Nilsson: *La
casa del angel.*
Argentina, 1957.
Elsa Daniel.

whose production had for years been largely confined to
sex films. The law of 24 March 1959 set up the Instituto
Cubano del Arte e Industria Cinematograficos (ICAIC)
through which was organised every aspect of cinema
activity – production, distribution and exhibition; export
and import; co-production, publicity, archive and publications. The problems faced were considerable. There was no
tradition of artistic or pedagogical film production. Moreover the new Cuban cinema had to rely for its existence –
apart from official subsidy – upon a population of a mere
seven million, which, culturally speaking, was far from
homogenous. Films had to address the large illiterate rural
population as well as the sophisticated urban audience.
A major asset was the fact that the production of blue
movies before the Revolution had reached the refinement
of Cinemascope and full colour, so that the new cinema
was able to draw on considerable technical expertise and
resources.

Though the new Cuban cinema was necessarily violently nationalistic, it never fell victim to the crippling xenophobic isolationism, or the rigid clichés of 'socialist realism' which from time to time have limited the Soviet cinema. The Cubans are, from geographical and historical circumstances, great cosmopolitans; and their cinema maintained an inquiring acquaintance with the international cinema, and particularly with movements in France and Britain. The young directors of the new cinema came largely from cinema-clubs in which they had acquired a solid foundation of film culture; and many were able to bring cosmopolitan backgrounds – education and training in London, Paris, Rome and New York – to their specifically Cuban tasks. From the start there was a policy of inviting participation from foreign film artists. Peter Brook and Tony Richardson both visited Cuba in the early days; Joris Ivens, Armand Gatti, Roman Karmen and Zavattini all worked on films there.

A large proportion of Cuban production was necessarily geared to direct propaganda and educational requirements; but even the most ferocious agit-prop shorts were made with flair and intelligence; and shorts and documentaries proved a valuable training ground for the new feature directors. The outstanding artist of the new Cuban cinema was clearly Tomás Gutiérrez Alea (born 1928), trained at the Rome Centro Sperimentale, and a director of remarkable versatility, turning with ease from revolutionary epic (*Historias de la revolucion*, 1960) to sophisticated comedy in *Las Doce sillas* (1962) and *Muerte de un burocrata* (1965), a truly classic black comedy, full of allusions and *homages* to all Alea's favourite film-makers, from Laurel and Hardy to Buñuel. *Memorias de subsedarollo* (1969) employed a different kind of humour in its treatment of a misfit, a man left over, like some prehistoric monster, from the old pre-revolutionary bourgeoisie. Still younger directors of the new Cuban cinema included Humberto Solas (born 1943) who made an auspicious feature debut with *Lucia* (1969) and Manuel Octavio Gomez (born 1939) whose *La primera carga al machete* (1969) was a brilliant if self-conscious exercise in style, a description of a Cuban rebellion of a hundred years before, done in the visual manner of early photo-

Tomás Gutiérrez Alea: *Muerte de un burocrata*. Cuba, 1969.

Manuel Octavio Gomez: *La primera carga al machete*. Cuba, 1969.

graphy. Gomez followed this film with *Las Dias del Agua* about a true incident in the 1930s when a peasant woman evinced miraculous healing powers.

In Brazil the focus of the *Cinema Nôvo* was from the start Glauber Rocha (born 1939). His critical writings, and in particular a history of Brazilian cinema, laid down the theoretical bases of the new movement, which was established in reaction against the phoney carnival folk-lore of the musical *Chanchadas* – a tradition that had dominated Brazilian films for decades, had produced Carmen Miranda, and survived an attempt in the early fifties to raise the standards of the Brazilian cinema by re-importing Alberto Cavalcanti, Brazil's most famous expatriate director, along with a host of foreign techniques and artists. The young men of the *Cinema Nôvo* however wanted a cinema which would acknowledge the political and social realities of a Brazil in which more than half the population were workless and half the population over fifteen illiterate. 'We realised that we were living in an underdeveloped society, historically excluded from the modern world. We also realised that we must discover this reality more profoundly in order to find the way to emancipation.' This presupposed a kind of film not naturally attractive to the commercial or the political establishment. The *Cinema Nôvo* directors had first to find means of raising the very small budgets on which they worked. They also started their own distributing organisation Difilm, whose profits were ploughed back into production. Despite difficulties – including political imprisonments – the *Cinema Nôvo* produced upwards of thirty new directors of promise, among whom the most prominent, apart from Rocha himself, were Joachim Pedro de Andrade, Carlos Diegues, Ruy Guerra and Nelson Pereira dos Santos.

In his own films Rocha developed an altogether individual amalgam of anthropology, folklore and political agitation, elevated always by a genuine lyrical quality. After an experimental film and a documentary, his first feature was *Barravento* (1962), followed by *Deus e o Diablo na terra do sol* (1964), *Terre im transe* (1967), *Antonio das Mortes* (1969). The pretentious and obscure political allegory, *Der Leone have sept cabecas* (1970), with its multi-

lingual title and its vague borrowings from Godard, fell considerably short of Rocha's previous work. Meanwhile the more direct political fables of Nelson Pereira dos Santos began to earn him a considerable international reputation. In 1970–71 he completed three feature films: *Lust for Love*, an almost conventional study of sexual permutations offered bitter and sophisticated political allegories. In *A Very Lunatic Asylum* he described how a local priest sets up his own madhouse to treat both the discontent of the rich and the disaffection of the poor. *How Good My Little Frenchman Was* was a strange, blackly comic morality about a sixteenth-century French adventurer who becomes the friend and later the food of a Brazilian tribe of cannibal Indians.

No other Latin-American cinema showed signs of such sustained revival in the 1960s, though in *Yawar Mallku* (1969) the Bolivian director Jorge Sanjinés (born 1937) created a film which combined ferocious political protest (against the exploitation and threatened extinction of the Bolivian Indian) with anthropological observation comparable in sympathy to that of Robert Flaherty.

Glauber Rocha:
*Deus e o Diablo
na terra do sol.*
Brazil, 1964.

In Sweden the film industry was stimulated by a deliberate, planned official effort. At the beginning of the sixties the introduction of television had started box office receipts on a sharp decline. Home takings were hit by a fairly heavy entertainments tax. Markets for Swedish films abroad suffered as the result of a decline in the fashionable reputation of Bergman. Outstanding directors like Alf Sjöberg and Arne Sucksdorff, director of some notable nature films, had practically ceased to work in the cinema.

The radical reforms introduced as measures to combat this situation, including the establishment of a Swedish Film Institute, were largely based on plans set out in a book, 'Can We Afford Culture?' by a successful engineer, Harry Schein, who was subsequently put in command of the Institute. The primary goal was to ensure a continuous and continuing production of Swedish films while at the same time guaranteeing the artistic as well as the economic solvency of the industry. The Government reckoned that since the industry's difficulties were largely due to the state-controlled television, it was reasonable to abolish the entertainment tax. In its place a 5 per cent levy was imposed on cinema takings to finance the work of the Swedish Film Institute.

More than half of the money thus raised was applied to direct support of Swedish films: 20 per cent in subsidy of features in relation to their income; 18 per cent for quality awards to feature films of special merit; 2 per cent for quality awards to short films; and 10 per cent to compensate losses on Swedish films which had won quality awards but fallen short of covering their cost in the home market. This exemplary system of compensation proved especially important by making it as profitable for producers to make films of quality as to embark on purely commercial adventures (though the test of quality applied was realistic: the representative award jury assessed films on results and not on ambitions or pretensions). Swedish producers in the sixties and early seventies were heartened to tackle offbeat subjects and to try out new directors.

A further 5 per cent of the levy was employed for public relations and promotional work; and not a little of the success enjoyed by Swedish films abroad could be attributed to the efficiency of this sector of the operation. The remainder of the Swedish Film Institute's finances was devoted to building up a fine film archive, establishing a school on 'workshop' principles; and the support and encouragement of film clubs, film criticism and amateur film-making which, it was optimistically hoped, might contribute new talents to the industry. In 1967 the Institute itself began production, its first work being *They Call Us Misfits*, an impressive first film by two students, Jan Lindquist and Stefan Jarl.

As a direct result of the film industry reforms production doubled after 1962 and a number of remarkable talents were able to come to the fore. Bo Widerberg (born 1930) had been one of the most forthright critics of reactionary elements in Swedish production before he made his first film, *The Pram* in 1963. Subsequently his work revealed a bitter-sweet romantic vision of the past (*Elvira Madigan*, 1967), and a particular fascination with the history of Swedish socialism; *Raven's End* (1963) and *Adalen 31* (1969). *Joe Hill* (1971), was the story of the Swedish immigrant who became the bard of the American labour movement. Vilgot Sjöman (born 1924), whilst evidently revelling in the *succès de scandale* of his individualistic blends of politics and sex in *I Am Curious – Yellow* (1967) and *Blushing Charlie* (1971), was a director of genuine ability, with films like the period piece *My Sister My Love* (1965) and a sensitive study of the effect of prison life on an intelligent delinquent, *You Are Lying!* (1970). The actress Mai Zetterling (born 1925), after making a number of documentaries in Britain for BBC television, directed a series of uneven but personal feature films in Sweden: *Loving Couples* (1964), *Night Games* (1966), *Dr Glas* (1968), *The Girls* (1969). Other notable debuts of the late sixties and early seventies were Kjell Grede (born 1936) with *Hugo and Josefin* (1968) and *Harry Munter* (1970); Jonas Cornell (born 1938) with *Hugs and Kisses* (1967) and *As Day and Night* (1968); Lasse Forsberg with *The Assault* (1969), an attack on mental health services and on the possibilities of censorship within a 'free' society; Roy Andersson, formerly Widerberg's assistant with *A Love Story* (1970).

Jörn Donner (born 1933) made his first films in this

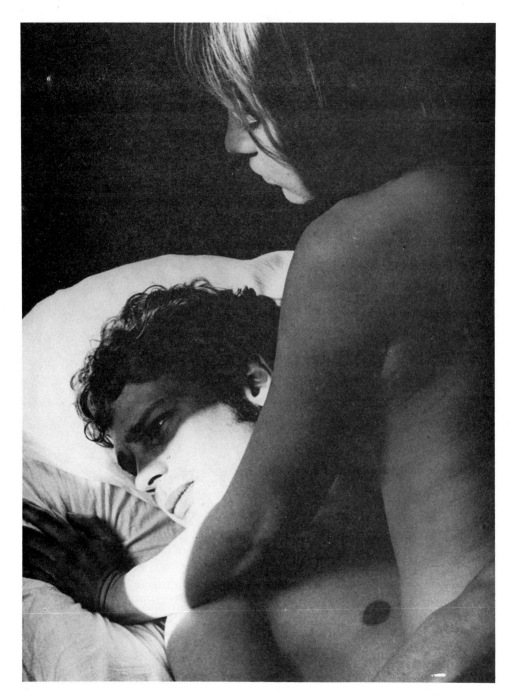

Vilgot Sjoman: *You are Lying!* Sweden, 1969. Stig Engström, Anita Ekström.

favourable Swedish climate (*Sunday in September*, 1963; *To Love*, 1964) before returning to his native Finland to enliven the industry there with his films on dedicatedly sexual themes: *Adventure Starts Here* (1965), *Black on White* (1967) and *Portraits of Women* (1970).

Denmark's best-known directors outside Dreyer had been the documentarist Jörgen Roos (born 1922) and the husband and wife team of Bjarne (born 1908) and Astrid (born 1914) Henning-Jensen, who specialised in films about childhood (*Ditte Child of Man*, 1946; *Palle alone in the World*, 1949). Although a large proportion of production in the late sixties, following the abolition of censorship, consisted in vapid sex films for export, a number of new, young directors made their first films in the last two or three years of the decade. The most notable film of the period however was Henning Carlsen's *Hunger* (1966) an inter-Scandinavian production with a notable performance by one of the best Swedish actors of his generation, Per Oscarsson.

Even West Germany, having failed signally to recapture the old German tradition of film culture, suddenly found itself possessed of a lively New Wave in the late sixties. In 1966 Alexander Kluge (born 1932), already known as a writer, made *Abscheid von Gestern*, a psycho-philosophical analysis of a delinquent girl. The following year Jean-Marie Straub's second film, the austere *Chronik der Anna Magdalena Bach* enjoyed an impressive critical success. Other young directors, Werner Herzog, Rainer Werner Fassbinder, Volker Schloendorff and a large and vociferous 'underground' (see page 346) also came to prominence as the decade ended.

Holland, with a strong documentary tradition, had always had a small but constant feature production – about four or five films per year. Notable older directors had been Fons Rademakers (born 1921), who made *Village on the River* (1959), *The Knife* (1961) and *Dance of the Heron* (1966), and the distinguished documentarists Bert Haanstra (born 1917), with *Fanfare* (1958) and *The M.P. Affair* (1960). In the late sixties, again, young directors sought opportunities to direct feature films. Harry Kümel (born 1940), a television director, made *Monsieur Hawarden* (1968) for the Parkfilm Company, established by the critic Rob du

Mee, and which also produced Erik Torpstra's (born 1937) *The Whipping Cream Hero* (1969). Wim Verstappen (born 1937) and Pim de la Parra (born 1940) collaborated on the feature productions *Joszef Katus* (1966), *Obsessions* (1969) and *Blue Movie* (1971). The writer Hugo Claus, who had written some of Rademaker's films, directed a Belgo-Dutch co-production *The Enemies* (1968). Philo Bregstein's (born 1932) *The Compromise* won the *prima opera* prize at the 1968 Venice Festival.

In Belgium André Delvaux made two films totally personal vision: *The Man Who Had His Hair Cut Short* (1966) and *Un soir . . . un train* (1969). His next film, a stylish and atmospheric recollection of the era of World War I, *Rendez-vous à*

Bray (1971), was a co-production with France and West Germany. In almost every country, it seemed, even where there were no existing cinema traditions, individual directors were finding the possibility of making films, turning to the cinema as, only ten or fifteen years before, they would have turned to the novel or poetry as a form of artistic expression.

In the socialist East also there was a time for change. Stalin died in 1953; and the Twentieth Party Congress in 1956 ushered in a much revised political and cultural ideology in the U.S.S.R. Even before 1956 there were signs of more human attitudes, in films like Heifet's *The Big Family* (1954) and *The Rumyantsev Case* (1955). But to the West, it was Grigori Chukrai's (born 1921) debut with *The Forty-First* (1956) – a remake of a Protazanov film of 1927 about the brief doomed passion of a Red girl partisan and her prisoner, a White officer – which revealed the real breakthrough. The following year the veteran Kalatozov (see page 142) who had practically vanished since *Salt of Svanetia* (1930), made a dramatic come-back with *The Cranes Are Flying* (1957), which used bravura without fear of 'formalism' and showed the Second World War in realistic instead of heroic terms. The war provided the theme for the directorial debut of the actor Sergei Bondarchuk (born 1920) with *Destiny of a Man* (1959) and for Chukrai's *Ballad of a Soldier* (1959). In 1961 Chukrai's *Clear Skies* broke more new ground by referring directly to the dark days and the relief brought by the death of Stalin. For the first time for many years Soviet films began to circulate in the West. A new generation of directors appeared: The Georgians Revez Chkheidze (*Our Yard*, 1957) and Tengiz Abuladze (born 1924: *Magdana's Donkey*, 1956; *Somebody Else's Children*, 1959); Lev Kulijanov (born 1924) and Yakov Segel (born 1923) who co-directed *The House I Live In* (1957), Alexander Alov (born 1923) and Vladimir Naumov (born 1927) who collaborated on *Peace to the Newcomer* (1961); Andrei Tarkovski (born 1932; *The Childhood of Ivan*, 1962; *Andrei Roublev*, 1967, *Solaris*, 1972), Andrei Konchalovsky (born 1937; *The First Teacher*, 1965) and the extravagant poetic talent of the Georgian-born, Kiev-based Sergei Paradjanov (born 1924; *Shadows of Our Forgotten Ancestors*, 1964).

There was a remarkable revival among the older genera-
tion also. Mikhail Romm made a fine war film *Nine Days of
One Year* (1961) and a compilation film about Nazism,
Ordinary Fascism (1965). Donskoi returned to Gorki for
Foma Gordeyev (1956) but failed to retrieve the simple epic
style of the Gorki trilogy, either in this or his films on the
childhood and youth of Lenin, *A Mother's Heart* and *A
Mother's Devotion* (both 1966). The FEKS group made some
of the best films of the period. Kozintsev followed a dazzling
Don Quixote (1959) with two Shakespeare adaptations of
notable intelligence: *Hamlet* (1964) and *King Lear* (1970).
Yutkevitch made a curious animated version of Maya-
kovsky's *The Bathhouse* (1962); returned to the problems of
recreating Lenin's image on the screen with *Stories of Lenin*
(1957) and *Lenin in Poland* (1966); and in 1969 recalled old
FEKS experimental days with an elegant, stylised examination of an episode in Chekhov's life, *Subject for a Short
Story.* Heifets' exquisite Chekhov adaptation, *The Lady*

With the Little Dog (1960) was, in its complete independence of all tradition, its own *nouvelle vague*.

With the later sixties however there were signs of a new tightening of control. Often the release of films was held up without explanation. Films on contemporary themes tended to be suspect; Tarkovsky's *Andrei Rublev* (1967) was not released on account of its 'negative' view of history. In these circumstances film-makers seemed unwilling to experiment, and despite rumours of interesting new activity in the national republics, little evidence of a progressive Soviet cinema was reaching the outside world at the turn of the seventies.

Hungary had always enjoyed a remarkably resilient cinematic tradition. Though driven underground for long periods, since before the time of Korda the Hungarian cinema seemed capable of constant revival. The turning-point after the grim Stalinist years of the regime of Mátyas Rákosi seemed to be Zoltán Fabri's *Fourteen Lives Saved* (1954). Fábri (born 1917) had made his first film in 1952; and thereafter a new group appeared: Károly Makk (born 1925), László Ránódy (born 1919), János Herskó (born 1926), Zoltán Várkonyi (born 1912), György Révézs (born 1927). Imre Féher (born 1926), Félix Máriássy (born 1919). The

Grigori Kozintsev: *Hamlet*. U.S.S.R. 1964.

years 1955–6 represented a peak of artistic achievement, with Fábri's *Merry-go-round* (1955) and *Professor Hannibal* (1956), Máriássy's *Spring in Budapest* (1955) and *A Glass of Beer* (1955) (revealing a strong neo-realist influence.) Ranódy's *Abyss* (1955) and Féher's exquisite first film, *A Sunday Romance* (1956–7). The political events of 1956 produced a temporary hiatus in artistic evolution as well as the temporary disappearance of one or two prominent artists; but the establishment of a second feature studio in 1957 made possible a sharp increase in production and a new variety of approach.

An identifiable revival around 1963 can be attributed, like the Swedish renaissance, to a deliberate official effort. The Hungarian Government remarked a degree of stagnation in Hungarian films at a time when in other countries the New Waves were breaking resoundingly. Consequently the Academy of Dramatic and Film Art was reformed and younger teachers appointed. The number of creative studios was increased to four from January 1963, with energetic young people placed in charge of their artistic policy. Additional stimulus had been provided by the creation of the Béla Balázs Studio in about 1961. Begun by a group of new graduates from the Academy, the studio was formed to overcome the old situation in which new directors might wait years before they had a chance to

Andrei Tarkovsky: *Andrei Roublev.* U.S.S.R., 1967.

direct their first films. The Béla Balász Studio offered possibilities for the young to prove their abilities on short films and their first productions clearly signalled a new wave when they were shown at international film festivals.

There were also political and philosophical reasons for this rebirth. The films which began to appear in 1962–3 – Miklós Jancsó's *Cantata*, Herskó's *Dialogue*, István Gaál's *Current*, András Kovács' *Difficult People* (1964) – treated recent history with a frankness which presupposed relaxation of official attitudes to a point which would have been unthinkable in the Soviet Union. Alongside the liberalisation went the high regard in which the young film-makers tended to hold the Marxist philosopher György Lukacs, with his emphasis on the need for frank self-criticism.

The resulting New Cinema was sharply divided from the previous era. A leading characteristic was the escape from a literary tradition which had dogged Hungarian cinema for better or worse since its earliest days. The new directors tended to be linked by strong mutual interest and admiration, helped by the fact that there were frequent close collaborations. Their films as a body had a remarkable cohesion. In contrast to the classic Soviet cinema, which was a cinema of political criticism and agitation, the New Hungarian film-makers endeavoured to use the film as a medium of socio-political *debate*.

Despite a community of interests, the styles of the directors of the new generation were strikingly individual. Miklós Jancsó (born 1921) made his first feature film, *Cantata* in 1962, but his characteristic style, with its extremely long, balletically composed shots, only began to appear with *The Round-up* (1965) and the start of a collaboration with the writer, Gyula Hernádi. Subsequent films – *The Red and the White* (1967), *The Silence and the Cry* (1968), *The Confrontation* (1968), *Sirocco* (1969), *Agnus Dei* (1971), *Red Psalm* (1972)–sometimes composed of barely a dozen shots of up to ten minutes each, marked the apogee of the *mise-en-scène* school of cinema, the conscious rejection of the old *montage* method. Stylistically András Kovács (born 1925) proved much more conventional, his innovations being rather in the matter of content, experiments with

film investigations of current social problems.

Jancsó and Kovács were reckoned the senior members of the New Hungarian Cinema. Its most talented younger directors included István Szábo (born 1938) whose films *The Age of Daydreaming* (1964), *The Father* (1966) and *Love Film* (1970) displayed a very personal combination of sentiment and historical intelligence; István Gaál (born 1933) with the austere, visually splendid *Current* (1964), *The Green Years* (1965) and *The Falcons* (1970); Imre Gyöngyössy (born 1930), Ferenc Kósa (born 1937), Sándor Sára (born 1933), János Rózsa (born 1937), Ferenc Kardos (born 1937), Pál Sándor (born 1939), Pál Gábor (born 1932), Judit Elek (born 1937) and Zsolt Kezdi-Kovács (born 1936).

In Poland Aleksander Ford's (born 1908) *Five Boys From Barska Street* (1953) seemed the breakthrough to more humane post-Stalinist attitudes, and was followed in 1954 by the first part of Andrzej Wajda's (born 1926) great trilogy: *A Generation* (1954), *Kanal* (1956) and *Ashes and Diamonds* (1958), which examined the psychological effects of the

Second World War upon those young men who had lived through and survived it. In Zbigniew Cybulski (1927–67), the Ukrainian-born actor, Wajda found and developed an archetypal hero. After Cybulski's death Wajda seemed to find a different kind of hero for Poland's sixties in Daniel Olbrychki (born 1945) who played in *Ashes* (1965), *Everything For Sale* (1968), a poetic search for the memory of Cybulski, and *Landscape after the Battle* (1970) which revisited, a decade further on, the historical scenes of Wajda's trilogy of the war.

Andrzej Munk (1921–61) had made only four feature films, all of large promise, before he died: *Man on the Tracks* (1956), *Eroica* (1957), *Bad Luck* (1960) and *Passenger* (1964, finished posthumously). Other directors of this period were Jerzy Kawalierowicz (born 1922); Wojiech Has (born 1925) whose best films were *How to be Loved* (1962) and *The Saragossa Manuscript* (1964), both with Cybulski; Kazimierz Kutz (born 1929); Jerzy Passendorffer (born 1923). In the sixties the climate seemed less propitious and several of the younger directors showed a preference for working abroad, among them the animated film-makers Jan Lenica (born 1928) and Walerian Borowczyk (born 1923), Roman Polanski (see page 316) and Jerzy Skolimowski (born 1938).

Andrjez Wajda: *A Generation.* Poland, 1954. Tadeusz Janczar, the future director Roman Polanski, Ryszard Kotas, Tadeusz Lomnicki.

A poet, actor, playwright and boxer as well as a film
director, Skolimowski collaborated on Wajda's *Innocent
Sorcerers* (1959) and Polanski's *Knife in the Water* (1962). His
own debut as a director was with *Marks of Identification –
None (Rysopsis)* (1964), a film which he made in sections, as
examination exercises at the Lodz Film School. In Poland
he also made *Walkover* (1965) *Barrier* (1966) and later *Hands
Up!* (1968, not released owing to censorship difficulties.) In
Belgium he made the brilliant character comedy *Le Départ*
(1967) with Truffaut's favourite actor Jean-Pierre Léaud;
for United Artists he made a Conan Doyle adaptation *The
Adventures of Gerard* (1970) in Britain, France and Switzerland; and for a German-American company he made the
brilliant *Deep End* (1970) with English actors and an English
setting, which further pursued his dominant theme of the
angry frustrations of young love, and *König, Dame, Bube*
(1972).

Czechoslovakia emerged from the Stalinist era with a
strong tradition of animated cinema but a rather conventional feature production. The early sixties however saw
the sudden appearance of a highly individual new wave in
which the most significant talent was Milós Forman (born
1932). His unique ability to observe ordinary human beings,
to perceive at once both their absurdity and their dignity,
was already displayed in a short, *Talent Competition* (1963)
and was developed in the feature films *Peter and Pavla*
(1963), a comedy about a boy's first job and first love affair;
A Blonde in Love (1965) about the frustrations love suffers
in the circumstances of contemporary urban life; and *The
Fireman's Ball* (1967) in which his comic observation of the
arrangements for a village celebration took on more
sombre symbolic meanings in relation to a bureaucratically
organised society. Forman's collaborator Ivan Passer (born
1933) directed his first feature film *Intimate Lighting* in
1967. Jiri Menzel (born 1938) attempted a style comparable
to Forman and Passer in *Closely Observed Trains* (1966).
Ewald Schorm (born 1931) whose *Courage for Every Day*
(1964) indicated a more severe approach, was regarded as
the ideologist of the new cinema. Vera Chytilova (born

Milós Forman:
The Firemen's Ball.
Czechoslovakia,
1967.

1929) and Jan Nemec (born 1936) adopted more avant-garde formal styles. Pavel Juracek's *Josef Kilian* (1963) was a Kafkaesque fantasy, but his subsequent *Every Young Man* (1965), about the experiences of a group of young soldiers, was nearer in feeling to the Forman-Passer style.

After the Soviet invasion of 1968 however the striking progress of the new Czech cinema was abruptly halted. Forman went to America where he made *Taking Off* (1971), in which he turned his characteristic comic and caustic vision upon American problems, in the story of a runaway child whose bourgeois parents are faced with a few of the temptations that confront the young, and emerge with scant credit. The directors who stayed behind seemed to have the choice of making anodyne and null comedies or adventure stories, or risking unemployment or (as happened in very many cases) the suppression of their films.

Until the middle sixties, Yugoslavia's main strength was the outstanding animated films – highly sophisticated in graphics and in content – produced at the Zagreb Studios, most notably by Vatroslav Mimica (born 1923) and Dusan Vukotic (born 1927), both of whom turned to feature direction in the sixties. The outstanding directors of a lively, independent emergent school of the late sixties, quite emancipated from the preoccupations of other Eastern states, were Aleksander Petrovic (born 1929) (*I Have Even Met Happy Gypsies*, 1967), and the former critic Dusan Makavejev (born 1932). Makavejev's first features, *A Man is Not A Bird* (1965) and *The Switchboard Operator* (1967) already showed an independent view of life in a socialist society and a philosopher's curiosity about the accidental nature of human affairs. *Innocence Unprotected* (1968) reconstituted a primitive film melodrama – the first Serbian feature – made during the war by Dragoljub Aleksič, a professional strong man and locksmith. Throughout these films Makavejev was developing a style of collage which he applied with notable brilliance in *WR: Mysteries of the Organism* (1971). Drawing upon his early training in psycho-

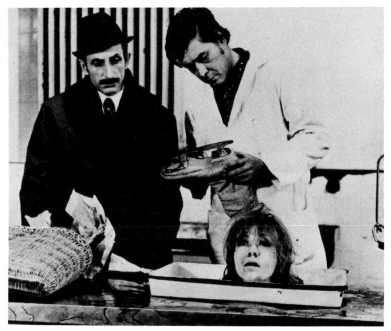

Dusan Makavejev: *W.R. Mysteries of the Organism.* Yugoslavia, 1971. Milena Dravic.

logy and philosophy, he devised a free-wheeling essay which took as its text the work of Wilhelm Reich, the Austrian-born psychoanalyst who endeavoured to reconcile the thought of Marx and Freud in his perception of the relationship between sexual and political repression.

Other Eastern countries had sporadic successes in the post-'thaw' years: Bulgaria with Vulo Radev's *The Peach Thief* (1964); Rumania with the animated films and live-action comedies of Ion Popescu-Gopo (born 1923); East Germany with the tendentious documentary compilations of Andrew and Annalie Thorndike and occasional notable features like Joachim Kunert's (born 1929) *The Adventures of Werner Holt* (1964). Among the major Communist states, only China showed no evidence of evolving beyond a primitive schematic socialist realism.

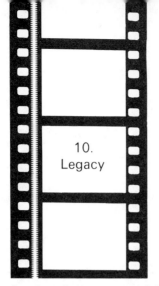

10.
Legacy

As the cinema moved into the 1970s and the final quarter of its first century, the future was as hard to predict as at any time in its history. One basic economic factor dominated all other considerations in the American and British cinemas, and was likely sooner or later to be of universal application. In the space of twenty-five years the cost of every aspect of making films had risen as much as four times. In the same period audiences had shrunk to as little as one sixth.* It was clear that the old economics of production were no longer valid. Yet the established cinema industries showed perilously little ability to adapt to the new circumstances. Attempts to reduce costs (hampered at every turn by trade unions' short term policies for the protection of the members of a notoriously underemployed industry), attempts to find new formulas to attract a wider and a different public seemed to solve no problems.

The profitability of films became more and more erratic and unpredictable, and film companies depended upon the occasional exceptional success – *The Graduate* and *Bonnie and Clyde* were examples in the sixties; *Love Story* and *The Godfather* the phenomena of the seventies – to offset the losses of the larger number of films which failed to recoup their production costs. As they had always done, the indus- trialists proceeded empirically, hoping to discover in the latest box-office success some secret for the salvation of the industry. Now they pinned their faith to multi-million

*In Britain the fall between 1945 and 1969 was from approximately thirty million to 4.7 million admissions per week.

dollar blockbusters; and when this magic failed them and an *Easy Rider* came along, they would decide that salvation lay, after all, in low-budget pictures. The industry seemed always to be seeking charms and omens: a characteristic peak of absurdity was reached when, at the beginning of the seventies, the coincident success of *Midnight Cowboy*, *Butch Cassidy and the Sundance Kid* and *Easy Rider* convinced many distributors and producers that the answer to all the problems of the box office lay in making films exclusively about friendships between two men.

It was a situation that clearly could not last forever, though the old companies and the old studios had survived much longer than anyone might reasonably have predicted in 1960. At the start of the new decade practically all the great old Hollywood companies had been taken over by new finance groups. It seemed a symbol of the fall of the old

Dennis Hopper: *Easy Rider*. U.S.A., 1969. Dennis Hopper, Peter Fonda.

·

empires when the legendary properties of MGM Pictures – furnishings, costumes, scenery and properties from half a century of American movies – were sold up in a colourful but melancholy auction sale in 1970. A few months later, in February 1971, Twentieth Century-Fox's store rooms were likewise emptied. Hollywood took stock, and a general, severe retrenchment had its effect upon film production in many other areas of the world – not least in Great Britain, whose cinema was driven into the worst crisis of her crisis-ridden history by the withdrawal of American money in the late sixties.

Another revolutionary change which affected the cinema, would have astonished and dismayed the old rulers of the industry – Louis B. Mayer with his public defence of the sanctity of all-American ideals of purity and patriotism, or Will Hays, whose office imposed upon the American cinema censorship codes that for years restricted its expression to the sort of limits acceptable in a Victorian Sunday School. The sixties saw an unprecedented relaxation in habits of social conduct, in what could be said and what could be done in public. The cinema, fighting to keep a hold over an audience which, it seemed, could only be retained by stronger and stronger sensations, led this general movement. The barriers of censorship crashed down. In Denmark censorship was formally abolished; in other countries it was relaxed to the extreme point at which it could still provide some protection or at least guidance for the very young or the very sensitive. By the end of 1971, it seemed that very little remained that could not be said or shown on the screen, at least in terms of sexual behaviour or expression.* What, in the long run, the effect of this would be, it was hard to say: generally the impression was that the short term effects – the exploitation of the new freedom by unscrupulous producers and distributors, the audiences that were attracted and those

*Not all western countries were equally permissive. Catholic Italy, post-Gaullist France, Franco's Spain were all very much more cautious. Eastern Europe (always excepting Yugoslavia) of course retained its decorum.

that were repelled for the wrong reasons – must ultimately be compensated by the gain in scope and freedom of discussion thus gained by the cinema.*

The temperamental polarisation between the young and the old, the dissenters and the establishment, more marked in this period than in any previous era, was especially reflected in the cinema. As the industrial establishments appeared to wane, a great many young people, in many different countries, chose to create their own cinemas. Deliberately rejecting the costly gloss and paraphernalia of industrial film-making, they carried a step further the lessons taught by the *nouvelle vague* in the fifties. Using minimal private resources of money, taking advantage of the ready availability of substandard (16 mm and 8 mm) equipment and film stock they sought to make the cinema an independent and personal expression, free from the traditional pressures applied by producers and the paying audience.

The 'underground' cinema first surfaced in America, in succession to the avant-garde pioneers of the forties and fifties. Its leading exponents were to become the already veteran Kenneth Anger, Stan Brakhage, Ed Emshwiller, Larry Kadish, Sandy Daley, Milton Moses Greenberg, Adolfas and Jonas Mekas, Paul Sharits, Robert Downey, Michael Snow, Gregory Markopoulos and above all the painter, Andy Warhol, whose films, from *The Chelsea Girls* (1966) onwards proved to have a very considerable box-office appeal. Made in complete freedom from formal rules, yet in a curious mood of homage to the lost eras of the star system, the best of the Warhol films were a continuation of the highly personal distillations of pop culture which had characterised the artist's graphic work. The earlier films were bold experiments in perception, some of which – *Sleep*, which observed a man sleeping for three hours and then repeated every shot to make a total running time of six hours; *Empire State*, which held a camera on the Empire

*In Britain a more interesting phenomenon was the handful of young directors who managed privately to raise sufficient money to make commercial films at a tiny fraction of current industrial budgets, among them Anthony Balch (*Secrets of Sex*, 1969) and Barney Platts-Mills (*Bronco Bullfrog*, 1970; *Private Road*, 1971).

Andy Warhol: *Flesh*. U.S.A., 1969. Joe Dallesandro.

State Building for eight hours – won their own notoriety. A change in orientation was evident in the Warhol films after Paul Morrissey joined Warhol as his principal collaborator-director. From *Flesh* (which Morrissey took over after Warhol was injured in a shooting incident) the characteristic technical *tics* became less evident: the films' style and subjects became a pastiche of commercial films and acquired a distinctive approach which might be described as 'documentary of the ridiculous'.

The 'underground' movement proved to be as international as the dissent of youth and students itself. In Italy Carmelo Bene (born 1937) was prominent with such extravagant narcissistic, baroque operatic abstractions as *Nostra Signora degli Turchi* (1968) and *Don Giovanni* (1970). In Germany there were individual groups in Heidelberg (Werner Schroeter), Berlin (Rosa von Praunheim, Rainer Boldt, Harun Farocki, K. P. Brehmer), Hamburg (Klaus Wyborny, Werner Nekes and his wife Dore O., Hellmuth Costard), Cologne (Wilhelm and Birgit Heln, Christian Michelis, Peter Kochenrath, Rolf Weist), Munich (Wim Wenders, Mattias Weiss, Vlado Kristl) and Stuttgart (Richard Besrodinoff, Ed Sommer, Lampert Winterberger) – each school with its own distinctive approach, aesthetic or activist. In Paris the underground centred mainly on three groups. S.L.O.N. and the Vertov Group, which was founded by Godard, had very positive social and political programmes. Zanzibar Productions – a company formed for convenience to fulfil the legal requirements for film production – loosely linked a group of underground filmmakers which included Philippe Garrel, creator of some highly personal, hallucinatingly boring film abstractions. There were underground cinemas in Canada (Gilles Groulx,

Marek Piwowski: *Fire, Fire, Something's Happening at Last!* Poland, 1969.

Michael Wadleigh: *Woodstock*. U.S.A., 1970.

Jean-Pierre Lefebvre), Austria, Switzerland, Holland and Japan where the avant-garde dramatist Shuji Terayama made two lively, scabrous films (*Emperor Tomato Ketchup*, 1971, *Throw Away Books: Let's Go into the Streets*, 1972). In Britain underground activity was tentative and imitative apart from the efforts of the U.S. born Steve Dwoskin who followed a series of shorts with two feature films, *Times For* (1971) and *Dynamo* (1972). Even in Eastern Europe where film-making was almost exclusively under state patronage, there were occasional murmurs of dissenting voices – in Poland in the short films of Marek Piwowski (*Fire! Fire! Something's Happening at last!*, 1969); in Hungary in the 'social' subjects which were being made in the Béla Balász Studio in 1970–71.

The Underground cinema took many forms. The *oeuvre* of some authors might consist of a single short short; others were prolific in feature length films. Some aimed at elegant professional standards; others made a virtue of hazy images and inaudible sound. The major importance of the underground however was that it found an audience. A generation – or at least a section of it – perhaps in revolt against television which they saw as the medium of their parents, turned to the cinema; and, in the cinema, rejected the products of the commercial establishment in favour of films which – however inadequate they sometimes were – seemed to express their feelings, to *belong to them*. To show the product of the underground, new clubs and private cinemas sprang up, to provide, national and international 'circuits' for independent, emphatically non-commercial production.

A characteristic phenomenon of the late sixties was the attempt of the commercial companies to take a lead from the underground cinema in trying to recapture the teenage and twenties audience. 1970 was a peak year for dissent and youth alienation as big box-office themes, with Arthur Penn's *Alice's Restaurant* (actually released in 1969), Stuart Hagmann's *The Strawberry Statement*, Richard Rush's *Getting Straight*, Haskell Wexler's *Medium Cool* and Michael Wadleigh's *Woodstock*. The anarchic scepticism of Robert Altman's *M.A.S.H.* and Mike Nichols' adaptation of Joseph Heller's *Catch 22* perhaps went deeper.

However misty the future, it was clear by the 1970s that nothing could ever be quite the same again. The cinema had been created as a mass medium; now it was a mass medium no longer, but had to make its appeal to a whole lot of minority audiences. The old industrial organisations were obsolete: if the cinema as we had known it were to survive to its second century, it could only be with new conceptions and new economies of film production, film exhibition, film, *tout court*.

Survival would depend on new techniques. The experience of the underground and the pressures of finance together forced the development of what had previously been dismissively styled 'sub-standard' equipment and film materials. In the fifties the fight against television had excited the development of bigger and clumsier film-stock – the 70 mm film. In the seventies there was accelerated experiment in the development and use of small-gauge film, 8 mm and 16 mm, previously confined to the amateur only.

Still more important, and even more imponderable in its probable results was the development of the video-cassette as a means of disseminating film or television material. When every kind of moving picture could be made readily and inexpensively available for home viewing, the mass audience would finally be splintered into its smallest individual units. Fast as was the technical development of the video-cassette no-one could foresee the ultimate effect upon the nature and the uses of the moving image.

The start of the seventies found us as blind before the future as our ancestors must have been. For Barker and Daguerre, Plateau and Muybridge, Reynaud and Edison can have had no idea what it was that – in their unknowing collaboration – they were creating. They cannot have guessed that, thanks to them, the image would become the primary and indispensable means of communication for the 20th century, whether for entertainment, education, propaganda, information or record. They cannot have imagined that for several of the most momentous decades in the history of the world, the instrument that would be created out of their labours would be the mirror and the medium of man's dreams and hopes, fears and tragedies; his master and his servant, his voice and his demon.

Appendix I:
A note on Animated Films

The animation of drawings actually predates the cinema proper. Plateau's Phenakisticope (page 10), its refinement in the Zoetrope (page 10) and above all Reynaud's Praxinoscope (page 10) all used a technique comparable to the modern cartoon film, employing series of drawings of successive stages of an action to produce the illusion of movement.

Before the turn of the century Méliès' camera tricks pointed the way to the frame-by-frame technique by which animated films are (generally) produced, and which seems to have been first fully exploited by J. Stuart Blackton at the Vitagraph Studios about 1907 (*Humorous Phases of Funny Faces*, *The Magic Paint Box*). The following year Emile Cohl, at Gaumont's Paris Studios, created the first of a series of films whose wit and brilliance still remain fresh after sixty years. In *Fantasmagorie*, *Drame chez les Fantoches*, *Le petit soldat qui devient dieu* and many other films Cohl used his economical and vivid draughtsmanship to create characters of charm and vivacity. He was followed by a distinguished school of French animation artists in silent films, including Robert Lortac, Benjamin Rabier and Joseph Hémard.

In the United States, where between 1910 and 1918 Winsor McKay created the endearing *Gertie the Dinosaur*, animated films drew upon the tradition of comic-strip characters; *Mutt and Jeff*, *The Katzenjammer Kids* and *Happy Hooligan* all originated in newspaper cartoons and in 1913 Emile Cohl went to America to create a series based on Mac-

Manus's *Snookums*. The most famous of the early American cartoon characters however was *Felix the Cat*, as much a personality of the twenties as Valentino or the Prince of Wales. Created by an Australian cartoonist, Pat Sullivan, and animated by Otto Mesmer, the Felix films discovered a vitality which had often eluded the earlier American cartoons, inhibited by their origins in static print. The same sort of vigour is discernible in the work of Max and Dave Fleischer. In their *Out of the Inkwell* series a cartoon clown, Koko, was associated with live actors. With sound, the Fleischers developed an inspired sexual caricature, Betty Boop, a creation lively enough to be condemned by the Legion of Decency, whereupon the Fleischers created the durable Popeye, together with his lady friend Olive Oil and their eccentric nautical entourage. (In 1939 the Fleischers were to follow Disney into feature length cartoon films with *Gulliver's Travels*).

Elsewhere in the silent period there were experiments with styles of animation which broke away from the traditional method of making individual drawings on paper. In Russia, Ladislav Starevitch had used stop action techniques as early as 1911 to animate exquisite little puppets – insects and animals which might have been conceived by Grandville. In the twenties, Lotte Reiniger in Germany adapted the principle of the *Ombres Chinoises*, and worked for three years with her husband Carl Koch to produce the world's first full-length animated film, *Die Abenteuer des Prinz Achmets* (1926).

The arrival of sound gave pre-eminence in the field to the American Walt Disney, who had hitherto (from 1923) had moderate success with the series *Alice in Cartoonland*, *Oswald the Lucky Rabbit*, and *Mortimer*, prototype of Mickey Mouse. Disney's appreciation of the possibilities of sound (*Steamboat Willie*, 1928; *Skeleton Dance*, 1929) and later his use of colour (*Flowers and Trees*, 1932); the vitality of his anthropomorphic animals – Mickey, Pluto, Donald Duck, Clarabelle Cow, Horace Horsecollar, Goofy – and the inventiveness of his gags (often close in feeling to Sennett originals) earned his work exaggerated admiration in the thirties, when he was reckoned America's outstanding cinema artist, the equal of Chaplin and Griffith. His popularity was further enhanced when *The Three Little Pigs* (1933), with its message of optimism ('Who's Afraid of the Big, Bad Wolf?') and of redemption through industriousness made it appear a rallying point and hymn of the New Deal Era.

The assertion implicit in Disney's work that animated film could be art stimulated experiment in Europe. Bertholt Bartosch made a politico-philosophical parable, *L'Idée* (1934). In *Nuit sur le mont chauve* (1933) Alexandre Alexeieff developed new graphic forms, employing light reflected off groups of pins to produce effects of stipple engraving. In the U.S.S.R. there were experiments with drawn sound tracks, while Alexander Ptushko made a feature film, the didactic *The New Gulliver* which employed live actors and cartoon figures in the same scenes.

Disney's decline was already however evident at the very peak of his celebrity, with the production of his first full-length cartoon, *Snow White and the Seven Dwarfs* (1938). The factory method of the Disney Studios at Burbank – then grown to immense size, and committed to the annual production of one feature film and forty-eight shorts, as well as to the commercial exploitation of innumerable by-products and copyright licenses – began to tell upon the films. Disney products had lost their individuality and charm: the characters had become stereotypes; the graphic style had succumbed to gloss and cliché, and was already beginning to seem archaic. The more seriously Disney took himself as an artist, the more unhappy the results tended to be. Writing of the commercial failure of *Fantasia* (1941) – an attempt to link animation to a series of popular musical classics – one critic wrote that 'It showed that crime does not always pay'.

In the forties and fifties there were violent reactions against the Disney style – for the most part led by former Disney artists. Paul Terry's *Terrytoons*, Leon Schlesinger's *Looney Tunes* and *Merry Melodies*, Bill Hanna and Joe Barbera's *Tom and Jerry*, Warners' *Bugs Bunny*, *Kiki* and *Sylvester* series (created by Freleng, Charles Jones, Robert MacKimson and others), Walter Lantz's *Woody Woodpecker*, and above all the creations of Tex Avery (notably *Chilly Willy the Penguin* and *Droopy*) all employed the Disney style of animation – a rather detailed and realist concept of anthropomorphism – but with a new energy, in surreal, anarchic, sadistic comedy altogether unlike the rather vapid tone of later Disney work.

Much more significant to the subsequent development of animated films throughout the world was the work of U.P.A. (United Productions of America), founded in 1945 by Stephen Bosustow, who had broken away from Disney to make *Brotherhood of Man*, a cartoon tract on racism. The graphic work of U.P.A. had a new sophistication and economy, derived from recent (i.e. *New Yorker*, Steinberg) traditions of humorous cartoon graphics. In place of the cluttered, naturalistic pictures of the Disney school, which often recalled old German oleographic illustrations in children's books, U.P.A. employed fresh, non-naturalistic colours in bold washes, and spare and vigorous drawing. The characters, too, had a new sophistication with whimsical and witty inventions like Robert Cannon's *Gerald McBoing Boing*, and above all Pete Burness's myopic busybody, *Mr Magoo*. Other U.P.A. artists were John Hubley, Art Babbitt, William Hurtz, Lew Keller, Ernest Pintoff, and Ted Parmelee, whose individual influences were widespread after the break-up of U.P.A.

Meanwhile in Canada, Norman McLaren, who had joined the National Film Board in 1941, was developing other individual lines in animation. A Scot, McLaren had been much influenced at the G.P.O. Film Unit by Len Lye, a New Zealand pioneer in techniques of drawing directly on to the film (*Colour Box*, 1935). McClaren himself experimented in various techniques, notably in stereoscopy (*Now is the Time, Around is Around*, both devised for the Festival of Britain, 1951); and later in applying animation techniques to human figures (*Neighbours*, 1952). McLaren's colleagues and followers at the National Film Board included Grant Munro, Gerald Potterton, Jim MacKay, Colin Low and George Dunning. Alexeieff was also an early collaborator of McLaren's at the National Film Board of Canada. Dunning later worked in Britain (*The Apple*, 1960; *The Yellow Submarine*, 1969).

The war period had seen the development in France of the delicate, traditional cartoon work of Jean Image and Paul Grimault. In England the films of John Halas and

Joy Batchelor offered another early and healthy reaction against the heavy Walt Disney baroque; and in later years the couple attempted unusual subjects for cartoon work: Orwell's *Animal Farm* (1954) and Gilbert and Sullivan's *Ruddigore* (1967). From the post-war period animated cinema flourished in Britain. David Hand's attempts to establish a cartoon studio for Rank were not successful; but in the fifties a number of individuals, working independently, were outstanding: Peter Földes, with his apocalyptic *A Short Vision*; the Canadian Richard Williams, combining wise and quirky humour with great graphic elegance and originality (*The Little Island*, etc); Bob Godfrey with an unique style of rich music hall vulgarity (*Polygamous Polonious, Henry 9 'til 5*); Biographic Films; Larkins Studios, and occasional outstanding work from art schools, notably Bristol College of Art. Elsewhere in Western Europe activity was sporadic, though the work of Joop Geesink's 'Dollywood' studios in Holland, and of Bruno Bozzetto in Italy was often notable.

While Soviet animators seemed stuck with the worst conventions of the Disney style (an exception was Yutkevitch's *The Bathhouse*, 1962, after Mayakowsky's play), elsewhere in Eastern Europe animated cinema was very highly developed. In Czechoslovakia an important group of artists collected around Jiří Trnka, from 1945. Trnka, a former puppeteer and cartoonist, had begun work on animated films the same year and turned to puppet films in 1947. With work ranging from folk-lore (*Czech Legends*, 1953) and national literature (*The Good Soldier Schweik*, 1954) to Shakespeare (*A Midsummer Night's Dream*, 1959), Hans Andersen (*The Emperor's Nightingale*, 1948) and haunting visions of present and future (*Obsession*, 1960; *The Hand* 1965), Trnka made the puppet film into a new and independent genre. His example was of inestimable importance to other fine puppet and cartoon film makers – Edward Hofman, Jiří Brdčka, Josef Kábrt, Václav Bedřich, Karel Zeman (*An Engine of Destruction*, 1957; *Baron Munchausen*, 1961) and Hermine Tyrlova. The Zagreb studios of Yugoslavia produced several distinguished cartoon makers – Vatroslav Mimica, Dusan Vukotić, Nikola Kostelac; in Rumania Ion Popescu-Gopo alternated animated films with live action comedies; In Poland Jan Lenica and Walerian Borowcyk devised new, anarchic and deeply disturbing uses for stop-action techniques (*Once Upon a Time*, 1957; *Dom*, 1958).

By the 1970s, the animated film – the oldest branch of the cinema – had become a remarkably varied and supple instrument, ranging in its possibilities from the lyrical documentary visions of John Hubley (*Of Stars and Men*) to the Rabelaisian farces of the Japanese, Yoji Kuri.

Appendix II:
Selected filmographies

NOTE

Complete filmographies are marked with an asterisk. Selective filmographies in all cases record the first and last recorded films of each director. Film dates are frequently problematic since there may be considerable periods between commencement, completion, first showings and public release. Whenever possible the date given in filmographies is the year of original release.

*Aldrich, Robert. (1918–). American.

1953: *The Big Leaguer*. 1954: *World For Ransom, Apache, Vera Cruz*. 1955: *Kiss Me Deadly, The Big Knife*. 1956: *Autumn Leaves, Attack*. 1957: *The Garment Jungle*. 1958: *Ten Seconds to Hell*. 1959: *The Angry Hills*. 1961: *The Last Sunset*. 1962: *Sodom and Gomorrah*. 1963: *Whatever Happened to Baby Jane, Four For Texas*. 1965: *The Flight of the Phoenix, Hush . . . Hush Sweet Charlotte*. 1967: *The Dirty Dozen*. 1968: *The Killing of Sister George*. 1969: *The Legend of Lyah Clare*. 1970: *Too Late the Hero*. 1971: *The Grissom Gang*.

*Alea, Tomás Gutiérrez. (1928). Cuban.

1959: *El megano* (documentary). 1960: *Esa tierra nuestra* (documentary). 1960: *Historias de la revolucion*. 1962: *Las 12 sillas*. 1964: *Cumbite*. 1965: *Muerte de un burocrata*. 1969: *Memorias de subsedarollo*.

*Alexandrov, Grigori Vasilievich. (né G. V. Mormonenko) (1903–). Soviet.

Co-directed with Eisenstein *October, The General Line, Que viva Mexico!* 1930: *Romance Sentimentale* (short). 1933: *Internationale* (documentary). 1934: *Jazz Comedy*. 1936: *Circus*. 1937: *Report by Comrade Stalin* (documentary). 1938: *Volga-Volga*. 1940: *The Bright Road*. 1943: *One Family*. 1944: *People of the Caspian*. 1947: *Spring, Meeting on the Elbe*. 1952: *The Composer Glinka*. 1957: *Russian Souvenir*. 1958: *From Man to Man*.

Alexeieff, Alexandre. (1901–). Russian-born, working in France as director of animated films.

1933: *Une Nuit sur le mont chauve*. 1935: *La Belle au bois dormant*. 1943: *En passant* (in Canada). 1963: *Le Nez*.

Allegret, Marc. (1900–   ). French.

1927: *Voyage au Congo.* 1932: *Fanny.* 1934: *Lac aux dames.* 1937: *Gribouille.* 1938: *Orage.* 1948: *Blanche Fury* (in Britain). 1954: *Femmina* (in Italy).

Allegret, Yves. (1907–   ). French.

1932: *Teneriffe.* 1936: *Vous n'avez rien à declarer.* 1946: *Les Démons de l'aube.* 1948: *Dédée d'Anvers.* 1949: *Une si jolie petite plage.* 1950: *Manèges.* 1953: *Les Orgeuilleux.* 1954: *Mam'zelle Nitouche.* 1956: *La Meilleure Part.* 1957: *Méfiez-vous fillettes.* 1959: *L'Ambitieuse.* 1963: *Germinal* (in Hungary).

Allio, René. (1921–   ). French.

1965: *La Vieille Dame indigne.* 1967: *L'Une et l'autre.* 1969: *Pierre et Paul.*

*__*Altman, Robert.__* (19–   ). American.

1957: *The James Dean Story.* 1968: *Countdown.* 1969: *That Cold Day in the Park.* 1970: *M.A.S.H.* 1971: *Brewster McCloud, McCabe and Mrs Miller.* 1972: *Images* (in Ireland).

Ambrosio, Arturo. (1869–1960). Italian pioneer director and producer.

1904: *La prima corsa automobilistica Susa-Moncenisio.* 1907: *Marcus Lycinus.* 1908: *Gli ultimi giorni di Pompei.* 1909: *Nerone.* 1910: *Lo schiave di Cartagine, La regina di Ninive.* 1920: *La nave.*

Anderson, Lindsay. (1923–   ). British.

1948: *Meet the Pioneers.* 1953: *Wakefield Express.* 1954: *O Dreamland, Thursday's Children* (co-directed with Guy Brenton). 1957: *Every Day Except Christmas.* 1963: *This Sporting Life.* 1966: *The White Bus.* 1967: *One Two Three* (in Poland), 1968: *If . . . .*

Andrade, Joachim Pedro De. (1932–   ). Brazilian.

1963: *Garrincha, alegria dopovo.* 1966: *O padre e a moca.* 1969: *Macunaima.*

*__*Antoine, André.__* (1858–1943). French. Creator of the Théâtre Libre.

1916: *Les Frères corses.* 1917: *Le Coupable.* 1918: *Les Travailleurs de la mer.* 1920: *Mademoiselle de La Seiglière.* 1921: *La Terre.* 1922: *L'Alouette et la mésange, L'Arlésienne.*

*__*Antonioni, Michaelangelo.__* (1912–   ). Italian.

1943–47: *Gente del Po.* 1948: *N.U., Superstizione,* 1949: *L'amoroza menzogna.* 1950: *Sette canne e un vestito. La villa dei mostri, La funivia del Faloria, Cronaca di un amore.* 1952: *I vinti.* 1953: *La signora seza camelie, L'amore in città* (one episode). 1955: *Le amiche.* 1957: *Il grido.* 1960: *L'avventura.* 1961: *La notte.* 1962: *L'eclisse.* 1964: *Il deserto rosso.* 1965: *I tre volti* (episode). 1966: *Blow-up* (in Britain). 1969: *Zabriskie Point* (in U.S.A.).

*__*Asquith, Anthony.__* (1902–68). British.

1928: *Shooting Stars.* 1929: *Underground.* 1930: *A Cottage on Dartmoor, Runaway Princess.* 1931: *Tell England, Dance Pretty Lady.* 1933: *Lucky Number.* 1934: *Unfinished Symphony.* 1935: *Moscow Nights.* 1938: *Pygmalion* (with Leslie Howard). 1939: *French Without Tears.* 1940: *Freedom Radio, Quiet Wedding.* 1941: *Cottage to Let.* 1942: *Uncensored.* 1943: *We Dive at Dawn, Demi-Paradise, Welcome to Britain.* 1944: *Two Fathers* (in France), *Fanny By Gaslight.* 1945: *The Way to the Stars.* 1946: *While the Sun Shines.* 1948: *The Winslow Boy.* 1950: *The Woman in Question, The Browning Version.* 1951: *The Importance of Being*

Earnest. 1953: *The Net, The Final Test.* 1954: *The Young Lovers.* 1955: *Carrington V.C.* 1958: *Orders to Kill.* 1960: *Libel.* 1961: *The Millionairess.* 1962: *Guns of Darkness, Two Living, One Dead.* 1963: *The V.I.P.s.* 1964: *The Yellow Rolls Royce.*

Astruc, Alexandre. (1923–). French.

1948: *Aller-retour.* 1952: *Le Rideau cramoisi.* 1955: *Les Mauvaises Rencontres.* 1958: *Une Vie.* 1960: *La Proie pour l'ombre.* 1961: *L'Education sentimentale.* 1963: *Le Puits et le pendule* (for TV). 1966: *La Longue Marche.* 1968: *Flammes sur l'Adriatique.*

Audry, Jacqueline. (1908–). French.

1943: *Les Chevaux de Vercors.* 1945: *Les Malheurs de Sophie.* 1949: *Gigi.* 1950: *Minne, l'ingénue libertine.* 1954: *Huis clos.* 1956: *Mitsou.* 1957: *La Garçonne.* 1959: *L'Ecole de cocottes.* 1962: *Les Petits Matins.* 1966: *Soledad.* 1971: *Le Lys de Mer.*

Autant-Lara, Claude. (1903–). French.

1923: *Faits divers.* 1925: *Construire un feu.* 1933: *Ciboulette.* 1939: *Fric Frac.* 1942: *La Mariage de Chiffon, Lettres d'amour.* 1943: *Douce.* 1945: *Sylvie et le fantôme.* 1947: *Le Diable au corps.* 1949: *Occupe-toi d'Amélie!* 1951: *L'Auberge rouge.* 1953: *Le Bon Dieu sans confession.* 1954: *Le Blé en herbe, Le Rouge et le noir.* 1955: *Marguerite de la nuit.* 1956: *La Traversée de Paris.* 1958: *En cas de malheur, Le Joueur.* 1959: *La Jument verte.* 1960: *Les Régats de San Francisco, Le Bois des amants.* 1963: *Tu ne tueras point, Le Magot de Josefa.* 1965: *Le Journal d'une femme en blanc.*

Baratier, Jacques. (1918–). French.

1955: *Paris la nuit.* 1958: *Goha.* 1962: *La Poupée.* 1963: *Dragées au poivre.* 1965: *L'Or du duc.*

Bardem, Juan Antonio. (1922–). Spanish.

1948: *Paseo sobre una guerra antigua* (collaboration with Berlanga), *Esa pareja feliz* (with Berlanga). 1954: *Comicos, Felices pascuas.* 1955: *Muerte de un ciclista.* 1956: *Calle mayor.* 1957: *La venganza.* 1959: *Sonadas.* 1960: *A las cinco de la tarde.* 1963: *Nunca pasa nada.* 1965: *Los pianos mecanicos.*

Barker, Will G. (1867–1951). British pioneer.

1897: actualities for Warwick Film Company, including *Queen Victoria's Diamond Jubilee.* 1911: *Henry VIII.* 1913: *Sixty Years a Queen, East Lynne.* 1914: *The German Spy Peril.* 1915: *Jane Shore.*

Barnet, Boris. (1902–65). Soviet.

1926: *Miss Mend.* 1927: *The Girl with the Hatbox.* 1928: *Moscow in October, The House on Trubnaya Square.* 1933: *Okraina.* 1940: *Stakhanov.* 1961: *Alionka.*

Baroncelli, Jacques de. (1881–1951). French.

1915: *La Maison de l'espoir.* 1919: *Ramuntcho.* 1921: *Le Père Goriot.* 1924: *Pêcheurs de l'islande.* 1929: *Le Femme et le pantin.* 1934: *Crainquebille.* 1937: *Michel Strogoff.* 1948: *Rocambole.*

Bartosch, Berthold. (1893–). Austro-Hungarian, active in France.

1934: *L'Idée* (animated film).

Batalov, Alexei Vladimirovitch. (1928–). Soviet.

1960: *The Overcoat*. 1964: *A Day of Happiness*. 1965: *The Light of Distant Stars*.

Bauer, Evgenii. (1865–1917). Russian.

1913: *Twilight of a Woman's Soul*. 1914: *Life in Death, Children of the Great City*. 1916: *A Life for a Life, Queen of the Screen*. 1917: *Puppets of Fate, The King of Paris, The Revolutionary*.

Bava, Mario. (1914–). Italian, formerly distinguished cameraman.

1960: *La maschera del demonio*. 1963: *I tre volti della paura, La frusta e il corpo*. 1964: *Sei donne per l'assassino*. 1968: *Diabolik*.

Becker, Jacques. (1906–60). French.

1939: *L'Or du Cristobal* (unfinished: credited to Jean Stelli). 1942: *Le Dernier Atout*. 1943: *Le Colonel Chabert, Goupi Mains-rouges*. 1945: *Falbalas*. 1947: *Antoine et Antoinette*. 1949: *Rendez-vous de juillet*. 1951: *Edouard et Caroline*. 1952: *Casque d'or*. 1953: *Rue de l'Estrapade*. 1954: *Touchez-pas au grisbi, Ali Baba et les 40 voleurs*. 1957: *Les Aventures d'Arsène Lupin*. 1958: *Montparnasse 19*. 1960: *Le Trou*.

Bellocchio, Marco. (1940–). Italian.

1965: *I pugni in tasca*. 1967: *La cina è vicina*. 1971: *Nel nome del padre*.

Benedek, Laszlo. (1907–). Hungarian-born; active in U.S.A., Germany, France.

1948: *The Kissing Bandit*. 1949: *Port of New York*. 1951: *Death of a Salesman*. 1952: *Storm Over Tibet*. 1953: *The Wild One*. 1954: *Bengal Brigade*. 1956: *Kinder, Mutter und ein General*. 1957: *Affair in Havana*. 1958: *Moment of Danger*. 1966: *Namu the Killer Whale*. 1968: *The Daring Game*.

Benoît-Levy, Jean. (1888–1959). French.

1920: numerous documentaries. 1933: *La Maternelle*. 1934: *Itto*. 1936: *Hélène*. 1937: *La Mort du cygne*. 1939: *Feu de paille*. (From 1926 generally worked in collaboration with Marie Epstein).

*Bergman, Ingmar. (1918–). Swedish.

1946: *Crisis, It Rains on Our Love*. 1947: *Ship For India, Music in Darkness*. 1948: *Port of Call*. 1949: *Prison, Thirst*. 1950: *To Joy, This Can't Happen Here*. 1951: *Summer Interlude*. 1952: *Waiting Women, Summer with Monika*. 1953: *Sawdust and Tinsel*. 1954: *A Lesson in Love*. 1955: *Journey into Autumn, Smiles of a Summer Night*. 1956: *The Seventh Seal*. 1957: *Wild Strawberries*. 1958: *So Close to Life, The Face*. 1959: *The Virgin Spring*. 1960: *The Devil's Eye*. 1961: *Through a Glass Darkly*. 1962: *Winter Light*. 1963: *The Silence*. 1964: *Now About these Women*. 1966: *Persona*. 1965–7: *Stimulantia*. 1968: *Hour of the Wolf, The Shame*. 1969: *The Rite, A Passion*. 1971: *The Touch*.

*Berkeley, Busby. (1895–). American.

Dance director in several Hollywood films, 1931 to 1935; then 1935; *Gold Diggers of 1935, Bright Lights, I Live For Love*. 1936: *Stagestruck*. 1937: *The Go-Getter, Hollywood Hotel*. 1938: *Men Are Such Fools, Garden of the Moon, Comet Over Broadway*. 1939: *They Made Me a Criminal, Babes in Arms, Fast and Furious*. 1940: *Strike Up the Band, Forty, Little Mothers*. 1941: *Babes on Broadway. Blonde Inspiration*. 1942: *For Me and My Gal*. 1943: *The Gang's All Here*. 1948: *Cinderella Jones*. 1949: *Take Me Out to the Ball Game*.

Berlanga, Luis Garcia. (1921–). Spanish.

1948: *Paseo sobre una guerra antigua* (with Bardem). 1949: *El circo.* 1951: *Esa pareja feliz* (with Bardem). 1952: *Bien venido, Mr Marshall!* (with Bardem). 1953: *Novio a la vista.* 1955: *Familia provisional.* 1956: *Calabuch.* 1957: *Los jueves, milagro.* 1952: *Placido.* 1964: *El Verdugo.*

*Bertolucci, Bernardo. (1941–). Italian.

1962: *La commare secca.* 1964: *Prima della rivoluzione.* 1965–6: *La via del petrolio* (for TV). 1967: *Vangelo '70* (episode). 1969: *Partner.* 1970: *Il conformista, La strategia del Ragno.* 1971: *I poveri muoiono prima, La petite mort.* 1972: *Last Tango in Paris.*

*Biberman, Herbert J. (1900–1971). American.

1953: *Salt of the Earth.* 1969: *Slaves.*

Blackton, J. Stuart. (1875–1941). British, mostly active in U.S.A.

1897: *The Burglar on the Roof, Tearing Down the Spanish Flag.* 1897–1912: several hundred short films. 1915: *The Battlecry of Peace.* 1922: *The Glorious Adventure.* 1923: *The Virgin Queen.* 1926: *Passionate Quest.*

Blasetti, Alessandro. (1900–). Italian.

1929: *Sole.* 1930: *Nerone.* 1932: *La tavole dei poveri.* 1934: *1860.* 1942: *Quattro passi fra le nuvole.* 1946: *Un giorno nella vita.* 1948: *Fabiola.* 1950: *Prima communione.* 1952: *Altri tempi, La fiammata.* 1954: *Tempi nostri.* 1955: *Peccato che sia una canaglia.* 1961: *Io amo, tu ami.* 1966: *Io, io, io . . . e gli altri.* 1967: *La ragazza del bersagliere.*

*Boetticher, Budd. (1916–). American.

1944: *One Mysterious Night, The Missing Juror, Youth on Trial.* 1945: *A Guy, a Gal and a Pal, Escape in the Fog.* 1948: *Assigned to Danger, Behind Locked Doors.* 1949: *Black Midnight.* 1950: *The Wolf Hunters, Killer Shark.* 1951: *The Bullfighter and the Lady, The Cimarron Kid.* 1952: *Red Ball Express, Broncho Buster, Horizons West.* 1953: *City Beneath the Sea, Seminole, The Man from the Alamo, Wings of the Hawk, East of Sumatra.* 1955: *The Magnificent Matador.* 1956: *The Killer is Loose, Seven Men From Now.* 1957: *Decision at Sundown, The Tall T.* 1958: *Buchanan Rides Alone.* 1959: *Ride Lonesome, Westbound.* 1960: *The Rise and Fall of Legs Diamond, Comanche Station.* 1959–68: *Arruza.* 1969: *A Time for Dying.*

*Bogdanovitch, Peter. (1939–). American.

1968: *Targets.* 1971: *The Last Picture Show.* 1972: *What's up, Doc?*

Boleslavski, Richard. (1889–1937). Polish, active in Russia, Poland, U.S.A.

1915: *Three Meetings, You Don't Know How to Love.* 1917: *Not Right, but Passion Rules, The Polenov Family, House on the Volga* (all in Russia). 1919: *Heroism of a Polish Scout.* 1921: *Miracle on the Vistula* (both in Poland). 1930: *Treasure Girl, The Last of the Lone Wolf.* 1933: *Rasputin and the Empress.* 1934: *The Painted Veil.* 1935: *Clive of India, The Hunchback of Notre Dame.* 1936: *The Garden of Allah, Theodora Goes Wild.* 1937: *The Last of Mrs Cheyney.*

Bolognini, Mauro. (1923–). Italian.

1953: *Ci troviamo in galeria.* 1957: *Giovani mariti.* 1960: *Il bel Antonio.* 1961: *La Viaccia.* 1962: *Senilità, Agostino.* 1966: *Madamigella di Maupin.*

Bondarchuk, Sergei. (1920–   ). Soviet.

1959: *Destiny of a Man*. 1963–7: *War and Peace*. 1970: *Waterloo*.

Borowczyk, Walerian. (1923–   ). Polish, active in Poland and France.

1957: *Once Upon a Time*. 1958: *Dom* (both in collaboration with Jan Lenica). 1959: *The School*. 1960: *The Magician*. 1966: *Le Dictionnaire de Joachim*. 1967: *Goto, île d'amour*. 1971: *Blanche*.

Borzage, Frank. (1893–1962). American.

1916: *Life's Harmony*. 1920: *Humoresque*. 1927: *Seventh Heaven*. 1928: *Street Angel*. 1929: *Lucky Star, The River*. 1930: *Song of My Heart, Liliom*. 1931: *Bad Girl*. 1932: *A Farewell to Arms, Secrets, A Man's Castle*. 1933: *No Greater Glory, Little Man, What Now?, Flirtation Walk*. 1936: *Desire*. 1937: *History is Made at Night, The Big City*. 1938: *Three Comrades*. 1940: *Strange Cargo, The Mortal Storm*. 1943: *Stage Door Canteen*. 1944: *Till We Meet Again*. 1948: *Moonrise*. 1958: *China Doll*. 1959: *The Big Fisherman*.

Boulting, John. (1913–   ). British.

1945: *Journey Together*. 1948: *Brighton Rock*. 1950: *Seven Days to Noon*. 1954: *Seagulls Over Sorrento* (with Roy Boulting). Produced many of Roy Boulting's films.

Boulting, Roy. (1913–   ). British.

1938: *The Landlady*. 1940: *Inquest*. 1943: *Desert Victory*. 1947: *Fame is the Spur*. 1949: *The Guinea Pig*. 1951: *High Treason*. 1954: *Seagulls Over Sorrento* (with John Boulting). 1957: *Brothers in Law*. 1960: *I'm All Right Jack*. 1967: *The Family Way*.

*Brando, Marlon. (1924–   ). American.

1960: *One-Eyed Jacks*.

Brenon, Herbert. (1880–1958). Irish, active in U.S.A. and Britain.

1913: *Ivanhoe*. 1914: *Neptune's Daughter*. 1916: *Daughter of the Gods, War Brides*. 1921: *The Garden of Allah*. 1925: *Peter Pan*. 1926: *The Great Gatsby, A Kiss for Cinderella, Beau Geste*. 1928: *Laugh, Clown, Laugh*. 1940: *The Flying Squad*.

*Bresson, Robert. (1907–   ). French.

1934: *Les Affaires publiques* (with Pierre Charbonnier). 1943: *Les Anges du péché*. 1945: *Les Dames du Bois de Boulogne*. 1950: *Le Journal d'un curé de campagne*. 1956: *Un condamné à mort s'est échappé*. 1959: *Pickpocket*. 1961: *Le Procès de Jeanne d'Arc*. 1966: *Au hasard, Balthasar, Mouchette*. 1969: *Une Femme douce*. 1971: *Quatre nuits d'un rêveur*.

Broca, Philippe de. (1933   ). French.

1960: *Les Jeux de l'amour*. 1961: *L'Amant de cinq jours*. 1962: *Le Farceur*. 1963: *L'Homme de Rio*. 1964: *Un Monsieur de compagnie*. 1967: *Les Fous de la ville*. 1972: *Chère Louise*.

Brook, Peter. (1925–   ). British.

1953: *The Beggar's Opera*. 1960: *Moderato Cantabile*. 1963: *Lord of the Flies*. 1967: *Marat-Sade*. 1968: *Tell Me Lies*. 1971: *King Lear*.

*Brooks, Richard. (1912–). American.

1950: *Crisis*. 1951: *The Light Touch*. 1952: *Deadline U.S.A.* 1953: *Battle Circus, Take the High Ground*. 1954: *The Flame and the Flesh, The Last Time I Saw Paris*. 1955: *The Blackboard Jungle, The Last Hunt*. 1956: *The Catered Affair*. 1957: *Something of Value*. 1958: *The Brothers Karamazov, Cat on a Hot Tin Roof*. 1960: *Elmer Gantry*. 1962: *Sweet Bird of Youth*. 1964: *Lord Jim*. 1966: *The Professionals*. 1967: *In Cold Blood*. 1970: *The Happy Ending*.

Brown, Clarence. (1890–). American.

1920: *The Great Redeemer, The Last of the Mohicans*. 1924: *Smouldering Fires*. 1925: *The Eagle, The Goose Woman*. 1926: *Kiki*. 1927: *Flesh and the Devil*. 1928: *A Woman of Affairs*. 1930: *Anna Christie, Romance*. 1931: *Inspiration, A Free Soul*. 1932: *Emma*. 1935: *Anna Karenina, Ah, Wilderness*. 1937: *Conquest (Marie Walewska)*. 1939: *The Rains Came*. 1940: *Edison the Man*. 1944: *National Velvet*. 1946: *The Yearling*. 1949: *Intruder in the Dust*.

*Brown, Karl. (c. 1895–). American. Formerly cameraman with D. W. Griffith etc.

1927: *Stark Love, His Dog*. 1930: *Prince of Diamonds*. 1932: *Flames*. 1936: *White Legion, In His Steps*. 1937: *Michael O'Halloran, Federal Bullets*. 1938: *Port of Missing Girls, Numbered Woman, Under the Big Top*. Continued as writer until 1953.

*Browning, Tod. (1882–1962). American.

1918: *The Brazen Beauty*. 1919: *The Wicked Darling*. 1920: *The Virgin of Stamboul*. 1921: *Outside the Law*. 1922: *Under Two Flags*. 1923: *The White Tiger, Drifting*. 1925: *The Unholy Three*. 1926: *The Road to Mandalay, The Blackbird*. 1927: *The Show, The Unknown, London After Midnight*. 1928: *West of Zanzibar*. 1929: *Where East is East, The Unholy Three* (remake), *The Thirteenth Chair*. 1930: *Outside the Law* (remake). 1931: *The Iron Man, Dracula*. 1932: *Freaks*. 1935: *The Mark of the Vampire*. 1936: *The Devil Doll*. 1939: *Miracles for Sale*.

*Brunius, Jacques. (1906–67). French.

1933: *Autour d'une évasion*. 1937: *Violons d'Ingres*. 1950: *Somewhere to Live*. 1952: *Brief City*. 1954: *The Blakes Slept Here*.

Brunius, John W. (1884–1937). Swedish.

1918: *Puss in Boots*. 1920: *Thora van Deken*. 1921: *A Wild Bird*. 1922: *The Eyes of Love*. 1925: *Karl XII*. 1928: *Gustav Wasa*. 1934: *False Greta*.

Buñuel, Luis. (1900–). Spanish.

1928: *Un Chien andalou*. 1930: *L'Age d'or*. 1932: *Las Hurdes*. 1947: *Gran Casino*. 1949: *El gran calavera*. 1950: *Los olvidados*. 1951: *Susana, La hija del engano, Una mujer sin amor, Sibida al cielo*. 1952: *El bruto, Robinson Crusoe, El.* 1953: *Cumbres borrascosas, La ilusion viaja en tranvia*. 1954: *El rio e la muerte*. 1955: *Ensayo de un crimen, Cela s'appelle l'aurore*. 1956: *La mort en ce jardin*. 1958: *Nazarin*. 1959: *La fièvre monte à El Pao*. 1960: *The Young One*. 1961: *Viridiana*. 1962: *El angel exterminador*. 1964: *Le Journal d'une femme de chambre*. 1965: *Simon del desierto*. 1966: *Belle de jour*. 1969: *La Voie lactée*. 1970: *Tristana*.

Cabanne, William Christie. (1888–1950). American.

1914: *The Sisters*. 1915: *The Lamb, Double Trouble*. 1937: *The Outcasts of Poker Flat*. 1948: *Back Trail*.

*Cacoyannis, Michael. (1922–). Greek.

1953: *Windfall in Athens*. 1954: *Stella*. 1957: *The Girl in Black*. 1958: *A Matter of Dignity*. 1959: *Our Last Spring*. 1961: *The Wastrel*. 1962: *Elektra*. 1966: *Zorba the Greek*. 1967: *The Day the Fish Came Out*. 1971: *The Trojan Women*.

Camerini, Mario. (1895–). Italian.

1923: *Jolly, clown del circo*. 1926: *Maciste contro lo sceicco*. 1929: *Rotaie*. 1932: *Gli uomini; che mascalzoni!* 1934: *Il capello a tre punte*. 1935: *Darò un milione*. 1942: *Una storia d'amore*. 1945: *Due lettere anonime*. 1948: *Molti sogni per le strade*. 1963: *Kali-Yug, la dea della vendetta, Il mistero del tempio indiano*.

Capellani, Albert. (1870–1931). French.

1906: *Aladin*. 1908: *Le Chat botté, Jeanne d'Arc, L'Homme aux gants blancs*. 1909: *L'Assommoir*. 1910: *Athalie, Les Deux Orphelines*. 1911: *Notre Dame de Paris, Les Mystères de Paris, Les Misérables*. 1913: *La Glu, Germinal*. 1914: *Les Quatrevingt-treize*. 1915: *Les Epaves de l'amour* (in U.S.A.). 1916: *The Common Law, La Bohème*. 1919: *Out of the Fog, The Red Lantern*. 1922: *Sisters, The Young Diana*.

Capra, Frank. (1897–). American.

1923: *Fultah Fisher's Boarding House*. 1926: *The Strong Man*. 1927: *Long Pants*. 1928: *Submarine, The Power of the Press*. 1929: *Flight*. 1931: *Dirigible, Platinum Blonde*. 1932: *Forbidden, American Madness*. 1933: *The Bitter Tea of General Yen, Lady for a Day*. 1934: *It Happened One Night, Broadway Bill*. 1936: *Mr Deeds Goes to Town*. 1937: *Lost Horizon*. 1938: *You Can't Take it With You*. 1939: *Mr Smith Goes to Washington*. 1941: *Meet John Doe*. 1942: *Prelude to War*. 1943: *Tunisian Victory*. 1944: *Arsenic and Old Lace*. 1946: *It's A Wonderful Life*. 1948: *State of the Union*. 1950: *Riding High*. 1951: *Here Comes the Groom*. 1959: *A Hole in the Head*. 1962: *A Pocketful of Miracles*.

Cardiff, Jack. (1914–). British. Former cinematographer.

1958: *Intent to Kill*. 1960: *Scent of Mystery* (abortive experiment with 'smellies'). *Sons and Lovers*. 1962: *My Geisha*. 1966: *Young Cassidy*. 1968: *Girl on a Motorcycle*.

Carné, Marcel. (1909–). French.

1929: *Nogent, eldorado du dimanche*. 1936: *Jenny*. 1937: *Drôle de drame*. 1938: *Quai des brumes, Hôtel du nord*. 1939: *Le Jour se lève*. 1942: *Les Visiteurs du soir*. 1943–5: *Les Enfants du paradis*. 1946: *Les Portes de la nuit*. 1948: *La fleur de large*. 1949: *La Marie du port*. 1951: *Juliette, ou la clé des songes*. 1953: *Thérèse Raquin*. 1954: *L'Air de Paris*. 1958: *Les Tricheurs*. 1961: *Le Terrain vague*. 1963: *Du mouron pour les petits oiseaux*. 1965: *Trois chambres à Manhattan*. 1971: *Les Assassins de l'ordre*.

Caserini, Mario. (1874–1920). Italian.

1907: *Otello, Garibaldi*. 1908–20: numerous spectacle films. 1920: *Fior di amore*.

Cassavetes, John. (1929–). American.

1960: *Shadows*. 1961: *Too Late Blues*. 1962: *A Child is Waiting*. 1968: *Faces*. 1970: *Husbands*. 1971: *Minnie and Moskowitz*.

Castellani, Renato. (1913–). Italian.

1941: *Un colpo di pistola*. 1942: *Zazà*. 1946: *Mio figlio professore*. 1948: *Sotto il sole di Roma*. 1949: *E primavera*. 1951: *Due soldi di speranza, Romeo and Juliet*.

1957: *I sogni nel cassetto*. 1958: *Nella città l'inferno*. 1961: *Il brigante*. 1963: *Mare matto*.

Cavalcanti, Alberto. (1897–). Brazilian, active in France, Britain, Brazil, Austria, Italy.

1926: *Rien que les heures*. 1927: *Yvette, En rade*. 1928: *Le Train sans yeux, La P'tite Lilie*. 1929: *La Jalousie de Barbouillé, La Capitaine Fracasse*. 1930: *Le Petit Chaperon Rouge*. 1923: *Le Tour de chant*. In Britain: 1934: *Pett and Pott*. 1936: *Coal Face*. 1942: *The Foreman Went to France*. 1944: *Champagne Charlie*. 1945: *Dead of Night* (one episode). *Nicholas Nickleby*. 1947: *They Made me a Fugitive, The First Gentleman*. 1948: *For Them that Trespass*. In Brazil: 1954: *O canto do mar, Mulher de Verdade*. In Austria: 1955: *Herr Puntila und sein knecht Matti*. In Italy: 1958: *La prima notte*. 1962: *Yerma*.

*Cayatte, André. (1909–). French.

1949: *Les Amants de Vérone*. 1950: *Justice est faite*. 1952: *Nous sommes tous des assassins*. 1954: *Avant le deluge*. 1955: *Le Dossier Noir*. 1956: *Oeil pour oeil*. 1960: *Le Passage du Rhin*. 1965: *Le Glaive et la balance*. 1964: *La Vie conjugale*. 1965: *Un Piège pour Cendrillon*.

*Chabrol, Claude. (1930–). French.

1958: *Le Beau Serge, Les Cousins*. 1959: *A Double Tour*. 1960: *Les Bonnes Femmes, Les Godelureaux*. 1961: *Les Sept péchés capitaux* (episode). 1962: *L'Oeil du Malin, Ophelia, Landru*. 1963: *Les plus belles escroqueries du monde* (episode). 1964: *Le Tigre aime la chair fraîche*. 1965: *Marie-Chantal contre le docteur Kha, Le Tigre se parfume à la dynamite*. 1966: *La ligne de demarcation, Paris vue par . . .* (episode), *Le scandale*. 1967: *La route de Corinthe*. 1968: *Les Biches, La femme infidèle*. 1969: *Que la bête meure, Le Boucher*. 1970: *La Rupture*. 1972: *La Décade Prodigieuse*.

Chaplin, Charles Spencer. (1889–). British, mostly active in U.S.A.

1914: *Making a Living* (acted only); 34 other films for Keystone, mostly directed by Chaplin himself. 1915: 15 films for the Essanay Company, all directed by Chaplin and including *The Champion, The Tramp, The Bank*. 1916: *The Floorwalker, The Fireman, The Vagabond, One A.M., The Count, The Pawnshop, Behind the Screen, The Rink*. 1917: *Easy Street, The Cure, The Immigrant, The Adventurer*. 1918: *A Dog's Life, The Bond, Shoulder Arms*. 1919: *Sunnyside, A Day's Pleasure*. 1921: *The Kid, The Idle Class*. 1922: *Pay Day*. 1923: *The Pilgrim, A Woman of Paris*. 1925: *The Gold Rush*. 1928: *The Circus*. 1931: *City Lights*. 1936: *Modern Times*. 1940: *The Great Dictator*. 1947: *Monsieur Verdoux*. 1952: *Limelight*. 1957: *A King in New York*. 1966: *A Countess from Hong Kong*.

Chenal, Pierre. (1903–). French.

1927: *Un Grand Illustré moderne*. 1932: *Le Martyr de l'obèse*. 1934: *La Rue sans nom*. 1935: *Crime et châtiment*. 1937: *L'Homme de nulle part, La Maison du Maltais*. 1939: *Le Dernier Tournant*. 1948: *Clochemerle*. 1951: *Sangre Negra (Native Son)* (in Argentina).

*Chiarini, Luigi. (1900–). Italian.

1942: *Via delle cinque lune, La bella addormentata*. 1943: *La locandiera*. 1946: *Ultimo amore*. 1948: *Patto con diavolo*.

Chiaureli, Mikhail. (1894–). Soviet.

1928: *First Lieutenant Streshnov*. 1929: *Saba*. 1933: *Last Masquerade*. 1937:

Arson. 1942–3: *Georgii Saakadze.* 1950: *The Fall of Berlin.* 1958: *Otar's Widow.* 1960: *Story of a Girl.*

*Christensen, Benjamin. (1879–1959). Danish, also active in U.S.A. and Germany.

1913: *The Mysterious X.* 1915: *Night of Vengeance.* 1922: *Häxan (Witchcraft Through the Ages).* In Germany: 1924: *Seine Frau, die Unbekannte.* In U.S.A.: 1926: *The Devil's Circus.* 1927: *Mockery.* 1928: *The Haunted House.* 1929: *The House of Horror, Seven Footprints to Satan.* In Denmark: 1939: *Children of Divorce.* 1940: *The Girl.* 1941: *Come Home With Me.* 1942: *Damen med ee lyse Handsker.*

Christian-Jaque. (1904–). French.

1932: *Bidon d'or.* 1936: *François premier.* 1938: *Les Disparus de St Agil.* 1941: *L'Assassinat du père Noel.* 1942: *Carmen* (in Italy). 1945: *Sortilèges.* 1946: *Boule de suif.* 1948: *La Chartreuse de Parme, D'homme à hommes.* 1949: *Singoalla.* 1950: *Souvenirs perdus.* 1951: *Fanfan la Tulipe, Barbe-bleue.* 1952: *Adorables créatures, Lucrèce Borgia.* 1954: *Madame Dubarry.* 1955: *Si tous les gars du monde . . ., Nana, Nathalie.* 1959: *Babette s'en va-t'en guerre.* 1961: *Madame Sans-Gêne.* 1964: *La Tulipe noire.*

Chukrai, Grigori. (1921–). Soviet.

1956: *The Forty-First.* 1959: *Ballad of a Soldier.* 1961: *Clear Skies.* 1965: *There Was an Old Man and an Old Woman.* 1969: *Stalingrad.*

*Chytilová, Věra. (1929–). Czech.

1962: *The Ceiling, A Bag of Fleas.* 1963: *Another Way of Life.* 1965: *Pearls of the Deep* (one episode). 1966: *Daisies.* 1969: *Fruits of Paradise.*

Ciampi, Yves. (1921–). French.

1945: *Les Compagnons de la gloire.* 1951: *Un Grand Patron.* 1955: *Les Héros sont fatigués.* 1961: *Qui êtes-vous, Monsieur Sorge?* 1962: *Liberté I* (in Senegal).

*Clair, René. (1898–). French.

1923: *Paris qui dort.* 1924: *Entr'acte.* 1925: *Le Fantôme du Moulin-Rouge, Le Voyage imaginaire.* 1926: *La proie du vent, La Tour.* 1927: *Un Chapeau de paille d'Italie.* 1928: *Les Deux Timides.* 1930: *Sous les toits de Paris.* 1931: *Le Million.* 1932: *A nous la liberté.* 1933: *Le Quatorze Juillet.* 1935: *Le Dernier Milliardaire.* 1936: *The Ghost Goes West.* 1938: *Break the News.* 1941: *The Flame of New Orleans.* 1942: *I Married a Witch.* 1944: *It Happened Tomorrow.* 1945: *And Then There Were None.* 1947: *Le Silence est d'or.* 1950: *La Beauté du diable.* 1952: *Les Belles-de-nuit.* 1956: *Les Grandes Manoeuvres.* 1957: *Porte des Lilas.* 1960: *La Française et l'amour* (one episode). 1961: *Tout l'or du monde.* 1963: *Les Quatre Vérités* (episode). 1966: *Les Fêtes galantes.*

*Clarke, Shirley. (1925–). American.

1960: *The Connection.* 1963: *The Cool World.* 1967: *Portrait of Jason.*

*Clayton, Jack. (1921–). British.

1955: *The Bespoke Overcoat.* 1959: *Room at the Top.* 1962: *The Innocents.* 1963: *The Pumpkin Eater.* 1967: *Our Mother's House.*

Clément, René. (1913–). French.

1937: *Arabie interdite.* 1946: *La Bataille du rail.* 1947: *Les Maudits.* 1949: *Au-delà des grilles.* 1950: *Le Château de verre.* 1952: *Jeux interdits.* 1954: *Monsieur Ripois.*

1956: *Gervaise*. 1958: *Barrage contre le Pacifique*. 1960: *Plein soleil*. 1961: *Che gioia vivere* (in Italy). 1963: *Le Jour et l'heure*. 1964: *Les Felins*. 1967: *Paris brûle-t'il?*

Cline, Eddie. (1892–). American.

1918: *Summer Girls*. 1921: *The Haunted House*. 1923: *The Three Ages*. 1926: *Ladies' Night in a Turkish Bath*. 1932: *Million Dollar Legs*. 1935: *Peck's Bad Boy*. 1940: *My Little Chickadee*. 1941: *The Bank Dick, Never Give a Sucker an Even Break*. 1948: *Jiggs and Maggie in Society*.

*Clouzot, Henri-Georges. (1907–). French.

1942: *L'Assassin habite au 21*. 1943: *Le Corbeau*. 1947: *Quai des orfèvres*. 1948: *Manon*. 1949: *Retour à la vie* (episode). 1950: *Brazil* (unfinished). 1952: *Le Salaire de la peur*. 1956: *Les Diaboliques, Le Mystère Picasso*. 1957: *Les Espions*. 1960: *La Vérité*.

*Cocteau, Jean. (1889–1963). French.

1930: *Le Sang d'un poète*. 1946: *La Belle et la bête* (co-directed with René Clément). 1948: *Les Parents terribles, L'Aigle à deux têtes*. 1950: *Orphée*. 1951: *La Villa Santo-sospir*. 1952: *Le Rouge est mis*. 1960: *Le Testament d'Orphée*.

Cohl, Emile. (1857–1923). French. The father of the animated film.

1907: *Course potirons, La Vie au rebours*. 1908: *Fantasmagorie, Drame chez les fantoches*. 1913–15: *Snookums* series (in U.S.A.). 1918: *Les Aventures des pieds-nickelés*.

Collins, Alfred. (?–?). British pioneer of chase films.

1903: *The Runaway Match, or, Marriage by Motor*. 1905: *Mutiny on a Russian Battleship* (early version of *Potemkin* mutiny).

Colpi, Henri. (1921–). French.

1921: *Des rails et des palmiers*. 1953: *Architecture de lumière*. 1961: *Une Aussi Longue Absence*. 1963: *Codine*.

Comencini, Luigi. (1916–). Italian.

1946: *Bambini in città*. 1948: *Proibito rubare*. 1950: *L'imperatore di Capri, L'ospedale del delitto*. 1953: *Pane, amore e fantasia*. 1954: *Pane, amore e gelosia*. 1960: *Tutti a casa*. 1963: *La ragazza de Bube*. 1966: *Incompreso*.

*Cooper, Merian C. (1893–). American.

In collaboration with Ernest Schoedsack: 1925: *Grass*. 1927:: *Chang*. 1929: *The Four Feathers, Rango*. 1933: *King Kong*.

Corman, Roger. (1926–). American.

1955: *Five Guns West*. 1956: *Apache Woman, The Day the World Ended, Swamp Woman, Gunslinger, It Conquered the World, Oklahoma Woman*. 1957: *The Undead, Teenage Doll, Naked Paradise, Attack of the Crab Monster, Not of this Earth, Rock All Night, Sorority Girl*. 1958: *Viking Women and the Sea Serpent, War of the Satellites, Teenage Caveman, She-Gods of Shark Reef, Machine Gun Kelly*. 1959: *Buckets of Blood, The Wasp Woman, I, Mobster*. 1960: *Ski-Troop Attack, Atlas, The Fall of the House of Usher, The Last Woman on Earth*. 1961: *The Little Shop of Horrors, The Pit and the Pendulum, The Creature from the Haunted Sea*. 1962: *The Intruder, The Premature Burial, Tales of Terror*. 1963: *The Terror, The Haunted Palace, The Man With the X-Ray Eyes, The Young*

Racers, Tower of London, The Raven. 1964: *The Tomb of Ligeia, The Masque of the Red Death, The Secret Invasion.* 1966: *The Wild Angels.* 1967: *The St Valentine's Day Massacre, The Trip.* 1970: *Bloody Mama.* 1971: *The Red Baron.*

Cornelius, Henry. (1913–58). British.

1949: *Passport to Pimlico.* 1951: *The Galloping Major.* 1953: *Genevieve.* 1955: *I Am a Camera.* 1958: *Next to No Time.*

*Cousteau, Jacques-Yves. (1910–   ). French.

1943: *Par 18 mètres de fond.* 1945: *Epaves.* 1947: *Paysages du silence.* 1949: *Au large des côtes tunisiennes, Autour d'un récif, Les Phoques du Rio de Oro, Dauphins et cétacés.* 1950: *Une Sortie du Rubis, Carnet de plongée.* 1952: *La Mer rouge.* 1953: *Un Musée dans la mer.* 1956: *Le Monde du silence* (with Louis Malle). 1964: *Le Monde sans soleil.*

*Crichton, Charles. (1910–   ). British.

1944: *For Those in Peril.* 1945: *Painted Boats, Dead of Night* (episode). 1947: *Hue and Cry.* 1949: *Against the Wind.* 1950: *Dance Hall, Train of Events.* 1951: *Another Shore, The Lavender Hill Mob.* 1952: *Hunted, The Titfield Thunderbolt.* 1954: *The Love Lottery, The Divided Heart.* 1956: *The Man in the Sky.* 1957: *Law and Disorder.* 1958: *Floods of Fear.* 1959: *The Battle of the Sexes.* 1960: *The Boy Who Stole a Million.* 1963: *The Third Secret.* 1965: *He Who Rides a Tiger.*

Crosland, Alan. (1894–1936). American.

1915: *Santa Claus versus Cupid* (with Will Louis). 1926: *Don Juan.* 1927: *The Jazz Singer, Old San Francisco.* 1935: *The Great Impersonation.*

Cruze, James. (1884–1942). American.

1918: *Too Many Millions.* 1923: *The Covered Wagon, Hollywood, Ruggles of Red Gap.* 1924: *Merton of the Movies, The Fighting Coward, The City That Never Sleeps.* 1925: *Beggar on Horseback, The Pony Express.* 1926: *Old Ironsides.* 1930: *The Great Gabbo.* 1938: *Come on Leathernecks.*

Cukor, George. (1899–   ). American.

1930: *Grumpy* (co-directed with Cyril Gardner). 1931: *Tarnished Lady.* 1932: *A Bill of Divorcement.* 1933: *Our Betters, Dinner at Eight, Little Women.* 1934: *David Copperfield.* 1935: *Sylvia Scarlett.* 1936: *Romeo and Juliet, Camille.* 1939: *The Women.* 1940: *The Philadelphia Story.* 1941: *Two-Faced Woman, A Woman's Face.* 1944: *Gaslight.* 1949: *Edward my Son, Adam's Rib.* 1950: *Born Yesterday.* 1951: *The Marrying Kind.* 1952: *Pat and Mike.* 1953: *The Actress.* 1954: *It Should Happen to You, A Star is Born.* 1955: *Bhowani Junction.* 1957: *Les Girls.* 1959: *Heller in Pink Tights.* 1960: *Let's Make Love.* 1961: *The Chapman Report, Something's Got to Give.* 1964: *My Fair Lady.* 1969: *Justine.*

Curtiz, Michael (Kertesz, Mihaly). (1888–1962). Hungarian, active in Hungary, Austria, Germany and U.S.A.

In Hungary: 1912: *Az utolsó behém, Ma és holnap.* 1919: *Jön az öcsém.* In Austria: 1919: *Der Stern von Damaskus.* 1922: *Sodom und Gomorrha.* 1924: *Samson und Dalila, Moon of Israel.* In U.S.A.: 1926: *The Third Degree.* 1929: *Noah's Ark.* 1932: *Cabin in the Cotton.* 1933: *20,000 Years in Sing-Sing, The Mystery of the Wax Museum.* 1936: *The Walking Dead, Charge of the Light Brigade.* 1938: *Angels With Dirty Faces.* 1942: *Casablanca.* 1946: *Mildred Pierce.* 1959: *The Hangman.* 1960: *The Adventures of Huckleberry Finn, A Breath of Scandal.* 1961: *Francis of Assisi, The Comancheros.*

Czinner, Paul. (1890–). Hungarian, active in Germany and Britain.

1924: *Nju.* 1927: *Doña Juana.* 1928: *Liebe.* 1929: *Fräulein Else.* 1930: *The Way of Lost Souls.* 1931: *Ariane.* 1932: *Der Traümende Mund.* 1934: *Catherine the Great.* 1935: *Escape Me Never.* 1936: *As You Like It.* 1937: *Dreaming Lips.* 1939: *Stolen Life.* 1957: *The Bolshoi Ballet.*

Daquin, Louis. (1908–). French.

1940: *Nous les gosses.* 1948: *Le Point du jour.* 1955: *Bel ami.* 1965: *La foire aux cancres.*

Dassin, Jules. (1911). American, active in U.S.A., France, Italy, Germany, Britain.

1941: *The Tell-Tale Heart.* 1944: *The Canterville Ghost.* 1947: *Brute Force.* 1948: *The Naked City.* 1949: *Thieves Highway.* 1950: *Night and the City.* 1955: *Rififi (Du Rififi chez les hommes).* 1957: *Celui qui doit mourir.* 1958: *La Loi.* 1960: *Never on Sunday.* 1962: *Phaedra.* 1964: *Topkapi.* 1966: *10-30 p.m. Summer.* 1968: *Survival, Uptight.* 1971: *Promise at Dawn.*

Decoin, Henri. (1896–1969). French.

1935: *Toboggan.* 1937: *Abus du confiance.* 1942: *Les Inconnus dans le maison.* 1946: *La Fille du diable.* 1950: *Trois telegrammes.* 1951: *La Vérité sur Bébé Donge.* 1952: *Les Amants de Tolède.* 1955: *Razzia sur la chnouf.* 1957: *Charmants garçons.* 1958: *La Chatte sort les griffes.* 1964: *Outcasts of Glory.*

Delvaux, André (1926–). Belgian.

1966: *The Man Who Had His Hair Cut Short.* 1969: *Un Soir . . . un train.* 1971: *Rendez-vous à Bray.*

Delluc, Louis. (1890–1924). French.

1920: *Fumée noire* (with Renê Coiffart), *L'Américain, Le Tonnerre, Le Silence.* 1921: *Fièvre.* 1922: *La Femme de nulle part.* 1924: *L'inondation.*

*De Mille, Cecil B. (1881–1959). American.

1913: *The Squaw Man, Brewster's Millions.* 1914: *The Call of the North, The Virginian, What's His Name, The Man From Home, Ready Money, Rose of the Rancho, The Circus Man, The Ghost Breaker, Cameo Kirby, The Girl of the Golden West.* 1915: *Goose Girl, The Warrens of Virginia, The Country Boy, Gentleman of Leisure, Governor's Lady, The Unafraid, The Captive, Snobs, The Wild Goose Chase, Chimie Fadden, Kindling, Carmen, The Cheat, Temptation.* 1916: *Maria Rosa, The Golden Chance, The Trail of the Lonesome Pine, The Heart of Nora Flynn, Dream Girl, Sweet Kitty Bellairs, Joan the Woman.* 1917: *A Romance of the Redwoods, The Little American, The Woman God Forgot, The Devil's Stone.* 1918: *The Whispering Chorus, Old Wives For New, You Can't Have Everything, Till I Come Back to You, The Squaw Man, Don't Change Your Husband.* 1919: *For Better or Worse, Male and Female, Why Change Your Wife?* 1920: *Feet of Clay, Something to think About, Forbidden Fruit.* 1921: *The Affairs of Anatol, Fool's Paradise.* 1922: *Saturday Night, Manslaughter.* 1923: *Adam's Rib, The Ten Commandments.* 1924: *Triumph, The Golden Bed.* 1925: *The Road to Yesterday.* 1926: *The Volga Boatman.* 1927: *The King of Kings.* 1928: *The Godless Girl.* 1929: *Dynamite.* 1930: *Madame Satan.* 1931: *The Squaw Man.* 1932: *The Sign of the Cross.* 1933: *This Day and Age.* 1934: *Cleopatra, Four Frightened People.* 1935: *The Crusades.* 1937: *The Plainsman, The Buccaneer.* 1939: *Union Pacific.* 1940: *Land of Liberty, North West Mounted Police.* 1941: *Reap the Wild Wind.* 1944: *The Story of Dr Wassell.* 1947: *Unconquered.* 1949:

Samson and Delilah. 1952: *The Greatest Show on Earth.* 1956: *The Ten Commandments.*

*Demy, Jacques. (1931–). French.

1956: *Le Sabotier du Val de Loire.* 1957: *Le bel indifférent.* 1958: *Musée Grevin.* 1959: *La Mère et l'Enfant, Ars.* 1961: *Lola, Les Sept Péchés Capitaux* (episode). 1963: *La Baie des Anges.* 1964: *Les Parapluies de Cherbourg.* 1966: *Les Demoiselles de Rochefort.* 1970: *Model Shop* (in U.S.A.). 1971: *Peau d'Ane.*

*De Robertis, Francesco. (1902–59). Italian.

1940: *Mine in vista.* 1941: *Uomini sul fondo.* 1942: *Alfa tau.* 1943: *Marinai senza stelle.* 1945: *Uomini e cieli.* 1945: *I figli della laguna, La vita semplice.* 1947: *La voce di Paganini.* 1948: *Fantasmi del mare.* 1949: *Il mulatto.* 1950: *Gli amanti di Ravello.* 1952: *Carica eroica.* 1953: *I sette dell'Orsa Maggiore.* 1954: *Mizar.* 1955: *Uomini-Ombra.* 1956: *La donna che venne del mare, Yalis, la vergine del Roncador.* 1958: *Ragazzi della marina.*

*De Santis, Giuseppe. (1917–). Italian.

1947: *Caccia tragica.* 1949: *Riso amaro.* 1950: *Non c'è pace tra gli ulivi.* 1951: *Roma, ore 11.* 1953: *Un marito per Anna Zazzheo.* 1954: *Giorni d'amore.* 1956: *Uomini e lupi.* 1958: *La strada lunga un anno* (in Yugoslavia). 1960: *La garçonnière.* 1964: *Italiani brava gente* (in U.S.S.R.).

De Seta, Vittorio. (1923–). Italian.

1954: *Pasqua in Sicilia, Lu tempu di li pisci spata, Isole di fuoco.* 1955: *Sulfurata, Contadini del mare, Parabola d'oro.* 1957: *Pescherecci.* 1958: *Un giorno in Barbagia.* 1959: *Pastori de Orgosolo* (all documentaries). 1961: *Banditi a Orgosolo.* 1966: *Un uomo a metà.*

*De Sica, Vittorio. (1901–). Italian.

1940: *Rose scarlette, Maddalena zero in condotta.* 1941: *Teresa venerdi.* 1942: *Un garibaldino al convento.* 1943: *I bambini ci guardano.* 1946: *La porta del cielo, Sciuscia.* 1948: *Ladri di biciclette.* 1951: *Miracolo a Milano.* 1952: *Umberto D.* 1953: *Stazione termini.* 1954: *L'oro di Napoli.* 1956: *Il tetto.* 1960: *La ciociara.* 1961: *Il giudizio universale, Boccaccio 70* (episode). 1962: *I sequestrati di Altona.* 1963: *Il boom, ieri, oggi, domani.* 1964: *Matrimonio all'italiana.* 1965: *Caccia alla volpe.* 1966: *Un mondo nuovo.* 1967: *Woman Times Seven.* 1969: *A Place for Lovers.* 1970: *Sunflower.* 1971: *Il giardino degli Finzi Contini.*

*Dickinson, Thorold. (1903–). British.

1936: *High Command.* 1939: *Arsenal Stadium Mystery.* 1940: *Gaslight.* 1941: *The Prime Minister.* 1942: *Next of Kin.* 1945: *Men of Two Worlds.* 1949: *The Queen of Spades.* 1950: *The Secret People.* 1954: *Hill 24 Doesn't Answer* (in Israel).

Dieterle, William. (1893–). German, active in Germany, U.S.A.

1923: *Menschen am Wege.* 1927: *Das Geheimnis des Abbe X.* 1928: *Geschlecht in Fesseln.* 1929: *Die Heilige und der Narr.* 1931: *Jewel Robbery, Man Wanted.* 1932: *The Last Flight, Six Hours to Live.* 1935: *A Midsummer Night's Dream* (in collaboration with Max Reinhardt). 1936: *The Story of Louis Pasteur.* 1937: *The Life of Emile Zola.* 1938: *Blockade.* 1939: *Juarez, The Hunchback of Notre Dame.* 1940: *Dr Ehrlich's Magic Bullet, This Man Reuter.* 1941: *All That Money Can Buy.* 1955: *The Magic Fire.* 1957: *Omar Khayam.*

Disney, Walt. (1901–66). American.

1923: *The Four Musicians of Bremen, Little Red Riding Hood.* 1924: *Alice in Cartoonland* series. 1926: *Oswald* series. 1927: *Mortimer Mouse* (prototype of Mickey Mouse). 1928: *Steamboat Willie* (first appearance of Mickey Mouse). 1929: *Skeleton Dance* (first 'Silly Symphony'). 1932: *Flowers and Trees* (first colour cartoon). 1933: *Three Little Pigs.* 1934: *The Band Concert* (first Mickey Mouse colour film). 1938: *Snow White and the Seven Dwarfs* (first full-length cartoon film). 1940: *Pinocchio.* 1941: *Fantasia, Dumbo, The Reluctant Dragon* (first mixture of live action and cartoon by Disney). 1942: *Bambi, Saludos Amigos.* 1944: *The Three Caballeros.* From 1950: 'True Life Adventure' series, produced by Disney.

Dmytryk, Edward. (1908–). Canadian, active in America and Britain.

1939: *Television Spy.* 1947: *Crossfire.* 1948: *Obsession* (in Britain). 1949: *Give Us This Day* (in Britain). 1952: *The Sniper.* 1954: *Broken Lance, The Caine Mutiny.* 1955: *The End of the Affair.* 1957: *Raintree County.* 1958: *The Young Lions.* 1959: *Warlock, The Blue Angel.* 1962: *Walk on the Wild Side.* 1963: *The Carpetbaggers.* 1964: *Where Love Has Gone.* 1965: *Mirage.* 1966: *Alvarez Kelly.* 1968: *Anzio, Shalako.*

Donen, Stanley. (1920–). American.

1949: *On the Town* (in collaboration with Gene Kelly). 1951: *Royal Wedding.* 1952: *Love is Better than Ever, Singin' in the Rain* (with Gene Kelly), *Fearless Fagan.* 1953: *Give a Girl a Break.* 1954: *Seven Brides for Seven Brothers, Deep in my Heart.* 1955: *It's Always Fair Weather* (with Gene Kelly). 1957: *Funny Face, A Blonde in Every Port, The Pajama Game.* 1958: *Indiscreet.* 1959: *Damn Yankees.* 1960: *Once More with Feeling.* 1961: *Surprise Package.* 1962: *The Grass is Greener.* 1964: *Charade.* 1966: *Arabesque.* 1968: *Two for the Road, Bedazzled.* 1969: *Staircase.*

*Doniol-Valcroze, Jacques. (1920–). French.

1960: *L'Eau à la bouche.* 1961: *Le Coeur battant.* 1962: *La Dénonciation.* 1968: *Le Viol.*

*Donner, Clive. (1920–). British.

1956: *The Secret Place.* 1967: *Heart of a Child.* 1959: *A Marriage of Convenience.* 1960: *The Sinister Man.* 1962: *Some People.* 1963: *The Caretaker, Nothing But the Best.* 1965: *What's New Pussycat?* 1967: *Luv, Here We Go Round the Mulberry Bush.* 1969: *Alfred the Great.*

Donner, Jorn. (1933–). Finnish, active in Sweden and Finland.

1954: *Morning in the City.* 1963: *Sunday in September.* 1964: *To Love* (both in Sweden). 1965: *Adventure Starts Here.* 1967: *Black on White.* 1969: *69.* 1970: *Portraits of Women* (all in Finland). 1971: *Anna.*

Donskoi, Mark. (1897–). Soviet.

1927: *Life.* 1928: *In The Big City.* 1938: *Childhood of Gorki.* 1939: *Among People.* 1940: *My Universities.* 1943: *The Rainbow.* 1947: *The Village Teacher.* 1956: *Mother.* 1959: *Foma Gordeyev.* 1966: *A Mother's Heart, A Mother's Devotion.*

*Dovzhenko, Alexander Petrovitch. (1894–1956). Soviet.

1926: *Vasya the Reformer, The Fruits of Love.* 1927: *The Diplomatic Bag, Zvenigora.* 1928: *Arsenal.* 1930: *Earth.* 1932: *Ivan.* 1935: *Aerograd.* 1939: *Schors.* 1940: *Liberation.* 1943: *Battle for the Ukraine.* 1948: *Michurin.*

After Dovzhenko's death, a number of his projects were realised by his widow, Julia Solntseva (qv).

*Dreyer, Carl Theodor. (1889–1968). Danish.

1919: *The President, Leaves From Satan's Book* (both in Denmark). 1920: *The Parson's Widow* (in Sweden). 1921: *Love One Another*. 1922: *Once Upon a Time*. 1924: *Mikaël* (all in Germany). 1925: *Master of the House* (in Denmark), *The Bride of Glomdal* (in Norway). 1928: *La Passion de Jeanne d'Arc* (in France). 1932: *Vampyr* (in Germany). 1943: *Day of Wrath* (in Denmark). 1944: *Two People* (in Sweden). 1954: *Ordet* (*The Word*) (in Denmark). 1964: *Gertrud* (in Denmark).

Duarte, Anselmo. (1920–). Brazilian.

1957: *Absolutely Sure*. 1962: *O pagador de promessas*.

*Dudow, Slatan. (1903–63). German.

1929: *Seifenblasen*. 1932: *Kühle Wampe*. 1949: *Unser tägliches Brot*. 1950: *Familie Benthin*. 1952: *Frauen Schicksale*. 1954: *Stärker als die Nicht*. 1956: *Der Hauptmann von Köln*. 1958: *Verwirrung der Liebe*.

*Dulac, Germaine. (1882–1942). French.

1916: *Les Soeurs ennemies*. 1917: *Géo mystérieux, Venus Victrix*. 1918: *Ames de fous*. 1919: *La Cigarette, La fête espagnole*. 1920: *Malencontre*. 1921: *La Belle Dame sans merci*. 1922: *La Mort du soleil, La Souriante Madame Beudet, Gossette* (serial). 1924: *Le Diable dans la ville*. 1925: *Ame d'artiste, La Folie des vaillants*. 1927: *L'Invitation au voyage, Antoinette Sabrier*. 1928: *La Coquille et le Clergyman, Princess Mandane*. 1929: *Etude cinematographique sur un arabesque, Disque 927*. 1930: *Thème et variations*.

Dunning, George. (1920–). Canadian, active in Canada and Britain.

1960: *The Apple*. 1962: *The Flying Man*. 1969: *The Yellow Submarine*.

Dupont, Ewald Andres. (1891–1956). German. Active in Germany, Britain and U.S.A.

1918: *Europa postlagernd*. 1925: *Variete*. 1927: *Love Me and the World is Mine*. 1928: *Moulin Rouge, Piccadilly*. 1930: *Atlantic*. 1933: *Ladies Must Love*. 1954: *Return to Treasure Island*.

Durand, Jean. (1882–1946). French.

1908: *Trop credule*. 1908–9: *Arizona Bill* series. 1911–13: *Calino* series. 1911–14: fauves' series. 1912–14: *Onésime* series. 1919–20: *Serpentin* series. 1921–22: *Marie* series. 1924: *La Chaussée des géants*. 1926: *Face aux loups*. 1927: *Palaces*. 1928: *L'Ile d'amour, La Femme rêvée*.

Duvivier, Julien (1896–1967). French.

1919: *Haceldama* (*Le Prix du Sang*). 1921: *L'Agonie des aigles* (in collaboration with Bernard Deschamps). 1924: *La Machine à refaire la vie*. 1925: *Poil de carotte*. 1930: *David Golder*. 1932: *Poil de carotte*. 1933: *La Tête d'un homme*. 1934: *Le Paquebot 'Tenacity'*. 1935: *Golgotha, Bandera*. 1936: *L'Homme du jour. La Belle Equipe, Le Golem*. 1937: *Pépé le Moko, Un Carnet de Bal*. 1938: *The Great Waltz* (in U.S.A.), 1939: *La Fin du jour, La Charette Fantôme*. 1940: *Un Tel Père et fils*. 1941: *Lydia*. 1942: *Tales of Manhattan*. 1943: *Flesh and Fantasy, The Imposter*. 1946: *Panique*. 1947: *Anna Karenina* (in Britain). 1949: *Au royaume des cieux*. 1950: *Sous le ciel de Paris*. 1951: *Don Camillo* (in Italy). 1952: *La Fête à Henriette.* 1955: *Marianne de ma jeunesse.* 1959: *La Femme et le Pantin.* 1962: *La Chambre ardente.* 1963: *Chair de poule.*

Dwan, Allan. (1885–   ). American. Perhaps the most prolific of all directors.

1911: *Brandishing a Bad Man, A Western Dreamer.* 1911–16: more than 300 films. 1916: *The Good Bad Man, The Half-Breed, Manhattan Madness.* 1917: *A Modern Musketeer.* 1918: *Mr Fix-It, Bound in Morocco, He Comes Up Smiling.* 1922: *Robin Hood.* 1923: *Zaza.* 1924: *A Society Scandal, Manhandled, Her Love Story, Wages of Virtue.* 1925: *Stage Struck.* 1929: *The Iron Mask.* 1937: *Heidi.* 1938: *Rebecca of Sunnybrook Farm.* 1949: *Sands of Iwo Jima.* 1952: *Montana Belle.* 1961: *Most Dangerous Man Alive.*

Dzigan, Yefim. (1898–   ). Soviet.

1928: *First Lieutenant Streshnov* (in collaboration with Chiaureli). 1936: *We From Kronstadt.*

Edwards, Blake. (1922–   ). American.

1955: *Bring Your Smile Along, He Laughed Last.* 1956: *Mr Cory.* 1958: *This Happy Feeling, The Perfect Furlough.* 1959: *Operation Petticoat.* 1960: *High Time.* 1961: *Breakfast at Tiffany's.* 1962: *Grip of Fear, Days of Wine and Roses.* 1963: *The Pink Panther.* 1964: *A Shot in the Dark, The Great Race.* 1966: *What Did You Do In the War, Daddy?* 1967: *Gunn.* 1968: *The Party.* 1969: *Darling Lili.*

Edwards, J. Gordon. (?–1925). Canadian, active in U.S.A.

1914: *Life's Shop Window.* 1915: *Anna Karenina, A Woman's Resurrection (Resurrection).* 1916: *Under Two Flags, Romeo and Juliet.* 1917: *The Tiger Woman, Camille, Cleopatra, Madame Dubarry.* 1918: *Salome, The She-Devil.* 1921: *The Queen of Sheba.* 1922: *Nero* (in Italy). 1924: *It is the Law.*

Eggeling, Viking. (1880–1925). Swedish, active in Germany.

1919: *Vertikal-Horizontal Mass.* 1920: *Vertikal-Horizontal Symphonie* (in collaboration with Hans Richter). 1922: *Diagonale Symphonie.*

*Eisenstein, Sergei Mikhailovitch. (1898–1948). Soviet.

1923: *Glumov's Diary.* 1924: *Strike.* 1925: *The Battleship Potemkin.* 1927: *October.* 1929: *The General Line.* 1930–32: *Que Viva Mexico!* (unfinished). 1935–7: *Bezhin Meadow* (unfinished). 1938: *Alexander Nevsky.* 1944–6: *Ivan the Terrible* (trilogy, only two parts completed).

*Ekk, Nikolai. (1902). Soviet.

1931: *The Road to Life.* 1936: *Nightingale, little Nightingale.* 1939: *Sorochinsk Fair.* 1941: *A May Night.*

Emerson, John. (1878–1936). American.

1915: *Old Heidelberg.* 1917: *In Again, Out Again.* 1918: *American Aristocracy.* 1919: *His Picture in the Papers, Down to Earth.* 1920: *Wild and Woolly.*

Emmer, Luciano. (1918–   ). Italian.

1941: *Racconto da un affresco.* 1941–9: series of documentaries in collaboration with Enrico Gras. 1949: *Domenica d'Agosto.* 1951: *Matrimonio alla moda, Parigi e siempre Parigi.* 1952: *Le ragazze di Piazza di Spagna.* 1956: *Il bigamo.* 1957: *Il nomento più bello.* 1960: *La ragazza in vetrina.*

Endfield, Cyril. (1914–). American.

1941–50: many second features. 1950: *Try and Get Me.* 1963: *Zulu.* 1965: *Sands of the Kalahari.* 1970: *De Sade.*

Engel, Morris. (1918–). American.

1953: *The Little Fugitive.* 1956: *Lovers and Lollipops.* 1958: *Weddings and Babies.*

*****Epstein, Jean.** (1897–1953). French.

1922: *Pasteur* (with Benoit-Levy). *Vendanges.* 1923: *L'Auberge rouge, Coeur fidèle.* 1924: *La Montagne infidèle, La Belle Nivernaise, Le Lion des mogols.* 1925: *L'Affiche, Le Double Amour.* 1926: *Les Aventures de Robert Macaire* (serial), *Mauprat.* 1927: *Six et demi onze, La Glace à trois faces, La Chute de la Maison Usher.* 1929: *Finis terrae, Sa tête.* 1930: *Mor Vran.* 1932: *L'Or des mers.* 1933: *L'Homme à l'Hispano, La Châtelaine du Liban.* 1934: *Chanson d'Amour.* 1936: *Coeur de queux.* 1937: *Vive la vie, La Femme du bout du monde.* 1938: *Les Batisseurs, Eau vive.* 1947: *La Tempestaire.* 1948: *Les Feux de la mer.*

*****Ermler, Friedrich.** (1898–1969). Soviet.

1924: *Skarlatina.* 1926: *Katka's Reinert Apples, Children of the Storm.* 1928: *House Across the Snow, The Parisian Shoemaker.* 1929: *Fragment of an Empire.* 1932: *Counterplan* (with Yutkevitch), *Peasants.* 1938–9: *The Great Citizen.* 1943: *She Defends Her Country.* 1945: *The Great Turning.* 1950: *The Great Power.* 1955: *Unfinished Story.* 1967: *Before the Judgment of History.*

*****Etaix, Pierre.** (1928–). French.

1961: *Rupture, Heureuse Anniversaire.* 1963: *Le Soupirant.* 1965: *Yoyo.* 1966: *Tant qu'on a la santé.* 1970: *Le Grand Amour.*

Fabri, Zoltan. (1917–). Hungarian.

1952: *The Storm.* 1954: *Fourteen Lives Saved.* 1955: *Merry-Go-Round.* 1956: *Professor Hannibal.* 1957: *Summer Clouds.* 1958: *Anna.* 1959: *The Brute.* 1961: *The Last Goal.* 1963: *Darkness in Daytime.* 1964: *Twenty Hours.* 1965: *A Hard Summer* (for TV). 1967: *Late Season.* 1968: *The Boys From Pal Street.* 1970: *The Toth Family.* 1972: *Ants' Nest.*

Fanck, Arnold. (1889–). German.

1919: *Wunder des Schneeschuhs.* 1924: *Berg des Schicksals.* 1925: *Der heilige Berg.* 1929: *Die weisse hölle von Piz Palu* (with G. W. Pabst). 1933: *S.O.S. Iceberg* (with Tay Garnett). 1940: *Ein Robinson.*

Farias, Roberto. (1935–). Brazilian.

1961: *Assalto ao tram pagador.* 1964: *Selva tragica.*

*****Feher, Imre.** (1926–). Hungarian.

1957: *A Sunday Romance.* 1958: *Bird of Heaven.* 1959: *On Foot to Heaven, The Sword and the Dice.* 1962: *Twenty Years in a New World, A Woman at the Helm.* 1966: *Harlequin and his Lover.*

Fejös, Paul. (1898–1963), Hungarian, active in Hungary, U.S.A., etc.

1920: *The Black Captain, Pan, Hallucinations.* 1923: *The Resurrected, Stars of Eger* (all in Hungary). 1927: *The Last Moment.* 1928: *Lonesome.* 1929: *Erik, the Great Illusionist, Broadway.* 1932: European versions of *The Big House* (directed by George Hill) (all in U.S.A.). 1932: *Fantomas* (in France). 1932: *Marie, Hungarian legend, Balaton condemned* (in Hungary). 1933: *Sonnenstrahl* (in

Austria), *Flight of Millions* (in Denmark). 1935: *Prisoner No. 1, The Outlaw, The Golden Smile* (all in Denmark). 1938: *A Handful of Rice* (in Siam). 1939–45: documentaries (in Sweden).

*Fellini, Federico. (1920–   ). Italian.

1951: *Luci del varietà* (co-directed with Lattuada). 1952: *Lo sceicco bianco.* 1953: *I Vitelloni, Amore in città* (episode). 1954: *La strada.* 1955: *Il bidone.* 1956: *Le notte di Cabiria.* 1960: *La dolce vita.* 1962: *Boccaccio 70* (episode). 1963: *Otto e mezzo.* 1965: *Giulietta degli spiriti.* 1968: *Histoires extraordinaires* (episode). 1969: *Fellini-Satyricon.* 1970: *I clowns.* 1972: *Fellini-Roma.*

*Ferreri, Marco. (1928–   ). Italian, active in Spain and Italy.

1956: *El pisito.* 1957: *Los cicos.* 1959: *El cochecito.* 1963: *L'ape regina, La donna scimmia.* 1965: *Oggi, domani, dopodomani* (episode), *Marcia nuziale.* 1968: *Dillinger è morto.*

Fescourt, Henri. (1880–1966). French.

1913: *Fantaisie de milliardaire, La Lumière qui tue, La Mort sur Paris.* 1918–19: *Mathias Sandorf* (serial). 1922: *Routetabille.* 1929: *Monte-Cristo.* 1931: *Serments.* 1942: *Retour de flamme.*

Feuillade, Louis. (1873–1925). French.

1906: *C'est papa qui prend la purge.* 1910: *Aux lions les chrétiens.* 1911: *Les Vipères.* 1910–12: *Bébé* series. 1911–13: *Le Vie telle qu'elle est* series. 1913–14: *Fantomas* (serial). 1914–17: *Bout-de-Zan* series. 1915: *Les Vampires* (serial). 1917: *Judex* (serial). 1918: *La Nouvelle Mission de Judex* (serial), *Tih Minh* (serial). 1920: *Barrabas* (serial). 1925: *Le Stigmate.*

Feyder, Jacques. (1888–1948). Belgian, active in France, U.S.A., etc.

1916: *Têtes de femmes, femmes de tête.* 1921: *L'Atlantide.* 1922: *Crainquebille.* 1925: *Visages d'enfants.* 1926: *L'Image, Gribiche.* 1928: *Thérèse Raquin.* 1929: *Les Nouveaux Messieurs.* 1930: *The Kiss.* 1931: *The Son of India, Daybreak, His Glorious Night, Si l'Empereur savait ça.* 1932: German version of Brown's *Anna Christie.* 1934: *Le Grand Jeu.* 1935: *Pension Mimosas, La Kermesse héroique.* 1937: *Knight Without Armour* (in Britain). 1938: *Fahrendes Volk* (in Germany). 1939–42: *La Loi du nord* (in France), *Une Femme disparaît* (in Switzerland).

Fischinger, Oscar. (1902–   ). German, active in Germany and U.S.A.

1926: *Studien* 7 and 8. 1927: *Komposition in Blau.* 1931: *Cinerhythme* (all in Germany). 1933–8: *Allegretto, Optical Poem, Rhapsody in Blue, An American March.* 1940: work on *Fantasia* (*Toccata and Fugue*). (all in U.S.A.).

*Flaherty, Robert J. (1884–1951). American, active in U.S.A. and Britain.

1918: *Eskimo.* 1922: *Nanook of the North.* 1924: *Twenty-Four Dollar Island, Story of a Potter.* 1926: *Moana of the South Seas.* 1928: initial work on W. S. Van Dyke's *White Shadows of the South Seas.* 1931: *Tabu* (collaboration with Murnau). 1932: *Industrial Britain.* 1934: *Man of Aran.* 1937: *Elephant Boy* (collaboration with Zoltan Korda). 1942: *The Land.* 1948: *Louisiana Story.*

Fleischer, Dave. (1894–   ) and **Max** (1889–   ). American.

1921: *Out of the Inkwell* series. 1923: *The Einstein Theory of Relativity.* 1939: *Gulliver's Travels.* 1941: *Mr Bug Goes to Town.*

Fleischer, Richard. (1916–   ). American (son of Max F.).

1946: *Child of Divorce.* 1952: *The Happy Time.* 1953: *Arena* (3-D). 1954: *20,000*

Leagues Under the Sea. 1955: *Violent Saturday, The Girl in the Red Velvet Swing.* 1956: *Bandido!* 1957: *The Vikings.* 1959: *Compulsion.* 1966: *The Fantastic Voyage.* 1968: *Doctor Doolittle.* 1969: *The Boston Strangler.* 1970: *Che!, Tora! Tora! Tora!* 1971: *Ten Rillington Place.* 1972: *The Last Run.*

Fleming, Victor. (1883–1949). American.

1919: *When the Clouds Roll By.* 1920: *The Mollycoddle.* 1926: *Mantrap.* 1927: *The Way of All Flesh.* 1929: *The Virginian.* 1931: *Around the World in Eighty Minutes.* 1932: *Red Dust.* 1933: *Bombshell.* 1934: *Treasure Island.* 1937: *Captains Courageous.* 1938: *Test Pilot.* 1939: *The Wizard of Oz, Gone With the Wind.* 1941: *Dr Jekyll and Mr Hyde.* 1942: *Tortilla Flat.* 1943: *A Guy Named Joe.* 1946: *Adventure.* 1948: *Joan of Arc.*

Forbes, Bryan. (1926–). British.

1961: *Whistle Down the Wind.* 1962: *The L-Shaped Room.* 1964: *Seance on a Wet Afternoon.* 1965: *King Rat.* 1966: *The Wrong Box, The Whisperers.* 1967: *Deadfall.* 1969: *The Madwoman of Chaillot.* 1970: *The Raging Moon.*

Ford, Aleksander. (1908–). Polish.

1929: *Morning, The Pulse of Poland's Manchester.* 1930: *Mascotte.* 1932: *Street Legion.* 1934: *Awakening, Sabra.* 1936: *Street of the Young.* 1937: *People of the Vistula.* 1948: *Border Street.* 1952: *The Young Chopin.* 1953: *Five Boys from Barska Street.* 1958: *Eighth Day of the Week.* 1960: *Knights of the Teutonic Order.* 1964: *The First Day of Freedom.* 1966: *Der Arzt stellt fest* (Swiss West German co-production).

Ford, John. (1895–). American.

1917: *Cactus, My Pal.* 1917–24: numerous two-reelers and features. 1924: *The Iron Horse.* 1926: *Three Bad Men.* 1928: *Four Sons.* 1930: *Men Without Women.* 1931: *Arrowsmith.* 1934: *The Lost Patrol, Judge Priest.* 1935: *The Whole Town's Talking, The Informer, Steamboat Round the Bend.* 1936: *The Prisoner of Shark Island, Mary of Scotland, The Plough and the Stars.* 1937: *Wee Willie Winkie, Hurricane.* 1938: *Four Men and a Prayer, Submarine Patrol.* 1939: *Stagecoach, Young Mr Lincoln, Drums Along the Mohawk.* 1940: *The Grapes of Wrath, The Long Voyage Home.* 1941: *Tobacco Road, How Green Was My Valley.* 1942: *The Battle of Midway.* 1943: *We Sail at Midnight.* 1945: *They Were Expendable.* 1946: *My Darling Clementine.* 1947: *The Fugitive.* 1948: *Fort Apache, Three Godfathers.* 1949: *She Wore a Yellow Ribbon.* 1950: *When Willie Comes Marching Home, Wagonmaster, Rio Grande.* 1951: *This is Korea.* 1952: *What Price Glory, The Quiet Man.* 1953: *The Sun Shines Bright, Mogambo.* 1955: *The Long Gray Line, Mr Roberts* (finished by Mervyn Leroy). 1956: *The Searchers.* 1957: *The Wings of Eagles, The Rising of the Moon.* 1958: *The Last Hurrah.* 1959: *Gideon's Day. The Horse Soldiers.* 1960: *Sergeant Rutledge.* 1961: *Two Rode Together.* 1962: *The Man Who Shot Liberty Vallance.* 1963: *Donovan's Reef.* 1964: *Cheyenne Autumn.* 1966: *Seven Women.*

*Forman, Milós. (1932–). Czech.

1963: *If There Were No Music, Talent Competition, Peter and Pavla.* 1965: *A Blonde in Love.* 1967: *The Firemen's Ball.* 1971: *Taking Off.*

*Franju, Georges. (1912–). French.

1934: *Le Métro* (co-directed with Henri Langlois). 1949: *Le Sang des bêtes.* 1950: *En passant par la Lorraine.* 1952: *Hôtel des Invalides, Le Grand Méliès.* 1953: *Monsieur et Madame Curie.* 1954: *Poussières, La Marine marchande.* 1955:

A propos d'une rivière, Mon chien. 1956: *T.N.P., Sur le pont d'Avignon.* 1957: *Notre Dame.* 1958: *La Première Nuit* (all short documentaries). 1958: *La Tête contre les murs.* 1960: *Les Yeux sans visage.* 1961: *Pleins feux sur l'assassin.* 1962: *Thérèse Desqueyroux.* 1964: *Judex.* 1965: *Thomas l'imposteur.* 1970: *La Faute de l'Abbé Mouret.*

*Frankenheimer, John. (1930–). American.

1956: *The Young Stranger.* 1961: *The Young Savages.* 1962: *All Fall Down, The Birdman of Alcatraz, The Manchurian Candidate.* 1964: *Seven Days in May, The Train.* 1966: *Seconds, Grand Prix.* 1968: *The Extraordinary Seaman.* 1969: *The Fixer, Gypsy Mothers.* 1970: *I Walk the Line.* 1971: *The Horsemen.*

Franklin, Sidney. (1893–1972). American.

1916: *Martha's Vindication* (with Chester Franklin). 1929: *Wild Orchids, The Last of Mrs Cheyney.* 1931: *Private Lives.* 1934: *The Barretts of Wimpole Street.* 1935: *The Dark Angel.* 1937: *The Good Earth.*

*Fuller, Samuel. (1911–). American.

1949: *I Shot Jesse James.* 1950: *The Baron of Arizona.* 1951: *The Steel Helmet, Fixed Bayonets.* 1952: *Park Row.* 1953: *Pickup on South Street.* 1954: *Hell and High Water.* 1955: *House of Bamboo.* 1957: *China Gate, Run of the Arrow, Forty Guns.* 1959: *The Crimson Kimono, Verboten!* 1961: *Underworld, U.S.A.* 1962: *Merrill's Marauders.* 1963: *Shock Corridor.* 1964: *The Naked Kiss.*

Gaál, Istvan. (1933–). Hungarian.

1957: *Surfacemen.* 1962: *To and Fro.* 1963: *Tisza–Autumn in Sketches.* 1964: *Current.* 1965: *The Green Years.* 1967: *Baptism.* 1970: *The Falcons.* 1972: *Dead Area.*

Gad, Urban. (1879–1947). Danish, active in Denmark and Germany. Husband and director of Asta Nielsen.

1910: *Afgrunden.* 1911–14: various films for Asta Nielsen. 1920–21: *Christian Wahnschaffe* (in Germany). 1922: *Henneles Himmelfahrt* (in Germany). 1927: *Likkehjulet* (in Denmark).

Galeen, Henrik. (1882– ?). Dutch, active in Germany.

1912: *Der Student von Prag* (in collaboration with Paul Wegener). 1914: *Der Golem* (with Paul Wegener). 1920: *Der Golem* (remake, also with Wegener). 1926: *Der Student von Prag* (remake). 1927: *Alraune.* 1928: *After the Verdict* (in Britain).

Gallone, Carmine. (1886–). Italian.

1914: *Turbine d'odio, La donna nuda;* then a prolific and unbroken production until 1955: *Madama Butterfly,* 1960: *Cartagine in fiamme.*

Gance, Abel. (1889–). French.

1911: *La Digue.* 1915: *La Folie du Dr Tube.* 1917: *La Zone de la mort, Mater Dolorosa.* 1918: *La Dixième Symphonie.* 1919: *J'accuse.* 1921–4: *La Roue.* 1923: *Au secours!* 1925–7: *Napoléon.* 1931: *La Fin du monde.* 1932: *Mater Dolorosa.* 1933: *Le Maître des forges.* 1934: *Poliche, La Dame aux camélias, Napoléon* (sound version). 1935: *Le Roman d'un jeune homme pauvre.* 1936: *Lucrèce Borgia, Un grand amour de Beethoven, Jerome Perreau–héros des barricades, Le Voleur de femmes.*

1938: *J'accuse*. 1939: *Louise*. 1940: *Le Paradise perdu*. 1941: *La Vénus aveugle*. 1943: *Le Capitaine Fracasse*. 1953: *Quatorze Juillet*. 1954: *La Tour de Nesles*. 1956: *Magyrama*. 1960: *Austerlitz*. 1964: *Cyrano et d'Artagnan*. 1972: *Bonaparte et la Révolution* (revised version of *Napoléon*).

Gardin, Vladimir. (1877–1965). Russian and Soviet.

1912: *The Keys of Happiness*. 1914: *Anna Karenina*. 1915: *War and Peace*. 1919: *Iron Heel*. 1921: *Hammer and Sickle, Hunger . . . Hunger . . . Hunger* (co-directed with Pudovkin). 1926: *Marriage of the Bear* (co-directed with Konstantin Eggert). 1927: *Poet and Tsar*. 1929: *Spring Song*.

Garmes, Lee. (1898–). American.

1937: *The Sky's The Limit* (with Jack Buchanan, in G.B.). 1940: *Angels Over Broadway* (with Ben Hecht).

Garnett, Tay (1892–). American.

1928: *Celebrity*. 1930: *Her Man*. 1935: *China Seas*. 1937: *Stand-in*. 1938: *Trade Winds*. 1944: *Bataan, Mrs Parkington*. 1945: *The Valley of Decision*. 1946: *The Postman Always Rings Twice*. 1956: *Seven Wonders of the World* (Cinerama). 1963: *Guns of Wyoming*.

Gasnier, Louis. (1882–1962). French, active in France and America.

1905: *La Première Sortie d'un collégien*. 1906–11: numerous Max Linder shorts. 1914: *The Perils of Pauline*. 1915: *The Exploits of Elaine, The New Exploits of Elaine, Romance of Elaine*. 1916–21: various serial films. 1921–40: numerous commercial feature films. 1941: *Stolen Paradise*.

Gatti, Armand. (1924–). French, active in France and Cuba.

1961: *L'Enclos*. 1963: *El otro Cristobal*.

Genina, Augusto. (1882–1957). Italian.

1913: *La moglie di Sua Eccellenza*. 1913–30: numerous feature films in Italy. 1930: *Prix de beauté* (in France). 1936: *Lo squadrone bianco*. 1939: *Castelli in aria*. 1940: *L'assedio dell'Alcazar*. 1942: *Bengasi*. 1949: *Cielo sulla palude*. 1950: *L'edera*. 1952: *Tre storie proibite*. 1953: *Maddalena*. 1955: *Frou-Frou* (in France).

*****Gerassimov, Sergei.** (1906–). Soviet.

1930: *Twenty-two Misfortunes* (co-directed with S. Bartenev). 1931: *The Forest*. 1932: *The Heart of Solomon*. 1934: *Do I Love You?* 1936: *The Bold Seven*. 1937: *Komsololsk*. 1939: *The Teacher*. 1941: *Maskarad, Film Notes on Battle No 1, The Old Guard*. 1942: *The Invincibles* (co-directed with Mikhail Kalatozov). 1943: *Cine-concert for the Twenty-Fifth Anniversary of the Red Army* (co-directed with Kalatozov and Yefim Dzigan). 1944: *The Great Earth*. 1948: *The Young Guard*. 1950: *Liberated China*. 1951: *Country Doctor*. 1954: *Nadezhda*. 1957–8: *Quiet Flows the Don*. 1959: *The Sputnik Speaks* (co-directed with E. Volk, V. Dorman and G. Oganissian). 1962: *Men and Beasts*. 1967: *The Journalist*.

Germi, Pietro. (1914–). Italian.

1946: *Il testimone*. 1947: *Gioventù perduta*. 1949: *In nome della legge*. 1950: *Il cammino della speranza*. 1951: *La città si difende*. 1952: *La presidentessa, Il brigante di Tacca del Lupo*. 1953: *Gelosia*. 1954: *Amori di mezzo secolo*. 1956: *Il ferroviere*. 1958: *L'uomo di paglia*. 1960: *Un maladetta imbroglio*. 1962: *Divorzio all'italiana*. 1964: *Sedotta e abbandonata*. 1966: *Signori e sig♪ore*. 1967: *L'immorale*.

*Godard, Jean-Luc. (1930-   ). French.

1954: *Operation Béton*. 1955: *Une Femme coquette*. 1957: *Tous les garçons s'appellent Patrick*. 1958: *Charlotte et son Jules, Une Histoire d'eau*. 1959: *A bout de souffle*. 1960: *Le Petit Soldat*. 1961: *Une Femme est une femme, Les Sept Péchés capitaux* (episode). 1962: *Vivre sa vie, RoGoPaG* (episode). 1963: *Les Carabiniers, Le Mépris, Les Plus Belles Escroqueries du monde* (episode), *Paris vue par . . .* (episode). 2964: *Bande à part, Une Femme mariée*. 1965: *Alphaville, Pierrot le fou*. 1966: *Masculin-féminin, Made in U.S.A.* 1967: *Deux ou trois choses que je sais d'elle. La Chinoise, Loin du Viêtnam* (episode), *Weekend, Le Plus Vieux Métier du monde* (episode), *Vangelo '70* (episode). 1968: *Le Gai Savoir, Un Film comme les autres, One Plus One* (in Britain). 1969: *One American Movie-1 a.m.* (uncompleted), *British Sounds (See You at Mao), Le Vent d'Est*. c. 1970: *Struggle in Italy, One French Movie* (begun in 1968).

Gosho, Heinosuke. (1902-   ). Japanese.

1925: *Spring in Southern Islands*. 1925-51: more than seventy feature films. 1953: *Four Chimneys*. 1954: *An Inn at Osaka*. 1960: *When a Woman Loves*. 1965: *An Innocent Witch*. 1966: *Our Wonderful Years*. 1967: *Rebellion of Japan*. 1968: *Woman and Bean Soup*.

Goulding, Edmund. (1891-1959). British, active in U.S.A.

1922: *Fury*. 1923: *The Bright Shawl*. 1925: *Sally, Irene and Mary*. 1926: *Dancing Mothers*. 1928: *Love*. 1931: *Reaching for the Moon*. 1932: *Grand Hotel*. 1938: *Dawn Patrol*. 1939: *Dark Victory*. 1943: *The Constant Nymph*. 1946: *Of Human Bondage, The Razor's Edge*. 1952: *We're not Married*. 1956: *Teenage Rebel*. 1958: *Mardi Gras*.

*Gregoretti, Ugo. (1930-   ). Italian.

1961: *I nuovi angeli*. 1962: *RoGoPaG* (episode), *Omicron*. 1964: *Le belle famiglie*. 1966: *I R.A.S.* (for television). 1967: *Il Circolo Pickwick* (for television).

*Gremillon, Jean. (1910-59). French.

1924-6: industrial documentaries. 1927: *Tour au large*. 1928: *Maldone, Bobs, Gratuites*. 1929: *Gardiens de phare*. 1930: *La Petite Lise*. 1931: *Dainah la métisse*. 1932: *Pour un sou d'amour, Le Petit Babouin*. 1933: *Gonzague*. 1934: *La Dolorosa*. 1935: *Centinela alerta!, Valse royale* (French version of *Königswaltz;* dir: Maisch). 1937: *Gueule d'amour*. 1938: *L'Etrange Monsieur Victor*. 1941: *Remorques*. 1943: *Lumière d'été*. 1944: *Le Ciel est à vous*. 1946: *Le Six Juin à l'aube*. 1948: *Pattes blanches*. 1949: *L'Apocalypse de Saint-Sèvres, Les Désastres de la guerre* (co-directed with Pierre Kast), *Les Charmes de l'existence* (with Kast). 1950: *L'Etrange Madame X*. 1951: *Caf'Conc', Alchimie*. 1953: *L'Amour d'une femme, Au coeur de l'Ile-_ France*. 1955: *La Maison aux images*. 1956: *Hautelice*. 1958: *André Masson et les quatre elements*.

Grierson, John. (1898-   ). British.

An inspired producer at the Empire Marketing Board, the GPO Film Unit, National Film Board of Canada and Group 3, Grierson's single essay as a director was: 1929: *Drifters*.

Griffith, D. W. (1875-1948). American.

1908: *The Adventures of Dollie*; and 46 other one-reel films. 1909: 138 films, including *The Lonely Villa, A Corner in Wheat*. 1910: 103 one-reelers. 1911: 67 films including *Enoch Arden, The Battle*. 1912: 60 films including *The*

Musketeers of Pig Alley, The Massacre, The New York Hat. 1913: 17 films including *Judith of Bethulia, The Battle of the Sexes.* 1914: *The Escape, The Avenging Conscience, Home Sweet Home.* 1915: *The Birth of a Nation.* 1916: *Intolerance.* 1918: *Hearts of the World, The Greatest Thing in Life, The Great Love.* 1919: *Romance of Happy Valley, The Girl Who Stayed at Home, True Heart Susie, Scarlet Days, Broken Blossoms, The Greatest Question.* 1920: *The Idol Dancer, The Love Flower, Way Down East.* 1921: *Dream Street, Orphans of the Storm.* 1922: *One Exciting Night.* 1923: *The White Rose.* 1924: *America, Isn't Life Wonderful.* 1925: *Sally of the Sawdust.* 1926: *That Royle Girl, The Sorrows of Satan.* 1928: *Drums of Love, The Battle of the Sexes.* 1929: *Lady of the Pavements.* 1930: *Abraham Lincoln.* 1931: *The Struggle.*

*Groulx, Gilles. (1931–   ). Canadian.

1955: *Les Héritiers.* 1958: *Les Raquetteurs.* 1959: *Normetal* (with Claude Fournier). 1960: *La France sur un caillou* (with Claude Fournier). 1961: *Golden Gloves.* 1962: *Voir Miami.* 1964: *Un jeu si simple, Le chat dans le sac.* 1969: *Où êtes-vous donc? Entre tu et vous.*

Guazzoni, Enrico. (1876–1949). Italian.

1909: *La nuova mammina.* 1910: *Adriana di Berton, Bruto, I Maccabei, Agrippina.* 1911: *San Francesco.* 1912: *Quo Vadis?* 1913: *La Gerusalemme liberta, Marcantonio e Cleopatra.* 1914: *Caius Julius Caesar.* 1941: *I pirati della Malesia.*

Guerra, Ruy. (1931–   ). Brazilian.

1962: *Os cafajestes.* 1963: *Os fuzis.* 1969: *Sweet Hunters.* 1970: *The Gods and the Dead.*

Guitry, Sacha. (1885–1957). French.

1914: *Ceux de chez nous.* 1932: *Les Deux Couverts.* 1935: *Pasteur.* 1936: *Mon Père avait raison, Le Nouveau Testament, Le Roman d'un tricheur, Faisons un rêve.* 1937: *Le Mot de Cambronne, Les Perles de la couronne.* 1938: *Quadrille, Remontons les Champs-Elysées.* 1939: *Ils étaient neuf célibataires.* 1948: *Le Diable Boiteux.* 1949: *Aux deux colombes, Toa.* 1954: *Si Versailles m'était conté, Napoléon.* 1955: *Si Paris nous était conté.* 1957: *Assassins et voleurs, Les Trois font la paire.*

Guy-Blaché, Alice. (1873–   ). French, active in France and U.S.A.

1900: *La Fée aux choux.* 1901: *Hussards et grisettes.* 1903: *Le Voleur sacrilège.* 1904: *Le Courrier de Lyons, Le Crime de la Rue de Temple.* 1906: *Vie de Christ* (co-directed with Jasset). 1912: *Fra Diavolo.* 1914: *Shadows of the Moulin Rouge.* 1917: *Behind the Mask.* 1918: *The Great Adventure.* 1920: *Tarnished Reputations.*

Haanstra, Bert. (1917–   ). Dutch.

1950: *Spiegel van Holland.* 1952: *Panta Rhei.* 1953: *Myrte en de Demonen.* 1955: *The Rival World.* 1956: *Rembrandt Painter of Man.* 1958: *Glass, Fanfare.* 1960: *The M.P. Affair.* 1962: *Zoo.* 1964: *The Human Dutch.* 1965: *The Voice of the Water.*

*Hamer, Robert. (1911–63). British.

1945: *Dead of Night* (episode), *Pink String and Sealing Wax.* 1948: *It Always Rains on Sunday.* 1949: *Kind Hearts and Coronets.* 1950: *The Spider and the Fly.* 1951: *His Excellency.* 1952: *The Long Memory.* 1954: *Father Brown.* 1955: *To Paris With Love.* 1959: *The Scapegoat.* 1960: *School for Scoundrels.*

*Harvey, Anthony. (1931–). British.

1966: *Dutchman.* 1968: *The Lion in Winter.* 1972: *There Were Giants.*

Has, Wojciech. (1925–). Polish.

1957: *The Noose.* 1958: *Farewells.* 1959: *One-room Tenants.* 1960: *Parting.* 1961: *Gold.* 1962: *How to be Loved.* 1964: *The Saragossa Manuscript.* 1966: *The Code.* 1968: *The Doll.*

Hathaway, Henry. (1898–). American.

1932: *Wild Horse Mesa.* 1934: *Now and Forever.* 1935: *The Lives of a Bengal Lancer.* 1936: *The Trail of the Lonesome Pine, Go West Young Man.* 1937: *Souls at Sea.* 1938: *Spawn of the North.* 1945: *Nob Hill.* 1947: *13, Rue Madeleine, Kiss of Death.* 1948: *Call Northside 777.* 1949: *Down to the Sea in Ships.* 1950: *The Black Rose, Fourteen Hours.* 1951: *Rawhide, The Desert Fox.* 1953: *Niagara.* 1954: *Prince Valiant.* 1958: *From Hell to Texas.* 1960: *North to Alaska.* 1962: *How the West Was Won* (episode). 1965: *The Four Sons of Katie Elder.* 1966: *Nevada Smith.* 1967: *The Last Safari.* 1968: *Five-Card Stud.* 1969: *True Grit.* 1970: *Airport.*

*Hawks, Howard. (1896–). American.

1926: *The Road to Glory, Fig Leaves.* 1927: *The Cradle Snatchers, Paid to Love.* 1928: *A Girl in Every Port, Fazil, The Air Circus.* 1929: *Trent's Last Case.* 1930: *The Dawn Patrol.* 1931: *The Criminal Code.* 1932: *The Crowd Roars, Scarface, Tiger Shark.* 1933: *Today We Live.* 1934: *Twentieth Century, Viva Villa!* (co-directed with Jack Conway). 1935: *Barbary Coast.* 1936: *Ceiling Zero, The Road to Glory, Come and Get it* (with William Wyler). 1938: *Bringing Up Baby.* 1939: *Only Angels Have Wings.* 1940: *His Girl Friday.* 1941: *Sergeant York, Ball of Fire.* 1943: *Air Force.* 1944: *To Have and Have Not.* 1946: *The Big Sleep.* 1948: *Red River, A Song is Born.* 1949: *I Was a Male War Bride.* 1952: *The Big Sky, Monkey Business, O. Henry's Full House* (episode). 1953: *Gentlemen Prefer Blondes.* 1955: *The Land of the Pharaohs.* 1959: *Rio Bravo.* 1962: *Hatari!* 1964: *Man's Favourite Sport.* 1965: *Red Line 7000.* 1967: *El Dorado.* 1970: *Rio Lobo.*

Heifets, Iosip. (1905–). Soviet.

In collaboration with Alexander Zarkhi: 1936: *Baltic Deputy.* 1940: *A Member of the Government.* 1946: *The Defeat of Japan.* 1947: *In the Name of Life.* 1948: *Precious Grain.* 1950: *Fires of Baku.* Heifets alone: 1953: *Spring in Moscow.* 1954: *The Big Family.* 1955: *The Rumyantsov Case.* 1958: *My Dear Man.* 1960: *Lady With the Little Dog.* 1961: *Horizon.* 1964: *A Day of Happiness.* 1966: *In the Town of S.*

Henning-Jensen, Astrid (1914–) and **Bjarne** (1908–). Danish.

1940–45: documentaries. 1946: *Ditte, Child of Man.* 1947: *De Pokker ungers.* 1948: *Kristinus Bergman.* 1950: *Vesterhavsdrenge.* 1953: *Sostik.* 1954: *Tivoligarden spiller.* Directed by Astrid H.-J. alone: 1949: *Palle alone in the world.* 1954: *Ballet Girl.* 1960: *Paw.*

Hepworth, Cecil. (1874–1956). British.

1899: *English Soldier Tearing Down the Boer Flag.* 1903: *Alice in Wonderland.* 1905: *Rescued by Rover, Falsely Accused.* 1906: *The Alien's Invasion.* 1912: *Blind Fate.* 1915: *Sweet Lavender.* 1924: *Coming Thro' the Rye.*

*Hill, George Roy. (1922–). American.

1963: *Period of Adjustment, Toys in the Attic.* 1964: *The World of Henry Orient.*

1966: *Hawaii*. 1967: *Thoroughly Modern Millie*. 1969: *Butch Cassidy and the Sundance Kid*. 1972: *Slaughterhouse Five*.

Hillyer, Lambert. (1889–   ). American.

1918: *Riddle Gawne*. 1919–21: numerous W. S. Hart westerns, including 1920: *The Tollgate, The Testing Block*. 1923: *The Spoilers*. 1923–4: several Tom Mix westerns. 1927–32: Buck Jones westerns. 1940–44: Bill Elliott Westerns. 1946–9: Johnny Mack Brown westerns. 1954: *Batman* (serial).

*Hitchcock, Alfred. (1899–   ). British, active in Britain and U.S.A.

1922: *Number Thirteen* (unfinished). 1925: *The Pleasure Garden*. 1926: *The Mountain Eagle, The Lodger*. 1927: *Downhill, Easy Virtue, The Ring*. 1928: *The Farmer's Wife, Champagne, The Manxman*. 1929: *Blackmail*. 1930: *Elstree Calling, Juno and the Paycock, Murder*. 1931: *The Skin Game*. 1932: *Rich and Strange, Number Seventeen, Lord Camber's Ladies*. 1933: *Waltzes From Vienna*. 1934: *The Man Who Knew Too Much*. 1935: *The Thirty-Nine Steps*. 1936: *The Secret Agent, Sabotage*. 1937: *Young and Innocent*. 1938: *The Lady Vanishes*. 1939: *Jamaica Inn*. 1940: *Rebecca, Foreign Correspondent*. 1941: *Mr and Mrs Smith, Suspicion*. 1942: *Saboteur*. 1943: *Shadow of a Doubt, Lifeboat*. 1944: *Bon Voyage, Aventure Malgache*. 1945: *Spellbound*. 1946: *Notorious*. 1947: *The Paradine Case*. 1948: *Rope*. 1949: *Under Capricorn*. 1950: *Stage Fright*. 1951: *Strangers on a Train*. 1952: *I Confess*. 1954: *Dial M For Murder, Rear Window*. 1955: *To Catch a Thief, The Man Who Knew Too Much*. 1956: *The Trouble with Harry*. 1957: *The Wrong Man*. 1958: *Vertigo*. 1959: *North by North-West*. 1960: *Psycho*. 1963: *The Birds*. 1964: *Marnie*. 1966: *Torn Curtain*. 1969: *Topaz*. 1972: *Frenzy*.

Howard, William K. (1889–1954). American.

1924: *The Border Legion*. 1927: *White Gold*. 1931: *Transatlantic*. 1932: *Sherlock Holmes*. 1933: *The Power and the Glory*. 1937: *Fire Over England*. 1944: *When the Lights Go On Again*.

Hubley, John. (1914–   ). American.

1946: *Brotherhood of Man*. 1949: *Mister Magoo* series (with Robert Cannon). 1951: *Rooty Toot Toot*. 1957: *Harlem Wednesday*. 1958: *Tender Game*. 1959: *Moonbird*. 1961: *Of Stars and Men*. 1962: *The Hole*. 1964: *The Hat*.

Hughes, Howard. (1905–   ). American.

1930: *Hell's Angels* (co-directed with James Whale). 1943: *The Outlaw*. 1946: *Vendetta*.

Hughes, Ken. (1922–   ). British.

1952: *Wide Boy*. 1953: *Black Thirteen*. 1954: *Little Red Monkey*. 1955: *The Brain Machine, Time Slip, Confession, Joe Macbeth*. 1956: *Wicked as they Come*. 1957: *Town on Trial*. 1960: *The Trials of Oscar Wilde*. 1963: *The Small World of Sammy Lee*. 1966: *Arrivederci Baby*. 1968: *Chitty Chitty Bang Bang*. 1969: *Cromwell*.

*Huston, John. (1906–   ). American.

1941: *The Maltese Falcon*. 1942: *In This Our Life*. 1943: *Report From the Aleutians, Across the Pacific*. 1944: *The Battle of San Pietro, Let There Be Light*. 1947: *The Treasure of the Sierra Madre*. 1948: *Key Largo*. 1949: *We Were Strangers*. 1950: *The Asphalt Jungle*. 1951: *The Red Badge of Courage. The African Queen*. 1953: *Moulin Rouge*. 1954: *Beat the Devil*. 1956: *Moby Dick*. 1957: *Heaven Knows Mr Alison*. 1958: *The Barbarian and the Geisha, The Roots of Heaven*. 1960: *The Unforgiven*. 1961: *The Misfits*. 1962: *Freud*. 1963: *The List of Adrian Messenger*.

1964: *Night of the Iguana*. 1966: *The Bible*. 1967: *Reflections in a Golden Eye*. 1969: *Sinful Davy, A Walk With Love and Death*. 1972: *Fat City*.

Ichikawa, Kon. (1915–). Japanese.

1945 6: *A Girl at Doho Temple*. 1952: *Mr Lucky*. 1953: *Mr Poo*. 1954: *Twelve Chapters About Women*. 1955: *The Heart*. 1956: *The Burmese Harp*. 1957: *The Crowded Train, The Hole*. 1958: *Conflagration*. 1959: *Odd Obsession, Fires on the Plain*. 1960: *Her Brother*. 1961: *Ten Dark Women, The Sin*. 1962: *Being Two Isn't Easy*. 1963: *An Actor's Revenge, Alone in the Pacific*. 1964: *Money Talks*. 1965: *Tokyo Olympiad*. 1966: *The Tale of Genji* (TV series). 1967: *Topo Gigio La Guerra del Missile* (in Italy). 1968: *Kyoto, Tournament*.

Imamura, Shohei. (1926–). Japanese.

1958: *The Stolen Desire, Lights of the Night, The Endless Desire*. 1959: *My Second Brother*. 1961: *Hogs and Warships*. 1963: *The Insect Woman*. 1964: *Unholy Desire*. 1966: *The Pornographer*. 1967: *A Man Disappears*. 1968: *Legends from a Southern Island*.

Ince, Thomas. (1882–1924). American.

Ince's great importance was as a supervising producer; and it is difficult to distinguish such films as he may have directed himself. The most likely of these are films made before 1913: 1910: *Their First Misunderstanding*. 1911: *The New Cook, Across the Plains, The Deserter, The Indian Massacre*. 1913: *The Battle of Gettysburg*.

Ingram, Rex. (1892–1950). Irish, active in U.S.A.

1919: *The Great Problem, The Chalice of Sorrow, Broken Fetters*. 1920: *The Reward of the Faithless, Under Crimson Skies, Hearts are Trumps*. 1921: *The Four Horsemen of the Apocalypse, The Prisoner of Zenda*. 1922: *Turn to the Right, The Conquering Power, Trifling Women*. 1923: *Where the Pavement Ends, Scaramouche*. 1924: *The Arab*. 1926: *Mare Nostrum*. 1927: *The Magician, The Siren of the Sea, The Garden of Allah*. 1929: *The Three Passions*. 1932: *Baroud*.

Ivens, Joris. (1898–). Dutch, active in Holland, U.S.S.R., Spain, Cuba etc.

1928: *De Brug*. 1929: *Regen*. 1930: *Zuiderzee*. 1932: *Komsomol*. 1934: *Borinage. New Earth*. 1937: *Spanish Earth*. 1939: *The Four Hundred Millions*. 1940: *The Power and the Land, New Frontiers* (incomplete). 1956: *Till Eulenspiegel* (co-directed with Gérard Philipe). 1957: *La Seine a rencontré Paris, Lettres de Chine*. 1965: *Le Ciel, la terre*. 1966: *Le Mistral*.

*Ivory, James. (1928–). American, active in India, America.

1962: *The Householder*. 1964: *Shakespeare Wallah*. 1969: *The Guru*. 1971: *Bombay Talkie*. 1972: *Savages*.

Jakubowska, Wanda. (1907–). Polish.

1932: *Reportaz* (in collaboration). 1939: *On the Niemen River*. 1948: *The Last Stage*. 1953: *Soldier of Victory*. 1954: *An Atlantic Story*. 1956: *Farewell to the Devil*. 1957: *King Macius I*. 1960: *Encounters in the Dark, It Happened Yesterday*. 1964: *Our World*. 1965: *The Hot Line*.

Jancsó, Miklós. (1921–). Hungarian.

1950: *We Hold Peace in Our Hands* (with Dezsö Koza and Gyula Meszaros). (short). 1953–71: many shorts. 1958: *The Bells Have Gone to Rome*. 1960: *Three Stars* (with Zoltan Varkonyi and Karoly Wiedermann). 1963: *Cantata*. 1964:

My Way Home. 1965: *The Round-up.* 1967: *The Red and the White, The Silence and the Cry.* 1968: *Confrontation.* 1969: *Sirocco.* 1970: *Angus Dei, The Pacifist* (in Italy). 1972: *Red Psalm, La tecnica e il rito* (in Italy).

Jasset, Victorin. (1862–1913). French.

1905: *Les Rêves d'un fumeur d'opium, La Esmeralda.* 1906: *La Vie de Christ.* 1908: *Ame corse, Nick Carter, Rifle Bill, Les Dragonards sous Louis XIV.* 1909: *Nick Carter, Morgan le Pirate, Mescal le contrebandier, Le Vautour de la sierra.* 1910: *Hérodiade.* 1911: *Zigomar, Zigomar contre Paulin Broquet, Zigomar contre Nick Carter, Nick Carter, La Fin de Don Juan.* 1912: *Au pays des ténèbres, Le Saboteur, Zigomar peau d'anguille, Le Cercueil de verre, Redemption, Un Cri dans la nuit.* 1913: *Balaoo, Protéa.*

*Jennings, Humphrey. (1907–50). British.

1935–6: *Birth of a Robot* (co-directed with Len Lye). 1939: *The First Days* (with Cavalcanti, Harry Watt, Pat Jackson etc), *Spare Time, Spring Offensive, Speaking From America, Her Last Trip.* 1940: *London Can Take It* (with Harry Watt), *Welfare of the Workers.* 1941: *Words For Battle, Heart of Britain, Listen To Britain.* 1943: *The Silent Village, Fires Were Started.* 1944: *The Story of Lilli Marlene.* 1944–5: *A Diary For Timothy.* 1945: *A Defeated People.* 1947: *The Cumberland Story.* 1949: *Dim Little Island.* 1950: *Family Portrait.*

Jessua, Alain. (1934–). French.

1964: *La Vie à l'envers.* 1967: *Jeu de massacre.*

Junghans, Karl. (1906–). German.

1924: *So ist das Leben.*

Jutzi, Piel. (c. 1902–). German.

1928: *Unser tägliches Brot.* 1928: *Kindertragödie.* 1929: *Mutter Krausens Fahrt ins Glück, Der Leben der Leichnam.* 1931: *Berlin-Alexanderplatz.* 1942: *So ein Früchtchen.*

Kadar, Jan. (1918–). Czech.

1950: *Katya.*
In collaboration with Elmar Klos: 1952: *Kidnapped.* 1954: *Music from Mars.* 1956: *Young Days.* 1957: *House at the Terminus.* 1958: *Three Wishes.* 1960: *Sparta-kiade, Youth.* 1963: *Death is Called Engelchen.* 1964: *The Dependent.* 1965: *Shop on the High Street.* 1969: *Adrift.*

Kalatozov, Mikhail. (1903–). Soviet (Georgian).

1930: *Salt for Svanetia.* 1950: *Conspiracy of the Doomed.* 1954: *Close Friends.* 1956: *The First Echelon.* 1957: *The Cranes are Flying.* 1960: *The Letter That Was Not Sent.* 1962: *I Am Cuba.* 1969: *The Red Tent.*

Kanin, Garson. (1912–). American.

1938: *A Man to Remember, Next Time I Marry.* 1939: *The Great Man Votes, Bachelor Mother.* 1940: *My Favourite Wife, They Knew What They Wanted.* 1941: *Tom, Dick and Harry.* 1945: *The True Glory* (co-directed with Carol Reed).

Karmen, Roman. (1906–). Soviet.

1932: *Moscow.* 1936–7: *On the Events in Spain.* 1938–9: *China in Conflict.* 1941: *In China.* 1945: *Berlin.* 1953: *Oilworkers of the Caspian Sea.* 1954: *Vietnam.* 1958: *How Broad is Our Country.* 1967: *Granada, My Granada.*

Kast, Pierre. (1920–). French.

1950: *Les Charmes de l'existence, Les Désastres de la guerre* (both co-directed with Jean Gremillon). 1951: *Les Femmes du Louvre, Je sème à tous vents.* 1952: *La Chasse à l'homme.* 1953: *A nous deux, Paris!* 1954: *Monsieur Robida, prophète et explorateur du temps, Nos ancêtres les explorateurs, Claude Ledoux, architecte maudit.* 1956: *La Brulure de mille soleils.* 1957: *Un Amour de poche.* 1958: *Images pour Baudelaire.* 1960: *Le Bel Age, Merci Natercia* (incomplete). 1961: *La Morte Saison des amours.* 1963: *Vacances Portugaises.* 1965: *Le Grain de sable.* 1972: *Les Soleils de l'Ile de Pâques.*

Kaufman, Mikhail. (1897–). Soviet.

1926: *Moscow.* 1929: *Spring.* 1933: *The Great Victory.* 1936: *March of the Air.* 1958: *Poem on the Life of the People.*

Kautner, Helmut. (1908–). German.

1939: *Kitty und die Weltkonferenz.* 1940: *Kleider machen Leute.* 1941: *Auf Wiedersehen, Franziska.* 1942: *Anuscka.* 1943: *Romanze in Moll.* 1945: *Unter den Brücken.* 1947: *In jenen Tagen.* 1948: *Der Apfel ist ab.* 1950: *Epilog.* 1954: *Die letzte Brücke.* 1955: *Des Teufels General, Himmel ohne Sterne.* 1956: *Der Hauptman von Köpenick, Ein Mädchen aus Flandern.* 1958: *Mompti, Der Schinderhannes.* 1959: *Der Rest is schweigen, Stranger in My Arms* (in U.S.A.).

Kawalerowicz, Jerzy. (1922–). Polish).

1950: *The Village Mill* (co-directed with Sumerski). 1953–4: *Celuloza.* 1956: *The Shadow.* 1957: *The Real End of the Great War.* 1959: *Night Train.* 1961: *Mother Joan of the Angels.* 1966: *Pharaoh.* 1969: *The Game.*

Kazan, Elia. (1909–). Turkish-born of Greek descent, active in U.S.A.

1937: *The People of the Cumberlands.* 1945: *A Tree Grows in Brooklyn.* 1947: *The Sea of Grass, Boomerang.* 1948: *Gentleman's Agreement.* 1949: *Pinky.* 1950: *Panic in the Streets.* 1951: *A Streetcar Named Desire.* 1952: *Viva Zapata!* 1953: *Man on a Tightrope.* 1954: *On the Waterfront.* 1955: *East of Eden.* 1956: *Baby Doll.* 1957: *A Face in the Crowd.* 1960: *Wild River.* 1961: *Splendour in the Grass.* 1964: *America! America! (The Anatolian Smile).* 1969: *The Arrangement.* 1972: *The Visitors.*

Keaton, Joseph Francis (Buster). (1895–1966). American.

1917: *The Butcher Boy,* (?) *A Reckless Romeo, Rough House, His Wedding Night, Oh, Doctor, Coney Island.* 1918: *Out West, The Bell Boy, Moonshine, Goodnight Nurse, The Cook.* 1919: *A Desert Hero, Backstage, The Hayseed, The Garage.* 1920: *The Saphead, The High Sign, One Week, Convict 13, The Scarecrow, Neighbours.* 1921: *The Haunted House, Hard Luck, The Goat, The Electric House, The Playhouse, The Boat, The Paleface.* 1922: *Cops, My Wife's Relations, The Blacksmith, The Frozen North, Daydreams, The Electric House.* 1923: *The Balloonatic, The Love Nest, The Three Ages, Our Hospitality.* 1924: *Sherlock Junior, The Navigator.* 1925: *Seven Chances, Go West.* 1926: *Battling Butler, The General.* 1927: *College.* 1928: *Steamboat Bill Jr., The Cameraman.* 1929: *Spite Marriage.*
This represents a complete check-list of the silent films in which Keaton *appeared.* Up to and including *The Garage* they were directed by Roscoe Arbuckle. *The Saphead* was directed by Herbert Blache. Although various director credits appear on the other films, it may be taken that Keaton's creative contribution was usually paramount.

Kelly, Gene. (1912–). American.

1949: *On the Town* (co-directed with Stanley Donen). 1952: *Singin' in the Rain* (with Donen). 1955: *It's Always Fair Weather* (with Donen). 1956: *Invitation to the Dance.* 1957: *The Happy Road.* 1958: *The Tunnel of Love.* 1963: *Gigot.* 1967: *A Guide for the Married Man.* 1969: *Hello, Dolly!* 1970: *The Cheyenne Social Club.*

King, Henry. (1892–). American.

1917: *Southern Pride.* 1921: *Tol'able David.* 1922: *Sonny, Fury* (in collaboration with Edmund Goulding). 1923: *The White Sister.* 1924: *Romola.* 1925: *Stella Dallas.* 1926: *The Winning of Barbara Worth.* 1930: *Lightnin'.* 1933: *State Fair.* 1935: *Way Down East.* 1936: *Lloyds of London, Ramona.* 1937: *Seventh Heaven.* 1938: *In Old Chicago, Alexander's Ragtime Band.* 1939: *Jesse James, Stanley and Livingstone.* 1940: *Little Old New York.* 1944: *The Song of Bernadette.* 1945: *Wilson, A Bell for Adano.* 1946: *Margie.* 1949: *Twelve O'Clock High, Prince of Foxes.* 1950: *The Gunfighter.* 1951: *David and Bathsheba.* 1952: *The Snows of Kilimanjaro.* 1955: *Love is a Many Splendored Thing.* 1956: *Carousel.* 1958: *The Sun Also Rises.* 1961: *Tender is the Night.*

Kinoshita, Keisuke. (1912–). Japanese.

1943: *The Blossoming Port.* 1955: *She Was Like a Daisy.* 1962: *New Year's Love, Ballad of a Workman.* 1963: *Sing Young People, A Legend or Was It?* 1964: *The Scent of Incense.* 1967: *Eyes, the Sea and a Ball.*

Kinugasa, Teinosuke. (1896–). Japanese.

1922: *Two Little Birds, Spark.* 1928: *Crossways.* 1953: *Gate of Hell.* 1958: *A Woman of Osaka.* 1963: *The Sorcerer.* 1967: *The Little Runaway* (Soviet-Japanese co-production).

Kirsanoff, Dmitri. (1890–1957). Estonian, active in France.

1923: *L'Ironie du destin.* 1925: *Ménilmontant.* 1926: *Sylvie-Destin.* 1927: *Sables.* 1929: *Brumes d'automne.* 1956: *Miss Catastrophe.*

Kluge, Alexander. (1932–). German.

1960: *Brutalität in Stein.* 1961: *Thema Amore, Rennen, Rennenfahrer.* 1963: *Lehrer.* 1965: *Portrat einer Bewahrung.* 1966: *Abschied von Gestern.* 1967: *Frau Blackburn wird gefümt, Feuerlöscher E. A. Winterstein.* 1968: *Die Artisten in der Zirkuskuppel: ratlos.* 1971: *Der grosse Verhau.*

Kobayashi, Masaki. (1916–). Japanese.

1952: *My Son's Youth.* 1959: *No Greater Love, Road to Eternity.* 1961: *A Soldier's Prayer.* 1962: *The Inheritance, Hara Kiri.* 1964: *Kwaidan.* 1967: *Rebellion.* 1968: *Hymn to a Tired Man.*

Konchalovsky-Mikhalkov, Andrei. (1937–). Soviet.

1958: *The Boy and the Pigeon.* 1959: *The Skating Rink and the Violin* (with Tarkovsky). 1964: *Andrei Rublev* (all shorts). 1965: *The First Teacher.* 1966: *The Story of Asya Klyachina, Who Loved but Did Not Marry.* 1969: *A Nest of Gentlefolk.* 1971: *Uncle Vanya.*

Korda, Alexander (Korda, Sándor). (1893–1956). Hungarian, active in Hungary, Austria, U.S.A., France, Britain.

1916: *White Nights.* 1917: *St Peter's Umbrella.* 1918: *Faun.* 1919: *The White Rose.* 1926: *Eine Dubarry von heute.* 1927: *The Private Life of Helen of Troy.* 1931:

Marius, Service For Ladies. 1932: *The Wedding Rehearsal.* 1933: *The Girl From Maxim's, The Private Life of Henry VIII.* 1934: *The Private Life of Don Juan.* 1936: *Rembrandt.* 1940: *Conquest of the Air.* 1941: *Lady Hamilton.* 1945: *The Perfect Strangers.* 1948: *An Ideal Husband.*

Korda, Zoltan. (1895–1961). Hungarian, active in Germany, U.S.A., and Britain.

1926: *Die elf Teufel.* 1935: *Sanders of the River.* 1936: *Elephant Boy.* 1939: *The Four Feathers.* 1942: *The Jungle Book.* 1943: *Sahara.* 1945: *Counter-attack.* 1947: *The Macomber Affair.* 1952: *Cry the Beloved Country.* 1955: *Storm Over the Nile* (with Terence Young).

Koster, Henry. (1905–). German, active in Germany and U.S.A.

1932: *Das Abenteuer einer schöne Frau.* 1936: *Three Smart Girls.* 1937: *One Hundred Men and a Girl.* 1953: *The Robe.* 1958: *Fraülein.* 1966: *The Singing Nun.*

*Kozintsev, Grigori. (1905–). Soviet.

Co-directed with Leonid Trauberg: 1924: *Adventures of Oktyabrina.* 1925: *Mishka Against Yudenich.* 1926: *The Devil's Wheel, The Overcoat.* 1927: *Little Brother, S.V.D.* 1929: *New Babylon.* 1931: *Alone.* 1934: *The Youth of Maxim.* 1937: *Return of Maxim.* 1938: *The Vyborg Side.* 1941: *Film Notes on Battles No. 1 and 2* (with Lev Arnshtam). 1945: *Plain People.* Kozintsev alone: 1947: *Pirogov.* 1951: *Belinsky.* 1957: *Don Quixote.* 1964: *Hamlet.* 1970: *King Lear.*

Kramer, Stanley. (1913–). American.

1955: *Not as a Stranger.* 1957: *The Pride and the Passion.* 1958: *The Defiant Ones.* 1959: *On the Beach.* 1960: *Inherit the Wind.* 1961: *Judgment at Nuremberg.* 1963: *It's a Mad, Mad, Mad, Mad World.* 1965: *Ship of Fools.* 1967: *Guess Who's Coming To Dinner.* 1969: *The Secret of Santa Vittoria.*

*Kubrick, Stanley. (1928–). American.

1949: *Day of the Fight.* 1951: *Flying Padre.* 1953: *Fear and Desire.* 1955: *Killer's Kiss.* 1956: *The Killing.* 1957: *Paths of Glory.* 1959: *Spartacus.* 1962: *Lolita.* 1964: *Doctor Strangelove.* 1968: *2001: A Space Odyssey.* 1972: *A Clockwork Orange.*

*Kuleshov, Lev. (1899–1970). Soviet.

1924: *The Strange Adventures of Mr West in the Land of the Bolsheviks.* 1925: *The Death Ray.* 1926: *Dura Lex.* (*By the Law*). 1927: *The Journalist Girl.* 1929: *The Happy Canary, Two-Buldi-Two.* 1931: *Forty Hearts.* 1933: *Horizon, The Great Consoler.* 1940: *The Siberians.* 1941: *Happening on the Volcano.* 1943: *Timur's Oath.* 1944: *We From the Urals.*

Kulidjanov, Lev. (1924–). Soviet.

1954: *Ladies* (co-directed with Oganissian). 1956: *It Started Like This* (co-directed with Segel). 1957: *The House I Live In* (with Segel). 1959: *Our Father's House, The Lost Photograph.* 1961: *When the Trees Grew Tall.* 1963: *The Blue Notebook.* 1969: *Crime and Punishment.*

*Kumel, Harry. (1940–). French.

1969: *Monsieur Hawarden.* 1971: *Daughters of Darkness.* 1972: *Malpertuis.*

*Kurosawa, Akira. (1910–). Japanese.

1943: *Judo Saga.* 1944: *The Most Beautiful.* 1945: *Judo Saga II, They Who Step on The Tiger's Tail.* 1946: *Those Who Make Tomorrow, No Regrets for Our Youth.* 1947: *One Wonderful Sunday.* 1948: *Drunken Angel.* 1949: *The Quiet Duel, Stray dog*. 1950: *Scandal, Rashomon*. 1951: *The Idiot*. 1952: *Ikira (Living)*. 1954: *Seven Samurai*. 1955: *Record of a Living Being*. 1957: *Throne of Blood, Lower Depths*. 1958: *The Hidden Fortress*. 1960: *The Bad Sleep Well*. 1961: *Yojimbo*. 1963: *High and Low*. 1965: *Red Beard*. 1970: *Dodeska Den*.

*Kutz, Kazimierz. (1929–). Polish.

1959: *The Cross of Valour*. 1960: *No-one Calls*. 1961: *People on a Train*. 1962: *Wild Horses*. 1963: *Silence*. 1964: *Heat*. 1966: *Whoever May Know*. 1968: *The Leap*. 1969: *Salt of the Black Earth*. 1972: *Pearls in the Crown*.

La Cava, Gregory. (1892–1952). American.

1924: *The New School Teacher*. 1926: *So's Your Old Man*. 1927: *Running Wild*. 1933: *Gabriel Over the White House*. 1936: *My Man Godfrey*. 1937: *Stage Door*. 1947: *Living in a Big Way*.

Laine, Edvin. (1905–). Finnish.

1943: *The Sin of Yrjänä's Wife*. 1955: *The Unknown Soldier*.

Lamorisse, Albert. (1922–70). French.

1947: *Djerba*. 1950: *Bim*. 1952: *Crin Blanc*. 1956: *Le Ballon rouge*. 1960: *Le Voyage en ballon*. 1964: *Fifi la plume*.

Lamprecht, Gerhardt. (1897–). German.

1923: *Die Büddenbrocks*. 1931: *Emil und die Detektive*. 1934: *Prinzessin Turandot*. 1937: *Madame Bovary*. 1955: *Oberwachtmeiser Bork*.

*Lang, Fritz. (1890–). Austrian, active in Germany, France, U.S.A.

1919: *Halbblut, Der Herr der Liebe, Die Spinnen* (two parts), *Harakiri*. 1920: *Das wandernde Bild, Vier un die Frau*. 1921: *Der Müde Tod (Destiny)*. 1922: *Dr Mabuse der Spieler*. 1924: *Die Nibelungen* (two parts). 1926: *Metropolis*. 1928: *Spione*. 1929: *Die Frau im Mond*. 1931: *M*. 1933: *Das Testament des Dr Mabuse*. 1934: *Liliom* (in France). 1936: *Fury*. 1937: *You Only Live Once*. 1938: *You and Me*. 1940: *The Return of Frank James*. 1941: *Western Union, Man Hunt*. 1943: *Hangmen Also Die*. 1944: *Ministry of Fear, The Woman in the Window*. 1945: *Scarlet Street*. 1946: *Cloak and Dagger*. 1948: *Secret Beyond the Door*. 1950: *House by the River, I Shall Return*. 1952: *Rancho Notorious, Clash By Night*. 1953: *The Blue Gardenia, The Big Heat*. 1954: *Human Desire*. 1955: *Moonfleet*. 1956: *While the City Sleeps, Beyond a Reasonable Doubt*. 1958: *Das indische Grabmal*. 1960: *Die 1000 Augen des Dr Mabuse*.

Lattuada, Alberto. (1914–). Italian.

1942: *Giacomo l'idealista*. 1945: *La freccia nel fianco*. 1946: *Il bandito*. 1947: *Il delitto di Giovanni Episcopo*. 1948: *Senza pietà*. 1949: *Il mulino del Po*. 1951: *Luci del varietà* (co-directed with Fellini), *Anna*. 1952: *Il cappotto*. 1953: *La lupa, Amore in città* (episode). 1954: *La spiaggia*. 1955: *Scuola elementare*. 1957: *Guendalina*. 1958: *La tempesta*. 1960: *I dolci inganni, Lettere di una novizia*. 1961: *L'imprevisto*. 1962: *Il mafioso, La steppa*. 1965: *La mandragola*. 1966: *Don Giovanni in Sicilia*. 1967: *Matchless*.

Laughton, Charles. (1899–1962). British, active as actor in Britain and U.S.A.

1955: *Night of the Hunter* (in U.S.A.).

Leacock, Richard. (1921–   ). British-born, active in U.S.A.

1956: *F.100, Bernstein in Israel.* 1960: *Primary, Yanqui No.* 1962: *Football.* 1963: *The Chair, Quint City, U.S.A., Jane.*

*Lean, David. (1908–   ). British.

1942: *In Which We Serve* (in collaboration with Noel Coward). 1943: *This Happy Breed.* 1944: *Blithe Spirit.* 1945: *Brief Encounter.* 1946: *Great Expectations.* 1947: *Oliver Twist.* 1949: *The Passionate Friends.* 1950: *Madeleine.* 1952: *The Sound Barrier.* 1953: *Hobson's Choice.* 1955: *Summer Madness.* 1958: *The Bridge on the River Kwai.* 1962: *Lawrence of Arabia.* 1966: *Doctor Zhivago.* 1970: *Ryan's Daughter.*

Le Chanois, Jean-Paul. (1909–   ). French.

1938: *La Vie d'un homme.* 1949: *L'Ecole buissonnière.* 1954: *Papa, maman, la bonne et moi.* 1958: *Les Misérables.*

Leenhardt, Roger. (1903–   ). French.

1933: *Lettre de Paris.* 1934: *L'Orient.* 1946: *Naissance du cinéma.* 1948: *Les Derniers Vacances.* 1962: *Le rendez-vous de minuit.*

*Lefebvre, Jean-Pierre. (1942–   ). French.

1964: *L'Homoman.* 1965: *Le Revolutionnaire.* 1966: *Patricia et Jean-Baptiste.* 1968: *Il ne faut pas mourir pour ça, Mon amie Pierette. Jusqu'au coeur.* 1969: *La chambre blanche.*

Léger, Fernand. (1881–1955). French.

1925: *Ballet mécanique.*

Leisen, Mitchell. (1898–   ). American.

1933: *Cradle Song.* 1934: *Death Takes a Holiday.* 1941: *Hold Back the Dawn.* 1944: *Lady in the Dark, Frenchman's Creek.* 1947: *Suddenly It's Spring, Golden Earrings.* 1953: *Tonight We Sing.* 1955: *Bedevilled.* 1957: *The Girl Most Likely.* 1963: *Here's Las Vegas.*

*Lelouch, Claude. (1937   ). French.

1960: *Le Propre de l'homme.* 1964: *L'Amour avec de si.* 1965: *Une Fille et des fusils.* 1966: *Les Grands Moments, Un Homme et une femme.* 1967: *Vivre pour vivre.* 1969: *A Man I Like.* 1970: *Le Rose et le noir.* 1971: *Smic, Smac, Smoc.* 1972: *L'Aventure c'est l'aventure.*

Leni, Paul. (1885–1929). German, active in Germany and U.S.A.

1918: *Dornöschen.* 1919: *Prinz Kuckuck.* 1921: *Fiesco, Hintertreppe.* 1924: *Das Wachsfigurenkabinett.* 1927: *The Cat and the Canary.* 1928: *The Chinese Parrot, The Man Who Laughs.* 1929: *The Last Warning.*

Lenica, Jan. (1928–   ). Polish.

Co-directed with Borowczyk: 1957: *Once Upon a Time, Requited sentiments.* 1958: *Dom.* Co-directed with Henri Gruel: 1959: *Monsieur Tête.* Lenica alone: 1961: *Janko the Musician.* 1962: *Labyrinth.* 1963: *Rhinosceros* (in Germany). 1965: *Femme fleur* (in France).

Leonard, Robert Z. (1889–   ). American.

1916: *The Plow Girl.* 1921: *Peacock Alley.* 1931: *Susan Lenox, Her Fall and Rise.* 1932: *Strange Interlude.* 1936: *The Great Ziegfeld.* 1937: *The Firefly, Maytime.* 1957: *Kelly and Me.*

Leone, Sergio. (1921–). Italian.

1964: *A Fistful of Dollars*. 1965: *For A Few Dollars More*. 1967: *The Good, the Bad and the Ugly*. 1969: *Once Upon a Time in the West*.

Lerner, Irving. (1909–). American.

1948: *Muscle Beach* (in collaboration with Joseph Strick). 1953: *Man Crazy*. 1959: *City of Fear, Murder by Contract*. 1960: *Studs Lonigan*. 1963: *Cry of Battle*.

Le Roy, Mervyn. (1900–). American.

1927: *No Place to Go*. 1929: *Hot Stuff*. 1930: *Little Caesar*. 1931: *Five Star Final*. 1932: *I Am a Fugitive From a Chain Gang*. 1933: *Gold-diggers of 1933*. 1936: *Anthony Adverse*. 1937: *They Won't Forget*. 1940: *Waterloo Bridge*. 1943: *Random Harvest, Madame Curie*. 1944: *Thirty Seconds Over Tokyo*. 1951: *Quo Vadis?* 1956: *The Bad Seed, Towards the Unknown*. 1958: *No Time For Sergeants*. 1959: *Home Before Dark, The F.B.I. Story*. 1960: *A Majority of One*. 1961: *The Devil at Four O'Clock*. 1962: *Gypsy*. 1963: *Mary, Mary*. 1965: *Moment to Moment*.

*Lester, Richard. (1932–). American-born; active in Britain.

1962: *It's Trad, Dad*. 1963: *The Mouse on the Moon*. 1964: *A Hard Day's Night*. 1965: *Help!, The Knack*. 1966: *A Funny Thing Happened on the Way to the Forum*. 1967: *How I Won the War, Petulia*. 1969: *The Bed-sitting Room*.

*Lewin, Albert. (1902–68). American.

1942: *The Moon and Sixpence*. 1945: *The Picture of Dorian Gray*. 1947: *The Private Affairs of Bel Ami*. 1951: *Pandora and the Flying Dutchman*. 1954: *Saadia*. 1957: *The Living Idol*.

Lewis, Jerry. (1926–). American.

1960: *The Bellboy*. 1961: *The Ladies' Man*. 1962: *The Errand Boy*. 1963: *The Nutty Professor*. 1964: *The Patsy*. 1965: *The Family Jewels*. 1966: *Three on a Couch*. 1970: *One More Time*. 1971: *Which Way to the Front?*

L'Herbier, Marcel. (1890–). French.

1919: *Rose France, Le Carnaval des vérités*. 1921: *Villa Destin, Prométhée banquier, Eldorado*. 1923: *Don Juan et Faust*. 1924: *L'Inhumaine*. 1925: *Feu Mathias Pascal*. 1926: *Le Vertige*. 1928: *Le Diable au coeur*. 1929: *L'Argent*. 1930: *Nuits de prince, L'Enfant de l'amour*. 1930: *Le Parfum de la dame en noir, Le Mystère de la chambre jaune*. 1936: *Veille d'armes*. 1937: *La Citadelle du silence*. 1939: *La Comédie du bonheur*. 1942: *La Nuit fantastique*. 1943: *L'Honorable Catherine*. 1951: *Gli ultimi giorni di Pompei*.

Litvak, Anatole. (1902–). Ukrainian-born, active in Germany, Great Britain, France, U.S.A.

1930: *Dolly macht Karriere*. 1931: *Nie wieder Liebe, Dover-Calais*. 1933: *Sleeping Car*. 1936: *Mayerling*. 1937: *The Woman I Love, Tovarich, The Amazing Dr Clitterhouse*. 1939: *Confessions of a Nazi Spy*. 1948: *Sorry Wrong Number, The Snake Pit*. 1955: *The Deep Blue Sea*. 1956: *Anastasia*. 1961: *Do You Like Brahms?* 1966: *The Night of the Generals*. 1971: *Lady in the Car with Glasses and a Gun*.

Lizzani, Carlo. (1922–). Italian.

1950: *Nel mezzogiorno qualcosa è cambiato*. 1951: *Achtung, banditi!* 1953: *L'amore in città* (episode). 1954: *Cronache di poveri amanti*. 1958: *La muraglia cinese*. 1960: *Il gobbo*. 1961: *L'oro di Roma*. 1963: *Il processo di Verona*. 1964: *La vita agra*. 1967: *Requiescant*.

Lloyd, Frank. (1888–1960). Scottish, active in America.

1916: *The Code of Marcia Gray*. 1918: *Les Misérables*. 1919: *Riders of the Purple Sage*. 1920: *Madame X*. 1922: *Oliver Twist*. 1924: *The Sea Hawk, Black Oxen*. 1927: *Children of Divorce*. 1929: *Drag*. 1930: *The Lash*. 1931: *East Lynne*. 1933: *Cavalcade, Berkeley Square*. 1935: *Mutiny on the Bounty*. 1936: *Under Two Flags, Wells Fargo*. 1955: *The Last Command*.

Loach, Ken. (1936–). British.

1967: *Poor Cow*. 1969: *Kes*. 1971: *Family Life*.

*Logan, Joshua. (1908–). American.

1938: *I Met My Love Again* (with Arthur Ripley). 1955: *Picnic*. 1966: *Bus Stop*. 1957: *Sayonara*. 1958: *South Pacific*. 1960: *Tall Story*. 1961: *Fanny*. 1964: *Ensign Pulver*. 1967: *Camelot*. 1969: *Paint Your Wagon*.

Lorentz, Pare. (1905–). American.

1936: *The Plow that broke the Plains*. 1937: *The River*.

*Lorre, Peter. (1904–64). Hungarian, active in Germany and U.S.A. (as actor).

1951: *Der Verlorene*.

*Losey, Joseph. (1909–). American, active in U.S.A. and Britain.

In U.S.A.: 1939: *Pete Roleum and his Cousins*. 1940–1: *A Child Went Forth, Youth Gets a Break*. 1945: *A Gun in His Hand*. 1948: *The Boy With Green Hair*. 1949: *The Dividing Line*. 1951: *The Prowler, M, The Big Night*. In Britain: 1953: *Stranger on the Prowl*. 1954: *The Sleeping Tiger*. 1955: *A Man on the Beach*, 1956: *The Intimate Stranger*. 1957: *Time Without Pity*. 1958: *The Gypsy and the Gentleman*. 1959: *Blind Date*. 1960: *The Criminal*. 1962: *The Damned, Eva*. 1963: *The Servant*. 1964: *King and Country*. 1966: *Modesty Blaise*. 1967: *Accident*. 1968: *Boom, Secret Ceremony*. 1970: *Figures in a Landscape*. 1971: *The Go-Between*. 1972: *The Assassination of Trotsky*.

*Lubitsch, Ernst. (1892–1947). German, active in Germany and U.S.A.

1915: *Blinde Kuh*. 1915–18: fourteen short comedies, starring Lubitsch as comedian. 1918: *Die Augen der Mumie Ma, Das Mädel vom Ballet, Carmen*. 1919: *Meier aus Berlin, Meine Frau, die Filmshauspielerin, Schwäbemadie, Die Austernprinzessin, Rausch, Madame Dubarry, Die Puppe*. 1920: *Kohlhiesel's Töchter, Romeo und Julia im Schnee, Sumurun, Anna Boleyn*. 1921: *Die Bergkatze*. 1922: *Das Weib des Pharao, Miss Julie*. 1923: *Die Flamme, Rosita*. 1924: *The Marriage Circle, Three Women, Forbidden Paradise*. 1925: *Kiss Me Again, Lady Windermere's Fan*. 1926: *So This is Paris*. 1927: *The Student Prince*. 1928: *The Patriot*. 1929: *Eternal Love, The Love Parade*. 1930: *Paramount on Parade* (part), *Monte Carlo*. 1931: *The Smiling Lieutenant*. 1932: *The Man I Killed, One Hour With You, Trouble in Paradise, If I Had a Million* (episode). 1933: *Design for Living*. 1934: *The Merry Widow*. 1936: *Desire*. 1937: *Angel*. 1938: *Bluebeard's Eighth Wife*. 1939: *Ninotchka*. 1940: *The Shop Around the Corner*. 1941: *That Uncertain Feeling*. 1942: *To Be or Not to Be*. 1943: *Heaven Can Wait*. 1946: *Cluny Brown*. 1948: *That Lady in Ermine* (posthumous; finished by Otto Preminger).

*Lumet, Sidney. (1924–). American.

1957: *Twelve Angry Men*. 1958: *Stage Struck, That Kind of Woman*. 1960: *The Fugitive Kind, A View From the Bridge*. 1962: *Long Day's Journey into Night*. 1963: *Fail Safe*. 1964: *The Pawnbroker*. 1965: *The Hill*. 1966: *The Group, The*

Deadly Affair. 1968: *Bye Bye Braverman, The Seagull.* 1969: *The Appointment,* 1971: *The Anderson Tapes.*

Lumière, Auguste (186   1954) and **Louis** (1864–1948). French.

1895–1903: numerous short films, among them *La Sortie du port, Arrivée d'un train, La Sortie des usines Lumière, Le Déjeuner de bébé, Démolition d'un mur.*

Lye, Len. (1901–   ). New Zealand-born, active in Britain.

1934: *Tusalava.* 1935: *Colour Box.* 1936: *Rainbow Dance, Kaleidoscope.* 1941: *Lambeth Walk.* 1941–5: war propaganda films. 1952: *The Fox Chase.*

Machaty, Gustav. (1901–63). Czech.

1929: *Erotikon.* 1932: *Extase.*

McCarey, Leo. (1898–1969). American.

1921: *Society Secrets.* 1931: *Indiscreet.* 1932: *The Kid From Spain.* 1933: *Duck Soup.* 1934: *Six of a Kind, Belle of the Nineties.* 1935: *Ruggles of Red Gap.* 1936: *The Milky Way.* 1944: *Going My Way.* 1945: *The Bells of St Mary's.* 1948: *Good Sam.* 1957: *An Affair to Remember.* 1958: *Rally Round the Flag Boys.* 1962: *Satan Never Sleeps.*

*****Mackendrick, Alexander.** (1912–   ). American-born, active in Great Britain and U.S.A.

1948: *Whisky Galore.* 1951: *The Man in the White Suit.* 1952: *Mandy.* 1954: *The Maggie.* 1955: *The Lady Killers.* 1957: *Sweet Smell of Success.* 1962: *Sammy Going South.* 1965: *A High Wind in Jamaica.* 1971: *Mary Queen of Scots.*

MacLaren, Norman. (1914–   ). British, active in Britain, U.S.A., Canada.

1937: *Book Bargain.* 1939: *Dots and Loops.* 1940: *Boogie Doodle.* 1942: *Hen Hop.* 1943: *Dollar Dance.* 1947: *Fiddle De Dee, La Poulette grise.* 1949: *Begone Dull Care.* 1951: *Around is Around.* 1952: *Neighbours.* 1956: *Rythmetic.* 1957: *A Chairy Tale.* 1958: *La Merle.*

McLeod, Norman Z. (1898–   ). American.

1931: *Monkey Business.* 1932: *Horse Feathers.* 1933: *If I Had a Million* (episode), *Alice in Wonderland.* 1937: *Topper.* 1938: *Merrily We Live, Topper Takes a Trip.* 1941: *Panama Hattie.* 1946: *The Kid From Brooklyn.* 1947: *The Secret Life of Walter Mitty, The Paleface.* 1951: *My Favourite Spy.* 1953: *Never Wave at a WAC.* 1954: *Casanova's Big Night.*

Makavejev, Dusan. (1932–   ). Jugoslav.

1953: *Jatagan Mata* (16mm short). 1953–64: Several shorts. 1962: *The Parade.* 1965: *A Man is not a Bird.* 1967: *The Switchboard Operator.* 1968: *Innocence Unprotected.* 1971: *WR: Mysteries of the Organism.*

Makk, Karoly. (1925–   ). Hungarian.

1952: *Liliomfi.* 1955: *Ward Number 9.* 1956: *Tale of the Twelve Points.* 1958: *The House Under the Rocks.* 1959: *Brigade Number 39.* 1960: *Don't Keep off the Grass.* 1961: *The Fanatic.* 1962: *The Lost Paradise.* 1963: *The Last But One.* 1964: *His Majesty's Dates.* 1968: *Before God and Man.* 1970: *Love.*

Malaparte, Curzio. (1898–1957). Italian writer, director of a single film:

1951: *Il Cristo proibito.*

*Malle, Louis. (1932–). French.

1955: *Le Monde du silence* (co-directed with Cousteau). 1957: *Ascenseur pour l'échafaud*. 1958: *Les Amants*. 1960: *Zazie dans le métro*. 1962: *Vie privée*. 1963: *Le feu follet*. 1965: *Viva Maria!* 1967: *Le Voleur*. 1971: *Le Souffle au Coeur*.

Malraux, André. (1901–). French.

1939: *L'Espoir*.

*Mamoulian, Rouben. (1898–). Armenian, active in U.S.A.

1929: *Applause*. 1931: *City Streets, Dr Jekyll and Mr Hyde*. 1932: *Love Me Tonight*. 1933: *Song of Songs, Queen Christina*. 1934: *We Live Again*. 1935: *Becky Sharp*. 1936: *The Gay Desperado*. 1937: *High, Wide and Handsome*. 1939: *Golden Boy*. 1940: *The Mark of Zorro*. 1941: *Blood and Sand*. 1942: *Rings on her Fingers*. 1947: *Summer Holiday*. 1957: *Silk Stockings*.

*Mankiewicz, Joseph L. (1909–). American.

1946: *Dragonwyck, Somewhere in the Night*. 1947: *The Late George Apley, The Ghost and Mrs Muir*. 1948: *Escape*. 1949: *A Letter to Three Wives, House of Strangers*. 1950: *No Way Out, All About Eve*. 1951: *People Will Talk*. 1952: *Five Fingers*. 1953: *Julius Caesar*. 1954: *The Barefoot Contessa*. 1955: *Guys and Dolls*. 1957: *The Quiet American*. 1959: *Suddenly, Last Summer*. 1963: *Cleopatra*. 1967: *The Honey Pot*. 1970: *There Was a Crooked Man*.

Mann, Anthony. (1907–67). American.

1942: *Doctor Broadway, Moonlight in Havana*. 1943: *Nobody's Darling*. 1944: *My Best Gal, Strangers in the Night*. 1945: *Two O'Clock Courage*. 1949: *Side Street*. 1950: *Winchester 73*. 1951: *The Tall Target*. 1953: *The Naked Spur*. 1954: *The Glenn Miller Story*. 1955: *The Far Country, Strategic Air Command, The Man from Laramie*. 1956: *The Last Frontier, Serenade*. 1957: *Men in War, The Tin Star*. 1958: *God's Little Acre, Man of the West*. 1960: *Cimarron*. 1961: *El Cid*. 1964: *The Fall of the Roman Empire*. 1965: *The Heroes of Telemark*. 1967: *A Dandy in Aspic* (finished by Laurence Harvey).

*Mann, Daniel. (1912–). American.

1952: *Come Back Little Sheba*. 1954: *About Mrs Leslie*. 1955: *The Rose Tattoo*. 1956: *I'll Cry Tomorrow*. 1957: *Teahouse of the August Moon*. 1958: *Hot Spell*. 1960: *The Last Angry Man, The Mountain Road, Butterfield 8*. 1961: *Ada*. 1962: *Five Finger Exercise*. 1963: *Who's been Sleeping in My Bed*. 1965: *Our Man Flint, Judith*.

*Mann, Delbert. (1920–). American.

1955: *Marty*. 1957: *Bachelor Party*. 1958: *Desire Under the Elms, Separate Tables, Middle of the Night*. 1960: *The Dark at the Top of the Stairs*. 1961: *Lover Come Back*. 1962: *That Touch of Mink*. 1963: *A Gathering of Eagles*. 1965: *Quick Before it Melts*. 1966: *Mister Buddwing*. 1967: *Fitzwilly*. 1969: *David Copperfield*. 1971: *Jane Eyre*. 1972: *Kidnapped*.

Mari, Febo. (1884–1939). Italian.

1912: *Il critico*. 1915: *L'emigrante*. 1916: *Cenere* (with Arturo Ambrosio; the only screen appearance of Eleanora Duse). 1917: *Fauno*. 1923: *Triboulet, la corte dei miracoli*.

Máriássy, Félix. (1919–). Hungarian.

1949: *Anna Szabó*. 1955: *A Glass of Beer, Spring in Budapest*. 1958: *Smugglers*.

1959: *Sleepless Years, A Simple Love.* 1960: *It is a Long Way Home, Test Trip.* 1962: *Every Day – Sunday.* 1964: *Goliath.* 1966: *Fig Leaf.* 1968: *Bondage.* 1970: *The Imposters.*

*Marker, Chris. (1921–). French.

1952: *Olympia 52.* 1956: *Dimanche à Pékin.* 1957: *Le Mystère de l'Atelier 15* (with Resnais). 1958: *Lettre de Sibérie.* 1959: *Les Astronautes* (with Borowczyk). 1960: *Description d'un combat.* 1961: *Cuba, si!* 1963: *Le Joli Mai, La Jetée.* 1965: *Le Mystère Koumiko.* 1966: *Si j'avais quatre dromedaires.*

Marshall, George. (1891–). American.

1928: *Smitty* series of comedy shorts. 1932: *Pack Up Your Troubles* (with Raymond McCarey). 1938: *The Goldwyn Follies.* 1939: *You Can't Cheat an Honest Man, Destry Rides Again.* 1940: *The Ghost Breakers, When the Daltons Rode.* 1941: *Texas.* 1943: *Star-spangled Rhythm.* 1947: *The Perils of Pauline.* 1948: *Tap Roots.* 1949: *My Friend Irma.* 1950: *Fancy Pants.* 1953: *Houdini.* 1954: *Red Garters.* 1955: *The Second Greatest Sex.* 1958: *The Sheepman.* 1960: *The Gazebo.* 1962: *How the West Was Won* (episode). 1969: *Hook, Line and Sinker.*

Martoglio, Nina. (1870–1921). Italian.

1913: *Il romanzo.* 1914: *Capitan Blanco, Sperduti nel buio.* 1915: *Teresa Raquin.*

Mattson, Arne. (1919–). Swedish.

1951: *One Summer of Happiness.* 1953: *Salka Valka.* 1958: *The Phantom Carriage.* 1962: *The Doll.*

May, Joe. (1880–1954). German, active in Germany, France and U.S.A.

1913: *Die geheimnisvolle Villa.* 1914: *Die Pagode.* 1916: *Veritas Vincit.* 1921: *Das Indische Grabmal.* 1922: *Die Herrin der Welt* (serial). 1928: *Heimkehr.* 1929: *Asphalt.* 1931: *Ihre Mäjestat die Liebe.* 1933: *Le Chemin de bonheur, Voyages de noces.* 1934: *Music in the Air.* 1940: *The House of the Seven Gables.* 1944: *Johnny Doesn't Live Here.*

Mayo, Archie. (1891–1968). American.

1926: *Money Talks.* 1929: *My Man, Sonny Boy.* 1935: *Go into your Dance.* 1936: *The Petrified Forest.* 1938: *The Adventures of Marco Polo.* 1941: *The Great American Broadcast, Charley's American Aunt.* 1942: *Moontide, Orchestra Wives.* 1946: *A Night in Casablanca, Angel on my Shoulder.*

Maysles, Albert. (1922–). American.

1963: *Showman.* 1969: *Salesman.* 1971: *Gimme Shelter.*

Mekas, Adolfas. (1925–). Lithuanian-born, active in U.S.A.

1963: *Hallelujah the Hills* (in collaboration with Jonas Mekas). 1965: *The Double-barrelled Detective Story.*

Mekas, Jonas. (1922–). Lithuanian-born, active in U.S.A.

1961: *Guns of the Trees, Secret Passions of Salvador Dali.* 1964: *The Brig, Flaming Creatures* (co-directed with Jack Smith). 1966: *Hare Krishna, The Circus Notebook.*

Méliès, Georges. (1861–1938). French.

1896–1912: several hundred short films, among them: 1896: *Une Partie de cartes, Escamotage d'une dame au Théâtre Robert-Houdin.* 1897: *L'Auberge ensorcelée*. 1898: *L'Homme de têtes*. 1899: *L'Affaire Dreyfus, Cendrillon*. 1900: *Jeanne d'Arc, Rêve de Noel, Le Deshabillage Impossible, Le Brahmane et le Papillon*. 1901: *Barbe Bleu, L'Homme à tête caoutchouc*. 1902: *Le Voyage dans la lune, Le Sacre d'Edouard VII*. 1903: *Le Mélomane, Le Royaume des fées, Bob Kick, l'enfant terrible, La Lanterne magique*. 1904: *Le Voyage à travers l'impossible*. 1906: *Jack le ramoneur, Les Incendiaires, Les 400 farces du Diable*. 1907: *Le Tunnel sous la manche*. 1908: *La Civilisation à travers les Ages, La Photographie electrique à distance*. 1911: *Les Hallucinations du Baron de Munchausen*. 1912: *A la conquête du Pole, Cendrillon*. 1913: *Le Chevalier des neiges, Le Voyage de la famille Bourrichon*.

Melville, Jean-Pierre. (1917–   ). French.

1946: *24 Heures dans la vie d'un clown*. 1949: *Le Silence de la mer*. 1950: *Les Enfants terribles*. 1953: *Quand tu liras cette lettre*. 1956: *Bob le flambeur*. 1959: *Deux hommes dans Manhattan*. 1961: *Léon Morin, Prêtre*. 1963: *Le Doulos*. 1964: *L'Aîné des Ferchaux*. 1966: *Le Deuxième Souffle*. 1967: *Le Samourai*. 1969: *L'Armée des ombres*. 1970: *Le Cercle rouge*.

Menzies, William Cameron. (1896–1967). American.

1932: *Chanda the Magician*. 1936: *Things to Come*. 1944: *Address Unknown*. 1951: *Drums in the Deep South*. 1953: *Invaders from Mars*.

Meyerhold, Vsevelod Emilievich. (1874–1940). Russian.

1915: *The Portrait of Dorian Gray, The Strong Man*.

Meyers, Sidney. (1894–   ). American.

1948: *The Quiet One*. 1959: *The Savage Eye* (co-directed with Joseph Strick).

Milestone, Lewis. (1895–   ). Russian, active in U.S.A.

1925: *The Cave Man*. 1927: *Two Arabian Knights*. 1929: *The Racket, Betrayal*. 1930: *Hell's Angels* (with James Whale and Luther Reed), *All Quiet on the Western Front, New York Nights*. 1931: *Front Page*. 1932: *Rain*. 1933: *Hallelujah, I'm a Bum*. 1934: *The Captain Hates the Sea*. 1935: *Paris in the Spring*. 1936: *Anything Goes, The General Died at Dawn*. 1939: *Of Mice and Men, The Night of Nights*. 1940: *Lucky Partners*. 1941: *My Life with Caroline*. 1942: *Edge of Darkness*. 1943: *The North Star*. 1944: *The Purple Heart*. 1945: *The Strange Love of Martha Ivers*. 1946: *A Walk in the Sun*. 1947: *Arch of Triumph*. 1948: *No Minor Vices*. 1949: *The Red Pony*. 1952: *The Halls of Montezuma*. 1953: *Kangaroo, Les Miserables*. 1954: *Melba*. 1955: *La Vedova X, They Who Dare*. 1959: *Pork Chop Hill*. 1960: *Ocean's Eleven*. 1962: *Mutiny on the Bounty*.

Mimica, Vatroslav. (1923–   ). Jugoslav.

1952: *In the Storm*. 1955: *Mr Ikl's Jubilee*. 1957–62: animated films, including *The Scarecrow, Happy End, The Egg*. 1961: *Suleiman the Conqueror*. 1965: *Prometheus from the Island of Viševica*. 1966: *Monday or Tuesday*. 1967: *Kaya, I'll Kill You*.

Minnelli, Vincente. (1913–   ). American.

1942: *Cabin in the Sky*. 1944: *Meet Me in St Louis*. 1945: *Under the Clock, Yolanda and the Thief*. 1946: *Ziegfield Follies*. 1948: *The Pirate*. 1950: *Father of the Bride*. 1951: *Father's Little Dividend, An American in Paris*. 1953: *Band Wagon*. 1954: *The Long, Long Trailer, Brigadoon*. 1955: *The Cobweb*. 1956: *Kismet, Lust for Life*. 1958: *Gigi*. 1959: *Some Came Running, The Bells are Ringing*. 1960: *The Four Horsemen of the Apocalypse*. 1966: *The Sandpiper*. 1969: *On a Clear Day You Can See For Ever*.

Mizoguchi, Kenji. (1898–1956). Japanese.

1922: *When Love Returns.* 1922–40: upwards of sixty feature films. 1940: *The Loyal Forty-seven Ronin.* 1952: *The Life of Oharu.* 1953: *Ugetsu Monogatari, Gion Music.* 1954: *Sansho the Bailiff, The Woman in the Rumour, Chikkamatsu Monogatari.* 1955: *Princess Yang Kwei Fei, New Tales of the Taira Clan.* 1956: *Street of Shame.*

Mocky, Jean-Pierre. (1929–). French.

1959: *Les Dragueurs.* 1960: *Un Couple.* 1961: *Snobs.* 1962: *Les Vierges, Un Drôle de paroissien.* 1964: *La Grande frousse.* 1965: *La Bourse et la vie.* 1966: *Les compagnons de la marguerite.* 1968: *La Grande Lessive.* 1969: *Solo.* 1970: *L'Etalon.* 1971: *L'Albatros.*

Molander, Gosta. (1888–). Finnish, active in Sweden.

1920: *King of Boda.* 1922: *Thomas Graal's Ward.* 1922: *The Amateur Film.* 1923–53: upwards of fifty feature films. 1954: *Herr Arne's Treasure* (remake). 1955: *The Unicorn.* 1956: *The Song of the Scarlet Flower.* 1965: *Stimulantia* (episode).

Mulligan, Robert. (1925–). American.

1957: *Fear Strikes Out.* 1961: *The Great Imposter.* 1962: *To Kill a Mocking Bird.* 1964: *Love with the Proper Stranger.* 1965: *Baby the Rain Must Fall, Inside Daisy Clover.* 1967: *Up the Down Staircase.* 1968: *The Stalking Moon.* 1970: *The Pursuit of Happiness.* 1971: *Summer of '42.*

Munk, Andrzej. (1921–61). Polish.

1949–55: various documentaries. 1956: *The Blue Cross, Man on the Tracks.* 1957: *Eroica.* 1960: *Bad Luck.* 1961: *The Passenger* (incomplete).

*Murnau, Friedrich Wilhelm. (1889–1931). German, active in Germany and U.S.A.

1919: *Der Knabe im blau, Satanas.* 1920: *Der Bucklige und die Tänzerin, Der Januskopf.* 1921: *Der Gang in die Nacht, Schloss Vogelöd, Sehnsucht.* 1922: *Maritza, Gennant die Schmuggler Madonna, Der brennende Acker, Nosferatu, Das Phantom.* 1923: *Austreibung, Die Finanzen des Grossherzogs.* 1924: *Der letzte Mann.* 1925: *Tartuffe.* 1926: *Faust.* 1927: *Sunrise.* 1929: *Four Devils.* 1930: *Our Daily Bread.* 1931: *Tabu.*

Neame, Ronald. (1911–). British.

1947: *Take My Life.* 1950: *The Golden Salamander.* 1952: *The Card.* 1953: *The Million Pound Note.* 1956: *The Man Who Never Was.* 1958: *The Horse's Mouth.* 1960: *Tunes of Glory.* 1962: *Escape From Zahrein.* 1963: *I Could Go On Singing.* 1964: *The Chalk Garden.* 1965: *Mr Moses.* 1966: *A Man Could Get Killed, Gambit.* 1969: *The Prime of Miss Jean Brodie.* 1970: *Scrooge.*

Negulesco, Jean. (1900–). Rumanian, active in U.S.A.

1934: *Kiss and Make Up.* 1944: *The Mask of Dimitrios.* 1946: *Humoresque.* 1948: *Johnny Belinda.* 1949: *Britannia Mews.* 1951: *The Mudlark.* 1953: *Titanic, How to Marry a Millionaire.* 1954: *Three Coins in the Fountain.* 1955: *Daddy Long Legs, The Rains of Ranchipur.* 1957: *Boy on a Dolphin.* 1970: *Hello and Goodbye.*

Neilan, Marshal (1891–1958). American.

1916: *Little Pal.* 1917: *Rebecca of Sunnybrook Farm.* 1918: *Stella Maris, Amarilly of Clothes-line Alley.* 1919: *Daddy Long Legs.* 1924: *Tess of the Durbervilles, Dorothy Vernon of Haddon Hall.* 1937: *Swing it Professor.*

Nemec, Jan. (1936–). Czech.

1960: *A Bite to Eat.* 1963: *Memory of our Day.* 1964: *Diamonds of the Night.* 1965: *Life After Ninety Minutes, Pearls of the Deep* (episode). 1966: *The Party and the Guests, Martyrs of Love.* 1967: *Mother and Son.*

Niblo, Fred. (1874–1948). American, of Italian parentage (Federico Nobile).

1918: *The Marriage Ring.* 1920: *The Mark of Zorro.* 1921: *The Three Musketeers.* 1923: *Blood and Sand.* 1924: *Thy Name is Woman.* 1924–6: *Ben Hur.* 1926: *The Temptress.* 1927: *Camille.* 1928: *The Mysterious Lady.* 1941: *Three Sons o'Guns.*

Nichols, Dudley. (1895–1960). American (writer; directed three films).

1943: *Government Girl.* 1946: *Sister Kenney.* 1947: *Mourning Becomes Electra.*

Nichols, Mike. (1931–). American.

1966: *Who's Afraid of Virginia Woolf?* 1968: *The Graduate.* 1970: *Catch 22.* 1971: *Carnal Knowledge.*

Okhlopkov, Nikolai. (1900–1967). Soviet actor: directed three films).

1927: *Mitya.* 1928: *The Sold Appetite.* 1930: *The Way of Enthusiasts.*

Olivier, Laurence. (1907–). British.

1945: *Henry V.* 1948: *Hamlet.* 1956: *Richard III.* 1970: *Three Sisters.*

Olmi, Ermanno. (1931–). Italian.

1954–61: industrial documentaries. 1959: *Il tempo si è fermato.* 1961: *Il posto.* 1963: *I fidanzati.* 1965: *E venne un uomo.* 1967: *Storie di giovani* (TV). 1970: *I ricuperanti, Un certo giorno.* 1971: *Durante l'estate.*

***Ophuls, Max.** (1902–57). German, active in Germany, Italy, France, U.S.A.

1930: *Dann schön lieber Lebertran.* 1931: *Die lachende Erben, Die verliebte Firma.* 1932: *Die verkaufte Braut, Liebelei,* 1933: *Une Historie d'amour, On a volé un homme.* 1934: *La Signora di Tutti.* 1935: *Divine.* 1936: *Comedie om Geld.* 1936: *Ave Maria of Schubert, La Valse Brillante, La Tendre Ennemie.* 1937: *Yoshiwara.* 1938: *Werther.* 1939: *Sans lendemain.* 1940: *De Mayerling a Sarajevo, L'Ecole des femmes* (unfinished). 1946. *Vendetta.* 1947: *The Exile.* 1948: *Letter From an Unknown Woman, Caught.* 1949: *The Reckless Moment.* 1950: *La Ronde.* 1951: *Le Plaisir.* 1953: *Madame de . . .* 1955: *Lola Montès.*

***Oshima, Nagisa.** (1932–). Japanese.

1959: *A Town of Love and Hope.* 1960: *A Story of Cruelty of Youth (Naked Youth), The Sun's Burial, A Foggy Night.* 1961: *The Catch.* 1962: *Amakusa Shiro Tokisada.* 1963: *A Small Adventure.* 1965: *Pleasures of the Flesh, Yunbogi's Diary.* 1966: *Violence at Noon.* 1967: *Sing a Song of Sex, Ninja Bugeicho, Double Suicide.* 1968: *Death By Hanging, A Sinner in Paradise.* 1969: *Diary of a Shinjuku Thief, Boy.* 1971: *He Died After the War, The Ceremony.*

Otsep, Fedor. (1895–1949). Soviet, active in U.S.S.R., France, Germany, U.S.A., Canada.

1926: *Miss Mend* (with Boris Barnet). 1929: *The Living Corpse.* 1931: *Die Mörder der Dimitri Karamazov.* 1932: *Mirages de Paris.* 1934: *Amok.* 1937: *La Dame de pique.* 1938: *Gibraltar.* 1943: *Le Père Chopin.* 1947: *Whispering City.*

Ozu, Yasujiro. (1903–63). Japanese.

1927: *Sword of Penitence.* 1929: *I Graduated but . . .* 1930: *A Straightforward Boy,*

I Flunked, but . . ., Luck Touched my Legs. 1932: *Spring Comes from the Ladies, I was Born but . . .* 1934: *A Mother Ought to be Loved, A Story of Floating Weeds.* 1935: *Tokyo is a Nice Place, An Inn in Tokyo.* 1936: *College is a Nice Place.* 1949: *Late Spring.* 1951: *Early Summer.* 1952: *A Flavour of Green Tea over Rice.* 1953: *Tokyo Story.* 1956: *Early Spring.* 1957: *Tokyo Twilight.* 1958: *Equinox Flower.* 1959: *Good Morning, Floating Weeds.* 1960: *Late Autumn.* 1961: *Early Autumn.* 1962: *An Autumn Afternoon.*

Pabst, Georg Wilhelm. (1885–1967). German.

1923: *Der Schatz.* 1925: *Die freudlose gasse.* 1926: *Geheimnisse einer seele.* 1927: *Die Liebe der Jeanne Ney.* 1928: *Abwege, Die Büchse der Pandora.* 1929: *Das Tagebuch einer Verlorenen, Die weisse Hölle von Piz Palu* (with Arnold Fanck). 1930: *Westfront 1918, Skandal um Eva.* 1931: *Die Dreigroschenoper, Kameradschaft.* 1932: *Atlantide.* 1933: *Don Quixote, Du haut en bas.* 1934: *A Modern Hero.* 1937: *Mademoiselle Docteur.* 1938: *Le Drame de Shanghai.* 1939: *Jeunes filles en détresse.* 1941: *Komodianten.* 1943: *Paracelsus.* 1945: *Der Fall Molander* (unfinished). 1948: *Der Prozess.* 1955: *Der letzte Akt.* 1956: *Durch die Wälder, durch die Auen.*

*****Pagnol, Marcel.** (1895–). French.

1934: *Angèle, Jofroi.* 1935: *Merlusse.* 1936: *César.* 1937: *Regain.* 1938: *Le Schpuntz, La Femme du boulanger.* 1940: *La Femme du puisatier.* 1951: *Topaze.* 1952: *Manon des sources.* 1954: *Lettres de mon moulin.*

Painlevé, Jean. (1902–). French.

1925: *La Pieuvre.* 1926–53: numerous scientific and nature documentaries. 1953: *Les Oursines.*

Pal, George. (1908–64). Hungarian, active in U.S.A.

1941: *Rhythm in the Ranks.* 1941–59: numerous puppet and animated shorts. 1959: *Tom Thumb.* 1961: *The Time Machine.* 1962: *The Wonderful World of the Brothers Grimm* (with Henry Levin).

Parrish, Robert. (1916–). American.

1951: *Cry Danger.* 1955: *The Purple Plain.* 1957: *Fire Down Below.* 1959: *The Wonderful Country.* 1964: *In The French Style.* 1967: *The Bobo.*

*****Pascal, Gabriel.** (1894–1954). Hungarian.

1941: *Major Barbara.* 1946: *Caesar and Cleopatra.*

*****Pasolini, Pier Paolo.** (1922–). Italian.

1961: *Accattone.* 1962: *Mamma Roma.* 1963: *RoGoPaG* (episode), *La Rabbia* (episode). 1964: *Il Vangelo secondo Matteo, Comizi d'amore.* 1965: *Sopraluoghi in Terra Santa.* 1966: *Uccellacci e Uccellini.* 1967: *Le Streghe* (episode), *Edipo Re, Vangelo 70* (episode). 1968: *Teorema.* 1969: *Porcile.* 1970: *Medea.* 1971: *Decamerone.* 1972: *I racconti di Canterbury.*

Passer, Ivan. (1933–). Czech.

1965: *A Boring Afternoon, Intimate Lighting.*

Pastrone, Giovanni. (1883–1959). Italian.

1910: *Agnese Visconti.* 1912: *Padre.* 1914: *Cabiria.* 1915: *Il Fuoco, Maciste.* 1916: *Maciste Alpino, Tigre Reale.* 1919: *Hedda Gabler.* 1923: *Povere bimbe.*

Pearson, George. (1875–   ). British.

1912: *Through Fair Sussex.* 1914: *Christmas Day in the Workhouse.* 1915: *Ultus* (series), *Ultus and the Gray Lady.* 1916: *Ultus and the Secret of the Night.* 1917: *Ultus and the Three Button Mystery.* 1921: *Squibs.* 1927: *Huntingtower.* 1955: *Springtime in England.*

*Peckinpah, Sam. (1926–   ). American.

1961: *The Deadly Companions.* 1962: *Guns in the Afternoon (Ride the High Country).* 1964: *Major Dundee.* 1969: *The Wild Bunch.* 1970: *The Ballad of Cable Hogue.* 1971: *Straw Dogs.* 1972: *Junior Bonner.*

*Penn, Arthur. (1922–   ). American.

1957: *The Left-handed Gun.* 1962: *The Miracle Worker.* 1964: *Mickey One.* 1965: *The Chase.* 1967: *Bonnie and Clyde.* 1969: *Alice's Restaurant.* 1971: *Little Big Man.*

Pereira Dos Santos, Nelson. (1938–   ). Brazilian.

1955: *Rio 40 graus.* 1957: *Rio zona norte.* 1960: *Mandacaru Vermelho.* 1963: *Bôca de ouro.* 1964: *Vidas secas.* 1967: *El justicero.* 1970–71: *Lust for love, A Very Lunatic Asylum, How Good My Little Frenchman Was.*

Perestiani, Ivan. (1870–1959). Georgian Soviet.

1917: *Goat . . . Kid . . . Ass . . ., Eva, Love . . . Hate . . . Death . . .* 1919: *Father and Son.* 1926: *Little Red Devils.* 1937: *Two Friends.*

Perret, Léonce. (1890–1935). French.

1909–20: numerous short films, directing and acting, including 'Léonce' series. 1912: *L'enfant de Paris.* 1917: *The Silent Master.* 1918: *Lest We Forget.* 1923: *Koenigsmark.* 1925: *Madame Sans-Gêne.* 1926: *La femme nue.* 1934: *Sapho.* 1935: *Les Précieuses Ridicules, Une séance à la Comédie Francaise.*

Petri, Elio. (1929–   ). Italian.

1961: *L'assassino.* 1962: *I giorni contati.* 1963: *Il maestro di Vigevano.* 1965: *La decima vittima.* 1967: *A ciascuno il suo, Tre pistole contro Cesare.* 1970: *Indagine su un cittadino al di sopra di ogno sospetto.* 1972: *La classe operaia va in Paradiso.*

Petrov, Vladimir. (1896–1966). Soviet.

1929: *The Address of Lenin.* 1934: *The Storm.* 1937–9: *Peter the Great.* 1949: *The Battle of Stalingrad.* 1957: *The Duel.*

Petrovic, Aleksandar. (1929–   ). Yugoslav.

1957: *Flight above the Marshes, Peter Dobrovic.* 1958: *The Roads.* 1960: *War against War.* 1961: *Where Love Has Gone.* 1963: *The Days.* 1964: *The Data, Fairs.* 1965: *Three.* 1967: *I Have Even Met Happy Gypsies.* 1969: *It Rains in My Village.*

Pichel, Irving. (1891–1954). American.

1932: *The Most Dangerous Game (The Hounds of Zaroff)* (with Schoedsack). 1935: *She.* 1946: *The Bride Wore Boots, O.S.S.* 1947: *They Won't Believe Me.* 1949: *The Great Rupert.* 1950: *Destination Moon.* 1953: *Martin Luther.*

Pick, Lupu. (1886–1931). Rumanian, active in Germany.

1918: *Der Liebe des Van Royk.* 1919: *Der Herr über Leben und Tod.* 1929: *Der Dummkopf.* 1922: *Scherben.* 1923: *Sylvester.* 1931: *Gassenhauer.*

Pietrangeli, Antonio. (1919–1969). Italian.

1953: *Il sole nelli occhi*. 1955: *Lo scapolo*. 1960: *Adua e le compagne*. 1962: *La parmigiana*. 1964: *Il magnifico cornuto*. 1965: *Io la conoscevo bene*.

Pintoff, Ernest. (1931–). American.

1958: *Flebus*. 1959: *The Violinist*. 1960: *The Interview*. 1962: *The Old Man, The Critic*. 1964: *Harvey Middleman, Fireman*.

Pires, Roberto. (1928–). Brazilian.

1962: *A grande feira*. 1963: *Tocaia no asfalto*.

Piscator, Erwin. (1893–1966). German.

1934: *Revolt of the Fishermen* (in U.S.S.R.).

Poirier, Léon. (1884–). French.

1913: *Cadette*. 1920: *Ames d'orient*. 1928: *Verdun, vision d'histoire*. 1948: *La Route inconnue*.

*****Polanski, Roman.** (1933–). Polish, active in Poland, France, Britain, U.S.A.

1958: *Two Men and a Wardrobe*. 1959: *When Angels Fall*. 1961: *Le Gros et le maigre*. 1962: *Ssaki, Knife in the Water*. 1963: *Les Plus Belles Escroqueries du monde* (episode). 1964: *Repulsion*. 1965: *Cul-de-Sac*. 1968: *Dance of the Vampires*. 1969: *Rosemary's Baby*. 1971: *Macbeth*.

*****Polonsky, Abraham.** (1910–). American.

1949: *Force of Evil*. 1970: *Tell Them Willie Boy is Here*. 1971: *Romance of a Horse Thief*.

Pontecorvo, Gillo. (1919–). Italian.

1956: *Die Windrose* (episode). 1957: *La grande strada azzurra*. 1959: *Kapo*. 1966: *La battaglia di Algeri*. 1970: *Queimada*.

Ponting, Herbert C. (1874–1936). British.

1912: *With Captain Scott R.N. to the South Pole*.

Popescu-Gopo, Ion. (1923–). Rumanian.

1950: numerous animation films. 1953: *The Little Liar*. 1954: *A Fly With Money*. 1956: *A Short History*. 1958: *Seven Arts*. 1960: *Homo Sapiens*. 1961: *A Bomb has been Stolen*. 1963: *Steps to the Moon*. 1965: *The White Moor*. 1966: *Faustus XX*. 1967: *My city*. 1968: *Sancta Simplicitas*.

Porter, Edwin S. (1870–1941). American.

1900: actuality films for Edison, including *McKinley's Inauguration, The Galveston Cyclone*. 1902: *The Life of an American Fireman*. 1903: *Uncle Tom's Cabin, The Great Train Robbery, The Bold Bank Robbery*. 1904: *The Ex-Convict, The Kleptomaniac*. 1905: *Dream of a Rarebit Fiend*. 1907: *Rescued from an Eagle's Nest*. 1912: *The Prisoner of Zenda*. 1913: *In the Bishop's Carriage* (with Dawley), *A Good Little Devil*. 1914: *Tess of the Storm Country, Eternal City*.

Potter, Henry C. (1904–). American.

1936: *Beloved Enemy*. 1939: *The Story of Vernon and Irene Castle*. 1941: *Hellza-poppin!* 1943: *Victory Through Air Power* (with Walt Disney). 1948: *Mr Blandings Builds his Dreamhouse*. 1950: *The Miniver Story*. 1955: *Three For the Show*.

Powell, Michael. (1905–   ). British.

1933: *The Night of the Party*. 1937: *The Edge of the World*. 1939: *Spy in Black*. *The Lion Has Wings* (with A. Korda). 1940: *Contraband, The Thief of Baghdad* (with Ludwig Berger and Tim Whelan.). In collaboration with Emeric Pressburger: 1941: *49th Parallel*. 1942: *One of Our Aircraft is Missing*. 1943: *The Life and Death of Colonel Blimp*. 1944: *A Canterbury Tale, I Know When I'm Going*. 1946: *A Matter of Life and Death*. 1947: *Black Narcissus*. 1948: *The Red Shoes. The Small Back Room*. 1949: *The Elusive Pimpernel*. 1950: *Gone to Earth*. 1951: *The Tales of Hoffman*. 1955: *Oh, Rosalinda*. 1956: *The Battle of the River Plate*. 1956: *Ill Met by Moonlight*. Powell alone: 1958: *Luna de miel* (in Spain). 1959: *Peeping Tom*. 1960: *The Queen's Guards*. 1966: *They're a Weird Mob*. 1969: *Age of Consent*.

*Preminger, Otto. (1906–   ). Austrian, active in U.S.A.

1932: *Die grosse Liebe*. 1936: *Under Your Spell*. 1937: *Danger, Love at Work*. 1943: *Margin for Error*. 1944: *In the Meantime Darling, Laura*. 1945: *A Royal Scandal, Fallen Angel*. 1946: *Centennial Summer*. 1947: *Forever Amber, Daisy Kenyon*. 1948: *That Lady in Ermine* (completed; begun by Lubitsch). 1949: *The Fan, Whirlpool*. 1950: *Where the Sidewalk Ends, The Thirteenth Letter*. 1953: *Angel Face, The Moon is Blue*. 1954: *River of No Return, Carmen Jones*. 1955: *The Court Martial of Billy Mitchell, The Man With the Golden Arm*. 1957: *Saint Joan*. 1958: *Bonjour Tristesse*. 1959: *Porgy and Bess, Anatomy of a Murder*. 1960: *Exodus*. 1962: *Advise and Consent*. 1963: *The Cardinal*. 1965: *In Harm's Way, Bunny Lake is Missing*. 1966: *Hurry Sundown*. 1968: *Skidoo*. 1970: *Tell Me That You Love Me, Junie Moon*. 1971: *Such Good Friends*.

Pressburger, Emeric. (1902–   ). Hungarian, active in Britain.

See Michael Powell.

Prévert, Pierre. (1906–   ). French.

1932: *L'Affaire est dans le sac*. 1935: *Le Commissaire est bon enfant* (with Becker). 1943: *Adieu Léonard*. 1947: *Voyage surprise*. 1958: *Paris mange son pain*. 1959: *Paris la belle*.

Protazanov, Yakov. (1881–1945). Russian and Soviet. Also active in France.

1909: *The Fountain of Bakhisarai*. 1912: *Anfisa*. 1913: *The Keys of Happiness*. (with Gardin). 1916: *The Queen of Spades*. 1917: *Father Sergius*. 1919: *L'Angoissante Aventure*. 1924: *Aelita*. 1925: *His Call*. 1926: *Trial of the Three Million*. 1927: *The Forty-first*. 1928: *The White Eagle, Don Diego and Pelagea*. 1929: *Ranks and Men*. 1931: *Tommy*. 1943: *Nasreddin in Bokhara*.

Ptushko, Alexander. (1900–   ). Soviet.

1928: *Occurrence in the Stadium*. 1935: *The New Gulliver*. 1946: *The Stone Flower*. 1953: *Sadko*. 1956: *Ilya Muromets*.

*Pudovkin, Vsevolod. (1893–1953). Soviet.

1921: *Hunger . . . Hunger . . . Hunger . . .* (with Gardin). 1925–6: *Mechanics of the Brain*. 1925: *Chess Fever* (with Shipkovsky). 1926: *Mother*. 1927: *The End of St Petersburg*. 1928: *Storm Over Asia*. 1930–32: *A Simple Case*. 1931–3: *Deserter*. 1935–38: *Victory* (with M. Doller). 1939: *Minin and Podzharsky* (with Doller). 1940: *Twenty Years of Cinema* (with Esther Shub), *Suvorov* (with Doller). 1941: *Feast at Zhirmukka*. 1942–3: *In the Name of the Fatherland* (with D. Vassiliev). 1944–6: *Admiral Nakhimov* (with D. Vassiliev). 1950: *Zhukovsky* (with D. Vassiliev). 1953: *The Return of Vasili Bortnikov*.

Pyriev, Ivan. (1901–68). Soviet.

1929: *The Strange Woman*. 1933: *The Death Conveyor*. 1936: *The Party Ticket*. 1938: *The Rich Bride*. 1939: *Tractorists*. 1941: *The Swine Girl and the Shepherd*. 1950: *Kuban Cossacks*. 1957: *The Idiot*. 1961: *White Nights*. 1969: *The Brothers Karamazov*.

Quine, Richard. (1920–   ). American.

1948: *Leather Gloves*. 1954: *Drive a Crooked Road, So This is Paris*. 1955: *My Sister Eileen*. 1956: *The Solid Gold Cadillac*. 1957: *Operation Mad Ball*. 1958: *Bell, Book and Candle*. 1961: *The Notorious Landlady*. 1965: *How to Murder Your Wife*. 1966: *Oh, Dad, poor Dad*.

Rademakers, Fons. (1921–   ). Dutch.

1959: *Village on the River*. 1961: *The Knife*. 1966: *Dance of the Heron*.

Radvanyi, Geza Von. (1907–   ). Hungarian, active in Hungary, Germany, Italy, France.

1940: *Trial Behind Closed Doors*. 1941: *Europe Doesn't Answer*. 1947: *Somewhere in Europe*. 1949: *Donne senza nome*. 1958: *Mädchen in Uniform*. 1959: *Douze heures d'horloge*.

Rahn, Bruno. (1898–1927). German.

1926: *Hölle der Liebe*. 1927: *Der Kleinstadtsünder, Dirnentragödie*.

Raisman, Yuli. (1903–   ). Soviet.

1927: *The Circle*. 1928: *Forced Labour*. 1930: *The Earth Thirsts*. 1937: *The Last Night*. 1942: *Mashenka*. 1944: *Moscow Skies*. 1945: *Berlin*. 1948: *Train for the East*. 1955: *Lesson of Life*. 1957: *The Communist*. 1967: *Your Contemporary*.

Ray, Man. (1890–   ). American, active as film-maker in France.

1923: *Le Retour à la raison*. 1927: *Emak Bakia*. 1928: *L'Étoile de mer*. 1929: *Les Mystères du chateau du Dé*. 1944–6: *Dreams that Money Can Buy* (episode).

*Ray, Nicholas. (1911–   ). American.

1948: *They Live By Night*. 1949: *Knock on Any Door, A Woman's Secret*. 1950: *In a Lonely Place, Born to be Bad*. 1951: *Flying Leathernecks, On Dangerous Ground*. 1952: *The Lusty Men*. 1954: *Johnny Guitar*. 1955: *Run For Cover, Rebel Without a Cause*. 1956: *Hot Blood, Bigger Than Life*. 1957: *The True Story of Jesse James*. 1958: *Bitter Victory, Wind Across the Everglades, Party Girl*. 1961: *The Savage Innocents, King of Kings*. 1963: *Fifty-five Days at Peking*.

*Ray, Satyajit. (1921–   ). Bengali.

1950–55: *Pather Panchali*. 1956: *Aparajito*. 1957: *Paras Pathar (The Philosopher's Stone)*. 1958: *Jalsaghar (The Music Room)*. 1959: *Apur Sansar (The World of Apu)*. 1960: *Devi (The Goddess)*. 1961: *Rabindranath Tagore, Three Daughters*. 1962: *Kanchenjunga, Abhijan*. 1963: *Mahanagar (The Big City)*. 1964: *Charulata*. 1965: *Kapurush-o-Mahaparush (The Coward and the Holy Man)*. 1966: *Nayak (The Hero)*. 1967: *Chiriakhana*. 1968–9. *Goopy Gyne and Bagha Byne*. 1969–70: *Days and Nights in the Forest*. 1970: *Pratidwandi (Siddhartha and the City)*.

*Reed, Carol. (1906–   ). British.

1934: *Midshipmen Easy*. 1936: *Laburnum Grove, Talk of the Devil*. 1937: *Who's Your Lady Friend, No Parking*. 1938: *Bank Holiday, Penny Paradise*. 1939:

Climbing High, A Girl Must Live, The Stars Look Down. 1940: *Night Train to Munich, The Girl in the News.* 1941: *Kipps, The Young Mr Pitt, Letter From Home.* c. 1942: *The New Lot.* 1944: *The Way Ahead.* 1945: *The True Glory* (with Garson Kanin). 1946: *Odd Man Out.* 1948: *The Fallen Idol.* 1949: *The Third Man.* 1951: *An Outcast of the Islands.* 1953: *The Man Between.* 1955: *A Kid For Two Farthings.* 1956: *Trapeze.* 1958: *The Key.* 1959: *Our Man in Havana.* 1963: *The Running Man.* 1965: *The Agony and the Ecstasy.* 1968: *Oliver!* 1970: *The Last Warrior.* 1972: *Follow Me.*

*Reeves, Michael. (1944–69). British.

1965: *Sorelle di Satana* (in Italy). 1967: *The Sorcerers.* 1968: *Witchfinder General.*

Reichenbach, François. (1922–). French.

1950–59: several documentaries. 1960: *L'Amérique insolite.* 1962: *Un Coeur gros comme ça.* 1964: *La Douceur du village, Les Amoureux du France.* 1966: *Hollywood.* 1970: *Rubinstein: L'Amour de la vie.*

Reinhardt, Max. (1873–1943). Austrian.

1935: *A Midsummer Night's Dream* (in U.S.A.).

Reiniger, Lotte. (1899–). German.

1919–20: *Das Ornament des verliebten Herzen.* 1923–16: *Die Abenteuer des Prinz Achmet.* 1928–33: *Dr Doolittle* series. 1932: *Sissi.* 1933: *Carmen.* 1934: *Das geraubte Herz.* 1935: *Kalif Storch, Der Graf von Carabas, Galathea, Papageno.* 1955: *The Brave Little Tailor.* 1956: *The Star of Bethlehem.*

*Reisz, Karel. (1926–). Czech-born, active in Great Britain.

1956: *Momma Don't Allow* (with Tony Richardson). 1958: *We Are the Lambeth Boys.* 1961: *Saturday Night and Sunday Morning.* 1963: *Night Must Fall.* 1966: *Morgan – A Suitable Case for Treatment.* 1968: *Isadora.*

*Renoir, Jean. (1894–). French.

1924: *La Fille de l'Eau.* 1926: *Nana, Charleston.* 1927: *Marquitta.* 1928: *La Petite Marchande d'allumettes, Tire au flanc.* 1929: *Le Tournoi dans la cité, Le Bled.* 1931: *On purge bébé, La Chienne.* 1932: *La Nuit du carrefour, Boudu sauvé des eaux.* 1933: *Chotard et cie.* 1934: *Madame Bovary, Toni.* 1936: *Le Crime de Monsieur Lange, La Vie est à nous, Une Partie de campagne, Les Bas-fonds.* 1937: *La Grande Illusion.* 1938: *La Marseillaise, La Bête humaine.* 1939: *La Règle du jeu.* 1941: *Swamp Water.* 1943: *This I ʼ ᵐd is Mine.* 1944: *Salute to France.* 1945: *The Southerner.* 1946: *Diary of a Chambermaid.* 1947: *The Woman on the Beach.* 1951: *The River.* 1953: *La Carozza d'oro.* 1955: *French Can Can.* 1956: *Eléna et les Hommes.* 1959: *Le Testament du Dr Cordelier* (TV), *Le Déjeuner sur l'herbe.* 1962: *Le Coporal épinglé.*

Resnais, Alain. (1922–). French.

1936–46: several 16 mm silent films. 1945: *Schéma d'une identification.* 1948: *Van Gogh, Malfray.* 1950: *Gauguin, L'Alcool tue, Guernica.* 1952: *Les Statues meurent aussi* (with Chris Marker). 1956: *Nuit et brouillard, Toute la mémoire du monde.* 1957: *Le Mystère de l'atelier 15* (with Marker). 1958: *Le Chant du Styrène.* 1959: *Hiroshima mon amour.* 1961: *L'Année dernière à Marienbad.* 1963: *Muriel, ou le temps de retour.* 1966: *La Guerre est finie.* 1970: *Je t'aime, je t'aime.*

*Richardson, Tony. (1928–   ). British, active in Britain, U.S.A. and France.

1956: *Momma Don't Allow* (with Karel Reisz). 1959: *Look Back in Anger*. 1960: *The Entertainer*. 1961: *Sanctuary, A Taste of Honey*. 1963: *The Loneliness of the Long Distance Runner, Tom Jones*. 1964: *The Loved One*. 1966: *Sailor From Gibraltar, Mademoiselle*. 1967: *Red and Blue* (episode). 1968: *The Charge of the Light Brigade*. 1969: *Laughter in the Dark*. 1970: *Hamlet, Ned Kelly*.

Richter, Hans. (1888–   ). German, active in Germany and U.S.A.

1921: *Rythmus 21*. 1923: *Rythmus 23*. 1925: *Rythmus 25*. 1926: *Filmstudie*. 1927: *Inflation*. 1928: *Vormittagspuk, Nachmittag zu den Wettrennen, Renn-Symphonie*. 1929: *Alles deht sich, alles bewent sich!* 1933: *Metall* (unfinished). 1930: *Une Nouvelle Vie*. 1944–6: *Dreams That Money Can Buy*. 1954: *Minotaure*. 1956: *Passionate Pastime*. 1957: *8 × 8* (with Cocteau and Calder).

Riefenstahl, Leni. (1902–   ). German.

1932: *Das blaue Licht* (co-directed with Béla Balázs). 1935: *Reichsparteitag*. 1935–6: *Des Triumph des Willens, Unserer Wehrmacht*. 1936–8: *Olympia*. 1940–53: *Tiefland*. 1956: *Schwarze Fracht*.

Risi, Dino. (1917–   ). Italian.

1945: *I bersaglieri della signora*. 1953: *Amore in città* (episode). 1955: *Pane, amore e . . .* 1962: *Il sorpasso, La marcia su Roma*. 1963: *I mostri*. 1967: *Il tigre, Sisignore*.

Ritt, Martin. (1920–   ). American.

1956: *Le Coup du berger*. 1960: *Paris nous appartient*. 1965: *La Religieuse*. 1968: *The Long, Hot Summer*. 1959: *The Sound and the Fury*. 1963: *Hud*. 1965: *The Spy Who Came in from the Cold*. 1967: *Hombre*. 1968: *The Brotherhood*. 1969: *The Molly Maguires*. 1971: *The Great White Hope*.

Rivette, Jacques. (1928–   ). French.

1956: *Le Coup du berger*. 1960: *Paris nous appartient*. 1965: *La Religieuse*. 1968: *L'Amour fou*.

Roach, Hal. (1892–   ). American.

1915: *Just Nuts*; then innumerable comedy shorts, mostly as producer.

Robbe-Grillet, Alain. (1922–   ). French.

1962: *L'Immortelle*. 1967: *Trans-Europ Express*.

Robison, Arthur. (1888–1937). German.

1915: *Knechte des Grauens*. 1922: *Schatten (Warning Shadows)*. 1923: *Zwischen Abends und Morgens*. 1929: *The Informer*. 1935: *Der Student von Prag*.

Robson, Mark. (1913–   ). American.

1943: *The Seventh Victim*. 1946: *Bedlam*. 1949: *Home of the Brave, Champion*. 1954: *Cell Below Zero, Phffft*. 1956: *The Harder They Fall*. 1957: *Peyton Place*. 1958: *The Inn of the Sixth Happiness*. 1960: *From the Terrace*. 1963: *Nine Hours to Rama, The Prize*. 1965: *Von Ryan's Express*. 1966: *Lost Command*. 1967: *Valley of the Dolls*. 1969: *Daddy's Gone A-Hunting*.

Rocha, Glauber. (1939–   ). Brazilian.

1959: *O Patio*. 1962: *Barravento*. 1964: *Deus e o Diablo na terra do sol*. 1967: *Terra im transe*. 1969: *Antonio das mortes*. 1970: *Der Leone have sept cabecas*.

404 · Selected Filmographies

Rogosin, Lionel. (1923–   ). American.

1957: *On the Bowery*. 1959: *Come Back Africa*. 1965: *Good Times, Wonderful Times*.

Rohmer, Eric. (1920–   ). French.

1950: *Journal d'un scélérat*. 1951: *Presentation ou Charlotte et son steak*. 1954: *Berenice*. 1956: *La Sonate à Kreutzer*. 1959: *Le Signe du lion*. 1962: *La Boulangère de Monçeau*. 1963: *La Carrière de Suzanne*. 1964: *Nadja à Paris* (all shorts). 1965: *Paris vu par . . .* (episode). 1967: *La Collectionneuse*. 1969: *Ma Nuit chez Maud*. 1971: *Le Genou de Claire*. 1972: *L'amour l'après-midi*.

Romm, Mikhail. (1901–71). Soviet.

1934: *Boule de Suif*. 1937: *The Thirteen, Lenin in October*. 1939: *Lenin in 1918*. 1948: *The Russian Question*. 1950: *Secret Mission*. 1953: *Admiral Usakov*. 1961: *Nine Days of One Year*. 1965: *Ordinary Fascism*.

Room, Abram. (1894–   ). Soviet.

1926: *The Hunt for Moonshine, Death Bay*. 1927: *Bed and Sofa*. 1930: *Plan of Great Works, The Ghost that Never Returns*. 1939: *Squadron No 5*. 1956: *The Heart Beats Again*.

Roos, Jorgen. (1922–   ). Danish.

1948: *Opus 1*. Numerous documentaries. 1960: *Copenhagen*. 1965: *Knud*.

Roshal, Grigori. (1899–   ). Soviet.

1927: *Messrs Skotinini*. 1928: *Salamander* (with M. Doller). 1939: *The Oppenheims*. 1949: *Academician Ivan Pavlov*. 1950: *Mussorgsky*. 1953: *Rimsky-Korsakov*. 1954: *Aleko*. 1957: *The Sisters*.

*Rosi, Francesco. (1922–   ). Italian.

1950: *Camicie rosse*. 1955: *Kean*. 1957: *La sfida*. 1959: *I Magliari*. 1961: *Salvatore Giuliano*. 1963: *Le mani sulla città*. 1965: *Il momento della verità*. 1967: *C'erà una volta*. 1970: *Uomini contro*. 1972: *Il Caso Mattei*.

*Rossellini, Roberto. (1906–   ). Italian.

1936: *Daphne*. 1937–40: five short films. 1941: *La nave bianca*. 1942: *Un pilota ritorna*. 1943: *L'uomo delle croce, Desiderio* (finished by Marcello Pagliero). 1945: *Roma, città aperta*. 1946: *Paisà*. 1947: *Germania, anno zero*. 1948: *Amore, La macchina amazzacattivi*. 1949: *Stromboli*. 1950: *Francesco giullare di Dio*. 1952: *Les Sept péchés capitaux*. (Episode), *Europa 51*. 1953: *Dov'è la libertà? Siamo donne* (episode), *Viaggio in Italia*. 1954: *Amore di mezzo secolo* (episode), *Angst, Giovanna d'Arco al rogo*. 1958: *India*. 1959: *Il generale della rovere*. 1960: *Era notte a Roma*. 1961: *Viva l'Italia, Vanina Vanini*. 1962: *Anima nera, RoGoPaG* (episode). 1964: *L'età del ferro* (TV series). 1966: *La Prise de pouvoir par Louis XIV*. 1970: *Socrate*.

*Rossen, Robert. (1908–66). American.

1947: *Johnny o'Clock, Body and Soul*. 1949: *All The King's Men*. 1951: *The Brave Bulls*. 1954: *Mambo*. 1956: *Alexander the Great*. 1957: *Island in the Sun*. 1959: *They Came to Cordura*. 1961: *The Hustler*. 1964: *Lilith*.

Rossi, Franco. (1919–   ). Italian.

1952: *I falsari*. 1954: *Il seduttore*. 1955: *Amici per la pelle*. 1959: *Morte di un amico*. 1960: *Odissea nuda*. 1962: *Smog*.

Rossif, Frédéric. (1922–   ). French.

1961: *Le Temps du ghetto*. 1963: *Mourir à Madrid*. 1964: *Les Animaux*. 1967: *La Révolution d'Octobre*.

Rotha, Paul. (1907–   ). British.

1932: *Contact*. 1934: *Rising Tide*. 1935: *The Face of Britain, Shipyard*. 1940: *The Fourth Estate*. 1943: *World of Plenty*. 1944: *Soviet Village*. 1945: *Britain can Make It*. 1946: *The World is Rich*. 1950: *No Resting Place*. 1953: *World Without End* (with Basil Wright). 1957: *Cat and Mouse*. 1961: *The Rise and Fall of the Third Reich*.

Rouch, Jean. (1917–   ). French.

1947: *Au pays des mages noirs*. 1949: *La Circoncision*. 1952: *Les Fils de l'eau*. 1955: *Les Maîtres fous*. 1957: *Jaguar* (unfinished). 1959: *Moi un noir*. 1961: *La Pyramide humaine, Chronique d'un été* (with Edgar Morin). 1963: *La Punition*. 1964: *La Fleur de l'âge* (episode), *La Chasse au lion à l'arc*. 1966: *Paris vu par . . .* (episode). 1970: *Petit à petit*.

Rouquier, Georges. (1909–   ). French.

1942: *Le Tonnelier*. 1943: *Le Charron*. 1947: *Pasteur, Farrébique*. 1949: *Le Chaudronnier*. 1950: *Le Sel de la terre*. 1953: *Sang et lumières*. 1955: *Arthur Honnegger*. 1957: *S.O.S. Noronha*.

Rozier, Jacques. (1926–   ). French.

1962: *Adieu Philippine*.

Ruggles, Wesley. (1899–   ). American.

1917: *For France*. 1931: *Cimarron*. 1933: *I'm No Angel*. 1946: *London Town*.

Russell, Ken. (1927–   ). British.

1964: *French Dressing*. 1967: *Billion Dollar Brain*. 1969: *Women in Love*. 1971: *The Music Lovers, The Devils*. 1972: *The Boy Friend*.

Ruttmann, Walther. (1887–1941). German.

1922–4: *Opus 1, 2, 3 and 4*. 1927: *Berlin, Symphonie einer Grosstadt, Hoppla, Wir leben*. 1929: *Melodie der Welt*. 1930: *Weekend*. 1931: *In der Nacht*. 1933: *Acciaio*. 1940: *Deutsche Panzer*. 1941: *Jeder Achte*.

Rybkowski, Jan. (1912–   ). Polish.

1949: *House on the Wastelands*. 1951: *First Days*. 1961: *A Town Will Die Tonight*. 1967: *When Love Was a Crime*.

Rydell, Mark. (1934–   ). American.

1968: *The Fox*. 1969: *The Reivers*.

Sagan, Leontine. (1889–   ). German.

1931: *Mädchen in Uniform*. 1932: *Men of Tomorrow*.

St Clair, Malcolm. (1897–1952). American.

1919: *Rip and Stitch, Tailors*. 1921: *The Goat*. 1922: *The Blacksmith*. 1925: *Are Parents People*. 1926: *The Grand Duchess and the Waiter*. 1928: *Gentlemen Prefer Blondes*. 1929: *The Canary Murder Case*. 1943: *Jitterbugs*. 1944: *Dancing Masters, The Big Noise*. 1948: *Fighting Back*.

Samsonov, Samson. (1921–). Soviet.

1955: *The Grasshopper, Shop Window*. 1957: *The Fiery Mile*. 1960: *As Old as the Century*. 1964: *The Optimistic Tragedy*. 1968: *The Arena*.

Saura, Carlos. (1932–). Spanish.

1960: *Los golfos*. 1966: *La caza*.

Schaffner, Franklin. (1920–). American.

1963: *The Stripper*. 1964: *The Best Man*. 1965: *The Warlord*. 1967: *The Double Man*. 1968: *Planet of the Apes*. 1969: *Patton*. 1971: *Nicholas and Alexandra*.

Schell, Maximilian. (1930–). German.

1968: *The Castle*. 1970: *First Love*.

Schlesinger, John. (1926–). British.

1961: *Terminus*. 1962: *A Kind of Loving*. 1964: *Billy Liar*. 1965: *Darling*. 1967: *Far From the Madding Crowd*. 1970: *Midnight Cowboy*. 1971: *Sunday, Bloody Sunday*.

Schoedsack, Ernest B. (1893–). American.

With Merian C. Cooper: 1926: *Grass*. 1927: *Chang*. 1929: *The Four Feathers* (with Lothar Mendes). 1931: *Rango*. 1932: *The Most Dangerous Game* (*The Hounds of Zaroff*). 1933: *King Kong*. Schoedsack alone: 1933: *Son of Kong*. 1935: *The Last Days of Pompeii*. 1940: *Dr Cyclops*. 1949: *Mighty Joe Young*.

*Schorm, Ewald. (1931–). Czech.

1959: *The One Who Doesn't Gain Paradise*. 1960: *Block 15*. 1961: *The Journal of F.A.M.U.* 1962: *The Tourist, Helsinki, Trees and People, Country of Countries*. 1963: *To Live One's Life, The Railwaymen, Why?* 1964: *Courage for Every Day*. 1965: *Pearls of the Deep* (episode), *Reflections*. 1966: *The Return of the Prodigal Son, Psalm, The Legs*. 1967: *Carmen not only according to Bizet, Five Girls to cope with*. 1968: *The End of a Priest, Prague Nights* (episode). 1969: *The Seventh Day, the Eighth Night*.

Sennett, Mack. (1880–1960). American.

1910–13: innumerable short films, mostly comedies, including *A Lucky Toothache* (1910), *The Masher, Comrades, A Dutch Goldmine, The Fickle Spaniard, An Interrupted Elopement, Cohen* series etc.

Shindo, Kaneto. (1912–). Japanese.

1951: *The Story of a Beloved Wife*. 1952: *Children of Hiroshima*. 1961: *The Naked Island*. 1964: *Onibaba*. 1969: *Heat Wave Island*.

Shub, Esfir (Esther). (1894–1959). Soviet.

1927: *Fall of the Romanov Dynasty, The Great Road*. 1928: *The Russia of Nikolas II and Leo Tolstoy*. 1930: *Today*. 1932: *Komsomol–Guide to Electrification*. 1934: *The Metro by Night*. 1938: *Land of the Soviets, Spain*. 1940: *Twenty Years of Cinema* (with Pudovkin).

Sidney, George. (1911–). American.

1938: *Our Gang* series: 1939: *Pete Smith* series. 1941: *Free and Easy*. 1945: *Anchors Aweigh*. 1946: *The Harvey Girls*. 1948: *The Three Musketeers*. 1950: *Annie Get Your Gun*. 1951: *Showboat*. 1952: *Scaramouche*. 1954: *Kiss Me Kate*. 1956: *The Eddie Duchin Story*. 1957: *Jeanne Eagels, Pal Joey*. 1959: *Who Was That Lady*. 1960: *Pepe*. 1963: *Bye Bye Birdie*. 1968: *Half a Sixpence*.

*Siegel, Don. (1912–). American.

1945: *Star in the Night, Hitler Lives.* 1946: *The Verdict.* 1949: *The Big Steal, Night unto Night.* 1952: *The Duel at Silver Creek, No Time for Flowers.* 1953: *Count the Hours, China Venture.* 1954: *Riot in Cell Block 11, Private Hell 36.* 1955: *An Annapolis Story.* 1956: *Invasion of the Body Snatchers, Crime in the Streets.* 1957: *Baby Face Nelson.* 1958: *Spanish Affair, The Lineup, The Gun-Runners.* 1959: *Hound Dog Man.* 1960: *Edge of Eternity, Flaming Star.* 1962: *Hell is For Heroes.* 1964: *The Killers, The Hanged Man.* 1967: *Madigan.* 1968: *Coogan's Bluff.* 1970: *Two Mules for Sister Sara.* 1971: *The Beguiled.* 1972: *Dirty Harry.*

Siodmak, Robert. (1900–). American-born, active in Germany, U.S.A. and France.

1929: *Menschen am Sonntag* (with Edgar Ullman and others). 1930: *Abscheid.* 1933: *Brennendes Geheimnis.* 1945: *The Spiral Staircase.* 1946: *The Killers.* 1948: *The Cry of the City, Crisis Cross.* 1952: *The Crimson Pirate.* 1954: *Le Grand Jeu.* 1955: *Die Ratten.* 1968: *Custer of the West.*

Sirk, Douglas (Detlef Sierck). (1900–). Danish-born German, active Germany, Spain, Africa, Australia, U.S.A.

1935: *April, April, Das Mädchen vom Moorhof.* 1943: *Hitler's Madman.* 1944: *Summer Storm.* 1946: *A Scandal in Paris, Lured.* 1948: *Sleep my Love.* 1949: *Shockproof, Slightly French.* 1950: *Mystery Submarine.* 1951: *The First Legion, Thunder on the Hill, The Lady Pays Off, Weekend With Father.* 1952: *Has Anybody Seen My Gal, No Room For the Groom.* 1953: *Meet Me at the Fair, Take Me To Town, All I Desire.* 1954: *Magnificent Obsession, Taza, Son of Cochise, Sign of the Pagan.* 1955: *Captain Lightfoot.* 1956: *All That Heaven Allows, There's Always Tomorrow,* 1957: *Battle Hymn, Written on the Wind, Interlude.* 1958: *Tarnished Angels, A Time to Love and a Time to Die.* 1959: *Imitation of Life.*

Sjöberg, Alf. (1903–). Swedish.

1929: *The Strongest.* 1940: *They Staked Their Lives.* 1942: *The Road to Heaven.* 1944: *Frenzy.* 1946: *Iris and the Lieutenant.* 1951: *Miss Julie.* 1953: *Barabbas.* 1954: *Karin Mansdotter.* 1955: *Wild Birds.* 1956: *Last Pair Out.* 1960: *The Judge.* 1964: *The Island.* 1969: *The Father.*

Sjöman, Vilgot. (1924–). Swedish.

1962: *The Mistress.* 1964: *491, The Dress.* 1965: *My Sister, My Love, Stimulantia* (episode). 1967: *I Am Curious–Yellow.* 1968: *I Am Curious–Blue, Journey With Father.* 1970: *You're Lying.* 1971: *Blushing Charlie.*

*Sjöstrom (in America, **Seastrom**), **Victor.** (1879–1960). Swedish, active in Sweden, U.S.A. and Britain.

1912: *The Gardener, A Secret Marriage, A Summer Tale.* 1913: *The Marriage Bureau, Smiles and Tears, The Voice of Blood, Lady Marion's Summer Flirtation, Ingeborg Holm, The Clergyman.* 1914: *Love Stronger than Hate, Half-Breed, The Miracle, Do Not Judge, A Good Girl Should Solve Her Own Problems, Children of the Street, Daughter of the High Mountain, Hearts that Meet.* 1915: *The Strike, One Out of Many, Expiated Guilt, Keep To Your Trade, Judas Money, The Governor's Daughters, Sea Vultures, It Was in May.* 1916: *At the Moment of Trial, Ships that Meet, She Was Victorious, Thérèse.* 1917: *The Kiss of Death, Terje Vigen, The Girl from Marsh Croft.* 1918: *The Outlaw and His Wife.* 1919: *The Sons of Ingmar, Parts I and II, His Grace's Will.* 1920: *The Monastery of Sendemir, Karin Ingmarsdotter, The Executioner.* 1921: *Thy Soul Shall Bear*

Witness. 1922: *Love's Crucible, The Hell Ship, The Surrounded House.* In America: 1923: *Name the Man.* 1924: *He Who Gets Slapped.* 1925: *Confessions of a Queen.* 1926: *Tower of Lies, The Scarlet Letter.* 1927: *The Divine Woman.* 1928: *The Wind, Masks of the Devil.* 1930: *A Lady to Love.* In Sweden: 1930: *Markurells i Wadköping.* In Britain: 1937: *Under the Red Robe.*

Skolimowski, Jerzy. (1938–   ). Polish, active in Poland, Belgium, Germany, Czechoslovakia and Italy.

1961: *Boxing.* 1964: *Marks of Identification–None (Rysopsis).* 1965: *Walkover.* 1966: *Barrier* (all in Poland). 1967: *Le Départ* (in Belgium), *Dialogue* (episode; in Czechoslovakia). 1968: *Hands Up!* (in Poland, unreleased). 1969: *The Adventures of Gerard* (U.S.A.–Italy). 1970: *Deep End* (West Germany). 1972: *King, Queen, Knave* (in Germany).

Smith, George Albert. (1864–1959). British.

1897: actuality films, *The Corsican Brothers.* 1898: *Cinderella, Faust and Mephistopheles, The Miller and the Sweep.* 1900: *Let Me Dream Again, Grandma's Reading Glass, As Seen Through a Telescope, Miss Ellen Terry At Home.* 1901: *The Little Doctor, Two Old Boys at the Music Hall.* 1902: *At Last that Awful Tooth, The Mouse in the Art School.* 1903: *Mary Jane's Mishap, Dorothy's Dream.* 1904: *The Free Trade Branch.* 1905: *The Little Witness.* 1909–14: *Kinemacolor films.*

Soldati, Mario. (1906–   ). Italian.

1938: *La principessa Tarakhanova* (with Otsep). 1940: *Piccolo mondo antico.* 1941: *Un colpo di pistola.* 1948: *Fuga in Francía.*

Solntseva, Julia. (1901–   ). Soviet.

1943–5: three documentaries. 1953: *Igor Bulichov* (with Lukyanov and Andreyeva). The wife of Dovzhenko, after his death Solntseva completed a series of his unrealised projects: 1958: *Poem of the Sea.* 1961: *Story of the Years of Flame.* 1965: *The Enchanted Desna.* 1970: *The Golden Gates.*

Starevitch, Ladislas. (1892–   ). Russian, active in Russia and France.

1912: *Beautiful Liukanida, The Insects' Aeronautic Week, Merry Scenes of Animal Life.* 1913: *The Grasshopper and the Ant.* 1923: *Les Grenouilles qui demandent un roi.* 1924: *Le Rat de ville et le rat des champs.* 1929: *La Petite Parade.* 1933: *Fetiche.* 1929: *Le Roman de renard.* 1949: *Zanzabelle à Paris.* 1950: *Fleur de fougère.*

Staudte, Wolfgang. (1906–   ). German.

1943: *Akrobat Sch-o-ön.* 1946: *Die Mörder sind unter uns.* 1949: *Rotation.* 1951: *Der Untertan.* 1954: *Mutter Courage und ihre Kinder.* 1957: *Rose Bernd.* 1959: *Rosen für den Staatsanwalt.* 1963: *Die Dreigroschenoper.*

Steinhoff, Hans. (1882 1945). German.

1921: *Bräutigam auf Kredit.* 1933: *Hitlerjunge Quex.* 1935: *Der alte und der junge König.* 1939: *Robert Koch.* 1941: *Ohm Krüger.* 1942: *Rembrandt.* 1945: *Shiva und die Galgenblume.*

*Sternberg, Josef Von. (1894–1969). Austrian, active in U.S.A., Germany and Britain.

1925: *The Salvation Hunters.* 1926: *The Exquisite Sinner, The Sea Gull.* 1927: *Underworld.* 1928: *The Last Command, The Drag Net, The Docks of New York.* 1929: *The Case of Lena Smith, Thunderbolt.* 1930: *Die Blaue Engel, Morocco.*

1931: *Dishonoured, An American Tragedy*. 1932: *Shanghai Express, Blonde Venus*. 1934: *The Scarlet Empress*. 1935: *The Devil is a Woman, Crime and Punishment*. 1936: *The King Steps Out, I, Claudius* (unfinished). 1939: *Sergeant Madden*. 1941: *The Shanghai Gesture*. 1943: *The Town*. 1950: *Jet Pilot*. 1951: *Macao*. 1953: *The Saga of Anatahan*.

*Stevens, George. (1905–). American.

1929–32: shorts in *Boy Friends* series. 1933: *Cohens and Kellys in Trouble*. 1934: *Bachelor Bait, Kentucky Kernels*. 1935: *Alice Adams, Laddie, Nitwits, Annie Oakley*. 1936: *Swing Time*. 1937: *Quality Street, A Damsel in Distress*. 1938: *Vivacious Lady*. 1939: *Gunga Din*. 1940: *Vigil in the Night*. 1941: *Penny Serenade*. 1942: *Woman of the Year, The Talk of the Town*. 1943: *The More the Merrier*. 1948: *I Remember Mama*. 1951: *A Place in the Sun*. 1953: *Shane*. 1956: *Giant*. 1959: *The Diary of Anne Frank*. 1964: *The Greatest Story Ever Told*. 1970: *The Only Game in Town*.

Stiller, Mauritz. (1883–1928). Finnish, active in Sweden and U.S.A.

1912: *Mother and Daughter, The Black Masks, The Tyrannical Fiancé*. 1913: *The Vampire, The Modern Suffragette*. 1914: *People of the Border, Because of Her Love*. 1915: *His Wife's Past, The Dagger*. 1916: *Love and Journalism, The Prima Ballerina*. 1917: *Thomas Graal's First Film, Alexander the Great*. 1918: *Thomas Graal's First Child*. 1919: *Song of the Scarlet Flower, Sir Arne's Treasure*. 1920: *The Vengeance of Jacob Vinda, Erotikon*. 1921: *Johan and the Exiles*. 1923: *Gunnar Hedes Saga*. 1924: *Gösta Berling's Saga*. In U.S.A.: 1926: *Hotel Imperial, The Temptress* (completed by Fred Niblo). 1927: *The Woman on Trial, The Street of Sin* (with Von Sternberg).

Storck, Henri. (1907–). Belgian.

1925: *Avec le Zinia au Danemark*. 1930: *Histoire du soldat inconnu*. 1931: *Idylle à la plage*. 1937: *Les Maisons de la misère*. 1946: *Le Monde de Paul Delvaux*. 1947: *La Joie de revivre*. 1948: *Rubens* (with Haesserts). 1951: *Le Banquet des fraudeurs*. 1962: *Le Bonheur d'être aimé*. 1971: *Paul Delvaux ou les femmes défendues*.

Strand, Paul. (1890–). American.

1921: *Manhattan, or New York the Magnificent* (with Charles Sheeler). 1935: *The Wave*. 1939: *China Strikes Back*. 1938–42: *Native Land* (with Leo Hurwitz).

*Straub, Jean-Marie. (1933–). French, active in Germany.

1963: *Machorka-Muff*. 1965: *Nicht versöhnt*. 1968: *Chronik der Anna Magdalena Bach, Der Bräutigam, die Komödiantin und der Zühalter*. 1969: *Les Yeux ne veulent pas en tout temps se fermer*. 1971: *Moses and Aaron*.

Strick, Joseph. (1923–). American.

1948: *Muscle Beach* (collaboration with Irving Lerner). 1959: *The Savage Eye* (collaboration with Meyers and Maddow). 1963: *The Balcony*. 1965: *Finnegans Wake*. 1967: *Ulysses*. 1969: *Tropic of Cancer*. 1970: *Interviews with My Lai Veterans*.

*Stroheim, Erich von. (1885–1957). Austrian, active in U.S.A.

1919: *Blind Husbands*. 1920: *The Devil's Passkey*. 1921: *Foolish Wives*. 1923: *Merry-go-round* (finished by Rupert Julian). 1923: *Greed*. 1925: *The Merry Widow*. 1927: *The Wedding March, The Honeymoon*. 1928: *Queen Kelly* (finished by Gloria Swanson). 1933: *Walking Down Broadway (Hello Sister)*.

Sturges, John. (1911–   ). American.

1946: *The Man Who Dared*. 1955: *Bad Day at Black Rock*. 1957: *Gunfight at O.K. Corral*. 1958: *The Old Man and the Sea*. 1960: *The Magnificent Seven*. 1961: *Sergeants Three*. 1963: *The Great Escape*. 1965: *The Satan Bug, The Hallelujah Trail*. 1967: *The Hour of the Gun*. 1968: *Ice Station Zebra*. 1969: *Marooned*.

*Sturges, Preston. (1898–1959). American.

1940: *The Great McGinty, Christmas in July*. 1941: *Sullivan's Travels, The Lady Eve*. 1942: *The Palm Beach Story*. 1943: *The Great Moment, The Miracle of Morgan's Creek*. 1944: *Hail the Conquering Hero*. 1946: *Mad Wednesday*. 1948: *Unfaithfully Yours*. 1949: *The Beautiful Blonde from Bashful Bend*. 1956: *Les Carnets du Major Thompson*.

Sucksdorff, Arne. (1917–   ). Swedish.

1939: *Rhapsody of August*. 1945: *Shadows on the Snow*. 1947: *Rhythm of a City*. 1948: *A Divided World*. 1951: *The Wind and the River*. 1953: *The Great Adventure*. 1957: *The Flute and the Arrow*. 1960: *The Boy in the Tree*. 1965: *My Home is Copacabana*.

Szábo, István. (1938–   ). Hungarian.

1961: *Concert, Variations on a Theme*. 1963: *You*. 1964: *The Age of Daydreams*. 1966: *The Father*. 1970: *Love Film*.

*Tashlin, Frank. (1913–1972). American.

1947: *The Way of Peace*. 1951: *The Lemon Drop Kid* (collaboration with Sidney Lanfield). 1952: *The First Time, Son of Paleface*. 1953: *Marry Me Again*. 1955: *Artists and Models*. 1956: *The Lieutenant Wore Skirts, Hollywood or Bust, The Girl Can't Help It*. 1957: *Will Success Spoil Rock Hunter?* 1958: *Rockabye Baby, Geisha Boy*. 1959: *Say One For Me*. 1960: *Cinderfella*. 1962: *Bachelor Flat, It's Only Money*. 1964: *The Man From the Diner's Club*. 1965: *The Alphabet Murders*. 1966: *The Glass-Bottom Boat*. 1967: *Caprice*. 1968: *The Private Navy of Sergeant O'Farrell*.

Tarkovski, Andrei. (1932–   ). Soviet.

1959: *There Will Be No Leave Today*. 1960: *The Skating Rink and the Violin* (with Konchalovsky-Mikhalkov) both short films). 1962: *Ivan's Childhood*. 1966: *Andrei Rublev*. 1972: *Solaris*.

Tati, Jacques. (1908–   ). French.

1932: *Oscar, Champion de Tennis*. 1938: *Retour à la terre*. 1946: *L'Ecole des facteurs*. 1947: *Jour de fête*. 1953: *Les Vacances de Monsieur Hulot*. 1958: *Mon Oncle*. 1967: *Playtime*. 1971: *Trafic*.

Taurog, Norman. (1899–   ). American.

1920: *The Fly Cop*; then, 1920–1972: innumerable films, mostly comedies, including 1931: *Skippy*. 1933: *Huckleberry Finn*. 1935: *Mrs Wiggs of the Cabbage Patch*. 1938: *The Adventures of Tom Sawyer, Boy's Town*. 1940: *Broadway Melody of 1940, Young Tom Edison, Little Nellie Kelly*. 1942: *A Yank at Eton*. 1943: *Presenting Lily Mars*. 1947: *The Beginning of the End*. 1948: *The Bride Goes Wild*. 1954: *Living it Up*. 1967: *Speedway*.

Terayama, Shuji. (1935–   ). Japanese.

1971–2: *Emperor Tomato Ketchup, Throw away books; Let's Go into the Streets!*

Teshigahara, Hiroshi. (1927–). Japanese.

1953: *Hokusai.* 1959: *José Torres.* 1962: *The Pitfall.* 1964: *Woman of the Dunes.* 1965: *La Fleur de large* (episode). 1966: *The Face of Another.* 1967: *Bakuso.* 1968: *Man Without a Map.* 1972: *Summer Soldiers.*

Thiele, Rolf. (1918–). German.

1951: *Primanerinnen* (with Alfred Braun). 1958: *Das Mädchen Rosemarie.* 1959: *Die Halbzarke, Labyrinth.* 1964: *Tonio Kröger.* 1969: *Komm nach Wien–ich zeig Dir was.* 1972: *Sex Olympics.*

Thiele, Wilhelm. (1890–). Austrian, active in Germany.

1923: *Carl Michael Ziehrers Märchen aus Alt-Wien.* 1930: *Die Drei von der Tankstelle.* 1960: *Sabine und die 100 Männer.*

Thorndike, Andrew. (1909–) and **Annelie.** (1925–). German.

1949: *Der 13 Oktober.* 1956: *. . . Du und mancher Kamerad.* 1957: *Urlaub auf Sylt.* 1963: *Das Russische Wunder.* 1965: *Tito in Deutschland.* 1969: *Du bist min, ein Deutsches Tagesbuch.*

*Torre-Nilsson, Leopoldo. (1924–). Argentina.

1947: *El muro.* 1950: *El crimen de Oribe* (co-directed with his father, Leopoldo Torre: *Rios*). 1953: *El hijo del Crack.* 1954: *Dias de odio, La Tigra.* 1955: *Para vestir santos, Graciela, Elprotegido.* 1957: *Precursores de la pintura Argentina, La casa del angel.* 1958: *El secuestrador.* 1959: *La caída.* 1960: *Fin de fiesta, Un guapo del '900.* 1961: *La mano en la trampa, Piel de verano.* 1962: *Setenta veces siete.* 1963: *Homenaje a la hora de la siesta, La terraza.* 1964: *El ojo de la cerradura.* 1966: *Cavar un foso, Monday's Child.* 1967: *The Traitors of San Anjel.* 1960: *Martin Fierro.* 1970: *El santo de la Espada.* 1971: *Güemes.*

Tourneur, Jacques. (1904–). French, active in France and U.S.A.

1931: *Tout ça ne vaut pas l'amour.* 1933: *Toto.* 1939: *Nick Carter, Master Detective.* 1942: *Cat People.* 1943: *I Walked with a Zombie, The Leopard Man.* 1949: *Easy Living.* 1955: *Wichita.* 1965: *City Under the Sea.*

Tourneur, Maurice. (1876–1961). French, active in France and U.S.A.

1913: *Le système du professeur Goudron.* 1915: *Alias Jimmy Valentine.* 1916: *The Whip, Trilby, Barbary Sheep.* 1917: *Poor Little Rich Girl.* 1918: *The Blue Bird, A Doll's House.* 1920: *The Last of the Mohicans* (with Clarence Brown). 1924: *The Isle of Lost Ships.* 1925: *Aloma of the South Seas.* 1927: *L'Equipage.* 1933: *Königsmark.* 1939: *Volpone.* 1943: *La Main du diable.* 1948: *Après l'amour.* 1949: *Impasse des deux anges.*

Trauberg, Ilya. (1905–48). Soviet.

1927: *Leningrad Today.* 1929: *The Blue Express.* 1936: *The Son of Mongolia.*

Trauberg, Leonid. (1902–). Soviet.

See **Kozintsev** for films made in collaboration. Trauberg alone: 1943: *The Actress.* 1947: *Pirogov.* 1958: *Soldiers on the March.* 1960: *Dead Souls.* 1961: *Free Wind.*

Trnka, Jiří. (1910–69). Czech.

1945: *Grandpa planted a Beet.* 1947: *The Czech Year.* 1948: *The Emperor's Nightingale.* 1953: *Czech Legends.* 1954: *The Good Soldier Schweik.* 1959: *A Midsummer Night's Dream.* 1962: *Cybernetic Grandma.* 1965: *The Hand.*

Troell, Jan. (1931-   ). Danish.

1960: *Stad*. 1961-65: shorts. 1966: *Here is Your Life*. 1968: *Who Saw Him Die?* (*Ole Dole Doff*). 1971: *The Emigrants, Unto a Good Land*.

*Truffaut, François. (1932-   ). French.

1955: *Une Visite*. 1958: *Les Mistons*. 1959: *Histoire d'eau* (with Godard), *Les Quatre Cents Coups*. 1960: *Tirez sur le pianiste*. 1961: *Jules et Jim*. 1962: *L'Amour à vingt ans* (episode). 1964: *La Peau douce*. 1966: *Fahrenheit 451*. 1967: *La Mariée etait en noir*. 1968: *Baisers volés*. 1969: *La Sirène du Mississippi*. 1970: *L'Enfant sauvage, Domicile conjugale*. 1971: *Les deux anglaises et le continent*.

Trumbo, Dalton. (1905-   ). American.

1971: *Johnny Got his Gun*.

Turin, Victor. (1895-1945). Soviet.

1925: *Order of the Day of October 8th*. 1929: *Turksib*. 1938: *Baku People*.

Tuttle, Frank. (1892-1963). American.

1922: *The Cradle Buster*. 1927: *Kid Boots*. 1933: *Roman Scandals*. 1945: *A Man Called Sullivan*. 1956: *A Cry in the Night*. 1958: *Island of Lost Women*.

Ustinov, Peter. (1921-   ). British.

1946: *School for Secrets*. 1948: *Vice Versa*. 1949: *Private Angelo*. 1961: *Romanoff and Juliet*. 1962: *Billy Budd*. 1965: *Lady L*.

Vadim, Roger. (1928-   ). French.

1956: *Et Dieu créa la femme*. 1957: *Sait-on jamais?* 1958: *Les Bijoutiers du clair de lune*. 1959: *Les Liaisons dangereuses*. 1960: *Et mourir de plaisir*. 1961: *La Bride sur le cou*. 1962: *Le Repos du guerrier*. 1963: *Le Vice et la vertu, Château en Suède*. 1964: *La Ronde*. 1966: *La Curée*. 1968: *Histoires extraordinaires* (episode). 1968: *Barbarella*. 1971: *Pretty Maids All in a Row*.

Van Dyke, Willard. (1906-   ). American.

1939: *The City* (with Ralph Steiner). 1940: *Design for Education, Valley Town, The Children Must Learn*. 1943: *War Town*. 1944: *The Bridge*. 1947: *Journey into Medicine*.

Van Dyke, Woodbridge S. (1887-1943). American.

1917: *The Land of Long Shadows*. 1926: *White Shadows of the South Seas*, (with Flaherty). 1930: *Trader Horn*. 1931: *Tarzan of the Apes*. 1933: *Eskimo*. 1934: *The Thin Man*. 1936: *San Francisco*. 1938: *Marie Antoinette*. 1942: *Journey for Margaret*.

Varda, Agnès. (1928-   ). French.

1955: *La Pointe courte*. 1956: *O saisons, o châteaux*. 1958: *Opéra Mouffe*. 1960: *Du côté de la côte*. 1962: *Cleo de 5 à 7*. 1964: *Le Bonheur, Salut les Cubains*. 1966: *Les Créatures*. 1969: *Lion's Love*.

Vassiliev, Georgi. (1899-1946) and **Sergei.** (1900-1959). Soviet. (Called 'The Vassiliev Brothers' although not related).

1928: *Footprint in the Ice*. 1934: *Chapayev*. Sergei V. alone: 1958: *In October Days*.

Vedrès, Nicole. (1911-65). French.

1947: *Paris 1900*. 1950: *La Vie commence demain*. 1953: *Aux frontières de l'homme*.

Velo, Carlos. (? –). Mexican.

1956: *Toro!* 1967: *Pedro Paramo.*

Vertov, Dziga. (1896–1954). Soviet.

1918–19: *Kinonedelia* (43 issues). 1922–5: *Kinopravda.* 1923: *Yesterday, Today, Tomorrow.* 1924: *Kino-Eye* (first series). 1926: *Stride, Soviet!, Sixth Part of the Earth.* 1928: *The Eleventh.* 1929: *The Man With the Movie Camera.* 1930: *Enthusiasm or Donbas Symphony.* 1934: *Three Songs of Lenin.* 1937: *Lullaby.* 1944–54: *News of the Day* (contributions to 55 issues).

Vidor, Charles. (1900–59). Hungarian, active in U.S.A.

1929: *The Bridge.* 1944: *Cover Girl.* 1945: *A Song to Remember.* 1946: *Gilda.* 1952: *Hans Christian Andersen.* 1957: *A Farewell to Arms, The Joker is Wild.* 1959: *A Song Without End* (finished by Cukor).

*Vidor, King. (1894–). American.

c. 1913–18: short and actuality films. 1918: *The Turn in the Road.* 1919: *Better Times, The Other Half, Poor Relations, The Jack-knife Man.* 1920: *Family Honour.* 1921: *The Sky Pilot, Love Never Dies, Conquering the Women, Woman Wake Up.* 1922: *The Real Adventure, Dusk to Dawn, Alice Adams, Peg o' my Heart.* 1923: *The Woman of Bronze, Three Wise Fools, Wild Oranges, Happiness.* 1924: *Wine of Youth, His Hour, Wife of the Centaur.* 1925: *Proud Flesh, The Big Parade, La Bohème.* 1926: *Bardelys the Magnificent.* 1928: *The Crowd, Show People, The Patsy.* 1929: *Hallelujah!* 1930: *Not So Dumb, Billy the Kid.* 1931: *Street Scene, The Champ.* 1932: *Bird of Paradise, Cynara.* 1933: *The Stranger's Return.* 1934: *Our Daily Bread, The Wedding Night.* 1935: *So Red the Rose.* 1936: *The Texas Rangers.* 1937: *Stella Dallas.* 1938: *The Citadel.* 1939: *North West Passage.* 1940: *Comrade X.* 1941: *H. M. Pulham Esq.* 1944: *An American Romance.* 1947: *Duel in the Sun, On our Merry Way.* 1949: *The Fountainhead, Beyond the Forest.* 1951: *Lightning Strikes Twice.* 1952: *Japanese War Bride, Ruby Gentry.* 1955: *Man Without a Star.* 1956: *War and Peace.* 1959: *Solomon and Sheba.*

*Vigo, Jean. (1905–34). French.

1929–30: *A propos de Nice.* 1931: *Taris, roi de l'eau.* 1933: *Zéro de conduite.* 1934: *L'Atalante.*

*Visconti, Luchino. (1906–). Italian.

1942: *Ossessione.* 1945: *Giorni di gloria* (co-directed with de Santis). 1948: *La terra trema.* 1951: *Bellissima, Appunti su un fatto di cronaca.* 1952: *Siamo donne* (episode). 1953: *Senso.* 1957: *Le notti bianche.* 1960: *Rocco e i suoi fratelli.* 1962: *Boccaccio 70* (episode). 1963: *Il gattopardo.* 1965: *Vaghe stelle dell'Orsa.* 1967: *Le streghe* (episode), *Lo straniero.* 1970: *The Damned.* 1971: *Death in Venice.* 1972: *Ludwig II.*

*Wajda, Andrzej. (1926–). Polish.

1954: *A Generation.* 1956: *Kanal.* 1958: *Ashes and Diamonds.* 1959: *Lotna, Innocent Sorcerers.* 1961: *Samson.* 1962: *L'Amour a vingt ans* (episode), *A Siberian Lady Macbeth.* 1965: *Ashes.* 1967: *Gates to Paradise.* 1968: *Everything For Sale.* 1969: *Hunting Flies.* 1970: *Landscape After the Battle.* 1971: *The Birch Wood.*

Walsh, Raoul. (1892–). American.

1912: *Life of Villa.* 1924: *The Thief of Bagdad.* 1926: *What Price Glory?* 1928: *Sadie Thompson.* 1933: *Going Hollywood.* 1939: *St Louis Blues, The Roaring Twenties.* 1940: *Dark Command.* 1941: *High Sierra, They Died With Their Boots*

On. 1947: *Cheyenne*. 1950: *White Heat*. 1951: *Distant Drums*. 1953: *A Lion is in the Streets*. 1955: *The Battle Cry, The Tall Men*. 1956: *The Revolt of Mamie Stover*. 1958: *The Naked and the Dead, The Sheriff of Fractured Jaw*. 1964: *A Distant Trumpet*.

Walters, Charles. (1912–). American.

1945: *Spreading' the Jam*. 1947: *Good News*. 1948: *Easter Parade*. 1949: *Barkleys of Broadway*. 1950: *Summer Stock*. 1953: *Lili*. 1955: *The Tender Trap*. 1956: *High Society*. 1960: *Please Don't Eat the Daisies*. 1962: *Billy Rose's Jumbo*. 1964: *The Unsinkable Molly Brown*. 1966: *Walk, Don't Run*.

Warhol, Andy. (1930–). American.

1963: *Kiss, Haircut, Eat, Blow-job, Sleep, Tarzan and Jane Regained, Sort of . . .* 1964: *Empire, Mario Banana, Harlot, 13 Most Beautiful Women, 13 Most Beautiful Boys, Taylor Mead's Ass*. 1965: *My Hustler, Camp, More Milk Yvette*. 1966: *Chelsea Girls*. 1967: *I, A Man, Bike Boy*. 1968: *Lonesome Cowboys*. 1969: *Blue Movie, Imitation of Christ, Flesh* (mainly directed by Paul Morrissey). 1971: *Trash* (entirely directed by Paul Morrissey), *L'Amour*. 1972: *Women in Revolt, Heat* (both directed by Morrissey).

Watt, Harry. (1906–). British.

1936: *Nightmail* (with Basil Wright), *6-30 Collection*. 1937: *The Saving of Bill Blewitt*. 1938: *Big Money, North Sea*. 1939: *The First Days*. 1941: *Target for Tonight*. 1943: *Nine Men*. 1944: *Fiddlers Three*. 1946: *The Overlanders*. 1949: *Eureka Stockade*. 1951: *Where No Vultures Fly*. 1954: *West of Zanzibar*. 1959: *The Seige of Pinchgut*.

Wegener, Paul. (1875–1948). German.

1912: *Der Student von Prag* (with Galeen). 1914: *Die Augen des Ole Brandes*. 1914: *Golem*. 1920: *The Golem*. 1937: *Unter Ausschluss der Oeffentlichkeit*.

*Welles, Orson. (1915–). American.

1934: *The Hearts of Age* (short). 1938: *Too Much Johnson* (short). 1941: *Citizen Kane*. 1942: *The Magnificent Ambersons, It's All True*. 1943: *Journey into Fear* (with Norman Foster). 1946: *The Stranger*. 1948: *The Lady From Shanghai, Macbeth*. 1952: *Othello*. 1955: *Mr Arkadin (Confidential Report)*. 1958: *Touch of Evil, The Fountain of Youth* (TV). 1962: *The Trial*. 1966: *Chimes at Midnight*. 1968: *Histoire Immortelle* (TV). 1970: *The Deep*. 1972: *The Other Side of the Wind*.

Wellman, William. (1896–). American.

1923: *The Man Who Won*. 1924: *Not a Drum Was Heard*. 1926: *When Husbands Flirt, The Boob, You Never Know Women*. 1927: *Wings*. 1928: *The Legion of the Condemned, Ladies of the Mob, Beggars of Life*. 1929: *Woman Trap*. 1930: *Young Eagles*. 1931: *Public Enemy, Night Nurse, Other Men's Women*. 1932: *The Hatchet Man. So Big*. 1933: *Central Airport, Wild Boys of the Road*. 1934: *Looking For Trouble, Stingaree, The President Vanishes*. 1935: *Call of the Wild, Small Town Girl*. 1936: *The Robin Hood of El Dorado*. 1937: *A Star is Born, Nothing Sacred*. 1938: *Men With Wings*. 1939: *Beau Geste, The Light that Failed*. 1940: *Reaching for the Sun*. 1942: *The Great Man's Lady, Roxie Hart, Thunderbirds*. 1943: *Lady of Burlesque, The Oxbow Incident*. 1944: *Buffalo Bill*. 1945: *This Man's Navy, The Story of G.I. Joe*. 1946: *Gallant Journey*. 1947: *Magic Town*. 1948: *The Iron Curtain, Yellow Sky*. 1949: *Battleground*. 1950: *The Happy Years, The Next Voice You Hear*. 1951: *Across the Wide Missouri, Westward the Woman, It's a Big Country*. 1952: *My Man and I*. 1953: *Island in the Sky*. 1954: *The High and the Mighty, Track of the Cat.* 1955: *Blood Alley.* 1956: *Goodbye My Lady.* 1957: *Darby's Rangers.* 1958: *Lafayette Escadrille.*

Werner, Gosta. (1908–). Swedish.

1945: *Early Morning, Midwinter Blood.* 1948: *The Train.* 1950: *Backyard.* 1952: *Meeting Life.* 1955: *Matrimonial Announcement.*

*Whale, James. (?1896–1957). British, active in U.S.A.

1930: *Journey's End.* 1931: *Waterloo Bridge, Frankenstein.* 1932: *Impatient Maiden, The Old Dark House.* 1933: *A Kiss Before the Mirror, The Invisible Man, By Candlelight.* 1934: *One More River.* 1935: *The Bride of Frankenstein, Remember Last Night?* 1936: *Showboat.* 1937: *The Road Back, The Great Garrick.* 1938: *Sinners in Paradise, Wives Under Suspicion, Port of Seven Seas.* 1939: *The Man in the Iron Mask.* 1940: *Green Hell.* 1941: *They Dare Not Love* (finished by Charles Vidor). 1949: *Hello Out There.* (never released).

Wicki, Bernhardt. (1919–). Swiss, active in Germany, U.S.A.

1959: *Die Brücke.* 1961: *Das Wunder des Malachias.* 1963: *The Visit.* 1965: *Morituri.*

*Widerberg, Bo. (1930–). Swedish.

1961: *The Boy and the Kite* (TV). 1963: *The Pram, Raven's End.* 1965: *Love, 65.* 1966: *Thirty Times Your Money.* 1967: *Elvira Madigan.* 1968: *The White Game.* 1969: *Adalen 31.* 1971: *Joe Hill.*

Wiene, Robert. (1881–1938). German.

1914: *Arme Eva* (co-directed with A. Berger). 1919: *Das Cabinet des Dr Caligari.* 1920: *Genuine.* 1923: *Raskolnikov, I.N.R.I., Orlacs Hände.* 1934: *Eine Nacht in Venedig.*

Wilcox, Herbert. (1891–). British.

1922: *Whispering.* 1923: *Chu Chin Chow.* 1926: *Dawn.* 1932: *Goodnight Vienna.* 1933: *Bitter Sweet.* 1937: *Victoria the Great.* 1938: *Sixty Glorious Years.* 1939: *Nurse Edith Cavell.* 1943: *The Yellow Canary.* 1945: *I Live in Grosvenor Square.* 1948: *Spring in Park Lane.* 1951: *Odette.* 1955: *King's Rhapsody.* 1956: *My Teenage Daughter.* 1959: *Heart of a Man.*

Wilder, Billy. (1906–). Austrian, active in France, U.S.A. and Britain.

1933: *La Mauvaise Graine.* 1942: *The Major and the Minor.* 1943: *Five Graves to Cairo.* 1944: *Double Indemnity.* 1945: *The Lost Weekend.* 1948: *The Emperor Waltz, A Foreign Affair.* 1950: *Sunset Boulevard.* 1951: *Ace in the Hole.* 1953: *Stalag 17.* 1954: *Sabrina Fair.* 1955: *The Seven Year Itch.* 1957: *Spirit of St Louis, Love in the Afternoon.* 1958: *Witness For the Prosecution.* 1959: *Some Like it Hot.* 1960: *The Apartment.* 1961: *One Two Three.* 1963: *Irma La Douce.* 1964: *Kiss Me Stupid.* 1966: *The Fortune Cookie.* 1970: *The Private Life of Sherlock Holmes.*

Williamson, James. (1855–1933). British pioneer.

1897: *The Naughty Boys.* 1901: *Attack on a China Mission, The Big Swallow, Are You There?* 1902: *The Soldier's Return, Fire!* 1905: *The True Serpent of the Sea.*

*Wise, Robert. (1914–). American.

1944: *Curse of the Cat People, Mlle Fifi.* 1945: *The Body Snatcher, A Game of Death.* 1946: *Criminal Court.* 1947: *Born to Kill.* 1948: *Mystery in Mexico, Blood on the Moon.* 1949: *The Set-up.* 1950: *Two Flags West, Three Secrets.* 1951: *The House on Telegraph Hill, The Day the Earth Stood Still.* 1952: *The Captive City, Something For the Birds.* 1953: *Destination Gobi, The Desert Rats, So Big.* 1954: *Executive Suite.* 1955: *Helen of Troy.* 1956: *Tribute to a Bad Man, Somebody Up There Likes Me.* 1957: *This Could Be the Night, Until They Sail.* 1958: *Run Silent, Run Deep, I Want to Live.* 1959: *Odds Against Tomorrow.* 1961: *West Side Story* (with Jerome Robbins). 1962: *Two For the Seesaw.* 1963: *The Haunting.* 1965: *The Sound of Music.* 1966: *The Sand Pebbles.* 1968: *Star!* 1971: *The Andromeda Strain.*

Wood, Sam. (1883–1949). American.

1917: *Justice.* 1920: *Double Speed.* 1923: *Bluebeard's Eighth Wife.* 1933: *The Late Christopher Bean.* 1935: *A Night at the Opera.* 1936: *A Day at the Races.* 1937: *Madame X.* 1939: *Goodbye Mr Chips.* 1940: *Our Town, Kitty Foyle.* 1943: *For Whom the Bell Tolls.* 1944: *Casanova Brown.* 1946: *Saratoga Trunk.* 1947: *Ivy.* 1949: *The Stratton Story.* 1950: *Ambush.*

Wright, Basil. (1907–). British.

1932: *O'er Hill and Dale, The Country Comes to Town.* 1933: *Windmill in Barbados, Cargo From Jamaica, Liner Cruising South.* 1934–5: *Song of Ceylon.* 1936: *Night Mail* (with Watt). 1937: *Children at School.* 1938: *The Face of Scotland.* 1939: *Evacuation.* 1945: *This Was Japan.* 1946: *Story of Omola.* 1948: *Bernard Miles on Gundogs.* 1951: *Waters of Time.* 1953: *World Without End* (with Paul Rotha). 1956: *The Stained Glass of Fairford.* 1957: *The Immortal Land.* 1960: *A Place for God.*

Wyler, William. (1902–). French-born, active in U.S.A.

1926: *Ridin' for Love, Lazy Lightning, Stolen Ranch.* 1927: *Blazing Days, Hard Fists, Straight Shooting, The Border Cavalier, Desert Dust.* 1928: *Thunder Riders, Anybody Here Seen Kelly?* 1929: *The Shakedown, Love Trap.* 1930: *Hell's Heroes, The Storm.* 1932: *A House Divided, Tom Brown of Culver.* 1933: *Her First Mate, Counsellor at law.* 1935: *The Good Fairy, The Gay Deception.* 1936: *Come and Get It* (with Howard Hawks), *Dodsworth, These Three.* 1937: *Dead End.* 1938: *Jezebel.* 1939: *Wuthering Heights.* 1940: *The Letter, The Westerner.* 1941: *The Little Foxes.* 1942: *Mrs Miniver.* 1945: *The Memphis Belle, The Fighting Lady.* 1946: *The Best Years of Our Lives.* 1949: *The Heiress.* 1951: *Detective Story.* 1952: *Carrie.* 1953: *Roman Holiday.* 1955: *The Desperate Hours.* 1956: *Friendly Persuasion.* 1958: *The Big Country.* 1959: *Ben Hur.* 1962: *The Loudest Whisper.* 1965: *The Collector.* 1966: *How To Steal a Million.* 1968: *Funny Girl.* 1970: *The Liberation of L. B. Jones.*

*Yutkevitch, Sergei. (1904–). Soviet.

1925: *Give Us Radio!* (episode). 1928: *Lace.* 1929: *The Black Veil.* 1931: *The Golden Mountains.* 1932: *Counterplan* (with Ermler and Arnshtam). 1934: *Ankora, Heart of Turkey.* 1937: *Miners, How the Elector Will Vote.* 1938: *The Man With the Gun.* 1940: *Yakov Sverdlov.* 1941: *Film Notes on Battle No 7.* 1942: *The New Adventures of the Good Soldier Schweik.* 1944: *Liberated France.* 1945: *Hello Moscow!* 1946: *Our Country's Youth.* 1948: *Three Meetings* (episode). 1951: *Prjevalski.* 1953: *Skanderbeg.* 1955: *Othello.* 1957: *Yves Montand Sings* (with M. Slutsky), *Stories of Lenin.* 1960: *Meeting With France.* 1962: *The Bathhouse.* 1963: *Peace to Your House.* 1966: *Lenin in Poland.* 1969: *Subject for a Short Story.*

Zampa, Luigi (1905–   ). Italian.

1933: *Risveglio di una città*. 1946: *Vivere in pace*. 1947: *Anni difficili*. 1967: *Le dolci signore*.

Zarkhi, Alexander. (1908–   ). Soviet.

See **Heifets**, for films made in collaboration. Zarkhi alone: 1952: *Pavlinka*. 1955: *Nesterka*. 1957: *The Heights*. 1960: *Men on the Bridge*. 1962: *My Younger Brother*. 1967: *Anna Karenina*.

Zecca, Ferdinand (1864–1947). French pioneer.

1898: *Mésaventures d'une tête de veau;* thereafter numerous short films for Gaumont and then Pathé, including *Histoire d'un crime*, (1901). *Les Victimes de l'alcoolisme* (1902), *La Passion* (1903, with Noguet), *Dix femmes pour un mari, La Course à la perruque, La Course aux tonneaux* (all 1905). 1912–14: *Scènes de la vie cruelle* (series).

Zeman, Karel. (1910–   ). Czech.

1945: *A Christmas Dream*. 1957: *An Engine of Destruction*. 1961: *Baron Munchausen*. 1966: *The Stolen Airship*. 1968: *Mr Servadac's Ark*.

Zinnemann, Fred. (1907–   ). Austrian, active in U.S.A.

1934–6: *Redes* (in Mexico with Paul Strand and Emilio Gomez Muriel). 1936–41: shorts for *Crime Does Not Pay* series. 1942: *Kid Glove Killer, Eyes in the Night*. 1944: *The Seventh Cross*. 1946: *Little Mr Jim*. 1947: *My Brother Talks to Horses*. 1948: *The Search*. 1949: *Act of Violence*. 1950: *The Men*. 1951: *Teresa*. 1952: *High Noon, The Member of the Wedding*. 1953: *From Here to Eternity*. 1955: *Oklahoma!* 1957: *A Hatful of Rain*. 1959: *The Nun's Story*. 1960: *The Sundowners*. 1964: *Behold a Pale Horse*. 1966: *Hawaii*. 1967: *A Man For All Seasons*.

Zurlini, Valerio. (1926–   ). Italian.

1950: *Storia di un quartiere*. 1951: *Pugilatore*. 1952: *Il blues della Domenica, Il mercato delle facce*. 1953: *Soldati in città*. 1954: *Le ragazze di San Frediano*. 1959: *Estate violenta*. 1961: *La ragazza con la valigia*. 1962: *Cronaca familiare*. 1965: *Le soldatesse*. 1967: *Vangelo '70* (episode).

Appendix III:
Bibliography

Until the 1950s, film books in any language were comparatively scarce. Since 1960 however an apparently insatiable appetite for literature on the cinema has induced a vast output – the bulk of it emanating from Britain and France. Inevitably much of this is of poor quality; and the reader will find himself losing a lot of time if he does not select with critical severity. This bibliography concentrates mainly on books available in English, but also includes some in other languages where no relevant American or British publications are available.

Works of General Reference
ENCICLOPEDIA DELLO SPETTACOLO (Rome, 1954–66). 11 volumes including *Aggiornamento* and Index
FILM LEXICON DEGLI AUTORI (Rome, 1959–67). 7 volumes.
    These two Italian works, although inevitably rapidly receding into obsolescence are still the most comprehensive reference sources available. The quality of the entries is variable however; and wherever possible facts should be cross-checked.
Halliwell, Leslie: THE FILMGOER'S COMPANION (New York, 3rd ed. 1970).
    A handy popular work, full of obscure and useful information.
Sadoul, Georges: DICTIONNAIRE DES CINEASTES (Paris 1965: later Italian edition.
    as IL CINEMA, in series Enciclopedie Pratiche Sansoni, Rome, 1967).
    The most convenient – and generally reliable – short guide.

Aesthetics of Film
Bazin, André: QU'EST-CE QUE LE CINEMA? (Paris, 1958).
Reisz, Karel *and* Millar, Gavin: THE TECHNIQUE OF FILM EDITING (New York, 2nd Enlarged Edition).

General Histories
Bardèche, Maurice and Brassillach, Robert: HISTORY OF THE FILM translated by Iris Barry (New York).
Knight, Arthur: THE LIVELIEST ART (New York, 1971).

Macgowan, Kenneth: BEHIND THE SCREEN (London, 1965).
Rotha, Paul: THE FILM TILL NOW (London, new edition, 1967).
Even the most recent of these English-language histories – the only reasonably authoritative and comprehensive available – are seriously out-of-date; and it might be better to consult any of the numerous general histories in other languages, notably those of Ulrich Gregor and Enno Patalas or F. von Sgilnicki in German; and of Pierre Leprohon or Georges Sadoul in French. Sadoul's HISTOIRE DU CINEMA MONDIAL (new edition, 1963) though partial and not always very accurate is a useful one-volume work.
Jacques Deslandes: HISTOIRE COMPAREE DU CINEMA (Paris, 1966–   ).
On completion, this meticulously documented work – which has so far reached only the second volume and 1906 – may well supersede all those presently existing.

Pre-History of Cinema
Ceram, C. W. ARCHAEOLOGY OF THE CINEMA (New York, 1965).
Cooke, Olive: MOVEMENT IN TWO DIMENSIONS (London, 1963).
Thomas, David B.: THE ORIGINS OF THE MOTION PICTURE (London, 1964).
None of these can be recommended entirely without reservation; and
Deslandes, op. cit. volume 1 (Paris, 1966).
is clearly preferable. Individual aspects of the origins of the cinema can be studied in
Gernsheim, Helmut and Alison: THE HISTORY OF PHOTOGRAPHY (New York, 1970).
Gernsheim, Helmut and Alison: L. J. M. DAGUERRE: THE HISTORY OF THE DIORAMA AND THE DAGUERREOTYPE (New York, 1969).
Pragnell, R. J.: THE LONDON PANORAMAS OF BARKER AND GIRTIN (London, 1968).

Studies of National Cinemas
Argentina
Nibila, Domingo di: HISTORIA DEL CINEMA ARGENTINO (Buenos Aires, 1960–   ).
Bulgaria
Hibbin, Nina: EASTERN EUROPE, AN ILLUSTRATED GUIDE (London, 1969).
China
Casiraghi, Ugo: IL CINEMA CINESA QUESTO SCONOSCIUTO (Turin, 1960).
Denmark
Hardy, Forsyth: SCANDINAVIAN CINEMA (New York, 1972).
various: 50 AAR I DANSK FILM (Copenhagen, 1958).
Czechoslovakia
Bocek, Jaroslav: LOOKING BACK ON THE NEW WAVE (Prague, 1967).
Bocek, Jaroslav: MODERN CZECHOSLOVAK FILM (1945–65) (Prague, 1967).
Dewey, Langdon: OUTLINE OF CZECHOSLOVAK CINEMA (London, 1971).
Hibbin, Nina: EASTERN EUROPE: AN ILLUSTRATED GUIDE (Cranbury, N.J., 1969).
Egypt
Khan, Mohammed: AN INTRODUCTION TO THE EGYPTIAN CINEMA (London, 1970).
France
Armes, Roy: FRENCH CINEMA SINCE 1946 (New York, 1970).
Graham, Peter: THE NEW WAVE (London, 1968).
Martin, Marcel: FRANCE: SCREEN GUIDE (Cranbury, N.J., 1971).
Sadoul, Georges: FRENCH FILM (New York, 1972).
Finland
Mäkinen, Aito and Pihlstrom, Bengt: THE FINNISH FILM TODAY (Helsinki, 1957).
Great Britain
Gifford, Denis: BRITISH CINEMA (Cranbury, N.J.).

420 · Bibliography

Low, Rachel: THE HISTORY OF THE BRITISH FILM, 4 volumes to date (1948–) (New York).

Oakley, Charles: WHERE WE CAME IN. (London, 1964).

Germany

Bucher: Felix: GERMANY: SCREEN GUIDE (Cranbury, N.J., 1970).

Eisner, Lotte: THE HAUNTED SCREEN (Berkeley, Ca., 1969).

Kracauer, Seigfried: FROM CALIGARI TO HITLER (Princeton, N.J.).

Hungary

Nemeskurty, István: WORD AND IMAGE (Budapest, 1968).

India

Barnouw, Erik and Krishnaswamy, S.: INDIAN FILM (1963).

Italy

Jarratt, Vernon: THE ITALIAN CINEMA (New York, 1972).

Lizzani, Carlo: CINEMA ITALIANO (Florence, 1953).

Prolo, Maria Adriana: STORIA DE CINEMA MUTO ITALIANO (Milan, 1951).

Rondi, Gian Luigi: ITALIAN CINEMA TODAY (1952–65) (Rome, 1966).

Japan

Anderson, J. L. and Richie, Donald: THE JAPANESE FILM (New York, 1959).

Richie, Donald: JAPANESE MOVIES (Tokyo, 1961).

Richie, Donald: THE JAPANESE MOVIE, an illustrated history (1966).

Svensson, Arne: JAPAN: AN ILLUSTRATED GUIDE (Cranbury, N.J., 1970).

Mexico

Custodio, Alvaro: NOTAS SOBRE EL CINE (Mexico, 1952).

Norway

Hardy, Forsyth: SCANDINAVIAN CINEMA (New York, 1972).

Poland

Hibbin, Nina: EASTERN EUROPE: AN ILLUSTRATED GUIDE (Cranbury, N.J., 1969).

Russia and U.S.S.R.

Leyda, Jay: KINO (New York, 1972).

Hibbin, Nina: EASTERN EUROPE: AN ILLUSTRATED GUIDE (Cranbury, N.J., 1969).

There is a very large literature on the cinema in Russian language – most of that published since 1960 being extremely well documented. Works of reference particularly recommended are

(filmography): SOVETSKII KHUDOZHESTVENII FILMII (4 vols to date; Moscow, 1961–).

Ginsburg, S.: KINEMATOGRAFIA DOREVOLUTSIONOI (Moscow, 1963).

(on pre-revolutionary cinema of Russia).

Sweden

Cowie, Peter: SWEDEN: AN ILLUSTRATED GUIDE (2 vols. London, 1970).

U.S.A.

A vast literature is available on the American cinema, and it is only possible to indicate a few basic texts. The most recent available publication is the series of volumes (eventually to number seven) in the *International Film Guide Series*:

Slide, Anthony: EARLY AMERICAN CINEMA (Cranbury, N.J., 1971).

O'Dell, Paul: GRIFFITH AND THE RISE OF HOLLYWOOD (Cranbury, N.J., 1970).

Robinson, David: HOLLYWOOD IN THE TWENTIES (New York, 1970).

Baxter, John: HOLLYWOOD IN THE THIRTIES (Cranbury, N.J.).

Greenberg, Joel and Higham, Charles: HOLLYWOOD IN THE FORTIES (New York, 1970).

Unfortunately not all the volumes maintain the same level of accuracy. Earlier and classic sources on American cinema are:

Griffith, Richard and Mayer, Arthur: THE MOVIES (New York, 1970).

Hampton, Benjamin: HISTORY OF THE AMERICAN FILM INDUSTRY (New York, new ed. 1970. Originally: A HISTORY OF THE MOVIES, N.Y. 1931).

Jacobs, Lewis: THE RISE OF THE AMERICAN FILM (N.Y. new ed. 1968).

Jobes, Gertrude: MOTION PICTURE EMPIRE (N.Y. 1966).

Ramsaye, Terry: A MILLION AND ONE NIGHTS (N.Y. new ed. 1964).
A classic source on early American film history, though not always completely reliable, owing to Ramsaye's special partiality for Edison.

Yugoslavia
Hibbin, Nina: EASTERN EUROPE: AN ILLUSTRATED GUIDE. (Cranbury, N.J., 1969).

Genres

Comedy
Durgnat, Raymond: THE CRAZY MIRROR (New York, 1972).

Lahue, Kalton C.: WORLD OF LAUGHTER (Norman, Okla., 1971).

Lahue, Kalton C. and Brewer, Terry: KOPS AND CUSTARDS (Norman, Okla., 1968).

Robinson, David: THE GREAT FUNNIES (New York, 1969).

Western
Eyles, Allen: THE WESTERN (Cranbury, N.J.).

Musicals
Taylor, John Russell and Jackson, Arthur: HOLLYWOOD MUSICALS (New York, 1971).

Horror
Clarens, Carlos: ILLUSTRATED HISTORY OF THE HORROR FILM (New York, 1968).

Gifford, Denis: MOVIE MONSTERS (New York).

Animation
Benayoun, Robert: *Le Dessin animé après Walt Disney* (Paris, 1961).

Underground and Avant-Garde Cinema
Ronan, Sheldon: THE UNDERGROUND FILM (London, 1968).

Tyler, Parker: UNDERGROUND FILM (New York, 1970).

Individual Directors
Generally this bibliography is confined to books currently in print – mostly in four popular paper-back series, indicated thus:
   (1) Movie Paperbacks series
   (2) International Film Guide series
   (3) Cinema One Series
   (4) Cinéma d'Aujourdhui (Paris).

Sussex, Elizabeth: LINDSAY ANDERSON (New York, 1970) (1).

Cameron, Ian and Wood, Robin: ANTONIONI (London, 1968) (1).

Donner, Jörn: The Personal Vision of INGMAR BERGMAN (New York, 1971).

Cowie, Peter: ANTONIONI, BERGMAN, RESNAIS (London, 1963) (2).

Wood, Robin: INGMAR BERGMAN (New York, 1969) (1).

Durgnat, Raymond, etc: The Films of ROBERT BRESSON (London 1969) (1).

Estève, Michel: BRESSON (Paris, 1962) (4).

BROWNLOW, KEVIN: How It Happened Here (London, 1968) (3).

Durgnat, Raymond: LUIS BUÑUEL (Berkeley, Ca., 1968) (1).

Kyrou, Ado: BUÑUEL (Paris, 1962) (4).

Aranda, J. Francisco: BUÑUEL (Madrid, 1969).

Wood, Robin and Walker, Michael: CHABROL (London, 1970) (1).

CHAPLIN, CHARLES: My Autobiography (New York).

Huff, Theodore: CHARLIE CHAPLIN (New York, 1972).

Simon, Karl Gunther: JEAN COCTEAU (Berlin, 1958).

DEMILLE, CECIL B. Autobiography (London, 1959).

Montagu, Ivor: WITH EISENSTEIN IN HOLLYWOOD (Berlin, 1968).

Geduld H. and Gottesman, R.: (EISENSTEIN): The Making and Unmaking of Que Viva Mexico (London, 1970).

Seton, Marie: EISENSTEIN (London, 1970).

Milne, Tom: The Cinema of CARL DREYER (Cranbury, N.J., 1970) (3).
Amengual, Barthelemy: DOVZHENKO (Paris, 1970) (4).
Haudiquet, Philippe: PAUL FEJÖS (Paris, 1968).
Calder-Marshall, Arthur: (FLAHERTY): The Innocent Eye (New York, 1970).
Bogdanovitch, Peter: JOHN FORD (Berkeley, Ca., 1968) (1).
Durgnat, Raymond: FRANJU (Berkeley, Ca., 1967) (1).
Jeanne, René and Ford, Charles: ABEL GANCE (Paris, 1963) (4).
Roud, Richard: JEANŒLUC GODARD (Bloomington, Ind., 1970) (3).
Barry, Iris and Bowser, Eileen: D. W. GRIFFITH: American Film Master (New York, 1965).
Wood, Robin: HOWARD HAWKS (London, 1968) (1).
HEPWORTH, CECIL: Came The Dawn (London, 1951).
Truffaut, François: HITCHCOCK (New York, 1969).
Wood, Robin: HITCHCOCK'S Films (Cranbury, N.J.) (2).
    KEATON, Buster and Samuels, Charles: My Wonderful World of Slapstick (London, 1967).
Robinson, David: BUSTER KEATON (Bloomington, Ind., 1969) (3).
Richie, Donald: The Films of AKIRA KUROSAWA (New York, 1965, 1971).
Bogdanovitch, Peter: FRITZ LANG in America (New York, 1969) (1).
Leahy, James: The Cinema of JOSEPH LOSEY (Cranbury, N.J.) (2).
Milne, Tom: LOSEY ON LOSEY (New York, 1972) (3).
Weinberg, Herman G.: The LUBITSCH Touch (New York, 1968).
Milne, Tom: ROUBEN MAMOULIAN (London, 1969) (3).
Bessy, Maurice/Duca, Lo: GEORGES MELIES MAGE (Paris, 1961).
Sadoul, Georges: GEORGES MELIES (Paris, 1961) (4).
Eisner, Lotte H.: F. W. MURNAU (London, 1972).
Stack, Oswald: PASOLINI ON PASOLINI (London, 1969) (3).
PEARSON, GEORGE: Flashback (London, 1957).
Wood, Robin: ARTHUR PENN (New York, 1970) (1).
Butler, Ivan: The Cinema of ROMAN POLANSKI (Cranbury, N.J., 1970) (2).
Leyda, Jay: Index to the creative work of V. I. PUDOVKIN (London, 1947).
Seton, Marie: Portrait of a Director: SATYAJIT RAY (Bloomington, Ind., 1971).
Armes, Roy: The Cinema of ALAIN RESNAIS (Cranbury, N.J.) (2).
Guarner, J. L.: ROSSELLINI (New York, 1971) (1).
Turconi, Davide: MACK SENNETT (Rome, 1961).
STERNBERG, JOSEF VON: Fun in a Chinese Laundry (London, 1966).
Sarris, Andrew: The Films of JOSEF VON STERNBERG (New York, 1966).
Finler, Joel: STROHEIM (Berkeley, Ca., 1968) (1).
Petrie, Graham: The Cinema of TRUFFAUT (Cranbury, N.J., 1970) (2).
Noel-Smith, Geoffrey: LUCHINO VISCONTI (London, 1967) (3).
McBride, Joseph: ORSON WELLES (New York, 1972) (3).
Gidal, Peter: ANDY WARHOL: Painting and Films (New York, 1971).
Higham, Charles: The Films of ORSON WELLES (Berkeley, Ca., 1970).
Madsen, Axel: BILLY WILDER (Bloomington, Ind., 1969) (3).

General Index

Note: This index does not refer to directors listed in the *Selected Filmographies.*

Film titles

Names

436 · Index

440 · Index